The Aesthetics of Grammar

CW00688909

The languages of Mainland Southeast Asia evidence an impressive array of elaborate grammatical resources, such as echo words, phonaesthetic words, chameleon affixes, chiming derivatives, onomatopoeic forms, ideophones, and expressives. Speakers of these languages fashion grammatical works of art in order to express and convey emotions, senses, conditions, and perceptions that enrich discourse.

This book provides a detailed comparative overview of the mechanisms by which aesthetic qualities of speech operate as part of speakers' grammatical knowledge. Each chapter focuses on a different language and explores the grammatical information of a number of well- and lesser-known languages from Mainland Southeast Asia. The book will be of great interest to syntacticians, morphologists, linguistic anthropologists, language typologists, cognitive scientists interested in language, and instructors of Southeast Asian languages.

JEFFREY P. WILLIAMS is Professor of Anthropology and Interim Dean of the College of Arts and Sciences at Texas Tech University.

The Aesthetics of Grammar

Sound and Meaning in the Languages of Mainland Southeast Asia

---

edited by

Jeffrey P. Williams

CAMBRIDGE
UNIVERSITY PRESS

CAMBRIDGE
UNIVERSITY PRESS

University Printing House, Cambridge CB2 8BS, United Kingdom

One Liberty Plaza, 20th Floor, New York, NY 10006, USA

477 Williamstown Road, Port Melbourne, VIC 3207, Australia

314-321, 3rd Floor, Plot 3, Splendor Forum, Jasola District Centre, New Delhi - 110025, India

79 Anson Road, #06-04/06, Singapore 079906

Cambridge University Press is part of the University of Cambridge.

It furthers the University's mission by disseminating knowledge in the pursuit of education, learning and research at the highest international levels of excellence.

www.cambridge.org
Information on this title: www.cambridge.org/9781108790383

© Cambridge University Press 2014

First published 2014
First paperback edition 2019

A catalogue record for this publication is available from the British Library

ISBN 978-1-107-00712-3 Hardback
ISBN 978-1-108-79038-3 Paperback

Contents

Figures

Tables

Maps

Contributors

GEOFFREY BENJAMIN is Senior Associate in the Centre for Liberal Arts and Social Sciences (CLASS), College of Humanities, Arts, and Social Sciences, at Nanyang Technological University. His research since 1964 has focused on the Orang Asli of Peninsular Malaysia, with an emphasis on the Temiars. He has also published more widely on the languages, societies and cultures of the Malay World, including the recent extensive study 'The Aslian languages of Malaysia and Thailand: an assessment' in Volume II of *Language documentation and description*. His book *Temian religion, 1964–2012* will be published by NUS Press in 2014.

MARC BRUNELLE is Associate Professor in the Department of Linguistics at the University of Ottawa. His publications have focused on aspects of Cham (Austronesian, Vietnam) and Vietnamese and have appeared in the *Journal of phonetics*, *Language documentation and conservation*, *Phonetica*, *Diachronica*, and the *Journal of the Aeoustical Society of America*.

JOHN HAIMAN is Professor and Director in the Linguistics Program at Macalester University. He is the author of several books including *Talk Is cheap* (1998), *Natural syntax* (1985), and *Hua, a Papuan language of the Eastern Highlands of New Guinea* (1980). Most recently he has published several articles on aspects of Khmer grammar as well as a reference grammar of the language with John Benjamins in 2012.

INGA-LILL HANSSON was Associate Professor of East Asian Linguistics at Lund University up until her retirement in 2010. She was elected an honorary member of the Linguistic Society of America in 2004. Professor Hansson is acknowledged as the leading international authority on Akha/Hani language and culture and she has authored numerous articles on Akha and Hani.

THOMAS JOHN HUDAK is Professor Emeritus in the School of Human Evolution and Social Change at Arizona State University. His recently funded research (NSF) on the Tai languages has resulted in several publications including *William J. Gedney's comparative Tai source book* (University of Hawaii, 2008).

WILAIWAN KHANITTANAN is Associate Professor and Head in the Linguistics Department of Thammasat University in Bangkok, Thailand where her research interests include the history of the Thai language, Thai sociolinguistics, and the language of the news media in Thailand. In 2007 she published her article 'Language of the News Media in Thailand' in the *International journal of the sociology of language*.

HÅKAN LUNDSTRÖM is Professor of Music and Society at Malmo Academy of Music at Lund University in Sweden. His research on the Kammu has resulted in several publications including his most recent book *I will send my song: Kammu vocal genres in the singing of Kam Raw* (2009), and is continuing in the interdisciplinary project *In the borderland between song and speech: vocal expressions in the oral cultures*.

TAM NGUYEN is a doctoral candidate in the Department of Linguistics at the University of Oregon. Her research interests are focused on the Chamic languages of Vietnam, especially Ede and Bih. She is the recent grant recipient from The Hans Rausing Endangered Languages Document Project grant for documentation of the endangered Bih language.

DAVID A. PETERSON is Associate Professor of Linguistics and Cognitive Science at Dartmouth College. His areas of research include morphosyntactic typology, language documentation, and comparative Tibeto-Burman. He has published widely and in *Language, Himalayan linguistics*, and *Linguistic typology*.

PAUL SIDWELL is an Australian Research Council Future Fellow at the Australian National University. Sidwell is a leading specialist in Mon-Khmer languages, especially the Katuic and Bahnaric branches. Most recently, he co-authored (with Philip Jenner), *Old Khmer grammar* for the Pacific Linguistics series.

LAP M. SIU is an Instructor in anthropology in the Department of Sociology, Anthropology and Social Work at Texas Tech University. Mr Siu, a native speaker of Jarai (Chamic, Austronesian), has research interests in language documentation, lexicography, and ethnomusicology.

JAMES N. STANFORD is Assistant Professor in the Program in Linguistics and Cognitive Science at Dartmouth University. He recently published *Variation in indigenous minority languages* (co-edited with Dennis Preston, 2009) and has authored several articles on Sui, a Tai-Kadai language of southern China.

ALICE VITTRANT is *Maître de Conférence* (Assistant Professor) in the Department of General Linguistics in Aix-Marseille University. Her specialisations are Burmese, typology, language contact and Southeast Asia

Languages in general. She is the author of several book chapters and articles on Burmese grammar in French and English. She is currently co-editing a book on Southeast Asian languages (with Justin Watkins) for Mouton de Gruyter.

JUSTIN WATKINS is Senior Lecturer in Burmese in the Department of the Languages and Cultures of South East Asia at SOAS, University of London. His publications include *The phonetics of Wa* (2002) and *Studies in Burmese linguistics* (2005) both published by Pacific Linguistics, Research School of Pacific and Asian studies at the Australian National University.

JULIAN K. WHEATLEY is currently an adjunct Associate Professor at Tulane University (Chinese), He also serves as chairman of the Burma Studies Foundation. He is author of book chapters on Burmese, articles on languages in the Tibeto-Burman family and author or co-author of several Chinese language textbooks.

JEFFREY P. WILLIAMS is Professor of Anthropology in the Department of Sociology, Anthropology and Social Work and Interim Dean of the College of Arts and Sciences at Texas Tech University. He has previously published *The lesser-known Varieties of English* (co-editor, Cambridge University Press, 2010), *Contact Englishes of the Eastern Caribbean* (co-edited with Michael Aceto, 2003) and a number of articles on language contact in the Caribbean and Papua New Guinea.

LÊ THỊ XUYẾN is Associate Professor in Vietnamese Language and Linguistics in the Department of Languages and Cultures of East Asia at Universtié Paris Diderot (Paris 7). She has published extensively on aspects of Vietnamese grammar, phonetics and phonology, the acquisition of Vietnamese, and Vietnamese language pedagogy. Most recently, she co-authored (with Marie-Claude Paris), *On conjunction and comitativity in Vietnamese* published by Mouton de Gruyter.

Abbreviations and conventions

AFF	affirmative
ALL	allative
ANAPH	anaphora
ANT	anterior
APP	applicative
AUG	augmentative
AUGVCL	augmentative verbal classifier
AUX	auxiliary
BEN	benefactive
CAUS	causative
CHIME	chiming constituent
CLF	classifier
COM	comitative
COMP	complementizer
COMPL	completive aspect
CONT	continuous aspect
COP	copula
CRS	constative modality, current relevant state
CS	conjunctive suffix
DAT	dative
DEIC	deictic
DEM	demonstrative
DIM	diminutive
DIMVCL	diminutive verbal classifier
DM	discourse marker
DSW	decorative 'servant word' (*bo'ri'va:sap* KHMER)
ECHO	echoant
ELAB	elaboration
EMOT	emotive
EMPH	emphatic
EVID	evidential
EXP	expressive

FGD	foregrounder
GEN	genitive
IDEO	ideophone
IMPFV	imperfective
INCEPT	inceptive
INDIC	indicative
INJ	injunction
INST	instrumental
INT	word-specific intensifier
INTERJ	interjection
INTERR	interrogative
INTNS	intensifier
IRR	irrealis
ITER	iterative aspect
LOC	locative
M	masculine
NEG	negative
NMLZ	nominalizer
OBJ	object
PFV	perfective
PL	plural
POL	politeness
POT	potential
PRF	perfect
PRS	present
PRT	particle
PST	past
PUNC	punctative
PURP	purposive
Q	question
QUOT	quotative
REAL	realis
RESP	respectful
S	source of the action (ablative or nominative)
SBJ	subject
SG	singular
SEQ	sequential
sfx	suffix
SUB	subordinator
SUPR	surprise
TOP	topic

VOC	vocative
VCBL	vocable
1	first person
2	second person
3	third person
♂	male speaker
♀	female speaker
(.)	brief pause

1   Introduction

Jeffrey P. Williams

1   Introduction

The languages of Mainland Southeast Asia (Map 1) are resplendent with elaborate grammatical resources for fashioning elaborative expressions that convey emotions, senses, conditions, and perceptions that enrich discourse – both everyday and ritualized – and are grammatical works of art.[1] Over time, a sizeable terminological lexicon has been created to categorize or classify these resources, including echo words, phonaesthetic words, chameleon affixes, chiming derivatives, onomatopoeic forms, ideophones, and most notably expressives. As Diffloth (1979: 50) pointed out some time back now, 'expressives are easy to formally identify due to their particular morphology'.

Speakers of these languages employ significant and complex strategies for the expression of qualities and attributes, feelings and thoughts, and meta-commentary through the use of these formatives as components of grammar.[2] These aesthetic qualities of language, which are formed from grammatical capital, are emergent in the poetry of everyday speaking.

When we speak of the 'aesthetics of grammar' from a linguistic perspective, we face challenges. Neither the term 'aesthetics' nor the term 'grammar' is unencumbered by semantic baggage, although most readers will share general agreement on 'grammar'. While other disciplines such as anthropology and folklore have confronted the issues of the aesthetic in speech, their approaches have tended to revolve around the communicative aspects and not the grammatical ones.[3] The intent of this volume is not to stand in reinforcement of such a distinction, but instead to explore the mechanisms by which aesthetic qualities of speech – involving the formal and functional manipulation of articulatory

---

[1] In fact it has been suggested that the class of expressives is one of the defining features of Mainland Southeast Asia as a linguistic area (Matisoff 2001) and may conjoin a larger macro-area of South and Southeast Asia (Williams 1991).

[2] Burenhult (2005) asserts that Jahai is lacking in the category of 'expressives' that are diagnostically found in the Aslian branch of Austroasiatic (cf. Sidwell and Benjamin this volume).

[3] For one such example, see Knoblauch and Kotthoff's *Verbal Art across Cultures* (Tübingen: Gunter Narr Verlag, 2001).

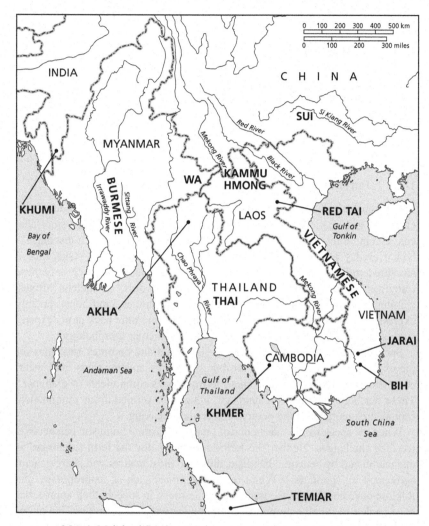

Map 1 Mainland Southeast Asia

features within phonotactic parameters by speakers and invoking patterns and principles whereby new and novel forms can be appreciated by listeners – are part of grammatical knowledge.

The essayists in this collection adopt an interpretative and explanatory stance in which 'aesthetics' holds fast to its original definition deriving from the Ancient Greek source αἰσθητικός; of or relating to sense perception, sensitive, perceptive – referring to 'things perceptible by the senses ... as opposed to things thinkable' (*The Oxford English Dictionary*, Third Edition, December 2011); interpreting their data with reference to sensory experience of one type or another as involved in a sound–meaning nexus. The cline of sensory experience is, in some cases, grammatically instantiated by a cline of allomorphy as shown by the Jarai (Chamic, Austronesian/Vietnam) examples (1a–c) that follow.

(1a)   anĕt   'small'
(1b)   anĕt aneo   'very small'
(1c)   anĕt anot   'extremely small'

The echoant[4] allomorphs in (1b) and (1c) are not governed by continuum of beautified expressions, so (1c) is not seen as more pleasing than (1b) or vice versa. Instead, the allomorphy in (1) is aesthetically governed along a continuum of intensity of feeling. It is this type of sensory motivated allomorphy that is at the heart of the aesthetics of grammar.

The fundamental concept of an aesthetic component of grammar was outlined in the concluding paragraph of Gérard Diffloth's essay on iconicity of Bahnar (Mon-Khmer, Cambodia/Vietnam) expressives:

Iconicity belongs to a different semiotic domain than the one usually described in our grammars. As far as expressives are concerned, the phonic and the meaning elements must be described in terms of certain elementary sensations. Iconicity consists here in exploiting similarities between the sensations of speech and other kinds of sensation. This kind of synaesthesia must be described in a distinct component of grammar, the esthetic component, which is distinct but not isolated, as it somehow must be plugged into the conventional components which have received much of the attention of theoreticians so far. (1994: 113)

As it will become evident from reading the essays collected herein, the authors are not all in agreement with Diffloth's suggestion that the aesthetic component is distinct within the grammar of a language. David Peterson and James Stanford, in particular, take a contrary view and contend that there is no need for a distinct component, even though their views are not necessarily in line with each other.

2   Defining the aesthetic in grammar

The following list provides a preliminary accounting of what features and properties are shared among the languages of the region in regards to what we are referring to as the aesthetic component of grammar.

---

[4] For echo word formation where roots and other non-meaningful morphs have multiple collocative allomorphs, I would suggest that a common term 'echoant' be used to categorize them on par with the use of the term 'reduplicants'.

The aesthetic component of grammar:

i. is referential in the areas of sensory or perceptual intensity;
ii. is a mechanism to beautify speech in socially and culturally appropriate and meaningful ways;
iii. is manifested in everyday speaking as well as in ritualized, named genres;
iv. is productive or semi-productive and rich in multiple exponents; and
v. is psychologically real.

Taking a broad anthropologically situated view, the aesthetics of grammar is an ethnoscience of perception that is encoded in grammar and emergent in discourse.

To some extent the reluctance on the part of linguists to fully address these phenomena relies on the fact that expressives, echo words, and other variants *break frame*, in the sense of Goffman (1974), whereby part of the focus on the communicative act shifts from the referential to the non-referential – the listener is directed to the form of the utterance, its elegance, and the skill of the speaker in her/his ability to create a nuanced, and possibly novel, form to represent a feeling, a sensation, or an opinion. In part these constructions are evaluated in such a way that links grammaticality with euphony.

Most linguists would assert that grammaticality is independent of euphony. The manifestation of euphonic considerations in native speaker grammaticality judgements can be disconcerting. It is clear to anyone who has experience with the grammars of the languages of Mainland Southeast Asia, however, that the distinction between grammaticality and euphony is difficult to establish with native speakers. The contributions by Lundström, Hudak, Williams and Siu, and Khanittanan in this collection provide evidence of and insights into that issue.

This component reaches far deeper into the cognitive realm than simply a manifest concern for pleasing utterances. Jacob (1966) has commented on the prevalence of phonaesthetic reduplicative compounds in the 'plain language' of Khmer; meaning, those varieties used in everyday discourse and not delimited by genre. As she states, the Khmer people are keenly observant of how individuals move their bodies and/or limbs to do tasks and have numerous forms from which to make commentary. As Haiman acutely analyses the Khmer data in his chapter, the function of many Khmer aesthetic forms is decorative and the meanings are derived from context and not from lexicality. One could interpret this as a sort of 'keying' in the sense of Goffman's frame analytic approach to discourse. It is too soon to tell if indeed this is what is happening since we have no full discourse analyses of the use of expressives and other grammatically aesthetic forms in extended social interaction.

Equally important in emerging discussions of euphony are the connections between the appreciation and evaluation of speech in relation to sung, chanted, lamented, or otherwise modified human vocal sound. There are significant relationships between the aesthetics of spoken and sung texts in the languages and cultures of Mainland Southeast Asia as Lundström's chapter on Kammu beautifying techniques exemplifies significant relationships between vocalic replacements in both text types.

In a detailed and insightful study of Thai classical singing, Swangviboonpong (2003) discusses the Thai term *ŷyan*. In most dictionaries, its definition includes 'the speaking of a word', 'a pronouncement', or 'speech in a pleasing voice'. However, in the vocabulary of Thai classical music, *ŷyan* refers to the 'wordless vocalizations' that are positioned between sung words (Swangviboonpong 2003: 32).[5] They are meaningless in terms of the text but are instead aesthetically charged.

The formal relationship between *ŷyan* in Thai music and echo morphology in Thai grammar is striking. In both *ŷyan* and in derisive/approximative echo words the Thai vowels *y* [ɣ] and *ə* [ə] are prominent as rhymes.[6]

Placing this in larger context and following the lead of scholars such as Feld (1990), we really must begin to seriously consider the anthropology of sound as a transdisciplinary field that is a reflection of the reality of cultural evaluations of the soundscape of human existence, inclusive of language.

One thing that is clear from the upcoming descriptions and analyses in this volume is that the aesthetic component of grammar is both productive and complex. In most of the languages covered here, some of these processes, specifically echo word formation, produces extensive allomorphy. Following the lead of Matthews (1972, 1974) and in the current path of Bermúdez-Otero (2012), we can speak of this in terms of multiple exponence. For echo word formation where roots and other non-meaningful morphs have multiple collocative allomorphs, I would contend that a common term 'echoant' be used to categorize them on par with reduplicants. Grammatically aesthetic processes such as echo word formation are not only sensitive to prosodic and phonological structure they are governed by them. For instance, minor syllables, or presyllables, do not participate in morphophonological processes of grammatical aesthetics in the languages of Mainland Southeast Asia and it is relatively straightforward to exclude these by the fact of their non-moraic qualities (see Cho and King (2003) on syllabification of minor syllables).

Given that we are dealing with linguistic structures and processes, it is important to provide evidence of the cognitive reality of the component of aesthetic grammar. Bermúdez-Otero (2012) provides a loose, operational definition of cognitive reality in which a morphophonological pattern is psychologically real

---

[5] The ability to use *ŷyan* is an important indicator of musical competency in Thai classical singing and organized *sătam chátn* competitions that measure this ability (Swangviboonpong 2003).

[6] According to Swangviboonpong (2003: 36) in *ŷyan*, *ə* [ə:] is most commonly used and can have the following variants: *əə, həə, ŋəə, əəŋ, and ŋəəj*.

if speakers broaden it to new items – even if only irregularly – whether evidenced in language change or in experimental tasks. While the contributors here do not tackle this issue directly in their chapters, the psychological reality of the aesthetic component of grammar is demonstrable through evidence of extension through language contact and change as Williams and Siu show for Jarai. Equally, the complex and nuanced patterns shown in all of the languages herein attest to the linguistically significant generalizations that can be made in this arena.

This volume links the aesthetic with the grammatical. The nexus of these two components of human cognition occupies a netherworld in regards to language description and theory, while as the contributors to this volume repeatedly demonstrate, the grammatically aesthetic devices that are employed by speakers are drawn from the traditional components of grammar, including phonetics, phonology, morphology, syntax, and semantics. Their contributions represent a modern linkage of Jakobson's (1960) emotive and poetic functions of language. Through the processes of reduplication and echo word formation we find grammatical – or morphological – level parallelism on par with sentential parallelism that is found in many Austronesian languages/cultures of insular Southeast Asia (see Fox 1988).

In his exposition of a discourse centred approach to language and culture, Sherzer (1987) focuses on the discourse contexts of echo word constructions in Bhojpuri as one of his extended examples of where meaningful intersections of language and culture are manifested. Sherzer is interested in the use of echo words as mediation between language and culture, as an enablement of culture through the resources of grammar (1987: 302). Sherzer's discourse instantiation echoes Diffloth's (1979: 55) comment that, 'Many Expressives are created on the spur of the moment, and their meaning is tied to a fleeting sensation which arose on a certain occasion.'

Treatments of the aesthetic component of grammar

While there are seemingly two disparate approaches to how to handle grammatically aesthetic forms in language, the overlap between the basic treatments is remarkably similar. On the one hand, there is the view espoused by Gérard Diffloth (1972, 1976, 1979), through his pioneering contributions to Mon-Khmer. He brought to the fore the opulent field of grammatical aesthetics in languages of Mainland Southeast Asia and was the first to use the term 'expressives' for a separate class of complex words in the languages of Southeast Asia that appeared to have no comparable class in the Indo-European language family (1972).[7]

---

[7] This assertion would prove false since many of the Indo-Aryan languages have equally complex and productive word formation processes that contribute to the aesthetic mode of utterances; typically, these are referred to as 'echo morphology' in the grammars of those languages.

The ephemeral and somewhat open-ended categorization of expressives has led to their seclusion and exoticization within the broad bin of grammatical categories. Diffloth's and some of his followers' approach has been to group these phenomena together into a single, large class within a distinct yet undefined aesthetic component of grammar. This has created, even within the field of Southeast Asian linguistics, a somewhat implicit attempt to relegate 'expressive morphology' to the realms of poetry and literary prose. In fact Judith Jacob (1979) stated that the occurrence of morphology devices, such as reduplication, in Khmer is only found in poetry. From what Haiman presents in this volume and elsewhere (2009), it is clear that the use of elaboration or decoration (in Haiman's terminology) is more widespread and productive in conversational Khmer than what has been purported in the literature.[8]

On the other hand, there are the formal grammarians – scholars such as Inkelas and Zoll (2005), McCarthy, Kimper, and Mullin (2012), Pullum and Rawlins (2007), Raimy (2009), and most dramatically Zwicky and Pullum (1987) – who seek to maintain strict compartmentalization of plain morphology from 'expressive' morphology. They contend that in most cases, these two types of morphology are not assumable under a single component.[9] Inkelas and Zoll (2005: 204) make the following claim regarding alliterative and rhyming processes in morphology:

While alliteration and rhyme clearly seem to play a role in processing and are aesthetically pleasing, the evidence suggests that rhyming, alliteration, and other similar correspondences do not play a significant role in productive morphology.

Formal modelling is difficult to capture although there is a quickly emerging body of formal accounts dealing with 'expressives' (cf. Potts et al. 2009, Zwicky and Pullum 1987, Cruse 1986, Potts 2007). The ill-starred conclusion of all of those accounts is that 'expressives' are somehow special and do not fit either within the traditional morphological component of grammar nor the descriptive dimension of meaning, or that they are not part of productive morphology as Inkelas and Zoll contend. In other words, expressives, which are only ill defined in most of these accounts, appear to be extragrammatical. If we allow ourselves to be convinced by these arguments, we will forever marginalize and exoticize languages (as well as speakers) such as Khmer, Vietnamese, Thai, and many other minority languages of Southeast Asia and

---

[8] Paul Sidwell also points out inconsistencies in the treatment of this kind of morphology in the Austroasiatic linguistics literature.

[9] Zwicky and Pullum (1987: 334) contend that Pacoh (a Bahnaric member of Mon-Khmer) possesses ideophonic formations akin to *shm-* reduplication in certain varieties of English. I would counter their claim that description of these formative processes calls for separate description from 'garden variety' morphology. It is more convenient in a purely formalistic account to remove these formative processes from consideration; however, it is completely arbitrary.

beyond where expressive morphology, in Zwicky and Pullum's sense, is central to the grammar. As Enfield (2005: 189) aptly states,

> The productivity and internal complexity of elaborative morpholexicon in MSEA languages should weaken claims that these languages lack morphology. One just has to know where to look.

In spite of the formal and functional richness and intricacy of these grammatical resources, they are relatively understudied and especially little understood from an areal, comparative perspective. The present collection provides a first step towards a comparative understanding of the aesthetics of grammar in the languages of the Mainland Southeast Asian linguistic area.

3   Organization of the volume

The authors of each chapter explore this distinct component of grammar – the aesthetic – in various ways, drawing on first-hand experiences either as native or near-native speakers or as field linguists with extensive research experience. Their contributions will provide the foundation for the architecture of theoretical infrastructure regarding the role of aesthetics in cognitive grammars.

The contributors were selected to provide data/analyses that cover the five major language families of the region; namely, Austroasiatic, Sino-Tibetan, Tai-Kadai, Hmong-Mien, and Austronesian. These contributions provide the descriptive and analytical foundation for the architecture of theoretical infrastructure regarding the role of aesthetics in cognitive grammars.

The range of approaches found in these chapters is great. Some contributors, like Stanford (Sui), cast the aesthetic phenomena in a formal mould while others, such as Khanittanan (Central Thai), provide a sociolinguistic account of the aesthetic. In spite of the variety of approaches and tacts, each contributor relies on first-hand linguistic experience either as a linguist native speaker or as a co-collaborator with native speakers. The threads that join this disparate grouping together are the phenomena themselves.

Part I leads off with chapters that document and analyse members of the Austroasiatic family in Southeast Asia and beyond. **Paul Sidwell** provides a timely and useful survey of what is known and not known about the broad and imprecisely defined category of 'expressives' in Austroasiatic. He includes data from the Munda family as well, relying on Anderson's (2008) documentation. The chapter presents some of the inconsistencies in description, characterization, and analysis of expressives as the grouping is referenced in the Austroasiatic literature. In spite of rather impressive linguistic documentation in some branches, such as Palaungic, the accounts are formally oriented and as such these kinds of phenomena go undiscussed. Sidwell stresses the need for more textured descriptions of representative speech in his chapter.

Geoffrey Benjamin adopts what would be for some a heretical approach to the relationship between sound and meaning in his nuanced analyses of grammatical aesthetics in Temiar. He makes a convincing case for the felt quality of iconicity as opposed to an intellectual, or cognitive, quality. Benjamin's contribution is the most anthropological of those included in this volume, going beyond the grammatical. He adopts the late Alfred Gell's (1979) notions of *a priori* and *a posteriori* iconic motivation, viewing these as condensed notions and not as fully articulated concepts.

In Temiar, expressives constitute a distinctive basic word-class parallel to verbs and nouns, and are concerned as much with connotational as with denotational meaning. Expressives in Temiar are voluntary additions to utterances that would still make sense without their appearance. As Benjamin points out, one can speak 'good' Temiar without ever using an expressive but such speech would risk sounding 'uninvolved and unemotional'.

In his chapter, **John Haiman** looks at non-referential morphology in Khmer. A passing but important point that he makes is in regards to the antiquity of the use of non-referential morphology in Khmer, citing the use of the decorative /-am-/ infix in Old Khmer inscriptions. Haiman provides a clever endolinguistic term for these kinds of pseudomorphemes: *bo'ri'va:sap*, which is derived from the Neo-Sanskrit *parivārasabda* 'retinue word'. Haiman refers to these as 'servant words' throughout his chapter. His claim is that this kind of morphology does not contribute to meaning but instead to elegance of expression. Haiman's contention is that these linguistic forms have their closest analogues in art, music, and ritual.

Marc Brunelle and **Lê Thị Xuyến** identify three types of sound symbolism in Vietnamese (ideophonic, phonaesthemic, and phonological), which are not mutually exclusive. The authors demonstrate that each type can and does interact with the others to form new constructions. Vietnamese grammar evidences a high frequency of sound symbolic mechanisms and Brunelle and Xuyến establish a typology of their distributions, proposing mechanisms to account for the development, maintenance, and widespread use of sound symbolic expressions in the language.

Justin Watkins explores aesthetic aspects of Wa grammar. Wa a member of the Palaungic branch of northern Mon-Khmer exhibits the typical Southeast Asian linguistic area of having extensive grammatical resources to describe the movement or manipulation of objects. Watkins' data is drawn heavily from the genre of proverbs as is Hudak's data for Red Thai in Chapter 8. As Watkins details in his contribution, Wa grammar permits a wide array of euphonic patterns in compounds that give speakers considerable creative licence to semantically hone constructions, such as the five possible four-syllable expressions that all mean 'neighbour'.

Håkan Lundström broadens the scope of this volume through his chapter 'Beautifying techniques in Kammu vocal genres' in which he examines the intimate linguistic relationships between poetic singing and eloquent speech. When the different vocal genres are ordered on a scale spanning from 'speech' to 'song' it becomes evident that there is no sharp boundary between the two. As Lundström points out, it might be more useful to conceptualize these issues in terms of degrees or levels or modes of speech – or degrees or levels or modes of song for that matter. He uses the term 'vocal genre' rather than 'song', making it easier to recognize the continuum that spans from daily speech via polite speech, prayer, recitation, and chant to song.

Part II represents accounts of grammatical aesthetics in the Tai-Kadai language family. The coverage of the family includes information on Central Thai (Siamese), several Tai languages (Red, Black, and others), as well as Sui, which is spoken widely in southern China as well. **Tom Hudak** explores the grammatical mechanisms used to frame single line proverbs in several Tai languages, including Central Thai (Siamese). He identifies three grammatical resources that are employed in Tai proverbs: (i) metricality, (ii) rhyme, and (iii) syntactic parallelism. As he points out in his chapter, some Tai languages employ only two of these while others employ all three. One important aspect of Hudak's analysis is his extension into the realm of larger narrative structures, which are made up of proverbs. Not surprisingly, these more substantial texts employ the same mechanisms of metricality, rhyme, and parallelism.

In his chapter 'Lexicalized poetry in Sui', **James Stanford** explores the use of adjective intensifiers in the genre of lexicalized poetry in Sui, a Tai-Kadai language of southwestern China. Sui adjective intensifiers are a frequent and vibrant part of daily discourse, commonly observed in everyday conversation as well as in traditional story telling. He presents extensive data from his fieldwork on Sui to document forms and patterns in other spatial and social dialects, including clan-based lects. As Stanford contends,

Not only is it the case that poetic devices are found in everyday speech in all languages, but certain languages have extensive poetic effects *systematically embedded within the lexicon*. For these languages, large and systematic sectors of the lexicon have 'poetic' patterns, e.g. Sui adjective intensifiers.

Sanford's study examines inter-speaker and cross-dialectal elaborations, consequently taking our understanding of Sui adjectives intensifiers beyond any single speaker's lexicon and into wider possibilities of community grammatical knowledge as a whole.

In her chapter **Wilaiwan Khanittanan** discusses how individual Thai speakers are continuously creating aesthetic expressions, especially those involving alliteration and vocalic rhyming, to capture meanings in context. The processes that give rise to forms are active and productive, and widely used in daily spoken Thai, applying to almost all verbals and many nominals. As she points out, in Thai these bases can be modified in more than one way to form new words and expressions, with the variation capturing slight changes in meaning.

Part III of this volume contains the single contribution to the Hmong-Mien language family, that of **Martha Ratliff**. Martha Ratliff's contribution examines the 'expressive-rich' White Hmong language. While she has published extensively on aspects of tonal manipulation in the language, her chapter here explores the iconicity of choice in relation to consonantal, vocalic, and pattern variation. Reduplicative expressives in Hmong, in contrast to some other languages represented herein, are derived from bases that lack referential meaning. Given that these bases have no referential meaning, it is a categorical stretch to refer to them even as morphemes, in the strict sense of the term. The place of expressives in everyday discourse in Hmong society is an important point that Ratliff makes.

Part IV provides the information on the Austronesian presence in Mainland Southeast Asia with contributions on Jarai and Bih. In their chapter, **Jeffrey Williams** and **Lap Siu**, who is a native speaker of Jarai, partially document the aesthetic aspects of Jarai grammar with an emphasis on echo word formations. The authors detail the types of echo word formation processes in the language, which are extensive. The poetics of *tơloi pơtuh* involve a complex rhyme and alliteration schema that link prosodic phrases together in a text. Equally complex are the principles of semantic relationships between words, reduplicative forms, and echo forms that govern the narrative cohesion in the texts. The authors conclude by briefly examining how grammatical aesthetics in Jarai provides insight into sociolinguistic aspects of code switching and code-mixing.

In her chapter, 'Expressive forms in Bih: a Highland Chamic language of Vietnam', **Minh Tam Nguyen** provides important preliminary documentation of Bih, which was previously believed to be simply a dialect of Rhade/Êđê. As she develops the typology of grammatical aesthetic forms in Bih, Nguyen points out the common characteristic of the semantics of expressives: the fact that expressive collocations are used to describe iconic events/situations, which would be expressed by independent clauses or phrases in languages without expressives. As Watkins and others in this volume, Nguyen makes a call for more data on these phenomena from the languages of the region. In the case of Bih, more data on expressives from other surrounding languages in the region, in particular Mnông, a Mon-Khmer language that is thought to have had significant influence on Bih, is needed to help determine whether or not the divergence between Bih and Êđê expressives may be a product of language contact and change.

Part V focuses on the languages of the Tibeto-Burman family represented in greater Southeast Asia. **David A. Peterson** develops an extensive documentation and analysis of reduplicative and sound symbolic aesthetic elements in Khumi, a language that straddles the South and Southeast Asian linguistic areas. He takes an inclusive stance on the issue of a specifically aesthetic component of grammar, and attempts to demonstrate that the elements of grammar most clearly related to aesthetics in Khumi show significant formal and functional overlap, and can in some sense be viewed as all arising from similar motivations.

In opposition to Thai as reported by Khanittanan in this volume, Peterson states that Khumi elaborate expressions are predominately formed from nouns. These sorts of comparisons are important to explore in future research into the Southeast Asian linguistic area and its genetic and contact histories. In fact, as with the chiming elements of Tedim and the ideophonic ones of Lai, verbal classifiers in Khumi show such idiosyncratic associations with particular verbal predicates, and they convey such subtle nuances, independent of any aesthetic effect they may have, that I think they are better regarded simply as part and parcel of the language's word-formation resources.

Julian K. Wheatley's chapter entitled 'Delight in sound: Burmese patterns of euphony' explores the vast resources in the Burmese lexicon for elaborating the monosyllabic Tibeto-Burman root. Through processes such as rhyme, chime (alliteration), prefixation, and pleonasm, speakers of the language are provided with a repertoire of euphonically balanced and rhythmically evocative expressions within both spoken and written genres. While English exploits its rich repertoire of initial and final clusters and weak syllables to animate its lexicon (higgledy-piggledy, mumble and mutter), Burmese makes use of the preponderance of syllabic or sesquisyllabic words and the ease of compounding. Both 'strategies' reflect the powerful communicative need to bridge the gap between the word and its referent, 'stirring dull roots with spring rain'. The most pervasive expressives in the Burmese lexicon are the four or six-syllable elaborate expressions. Many involve reduplication, either clustered, or interleaved.

In her chapter, 'Psycho-collocational expressives in Burmese' **Alice Vittrant** delves deeply into the world of psycho-collocations as they are defined by Matisoff (1986):

Psycho-collocation [is] a polymorphemic expression referring as a whole to a mental process, quality, or state, one of whose constituents is a psycho-noun, i.e. a noun with explicit psychological reference (translatable by English words like heart, mind, spirit, soul, temper, nature, disposition, mood).

She provides a detailed, sophisticated accounting of the broad class of psycho-collocations that make explicit reference to body parts or organs as the locus of emotions or psychological states. Vittrant distinguishes between elaborate expressions and psycho-collocations in Burmese and points out differences in respect to their structural attributes. While elaborate expressions have a tendency for creation via rhyme, repetition, and alliteration, these resources are not aspects of the construction of psycho-collocations. She also points out the semantic differences between the two types, whereby elaborate expressions develop nuanced meanings via imitative or evocative sounds and psycho-collocations describe emotions, feelings, mental states or processes.

Inga-Lill Hansson documents aesthetic devices within the grammatical structure of Akha ritual texts and compares those texts with versions in modern, vernacular Akha. In the course of her presentation, Hansson develops a typological analysis of ritual texts in Akha. As she states, the largest number of ritual texts belongs to the *phirma*, who holds the role of reciter in connection with personal rituals at death, sickness, and securing of good health. The language of the texts is believed to be the 'words of the ancestors' and as such is taught and memorized by apprentices. The aesthetic devices therein are not productive in ways that we find other languages represented in this volume.

References

Anderson, Gregory (ed.). 2008. *The Munda languages*. London: Routledge.

Bermúdez-Otero, Ricardo. 2012. 'The architecture of grammar and the division of labour in exponence'. In Jochen Trommer (ed.), *The morphology and phonology of exponence*. Oxford University Press, pp. 8–83.

Burenhult, Niclas. 2005. *A grammar of Jahai*. Pacific Linguistics 566. Canberra: Australian National University.

Cho, Young-mee Yu and Tracy Holloway King. 2003. 'Semisyllables and universal syllabification'. In Caroline Féry and Ruben van de Vijver (eds.), *The syllable in optimality theory*. Cambridge University Press, pp. 183–212.

Cruse, David A. 1986. *Lexical semantics*. Cambridge University Press.

Diffloth, Gérard. 1972. Notes on expressive meanings. *Chicago linguistic society* 8: 440–447.

1976. Expressives in Semai. *Oceanic linguistics special publications* 13: 249–264.

1979. 'Expressive phonology and prosaic phonology in Mon-Khmer'. In Theraphan L. Thongkum et al. (eds.), *Studies in Tai and Mon-Khmer phonetics and phonology in honor of Eugenie J. A. Henderson*. Bangkok: Chulalongkorn University Press, pp. 49–59.

1994. 'i:big, a: small'. In L. Hinton, J. Nichols, and J. Ohala (eds.), *Sound symbolism*. New York: Cambridge University Press, pp. 107–114.

Enfield, N. J. 2005. Areal linguistics and Mainland Southeast Asia. *Annual review of anthropology* 34: 181–206.

Feld, Steven. 1990. *Sound and sentiment: birds, weeping, poetics, and song in Kaluli expression*. Second edition. Philadelphia: University of Pennsylvania Press.

Fox, James J. (ed.) 1988. *To speak in pairs: essays on the ritual languages of Eastern Indonesia*. Cambridge University Press.

Gell, Alfred. 1979. The Umeda language-poem. *Canberra anthropology* 2(1): 44–62.

Goffman, Irving. 1974. *Frame analysis: an essay on the organization of experience*. London: Harper and Row.

Haiman, John. 2009. 'Formulaic language in ritual (and everyday) speech'. In Corrigan et al. (eds.), *Formulaic language*, volume II. Amsterdam: John Benjamins, pp. 567–587.

Inkelas, Sharon and Cheryl Zoll. 2005. *Reduplication: doubling in morphology.* Cambridge University Press.

Jacob, Judith M. 1966. 'Some features of Khmer versification'. In C. E. Bazell et. al. (eds.), *In memory of J. R. Firth*. London: Longmans Green and Co., pp. 227–241.

1979. 'Observations on the uses of reduplication as a poetic device in Khmer'. In Theraphan L. Thongkum et al. (eds.). *Studies in Tai and Mon-Khmer phonetics and phonology in honor of Eugénie J. A. Henderson*. Bangkok: Chulalongkorn University Press, pp. 111–130.

Jakobson, Roman. 1960. 'Closing statement: linguistics and poetics'. In T. A. Sebook (ed.), *Style in language*. Cambridge, MA: MIT Press, pp. 350–377.

Matisoff, James A. 1986. Hearts and minds in Southeast Asian languages and English: an essay in the comparative lexical semantics of psycho-collocation. *Cahiers de linguistique d'Asie Orientale* 15(1): 5–57.

2001. 'Genetic versus contact relationship: prosodic diffusibility in Southeast Asian languages'. In Aikhenvald, Alexandra and Dixon, R. M. W. (eds.), *Areal diffusion and genetic inheritance: problems in comparative linguistics*. Oxford University Press, pp. 291–327.

Matthews, Peter. 1972. *Inflectional morphology: a theoretical study of aspects of Latin verb conjugation*. Cambridge University Press.

1974. *Morphology: an introduction to the theory of word-structure*. Cambridge University Press.

McCarthy, John J., Wendell Kimper, and Kevin Mullin. 2012. Reduplication in harmonic serialism. *Morphology* 22: 173–232.

Potts, Christopher. 2007. The expressive dimension. *Theoretical linguistics* 33: 165–197.

Potts, Christopher, Ash Asudeh, Seth Cable, Yurie Hara, Eric McCready, Luis Alonso-Ovalle, Rajesh Bhatt, Christopher Davis, Angelika Kratzer, Tom Roeper, and Martin Walkow. 2009. Expressives and identity conditions. *Linguistic inquiry* 40: 356–366.

Pullum, Geoffrey and Kyle Rawlins. 2007. Argument or no argument? *Linguistics and philosophy* 30: 277–287.

Raimy, Eric. 2009. 'Deriving reduplicative templates in a modular fashion'. In Eric Raimy and Charles E. Cairns (eds.), *Contemporary views on architecture and representations in phonology*. Cambridge, MA: MIT Press, pp. 383–404.

Sherzer, Joel. 1987. A discourse-centered approach to language and culture. *American anthropologist* 89(2): 295–309.

Swangviboonpong, Dusadee. 2003. *Thai classical singing: its history, musical characteristics and transmission*. Hampshire: Ashgate Publishing.

Williams, Jeffrey P. 1991. A note on echo word morphology in Thai and the languages of South and Southeast Asia. *Australian journal of linguistics* 11: 107–111.

Zwicky, Arnold M. and Geoffrey K. Pullum. 1987. 'Plain morphology and expressive morphology'. In Aske, Natasha Beery, Laura Michaelis, and Hana Filip (eds.), *Berkeley Linguistics Society: Proceedings of the Thirteenth Annual Meeting, General Session and Parasession on Grammar and Cognition*. Berkeley: Berkeley Linguistics Society, pp. 330–340.

Part I

Austroasiatic

2 Expressives in Austroasiatic

Paul Sidwell

1 Introduction

The Austroasiatic languages have often been recognized as showing a significant amount of transparently sound symbolic lexicon, although this alone is not a remarkable fact. However, since the 1960s, some scholars (e.g. Watson 1966, Diffloth 1976a, 1979 and others) have characterized various Austroasiatic (AA) languages (especially some Mon-Khmer languages[1]) as having a special class of motivated forms. These are forms not immediately imitative or otherwise directly sound symbolic (in the way that, for example, the AA root for 'bird' *cim[2] and similar forms are imitative of a bird's cheeping), but through the use of strategies such as reduplication and unusual segmental collocations, index descriptive or expressive meanings. These so-called 'expressives' are claimed to effectively form a third major open class with distinct phonological, morphosyntactic, and semantic characteristics.

Subsequently, within Austroasiatic (AA) studies, the term 'expressives' has gained wide currency, and attracted attention from time to time. For example, Burenhult (2005), introducing the topic of descriptives in the Aslian language Jahai,[3] writes:

Expressives, a category of words which forms a distinct word-class in many Austroasiatic languages, denote sensory perceptions of the speaker – visual, auditory, tactile, olfactory, gustatory, emotional or other – in relation to a particular phenomenon (Diffloth 1972, 1976a). . . . They often display peculiar phonological and morphological features, and they function syntactically like sentence adjuncts. (Burenhult 2005: 113)

Also in a discussion of Aslian languages, Matisoff explains:

---

[1] This writer does not treat Mon-Khmer as a real taxon (e.g. see Sidwell 2010), but simply a convenient term for Austroasiatic languages not including the typological aberrant Munda branch.

[2] See Shorto (2006) entry #1324.

[3] In fact, such a class of expressives does, 'not appear to be as evident in Jahai as in other Aslian languages' (Burenhult 2005: 113) and Burenhult's treatment focuses largely on straighforwardly onomatopoeic forms.

Perhaps the greatest single sweller of the Aslian vocabulary is the class of words Diffloth calls expressives. These words exist throughout Austroasiatic, though they have largely escaped notice in prestige languages like Khmer, Mon and Vietnamese. Their formation is a fully productive process only in nonliterate societies, where expressives constitute a third major form-class comparable in magnitude to nouns and verbs.

... Unlike the classes of nouns and verbs, which are 'lexically discrete' (Diffloth's term), expressives are lexically non-discrete, in that they are subject to a virtually unlimited number of semantic nuancings that are conveyed by small changes in their pronunciation. (Matisoff 2005: 50)

A strong feature of these expressives is reduplication, either full or partial, often with segmental substitutions or alternations that behave like pseudo-morphemes but are difficult or impossible to systematize (also sometimes characterized as *phonaesthemes*). And this association with reduplication is so strong that in some writings expressives and reduplications are treated synon-ymously (see for example various entries under *expressives* in Anderson 2008). In fact, reduplication is a common strategy across all Austroasiatic branches for encoding, for example, plurality, augmentation, distributed action, etc. across word classes (verbal, adverbial/adjectival, nominal). Other scholars simply fail to distinguish expressives and ideophones; for example this is the approach taken by Kruspe (2004) in her grammar of Semai. Generally we can say that among scholars of Austroasiatic languages, attitudes towards discussing expressives are mixed, and have been for sometime:

many linguists are ill at ease with iconicity, and no models have been devised to describe it. And even in languages where it is quite prominent, western investigators simply ignored the annoying fact, as in the case of Sre, for instance (Diffloth 1979: 49).

This leads to very curious anomalies; for example, whereas Watson's (1966) Master's thesis, 'Reduplication in Pacoh', is largely devoted to the analysis of a set of over 600 expressives, the more recent (2006) *A grammar of Pacoh* by Alves makes no mention of them, and similar observations can be made for the literature in respect to most branches of AA. Consequently, while a distinct class of expressives may or may not be strongly represented in any particular language, the lack of a mention in the regular descriptive or typological sources is no indication either way.

In the immediately following text, I review expressives as reported for various AA branches, revealing something of their scope and extent, and the different ways they have been treated, before offering some concluding remarks.

2   Bahnaric

The Bahnaric branch is a large and rather well-known group that is spread over a wide zone of Indo-China. However, most language documentation available for Bahnaric consists of lexicons, and some grammars written in formal frameworks that pay scant attention to descriptives. None the less, the analytical work by Banker in the 1960s does reveal an elaborate system of expressives in Bahnar, and one can find indications that a similar state of affairs pertains throughout the branch by perusing the available lexicons and dictionaries.

2.1 Bahnar

Banker (1964) discusses replication in Bahnar, across a range of word classes and functions, including a category *descriptives*, which is equivalent to the later use of expressives by Watson and others. Banker distinguishes several categories:

i. full reduplication or reduplication with vowel of the initial syllable reduced to schwa (ơ in Banker's notation); e.g.:

> *'dit* 'describes movement of chest breathing'
> *'dit-'dit, 'dơt-'dit* 'describes very rapid movement of chest breathing quickly'
> *prâ* 'describes noise of coin being laid down'
> *prâ-prâ, pơ-prâ* 'describes noise of many coins being laid down'

ii. as above, but the base form does not occur independently; e.g.:

> *nĭng-nĭng, nơnĭng* 'describes something very heavy'
> *giot-giot, gơgiot* 'describes the hop of a rabbit'
> *glăk-glăk, gơglăk* 'describes heavy laughter'

iii. three word reduplicative formations; those with the pattern CVC-CaC-maC have extensive meaning, while CV-Cônh-mônh) give distributive meaning; e.g.:

> *hlêl* 'of a jar to be full'
> *hlêl-hlal-mal* 'of many jars to be full'
> *blư* 'of a few people to arrive'
> *blư-bla-ma* 'of many people to arrive'
> *grôk* 'noise of stomach rolling'
> *grôk-grak-mak* 'noise of stomach rolling many times'

Bahnar word classes are discussed by Banker (1965, unpublished, not seen by this writer), although Watson (1966: 11–12) offers the following quote:

> For Bahnar, John Banker (1965: 22, 35) includes words similar to Pacoh Descriptives under two word classes. He considers Nominative Descriptives to belong to Adjectives in the Noun Phrase, and Descriptive Adverbs to belong to Adverbs in the Verb Phrase. However, Banker states that Nominal Descriptives have certain features of form (...) and function that are similar to Descriptive Adverbs (3.4.1) and another analysis might have classed these two together.

2.2   Tampuon

Tampuon is closely related to Bahnar within Central Bahnaric, yet is separated
geographically, being spoken in NE Cambodia. Although a grammar is not
available, the dictionary by Crowley, Tieng, and Churk (2007) lists three pages
of entries for descriptives. Most of the entries are simply full reduplications, but
some show alternations of the kind Banker described for Bahnar, e.g:

(1)   *kəŋ krəiŋ* 'descriptive of great strength'

(2)   *bləŋ bləiʔ* 'descriptive of noise made by splashing'

(3)   *krail krɔm* 'descriptive of scattered abundance'

(4)   *rañțiŋ rañaaŋ* 'descriptive of trees fallen in disorder'

2.3   Sre

Diffloth (1979) extracted Sre expressives from the dictionary of Dournes (1950),
identifying various morphological patterns:

i.   Reduplication; full reduplication of monosyllables and partial, e.g.:
     ŋɛɛ- srŋɛɛ 'in slanted patterns'
     pɔh-smpɔh 'seriously, not halfway'

ii. Reduplication with *r-* substitution, e.g.:
     riw-wiw 'denying movements'
     rik-mhik 'softened (earth)'

iii. Reduplication with *-rə-* insertion, e.g.:
     ŋuu-rə-ŋuu 'livid'
     ʔɛɛw-rə-ʔɛɛw 'feeling of weakness'

iv. Reduplication and replacement with *-h*, e.g.:
     dah-daat 'vacillating'
     dɛd-dwɛɛw '(walking) legs widely apart'

v.   Triplication and replacement by initial *t-*, e.g.:
     tul-hul-hul 'feeling of heat'
     tun-plun-plun '(dog's) dangling ears'

3   Katuic

The Katuic languages are also spoken in Indo-China, generally to the north and
west of Bahnaric. Fortunately special attention has been paid to expressives in
Katuic languages, and in particular the detailed study of Pacoh reveals an
elaborate system with echoes in the most far-flung branches of the AA phylum.

3.1   Pacoh

The canonical text concerning expressives in Austroasiatic is Watson (1966) 'Reduplication in Pacoh' (spoken in the Lao-Vietnam borderlands), which seeks to exhaustively identify and analyse the reduplicative constructions he recorded in the language and in the process provides a critical documentation and analysis.[4] Throughout Watson uses the term 'descriptives' (following Banker 1964), which was later displaced by 'expressives' due its extensive usage among fellow Summer Institute of Linguistics researchers.

Watson offers an early characterization that includes syntactic specifications:

In this present study Descriptives are interpreted as belonging to a distinct word class on the clause level as well as on the phrase level, ...

On the phrase level, Descriptives are distinguished from Adverbs in that Adverbs can be modified but Descriptives cannot. Descriptives can occur in expanded phrases only in the sense that two or three Descriptives can occur in sequence, as Adverbs, Nouns, and Verbs also can.

On the clause level, Descriptives and Adverbs are similar in the following ways: they can occur in the same positions in clauses, and certain Descriptives and Adverbs can be substituted for each other. . . .

However, Descriptives and Adverbs are distinguished by their occurrence in non-adjacent positions in a clause, Descriptives and Adverbs can occur in clause initial or clause final positions but neither can occur in both positions in the same clause. (Watson 1966: 12–13)

His analysis divides 610 examples into nine sets according to phonological shapes; e.g.:

i.   tR ± R–VR ± R:
     tén-bén 'a sudden or unexpected arrival'
     top-hop 'ajar, not closed tightly'

ii. RR ± R–RR ± R:
     nhôk-nhôk 'walking bouncily'
     pléb-pléb 'speaking or acting presumptuously'

iii. (CV)RR±R–(CV±C)RR±R:
     klék-qiklék 'sound of blacksmithing'
     râh-nurâh 'on and on'

iv. (RR)RV±R–(RR±R)RV±R:
     pârngop-pârngap 'extreme difficulties'
     qârqiq-qârqŏaq 'sunnier pleasant weather'

---

[4] It is striking that Diffloth, in his widely cited (1976a, 1979) papers on descriptives, fails to mention this thesis.

v.   Ráh–(CV±C)R±C:
     cháh-kichát 'something stuck between teeth'
     klâh-kliang 'in the middle'

vi. (CV±C)RV±C–(CV±C)RV±C:
     pikhɨ-pikhɨm 'haughty, doesn't reply to others'
     qângngúk-qângngur 'too bitter (angry) to speak'

vii. (CVC)CR±C–(CVC)CR±C:
     qâllɨt-qɨt 'loaded down as with produce on head'
     qârling-ting 'a sound of something approaching'

viii. Residue of reduplicative words: seven words only with no particular
      structural commonalities, e.g.:
      pel-klɨ́p 'hobbling lamely'
      kârmay-qapoh 'curly hair'

ix. RV±RCV±C:
     bâmbual 'water bubbling strongly'
     chânhchúl 'uninhibited'

The above classification is principally structural, and does not go to the motivation for the observed data, but does potentially establish a basis for wider
comparative analyses.

3.2   Ngeq

The Ngeq language is spoken near Salavan in southern Laos, to the west
of Pacoh, and is also known as Kriang. Smith's (1973) paper on reduplication
in Ngeq presents an exhaustive compilation of reduplicative forms from
his lexicon, with some semantic and structural categorization, indicating a
state of affairs more or less directly comparable to Pacoh. However, unlike
Watson, Smith does not distinguish between expressives/descriptives and reduplication across word classes in his listing of examples. Nevertheless, Smith is
aware of the distinction, and offers an important cultural observation:

Adverbial descriptives modify verbs and adjectives. These are an important distinctive in
Ngeq as well as other related languages of the area. To speak "Brou" as they do one must
use these descriptives. One can communicate freely and still not use these couplets of
reduplication. But to use the language idiomatically, one must use these freely because
they have a description for nearly every kind of action and every kind of "goodness" and
"badness". (Smith 1973: 86)

Here we find a specific indication of the value speakers place upon such
motivated expressions. I suspect the underlying importance of iconicity with

these expressives is somewhat limited, whereas their role in respect of in-group/ out-group marking is more crucial. While much of Southeast Asia reflects a linguistic area in which diverse peoples speak languages that are structurally similar, I suggest that a mastery of local/identifying expressive vocabulary, which is to a great extent syntactically independent, can communicate more about one's ethnic and familial affiliations and loyalties.

3.3   So

Migliazza (2005) discusses expressives in So, a Katuic language spoken in Northeast Thailand and Salavan Province of Laos, although he uses the term in the broader sense encompassing all onomatopoeia and reduplications. The number of examples is modest, such that there is insufficient morphosyntactic detail to establish whether a special class of expressives is present. None the less, examples are provided that indicate that So speakers use both partial reduplications and reduplications with segmental substitutions, much as found throughout Austroasiatic as examples (5) through (7) demonstrate.

(5)   *pịŋ dịŋ* 'very still'

(6)   *la.ɲit la:ŋa:t* 'to act lazily'

(7)   *sa.baw sa.bot* 'to speak loudly'

4   Munda

Thanks to Anderson (2008) we now have brief descriptions of expressives in several Munda languages, and I draw on that volume to present details for four of these. Generally the approach of the authors is to use the term expressives either synonymously with reduplications, or simply to cover all forms with some apparent sound symbolic component.

4.1   Mundari

Osada (2008: 138) informs us that, 'Mundari has a rich system of expressives'. These can be divided into three types according to their formation:
a. full reduplication
b. partial reduplication
c. vowel mutation
Type (a) is distinguished from verbal reduplication in that in this case the reduplicated base has no independent meaning. Osada's examples include:

(8)   *cakob cakob*   'to eat noisily'

(9)   *hayam hayam*   'to talk in whispers'

(10)   *kase kase*   'to look askance at (a person)'

(11)   *mogo mogo*   'a smell of flowers'

Type (b) similarly involves the reduplication of an otherwise meaningless word, but the initial consonant of the second iteration is replaced, most frequently with a labial consonant, although others are possible, e.g.:

(12)   *laṭa paṭa*   'to make a stew thick, pasty'

(13)   *cali bali*   'trickiness'

(14)   *gero mero*   'a shamed face or a crying face'

(15)   *runu junu*   'to go or walk with difficulty due to handicap'

(16)   *boro soro*   'cowardice'

Although such forms can be grouped according to the substitutions, no particular semantic or phonological correlations are apparent.

In type (c) the second iteration is marked by vowel substitution. Osada distinguishes six patterns; what they all have in common is that the substituted vowel is not found in the base form and occurs in all syllables of the reduplicate.

(17)   *lada ludu*   'a fat child'

(18)   *ṭarad ṭorod*   'a sound of frog'

(19)   *gida godo*   'semi-liquid things'

(20)   *pica poco*   'to empty a soft or pasty substance by compression'

Syntactically, there are few restrictions; according to Osada, 'Expressives can occupy any place, that is, in a predicate, complement, or argument slot' (2008: 143).

4.2   Ho

The Ho language, a close relative of Mundari within the Kharwarian (North Munda) group, is described by Anderson, Osada, and Harrison (2008) as having expressives that serve as verb stems plus a range of lexical items, especially with distributed or collective semantics. They report that,

A preliminary survey of the Ho lexical materials (e.g. Deeney 1978) reveals rich use of expressive, mimetic or echo reduplication patterns of the type found across the Munda family, and more broadly across the Eurasian continent as an areal feature. These include (128) full reduplication, (129) full reduplication with overwriting of one or more vowels, and (130) full reduplication with overwriting (or protheisi) on an initial consonant, typically [s], [m] or [b] (Anderson, Osada, and Harrison 2008: 230–231).

It is clear from this characterization that the Ho expressives distribute and pattern very similarly to Mundari. The examples provided, although not sub-classified as expansively as Osada does for Mundari, none the less can be compared directly.

4.3   Sora

Sora, one of the more important South Munda languages, is described by Anderson, Osada, and Harrison (2008). They describe four kinds of expressive formations:

i.   full reduplication, e.g.:
     yub yub   'sounds of footsteps'

ii. full reduplication with consonant overwriting, e.g.:
     mandi:n tadin   'plates, dishes' (< *mandi:n* 'a dish')

iii. full reduplication with vowel overwriting, e.g.:
     run ram   'to trot or prance, as horses'

iv. full reduplication with both vowel and consonant overwriting, e.g.:
     mode:te padde:te 'twists'

Note the 'dishes' example (ii) in which the base is a meaningful lexeme. Anderson, Osada, and Harrison also list some verbs that only appear in redu-plicated form, such as (21) and (22) and some others, clearly with a distributed or iterative meaning.

(21)   *mel mel* 'to inspect'

(22)   *ɲaŋ ɲaŋ* 'to teach, admonish'

Additionally, there are various semantically distinct plain and reduplicated forms, e.g.:

(23)   *guŋ-* 'to fall, tumble'

(24)   *guŋ guŋ-* 'to strike, knock'

(25a)   *jun-* 'to escort'

(25b)   *jun jun-* 'to take back, return, restore'

Thus it would appear that Sora reduplication is not strictly confined to expressive vocabulary, but is rather one strategy for encoding plural, augmentative, and distributive meanings across various lexical categories.

4.4   Remo

Remo is a South Munda language that is not extensively documented; it remains unwritten, and the speakers have a reputation for being somewhat uncivilized and ferocious. According to the discussion by Anderson & Harrison (2008), citing Bhattachraya (1968), many Remo nouns are reduplicated, with overwriting of V and V.; e.g.:

(26)   *titi tata*   'hand'

(27)   *gusɔʔ gusɔʔ*   'dog'

(28)   *siram sirim*   'sambar'

(29)   *musri musra*   'lentil'

It is immediately evident that Bhattachraya's list includes many nouns with good Austroasiatic heritage (note 'hand' and 'dog' forms above). There is no discussion concerning the semantic impact, if any, of these reduplications, nor mention of verbal or abverbial reduplication.

5   Khasian

The Khasian languages of Meghalaya State (India) are not closely related to Munda, but quite likely reflect an early split from the Palaungic group, now largely spoken in Myanmar (see Sidwell 2011). One language, Standard Khasi, is well documented, and widely written and understood; others such as Lyngngam, Pnar, and War are not yet represented in detailed grammars, and the limited descriptive accounts that are available do not discuss descriptives (with a minor exception discussed below). However, the literature on Standard Khasi is extensive, and indicates a richness of descriptives, especially adverbials with reduplicated and sound symbolic forms.

5.1   Standard Khasi

Rabel-Heymann (1976) describes reduplication of adverbs, both with and without vowel overwriting ('ablaut' on her description). Likewise, Nagaraja's (1985) grammar of Khasi provides a similar picture of the adverbial system.

The following examples from Nagaraja illustrate various reduplication types:

i. Reduplicated without modification:
    khalakhala   'at once'
    ŋeŋŋeŋ   'drowsily'

ii. Reduplicated with vowel change in the second member:
    jɨrwitjɨrwat   'unwillingly'
    phuʔmatphuʔmut   'cheerfully'

iii. Triplicated forms with initial consonant lost in the repetitions:
    jraŋ-raŋ-raŋ   'resoundingly' (*jraŋ* 'with sound')
    thlip-lip-lip   'very very dark' (*thlip* 'completely')

iv. Quadruplicated forms with vowel change:
    sipsip sapsap   'in an underhand way'
    luŋluŋ leŋleŋ   'hurriedly'

Rabel-Heymann is sure that the vowel alternations are meaningful, and suggests an elaborate and productive ablaut series, such that, 'it is my feeling that proficient Khasi speakers can make up new words on the spur of the moment using the vocalic associations' (1976: 257–258). She proposes these associations as follows:

i , ie   small, light, dainty, cute;
ia   young, tender, thin, flat, pretty, modest, quick, attractive;
o, o:, uo   small, short, smooth, tender, delicate, feeble, pertaining to babies;
a, a: medium-sized, small and flat, pertaining to stout persons;
e, e: big, strong, tall, pertaining to grown-ups;
u   big, large, fat, ungainly, plump, fleshy, heavy, pertaining to old persons.

Rabel-Heymann also finds that adverbs with initial clusters, monosyllables, and reduplicates show especially frequent initial *j*- and *l*-, with apparent semantic associations. For example, on the basis of forms such as:

(30)   *lmoɲ*   'cut short (of small things)'

(31)   *lmuɲ*   'cut short (of big things)'

(32)   *lman-lman* 'fleshy (of a young baby)'

(33)   *lmum-lmum* 'fleshy and plump (of an adult)'

(34)   *lmeʔ*   'young looking in spite of old age'

Rabel-Heymann (1976: 254) proposes a morpheme *lm*- meaning 'short and fleshy', and goes on to list a total of twenty-nine proposed 'morphemes'. These are clearly not morphemes in the regular sense, since Khasi words do not otherwise divide morphologically into initials and rhymes; consequently I would characterize them as phonaesthemic constructs, in various cases probably real form–meaning associations that are understood and manipulated by speakers.

The major force of Diffloth's (1979) discussion of Rabel-Heymann (1976) is to make the point that the proliferation of consonant clusters in Khasi that show sound symbolic associations fill out phonological possibilities not utilized elsewhere in the lexicon.

5.2   Amwi

The Amwi dialect of War is the subject of a little known grammar by Weidert (1975), written in German. Strikingly, although Amwi has undergone extensive phonological change and restructuring (compared to Standard Khasi) Weidert's account indicates very similar patterning. For example, in relation to the sound symbolic initial clusters, Weidert (1975: 44) identifies groups of expressive forms with initial clusters *cw-, ch-, lb-, lh, sph-*, 'viele Ks.gruppen zeigen in der Mehrheit Expressiva als Beispiele' (...*the majority of examples of expressives show in this group*). Amwi has undergone a devoicing of initial palatal stops, so the forms with initials *c-* and *l-* correspond to Standard Khasi forms with initials *j-, l-* discussed above.

Amwi also shows the Khasi style of vowel ablaut, especially encoding augmentation/diminution. Weidert (1975: 104) explains:

Die als Nuclei aufgefaßten vokalischen Ableitungssuffixe sind:
/a/, /e/, /ɛ/ und /u/: bezeichnen alles, was groß, erwachsen, alt, stark, gewalttätig, dick, schwerfällig, grob, laut, breit, hoch, lang, tief, schwerflüssig, allgemein von großer Dimension ist;
/i/, /ɔ/, /a/ und /ia/: bezeichnen alles, was klein, jung, leicht, dürr, leise, zart, hübsch, niedlich, niedrig, schwach, leichtfüßig, heiter, allgemein von kleiner Dimension ist.
Conceived as the nuclei vowel suffixes are:
/a/, /e/, /ɛ/ *and* /u/: *describe anything that is large, grown-up, old, strong, violent, thick, heavy, coarse, loud, wide, high, long, deep, heavy liquid, generally of large dimension;*
/i/, /ɔ/, /a/ *and* /ia/: *describe anything small, young, light, thin, soft, delicate, pretty, cute, low, weak, light-footed, cheerful, or generally of smaller dimension.*

For example, with adverbs using specific verbs such as *chəliaŋ* and *dɔr* 'be deformed, inclined at an angle' or *bo* 'to eat', examples (35) through (38) show vowel overwriting correlating with characteristics of the object.

(35)   *chəkrwɔc*   'large object'

(36)   *chəkrwãc*   'small object'

(37)   *chəkrwĩãc* 'very small object'

(38)   *chəkrwuc* 'large object'

And expressive reduplication with segmental substitution is reported, although Weidert characterizes it as verb followed by an adverb that shows '*phonemische Ähnlichkeit*' ('phonemic similarity') to the verb.

(39)   *khãt, khĩãt* expressive with *crkhãt* 'to pinch'

(40)   *ŋaŋ-ŋaŋ, ŋəŋ-ŋəŋ* expressive with *kəŋaŋ* 'to shake head'

(41)   *tʔəŋ, tʔãŋ* expressive with *tŋʔĩãŋ* 'high, to look up'

So it would appear that both Standard Khasi and Amwi, which do not closely sub-group within Khasian, show directly comparable expressive formations, which one would predict are characteristic of the branch as a whole.

6   Palaungic

The Palaungic branch is a typologically diverse diaspora of small groups across hilly areas of Myanmar, Yunnan, Thailand, and Northern Laos. Much descriptive work has been done in recent decades, although it is mostly in the form of dissertations that emphasize phonetic and phonological description and lexicon, rather than morphosyntactic detail. Even the recent (2008) grammar of Man Noi Plang by Lewis makes no mention of reduplication or other expressive forms, continuing the tendency for 'formal' grammar rather than rich description of representative speech.

Consequently, one of the best sources for grammar is still Milne's (1921) *An elementary Palaung grammar*, which is not written to contemporary linguistic standards, but is none the less insightful.

Milne's chapter on adverbs (1921: 86–113) contains examples of reduplication and clues to the use of expressive forms. It begins:

Many adjectives and verbs become adverbs by reduplication: the word is used alone for the adjective or for the verb, and is repeated for the adverb. Although this is often the case, it is not always so. Verbs are very often the same as adjectives, and are sometimes reduplicated for the sake of emphasis, and the adjective is also used occasionally in a reduplicated form.

a)   lă   *good, to be good*
b)   lă lă   *well*
c)   rēng   *loud, to be loud*
d)   rēng rēng   *loudly*

Under the discussion of verbs (p. 67), we are told:

The reduplication of a verb, however, does not always express a more emphatic command, it sometimes entirely changes the meaning of the word, as:

to hide *blōŋg*; to throw water (on a floor) *blōŋg blōŋg*

to hang without movement *jwǫ̀*; to hang with a swinging movement, to dangle *jwǫ̀ jwǫ̀*.

and other examples, suggesting distributed adverbial meanings. Unfortunately, this is where the trail grows cold, absent richer documentation of Palaungic languages.

7   Khmuic

The Khmuic branch consists of a large Khmu' dialect chain distributed over much of northern Laos, and ten or a dozen lesser Khmuic languages about the periphery. Much descriptive work has been done, and we are fortunate to have some sources that have paid close attention to the subject of expressives.

7.1   Mlabri

Rischel's (1995) quirky but informative grammar of Minor Mlabri devotes some seven pages to discussing reduplication and expressives. His discussion on page 92 begins:

Reduplication, with or without vowel alternation between the reduplicating and the reduplicated syllable, is a frequent phenomenon in Mlabri words. It is a word formation device, but words with reduplications are in most cases not synchronically derivable from simple stems.

Thus Rischel's characterization of Mlabri immediately suggests commonalities with languages discussed above, such as Mundari. Rischel provides various examples, some of which have clear sound symbolic value, others less obviously, e.g.:

(42)   *muŋmo:ŋ*   'gong'

(43)   *dumdum:m*   'to rock a child in one's arms'

(44)   *pjurpjuːr*   'to stare'

(45)   *dɨwdɨw*   'to look upwards'

(46)   *kutke:t*   'spout (of kettle)' (< ke:t 'ear')

(47)   *micmɛ:c*   'ant'

Rischel classifies reduplicates into three types phonologically:

i.   full syllable reduplication
ii. when coda is a voiced sonorant becomes syllabic, with or without insertion
     of -r-: e.g.: *krlki:l* 'knee'
iii. pretonic syllable with short vowel that harmonizes with the main vowel,
     e.g.: *prijhprɛjh* 'crisp'.

All of the above are frequent. However, Rischel (p. 97) advises that, 'sometimes
there are substantial discrepancies in vowel quality, ... It is certainly not all
reduplicatives that follow the regular patterns (i)–(iii).'

7.2   Khmu' / Kammu

Khmu' has been the subject of tremendous scholarship, which has revealed
extensive and highly elaborated use of expressive formations. Despite this,
Khmu' studies have not been free from the blind spot for expressives that
seems to curse much of the AA research community, and there are extraordinary
examples, such as the fact that Suwilai Premsrirat's otherwise magisterial
(2002) *Thesaurus of Khmu dialects in Southeast Asia* barely records the fact
that such things exist. It is simply an outcome of a mode of working that has
emphasized the recoding of lists of lexical items over other aspects of language
documentation.

    Fortunately, in respect of Khmu', there is Svantesson's (1983) *Kammu
phonology and morphology*, and Proschan's (1993) 'Khmu play languages'
(which also extensively references the former). Proschan (1993: 44) points out
that:

In his authoritative account of Khmu morphology, Svantesson identifies five kinds of
reduplication (1983: 84); the symbols and definitions are his but the examples are my
own:
R(Ø), reduplication without any change *caac caac* 'sound of liquid dripping to ground'
R(O), onset-changing reduplication *tlot tot* 'name of a bird species'
R(P), peak-changing reduplication *kvlaav kvlav* 'manner of shivering'
R(C), coda-changing reduplication *hvɔɔy hmɔt* 'flute sound flutters'
R(R), rhyme-changing reduplication *sŋglɔŋ sŋbooŋ* 'smooth-skinned and light-skinned'
    In each case, certain phonological sequences are repeated without change, while
others are altered or introduced. The first case involves simple repetition, while the
others clearly involve partial repetition with variation.

Strikingly, on the same page we are told that:

With a few interesting exceptions, the basic lexicon of Khmu is common to all dialects,
while the expressive vocabulary is far more diverse. But because the morphological
structure of the language and the techniques of reduplication are well known to speakers,
newly encountered reduplicative words can be understood even if they are not present in
a particular dialect.

This fact resonates with Rabel-Heymann's (1976) remark, discussed above, to the effect that Khasi speakers can invent on the spot new expressive forms, and yet expect to be understood. It is clear that speakers must have at least an intuitive grasp of a set of common form–meaning associations which they can deploy productively, if perhaps idiosyncratically.

Proschan's paper goes on to give examples of word play in Khmu' poetry and song, demonstrating multiple degrees of parallel reference more removed than reduplication, where the corresponding word may be in a contiguous line or verse, or even be absent. This is not so far from our own experience: consider English rhyming slang, in which a rhyming word may be deleted completely, or replaced with a semantic correspondent (*raspberry* < *raspberry tart* < *fart*; see Anttila and Embleton 1992 for discussion).

8   Aslian

Attention has been drawn to expressives in Aslian languages, particularly since Diffloth (1972, 1976a, 1976b). An interesting characteristic in Aslian is the special kind of reduplication, called 'incopyfixation' by Matisoff (2003), in which the word final consonant is copied into the coda of the presyllable. While this strategy is employed in the elaboration of expressives, and one finds traces in other branches (such as Khmuic), it is not restricted to that function, and not all Aslian languages can be said to evidence a distinct class of expressives (see Burenhult 2005: 113).

8.1   Semai

Diffloth's studies of Semai (1972, 1976a) drew special attention to expressives as a distinct word class, and considered to some extent sensory and cognitive bases for regarding them as sound symbolic forms. His analyses lead him to make strong theoretical claims that ran directly counter to the dominant structuralist thinking of the times:

It should be clear from these examples that expressives are not subject to the condition of "lexical discreteness" and that the same exemption may apply to certain verbs and nouns related to expressives. It follows that the "roots" of expressives have to be analysed into very small "morphemes"–elements as small, perhaps, as distinctive features. We must be prepared to see the expressives as a whole decomposed in such manner to discard the conventional notions of root and morphology, and to treat expressives as micro-sentences made up of distinctive features. (Diffloth 1976a: 261)

Within Semai it is apparent that there are specific word-formational strategies that are particular to the expressive. In particular, Diffloth mentions *minor reduplication* which 'consists in prefixing a minor syllable made of two consonants identical respectively to the first and last consonants of the root' (1976a: 253).

(48)   *dldyɔ̃:l* 'appearance of an object which goes on floating'

(49)   *dhdŋɔh* 'appearance of nodding constantly'

Two other types of reduplication are discussed:
- full copy reduplication with modified vowel, e.g.: *klcwẽc > klcwũc klcwẽc* 'irregular flapping circular movements'
- a prefixing reduplication restricted to the Kampar basin dialect, e.g.: *r(ŋ)rŋʔaŋ > r(ŋ)rŋʔaŋ maʔaŋ* 'appearance of irregular cracks'.

8.2   Temiar

Benjamin (1976: 177) offers the following definition of expressives in Temiar.

This is a heterogeneous category of adjuncts many of which are formed from real or imaginary verb roots by what can only be described as 'reduplicative play'. Syntactically they stand in apposition to the whole verb phrase, or even to the whole sentence. Semantically they serve as a kind of expressive mirror-phrase, summing up in a word or two the 'feelings' that are stereotypically supposed to be aroused in the interlocutors' minds.

Benjamin reports that expressives are common in conversation, and form essential elements in stories and song lyrics, with examples (50) through (52).

(50)   *gɛngɛrlʉt* 'spindly-ness' (<*gɛrlʉt* 'long and thin')

(51)   *cəraʔŭk ʔŭk* 'stomach queeziness' (no root *cəʔŭk* known)

(52)   *kərahab hab* 'lip smacking' (*kɛrhab* 'to eat noisily')

Although aware of Diffloth's treatment of expressives as a distinct class, Benjamin prefers to characterize them as 'verbal derivatives'.

9   Conclusion

The above survey, although necessarily sketchy, does allow us to make some observations. Broadly, it is evident that there is a huge, far from fully documented aspect of Austroasiatic languages, namely descriptive and sound-symbolic lexicon and related word-formational strategies that are recognized under the rubric of expressives. In some cases one can identify the phenomenon with a discrete word class, in other cases it is more generalized. However, there is a widespread under-appreciation, even a reluctance, stretching back at least four decades, to even recognize expressives as part of the grammar, resulting in unfortunate gaps in the otherwise increasing descriptive literature. The study of Austroasiatic expressives thus presents fertile ground for investigation, with much promise for informing our understanding of sound-symbolism, word play and even glottogenesis.

References

Alves, Mark. 2006. *A grammar of Pacoh: a Mon-Khmer language of the central highlands of Vietnam*. Canberra: Pacific Linguistics, The Australian National University.

Anderson, Gregory (ed.). 2008. *The Munda languages*. London: Routledge.

Anderson, Gregory, Toshiki Osada and K. David Harrison. 2008. 'Ho and the other Kherwarian languages'. In G. D. S. Anderson (ed.), *The Munda languages*. Routledge Language Family Series. London: Routledge, pp. 195–255.

Anttila, Raimo and Sheila Embleton. 1992. 'The iconic index: from sound change to rhyming slang'. In Raffaele Simone (ed.), *Iconicity in language*. Amsterdam: John Benjamins, pp. 87–118.

Banker, Elizabeth M. 1964. Bahnar affixation. *Mon-Khmer studies* 1: 99–117.

Banker, John A. 1965. Bahnar word classes. Hartford Seminary Foundation, unpublished Master's thesis.

Benjamin, Geoffrey. 1976. 'An outline of Temiar grammar'. In Philip N. Jenner, Laurence C. Thompson, and Stanley Starosta (eds.), *Austroasiatic studies*, Part I. (Oceanic Linguistics Special Publications, No. 13.) Honolulu: University of Hawaii Press, pp. 129–188.

Burenhult, Niclas. 2005. *A grammar of Jahai*. Canberra: The Australian National University.

Crowley, James Dale, Vay Tieng, and Wain Churk. 2007. *Tampuan Khmer English dictionary: with English Khmer Tampuan glossary*. Cambodia: EMU International and National Language Institute of the Royal Academy of Cambodia.

Deeney, J. J. 1978. *Ho-English dictionary*. Chaibassa: Xavier Ho Publications.

Diffloth, G. 1972. 'Notes on expressive meaning'. In *Papers from the Eighth Regional Meeting of the Chicago Linguistics Society*. Chicago Linguistic Society, pp. 440–447.

1976a. 'Expressives in Semai'. In Philip N. Jenner, Laurence C. Thompson, and Stanley Starosta (eds.), *Austroasiatic studies*, Part I. (Oceanic Linguistics Special Publications, No. 13.) Honolulu: University of Hawaii Press, pp. 249–264.

1976b. 'Jah-Hut: an Austroasiatic language of Malaysia'. In Nguyen Dang Liem (ed.), *Southeast Asian linguistic studies* vol. 2 (Pacific Linguistics series C, no. 42). Canberra: The Australian National University, pp. 73–118.

1979. 'Expressive phonology and prosaic phonology in Mon-Khmer'. In Theraphan L. Thongkum et al. (eds.), *Studies in Tai and Mon-Khmer phonetics and phonology in honour of Eugénie J. A. Henderson*. Chulalongkorn University Press, pp. 49–59.

Dournes, Jacques. 1950. *Dictionnaire Srê (Köhö)-Français*. Saigon: Des Missions Etrangères de Paris.

Kruspe, Nicole. 2004. *A grammar of Semelai*. Cambridge University Press.

Lewis, Emily Dawn. 2008. Grammatical studies Man Noiplang. Master's thesis. Payap University.

Matisoff, James. 2003. Aslian: Mon-Khmer of the Malay Peninsula. *Mon-Khmer studies* 33: 1–58.

2005. *English–Lay lexicon*. University of California Press.

Migliazza, Brian. 2005. Some expressives in So. *Ethnorêma* 1(1): 1–18.

Milne, Leslie. 1921. *An elementary Palaung grammar*. Oxford: Clarendon Press.

Nagaraja, K. S. 1985. *Khasi – a descriptive analysis*. Poona: Deccan College Postgraduate Research Institute.

Osada, Toshiki. 2008. 'Mundari'. In Gregory D. S. Anderson (ed.), *The Munda languages* (Routledge Language Family Series). London, New York: Routledge, pp. 99–164.

Premsrirat, Suwilai. 2002. *Thesaurus of Khmu dialects in Southeast Asia*. Bangkok: Institute of Language and Culture for Rural Development, Mahidol University.

Proschan, Frank. 1993. Khmu play languages. *Mon-Khmer studies* 23: 43–65.

Rabel-Heymann, Lili. 1976. 'Sound symbolism and Khasi adverbs'. In Nguyen Dang Liem (ed.), *Southeast Asian linguistic studies* vol. 2. (Pacific Linguistics series C, no. 42). Canberra: The Australian National University, pp. 253–262.

Rischel, Jørgen. 1995. *Minor Mlabri: a hunter-gatherer language of northern Indochina*. Copenhagen: Museum Tusculanum Press.

Shorto, Harry L., Paul Sidwell, Dong Cooper and Christian Bauer (eds.). 2006. *A Mon-Khmer comparative dictionary*. Canberra: Pacific Linguistics, The Australian National University.

Sidwell, Paul. 2011. 'Katuic-Bahnaric: Austroasiatic sub-family or convergence area?'. In Sophana Srichaupa, Paul Sidwell, and Kenneth Gregerson (eds.), *Austroasiatic studies: papers from the ICAAL4, Man-Khmer studies* (Journal Special Issue no. 3). Dallas: SIL International; Canberra-Pacific Linguistics; Salaya: Malidol University, pp. 23–37.

Smith, Ronald L. 1973. 'Reduplication in Ngeq'. *Mon-Khmer studies* 4: 85–111.

Svantesson, Jan-Olof. 1983. *Kammu phonology and morphology*. Lund: CWK Gleerup.

Watson, Richard L. 1966. Reduplication in Pacoh. Hartford Seminary Foundation, unpublished Master's thesis.

Weidert, Alfons K. 1975. *Itkong Amwi. Deskriptive Analyse eines Wardialekts des Khasi*. Wiesbaden: Harrassowitz.

3   Aesthetic elements in Temiar grammar

Geoffrey Benjamin

1   Introduction

Temiar is a Mon-Khmer (Austroasiatic) language of the Central Aslian division, spoken by almost 30,000 people in the interior of northern Peninsular Malaysia (Map 2). Until recently, the Temiars were living in relatively autonomous tribal circumstances. Currently, their lifeways are changing rapidly, involving a shift from their former subsistence-based existence to a cash-based one. For younger Temiars, this has been associated with almost universal primary education, resulting in basic literacy in Malay, the (unrelated) national language, as well as with shifts in their social and religious orientations. The Temiar language, however, is still employed in all domains of daily life except those that require formal literacy, and it therefore remains essentially unwritten.

2   Aesthesis and iconicity in language

People who lack writing necessarily have a different sense of what a language is than do literate people. Roy Harris (1987: 51ff.) relates this difference to what he calls 'scriptism' – the tyranny of the written word. For non-literate people, a language consists primarily in the sounds and/or oral (articulatory) gestures of speech. Approaches to linguistic analysis that commence by declaring any connection between sounds and meanings to be arbitrary are therefore methodologically questionable. On the contrary, such iconicity should be searched for and, if found, incorporated into the analysis, along with an investigation of its relation to the social circumstances of the language's speakers.

A major reason for linguistic iconicity is economy of expression. If a language were to permit direct one-to-one expression to all of its underlying semantic features, the resulting grammar would be too complex for its speakers to cope with. Consequently, shunts or syncretisms develop, in which several different features are mapped onto a single overt surface expression – phonic, morphosyntactic, or lexical. A degree of semantic condensation is therefore an inevitable, though variable, feature of all grammars, but it is especially marked in languages such as Temiar, where syncretisms of this kind are frequent. Since

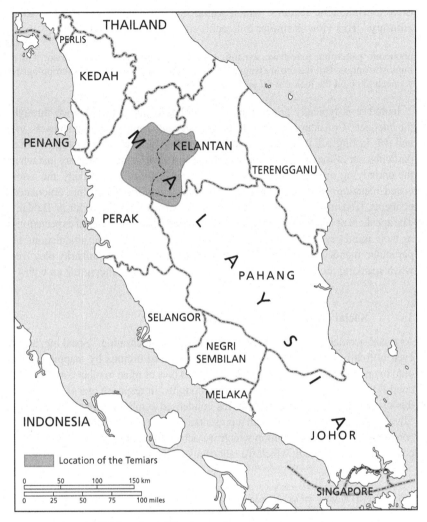

Map 2 The location of Temiar speakers

semantic condensation reduces arbitrariness, it necessarily results in a degree of iconicity, phonaesthetic or otherwise.

There may well be a universal tendency towards *a priori* phonaesthetic expression – of deictic and quantitative contrasts especially – that has become submerged or not taken up in a systematic manner in some languages. But if the speakers of a language do take up phonic iconicity they may then in a secondary, *a posteriori*, manner proceed to elaborate the lexical or grammatical motivation of certain phonetic features, which would thereby become iconic rather than arbitrary.[1] This view is similar to Leach's suggestion (1971: 83) that

phonemic patterning may have semantic significance, not that it must do so; it is a linguistic option. But if there are languages which work that way then as anthropologists we need to be on the look out for such a possibility.

Iconicity is typically *felt* (a matter of aesthesis) rather than known through the intellect.[2] Consider, for example, the *a posteriori* iconic phonaesthemes *th-*, *gl-* and *wh-* in English, where an iconic form is felt to be peculiarly appropriate to a particular set of meanings even though most speakers cannot easily say just what the underlying meaning is. In both *a priori* and *a posteriori* iconicity, the associated meanings are held in mind as condensed *notions* rather than articulated concepts. (Examples of both *a priori* and *a posteriori* iconicity occur in Temiar.) The speakers of a language thereby generate inchoate but meaningful expectations in their minds as to the appropriateness of particular phonetic articulations to particular intended meanings. This is a primary source of the familiarity they feel when speaking the language, especially if it is the language they grew up with.

3   Social dimensions of linguistic iconicity

As noted, iconicity necessarily involves symbolic condensation.[3] Speaking, however, normally forces us to *articulate* our condensed notions by mapping them onto overt conventionalized concepts. This then lays us open to others' attempts to control the way in which we express our thoughts. In response, we seek to resist this by holding on to our notions in the condensed symbolic forms in which we 'dwell'. Consequently, our mental representations constantly flip-flop between the condensed notional forms upon which we act (unthinkingly) and the articulated conceptual ones through which we talk (thinkingly) to others.[4]

---

[1]   On *a priori* and *a posteriori* iconic motivation, see Gell (1979). Tufvesson (2011: 89), following Peirce, refers to the latter as 'diagrammatic, or second-order, iconicity, where likeness between form and meaning is driven by the aligning of similar forms with similar meanings'.

[2]   I take 'iconic' in its normal linguistic sense of 'non-arbitrary'; but I employ 'aesthetic' in its etymological sense as having to do with what is *felt* or *perceived*, rather than with the later view that it is concerned with 'beauty'. The source is Greek αἴσθησις, αἰσθητικός, referring to 'things perceptible by the senses ... as opposed to things thinkable' (*The Shorter Oxford English Dictionary*, Third edition, I: 32).

[3]   On symbolism – or better, 'symboling' – as being the *willed* condensing together of subjectively held notions, see Sperber (1979).

[4]   This view derives from Michael Polanyi's work on 'tacit' and 'explicit' knowledge (Polanyi 1959: 31). Levinson (2000: 28) implies that we are four times as reluctant to articulate our meanings in speech than we are to parse what others are saying. He suggests that this results from a physiological constraint on the speech organs, but I believe it may also relate to a desire to *keep* our meanings unarticulated. For a more extended presentation of the views expressed in the next few paragraphs, see Benjamin (1993: 344–350).

Socio-cultural traditions vary considerably in this regard. In some communities speech is relatively infrequent, being regarded as just one of several communication modes, most of which (eating and cooking, body decoration, vernacular architecture, ceremonial, music, dance, odours, bodily stance, manual gesture, facial expression – to name a few) fall towards the symbolically condensed end of the spectrum. Such communities often display a non-interfering ethos of interpersonal behaviour. Thus, in relatively non-interfering situations, or in situations where no preference is directed towards articulate speech as opposed to other modes of communication, people tend to be more favourably disposed towards the condensed 'symbolic' modes of expression – including iconic modes. The more interfering and language-valuing situations, however, make greater demands on individuals to articulate their thoughts as fully as possible into language, thereby reducing the likelihood that iconicity will invade the grammar.

The alternation between articulated and condensed modes of expression should not be misconstrued. It has no obvious connection to the complexity of what is in individuals' minds, but it has much to do with differences in social complexity. As Ernest Gellner argued (1989: 45ff.), the crucial issue is the contrast between the *many-strandedness* of social relations in less complex societies and the relative *single-strandedness* of social relations in more complex societies, especially those embedded in modernity. In the latter case people typically believe it possible to talk about just one thing at a time, in what Max Weber would have recognized as a display of 'formal rationality'. This predisposes people to a view of linguistic meaning as primarily referential, in what Roy Harris calls 'reocentric surrogationalism'.[5] The more implicational and allusive kinds of meaning then come to be seen as secondary or trivial. In many-stranded circumstances, on the other hand, these forms of expression are seen as no less normal than the more referential meanings that the people also employ on occasion. In other words, ways of speaking that might be regarded as metaphorical in a 'single-stranded' context are seen as nothing out of the ordinary by people operating in 'many-stranded' contexts (Gellner 1989: 45ff.).

Consequently, at the many-stranded end of the scale, speech is typically more embedded in its context, less articulated, more allusive, and more liable to imply several different meanings in a single expression. This 'poetic' tendency may then come to be matched by aesthetic properties in the language itself, as expressed in certain morphological patterns or in the linked meanings generated

---

[5] In Harris's framework (1987: Chapter 2) there are, besides 'reocentric' thing-orientation, at least two other configurations of linguistic surrogationalism: *logocentric*, in which 'words' are seen as the really real (as in the classical Chinese principle of 'the rectification of names'); and *psychocentric*, in which consciousness itself serves as the ultimate reality upon which language rests. The Temiar pattern of cultural and linguistic organization fits into the psychocentric framework.

by the homophony of apparently unrelated forms. In such cases it is the iconic properties of the sounds and vocal gestures that carry the language-poem, as Gell (1979) called it. The 'meaning' then pertains not solely to the ostensible referential meaning of the speakers' utterances, but also to the cultural and psychological 'figure' (Becker 1979) presented by the language's grammatical and lexical patterns.[6] Temiar is one such language.

4   Iconic aesthesis in Temiar

In previous studies of Temiar (Benjamin 2011a: 14; 2012) I discussed a set of grammatical and lexical features that display the iconic-aesthetic effects of contrasting deictic gestures made by the vocal organs:[7]

- Opening the mouth wide, as if addressing oneself to OTHER, the rest of the world[8]
- Closing the mouth in SELF-contemplation, as if in temporary retreat from the world.

The relatively open mouth position, manifested in Temiar by the low vowel *a*, the back consonants *ʔ* and *h*, and vowel nasality (i.e., velic opening), underlies the OTHER-referring features – a generalization, perhaps, of 'you (*hãã ʔ*)'-deixis. The low vowel *-a-* is employed on its own as an object-referring infix in the middle-voice inflection of the verb, as well as in a series of semantically similar but non-inflecting 'deponent' verbs and 'middle-voice' nouns. The same open-mouth articulation is also employed in the second- and third-person pronouns, the objective case-marking particles and in a few other idiomatic expressions. A partial list is given in Table 3.1.

The relatively closed mouth position, on the other hand, signifies the more subjective SELF-focused, 'I (*yee ʔ*)'-deixis realm. This is expressed phonically by the high vowel *i* and the front consonants *y*, *c*, *m*, and *r*. The high vowel *i* is employed in a series of first-person proclitic pronouns. The same closed articulation is also employed in nominative and instrumental case-marking particles. Table 3.2 lists the forms discussed in the rest of this chapter.

There is no room here to discuss the SELF-referring features indicated by the consonants *m* and *r*. These include: (i) the employment of the closed-mouth

---

[6] A similar suggestion has been proffered by Levinson and Burenhult (2008: 169), in pointing to the relatively frequent occurrence of the symbolically condensed linguistic figures they refer to as 'semplates' in 'small, traditional societies without elaborate divisions of labor, in domains that are central to their way of life'.

[7] For a description of the Temiar sound-system see Benjamin (1976: 130–153). Note that the iconicity under discussion here relates to oral-articulatory gesture rather than the acoustic properties of the sounds produced by those gestures (cf. Jakobson and Waugh 1979: 182). See also Benjamin (2009: 301–303) on related features in Malay.

[8] Non-articulated notional meanings, such as SELF and OTHER, are indicated in small caps.

Table 3.1 *Articulatorily open forms*

-a-	the middle-voice verbal affix
hãã²	the pronoun 'you (singular)' (free-standing, stressed)
hah	the pronoun 'you (singular)' (free-standing, unstressed, phrase-final clitic form of *hãã²*)
ha-	the pronoun 'you (singular)' (proclitic, unstressed form of *hãã²*)
ha-	the accusative (affected-patient) object-marker (optional, proclitic, unstressed)
²aar	the inclusive dual pronoun 'you-and-I' (free-standing, stressed)
²ah	the inclusive dual pronoun 'you-and-I' (free-standing, unstressed, phrase-final clitic form of *²aar*)
²a-	the inclusive dual pronoun 'you-and-I' (proclitic, unstressed form of *²aar*)
²a-	the delimiting determiner (proclitic to demonstratives, and to proper nouns in direct address)
²a-	the negative-imperative marker 'don't!'
na²	the demonstrative 'there, near you' (free-standing)
na-	the third-person pronoun 'he/she/it' (proclitic, unstressed)

Table 3.2 *Articulatorily closed forms*

cee²	the pronoun 'I' (emphatic, free-standing, stressed)
cə-	the contrastive topic-marker 'as for . . .' (optional, proclitic, unstressed)
yee²	the pronoun 'I' (free-standing, stressed)
yeh	the pronoun 'I' (free-standing, unstressed, phrase-final clitic form of *yee²*)
yi-	the pronoun 'I' (contrastive, proclitic, unstressed form of *yee²*)
yi-	the nominative (agent/statant) subject-marker (contrastive, optional, proclitic, unstressed)
yi-	the instrument (accessory agent) marker (proclitic, unstressed)
yə²-	the instrument (inanimate accessory agent) marker (proclitic, unstressed); sometimes 'locative' in meaning ('[other] place')
²i-	the pronoun 'I, my, me' (proclitic, unstressed)
²i-	the nominative (agent/statant) subject-marker (optional, proclitic, unstressed)
²i-	the instrument (accessory agent) marker (proclitic, unstressed)

pre-verbal clitic *-m-* to indicate a range of subjective irrealis meanings – intentive, purposive, future, imperative, counterfactual, conditional, avertive, and proximative (Benjamin, under review); and (ii) the incorporation of the front consonant *r* in a set of forms to carry the notional meaning REPLICATION (OF SELF) – the intensifier *rii²* 'self(same)', the preposition *rɛ²-* 'like', the pronoun-anaphor *rə-* 'who', and the causative verbal affix *-r-* (*~tɛr-*) (Benjamin 2012).[9]

The salience accorded in Temiar grammar to the SELF–OTHER dialectic directly reflects the prominence of this dialectic as an organizing principle of the Temiar cultural regime,[10] which is calqued psychocentrically upon the

---

[9] For discussion of the semantically somewhat similar iconic status of [m] and [r] in Malay, see Benjamin (2009: 301–305).

[10] On 'cultural regime' as opposed to 'a culture', see Benjamin (1993: 348–350, 2011b: 176). For more extended discussions of Temiar dialecticism, see Benjamin (1994, 2011a: 22–23). For a detailed study of its expression in musical performance, see Roseman (1984: 421–427).

direct experience that individual human beings have of their own subjectivity as simultaneously a controlling actor and an undergoing patient. Consciousness itself then serves as the ultimate surrogational reality upon which language (and the cosmos) rests, and upon which meaning is constructed. This dialectical framework did not just 'happen', but was deliberately (though inchoately) *cultivated* in response to the specific societal and environmental circumstances of Temiar life, and as part of the means by which they generated a complementarity between themselves and the neighbouring populations (Benjamin 2011b). The specific iconic patterning of certain sections of Temiar grammar has had a major role in the maintenance of this dialectical mode of orientation, by embedding it more deeply into the cultural framework than could have been achieved by explicit articulation.[11]

In the rest of this chapter I examine the semantic and iconic properties of the various affixes, clitics and reduplicative patterns that modify the meaning of words and utterances in Temiar, and which display a combination of *a priori* and *a posteriori* motivations. I also briefly discuss the iconic aspects of the special class of words known as expressives.

5   Phonaesthetic iconicity

Tables 3.1 and 3.2 display some of the pronoun-linked syncretisms that affect the surface expression of some key features of Temiar grammar. Illustrations of their usage are presented in examples (1)–(6), which are mostly taken from texts that I collected by tape-recording and direct dictation or from notes of overheard conversations, at various times between 1964 and 2010. Several of the sentences are taken from traditional tales concerning the doings of ʔɛŋkã̃ãy or ʔɛŋkuuʔ (the thunder deity) and his younger brother ʔalʉj (the first human). Each of the examples contains identical or closely similar forms that serve different grammatical functions.

Examples (1)–(3) disclose a subjective (SELF) semantic, as indicated by their phonically high and closed character, linked with the first-person pronoun forms. In (1a), *cə*- 'as for ...' is the contrastive topic-marker (CTRS). In (1b), *ceeʔ* is the emphatic contrastive form of the first-person singular pronoun:[12]

---

[11] Most Temiars find it difficult to talk about language in ways that would involve abstracting it away from this dialectical imagery. The Temiar word for '(a) language', *kuy*, which basically means 'head', well encapsulates this view, for it implies a dialectical conjoining of ears and tongue, hearer and speaker. Temiar, unlike many (most?) other languages, therefore does not derive the word for 'language' from a word meaning 'tongue' (as with the English word 'language' or the Arabo-Malay *lisan*).

[12] To increase legibility the orthography used here indicates the fully determined epenthetic vowels (*ə*, *ɛ*) that would be omitted in a strictly phonemic transcription. But I also omit them when

(1)   a. *Ɂaluj, ɂe-loɁ cə-hãã̃Ɂ   ha-pɔɁ?*
         Ɂalʉj, what <u>CTRS</u>-2SG 2SG-dream.PFV?
         'Ɂalʉj, what did *you* dream?'

      b. *Hɔ̃y TataaɁ,   ceeɁ tɔɁ   Ɂi-pɛɁpɔɁ.*
         No Old.man, <u>1SG</u> NEG 1SG-dream.IPFV.
         'No Sir, *I* didn't dream.'

In (2a), *yi-* is the emphatic proclitic form of the pronoun *yeeɁ* 'I'. In (2b), *yi-* is the contrastive form of the 'nominative' subject-marker (NOM), indicating that it was specifically the younger of the two brothers who slept. In (2c), *yi-* is an 'instrument' marker (INS); in (2d), *yəɁ-* is an 'instrument' (or possibly a 'location') marker:

(2)   a. *Yi-ciib   ma-tiiw rɛh.*
         <u>1SG</u>-go.PFV to-river below.
         'I went down to the river.'

      b. *Na-səlɔg   yi-Ɂalʉj   Ɂəh.*
         3SG-sleep.PFV <u>NOM</u>-Ɂalʉj 3SG.
         'Ɂalʉj slept.'

      c. *pɛnɁɔɔl   yi-Ɂawaat.*
         cook.NMLZ <u>INS</u>-bamboo
         'cooking with a bamboo tube'

      d. *Ɂɛ-siih   yəɁ-rɛntiɁ.*
         1PL.INCL-pound.PFV <u>INS</u>-pestle.
         'We pound it with a pestle.'[13]

necessary to clarify the morphological processes, as in Tables 3.3 and 3.4, below. In the glosses, full-stops separate the lexical and grammatical components of each word: *tərɛngəl* (sit.CAUS. NMLZ.IPFV) 'causing to sit down (imperfective)'. The following abbreviations are employed: * 'non-occurring form' or 'proto-language reconstruction'; 1 'first-person'; 2 'second-person'; 3 'third-person'; ACC 'accusative'; CAUS 'causative'; Cⁱ 'initial consonant'; Cᶠ 'final consonant'; Cᵐ 'medial consonant'; CTRS 'contrastive'; DU 'dual'; EMP 'emphatic'; EXCL 'exclusive'; INCL 'inclusive'; INS 'instrument'; IPFV 'imperfective'; IRR 'irrealis'; MID 'middle voice'; NEG 'negative'; NMLZ 'nominalizer'; NOM 'nominative'; PFV 'perfective'; PSTV 'presentative'; PL 'plural'; PROG 'progressive'; SG 'singular'.

[13] Sentence (2d) is taken from one of the very few published Temiar texts (Noone 1949: 5), where it reads *e si:h iĕ rentĭ*. Sentence (3c) is also taken from that text (p. 6), where it reads *e jĕlog ijuk*. I suspect that the proclitic *yəɁ-* is an example of grammaticization, reinforced in this function by *a posteriori* iconicity. As an independent (prosodic) word, *yəɁ* means 'place', 'near', 'somewhere else', or simply 'at'. But, when unstressed, its similarity to *yi-* has allowed the 'at' meaning to develop into an 'instrumental' proclitic. In some instances, however, *yəɁ-* still retains a 'locative' meaning and might then be better treated as a separate word (as Noone did in this instance).

In (3a), *ʔi-* is the unstressed proclitic form of the first-person singular pronoun. In (3b), *ʔi-* is the 'nominative' subject-marker (NOM), referring to an already mentioned entity.[14] In (3c), *ʔi-* is an 'instrument' marker (INS):[15]

(3)　a. *ʔi-ciib　　　ma-tuuy.*
　　　　1SG-go.PFV　to-there.
　　　　'I went there.'

　　　b. *ʔɛn-lɔɔʔ　ʔi-deek　　　ʔun.*
　　　　at-where　NOM-house　3SG.
　　　　'Where is their house?'

　　　c. *ʔɛ-jəloog　　　　ʔi-juk.*
　　　　1PL.INCL-tread.PFV　INS-foot.
　　　　'We tread it out with our feet.'

The following examples, (4)–(7), illustrate the objective (OTHER) semantic, linked with the second- and third-person pronouns, as indicated in Table 3.1. These all contain the criterial vowel *a*, either alone or in combination, which is discussed in greater detail later as the marker of the middle-voice in verbs and some nouns.

In (4a), *ha-* is the unstressed proclitic form of the second-person singular pronoun *hãã*ʔ 'you', which also occurs at the end of the same sentence in its fully stressed form. In (4b), *ha-* is again the second-person singular pronoun, but this time as the object of a verbal phrase. In (4c), *ha-* (twice) is the 'accusative' (affected-patient) definitizing object-marker (ACC):

(4)　a. *ʔalɨj, hɔj　　ha-təʔɛl　　　cə-hãã*ʔ?
　　　　ʔalɨj, already　2SG-make.PFV　CTRS-2SG
　　　　'ʔalɨj, have *you* made yours?'

　　　b. *Yam-bar-lɛh　　　　　ha-lah.*
　　　　1DU.EXCL.IRR-PROG-wife　2SG-EMP.
　　　　'We both want to marry you.'[16]

---

[14] An important correction must be inserted here. Matisoff (2003: 36, 38–41), through no fault of his own, reports my previous characterization of *cə-* as the 'statant role-marker' and *ʔi-* as the 'actor role-marker'. Unfortunately, this has turned out to be incorrect, being based on errors in an unpublished ancestor of the present study. As the examples in this chapter make clear, *cə-* 'contrastive' and *ʔi-* 'nominative' mark syntactic and discourse relations rather than participant roles.

[15] Shorto (2006: 69) suggests that Temiar *yee*ʔ 'I' derives from Proto-Mon-Khmer *ʔiiʔ 'person'. This might explain why the proclitic form of *yee*ʔ is *ʔi-*; if so, the latter would be the more 'original' form, masquerading as a reduced form. If this linkage can be sustained, it would lend further support to the iconic connection made here between some of the phonetically closed forms listed in Table 3.2.

[16] Polyandry is permitted by Temiar kinship rules, but such marriages are rare in practice.

c. *Na-wɔg*   *ʔi-Paluj,*   *siyab*   *ha-ranɔʔ*   *ʔəh,*
3SG-wake.PFV   NOM-Paluj,   prepare.PFV   ACC-backbasket 3SG,

cap   *ha-kayuuh*   *naar*   *kɛnlɔk.*
pack.PFV   ACC-cassava   two   tuber.
'Paluj woke up, prepared his [aforementioned] back-basket, packed the two tubers of cassava.'

In (5a) there occur three variant forms of the first-person dual inclusive pronoun 'you and I': the free-standing form *ʔaar*, the unstressed proclitic form *ʔa-* (twice), and the unstressed postposed form *ʔah*. In (5b) the proclitic *ʔa-* forms the direct-address versions of names and kin-terms; in (5c) it delimits demonstratives; and in (5d) it forms the negative imperative with verbs:

(5)   a. *Padaaʔ*   *ʔa-lah*   *cə-ʔaar,*   *ʔam-maaʔ,*
        Come   1DU.INCL-EMP   CTRS-1DU.INCL,   1DU.INC.IRR-return.PFV,

        mɛn-ʔambooʔ   *ʔun-pət*   *ʔah.*
        PL-Mother   3PL-miss.PFV   1DU.INCL.

        'Come, let's both return home, Mother and the others are missing us.'

   b. *bəəh* '(one's) father' (reference)
       Pabəəh!   'Father!' (direct address)

   c. *teeʔ* 'earlier today'
       ʔa-teeʔ 'just now'

   d. *ciib* 'go'
       ʔa-ciib! 'don't go!'

As a clitic, therefore, *ʔa-* fulfils a diverse range of surface functions. What meaning could they possibly have in common? The answer is that *ʔa-* not only carries the meaning OTHER but also the implication that the Other it refers to is the *object* of some special marking: it is *salient*. There is, of course, a psychological ambivalence about something that has been declared to be both Other *and* salient, for, while it falls outside one's own subjective domain, it still remains the object of one's attention. (Indeed, the English word 'object' implies precisely this ambivalence.) Thus, in addressing someone as 'Father!' (*Pa-bəəh*) one treats him as an Other (to one's own status as 'child') and yet acknowledges that he holds a special relationship to oneself. In 'just now' (*ʔa-teeʔ*) one's attention is directed to an objective point in time, already past and done with, which nevertheless still holds relevance to the more subjective concerns of what one is doing now. In 'don't go!' (*ʔa-ciib!*) one is adjured to put the act away from oneself and yet to hold it in mind as something forbidden.

The same feature is found in the transparently OTHER-referring forms, the proclitic pronoun *na-* 'third-person singular' and the demonstrative *na?* 'that'. Both occur in (6):

(6)   *Gɔb   na?   na-piɲjam   motooh   kəloo?   ?əh.*
        Malay that   3SG-borrow   motorbike elder.sibling 3SG.
        'That Malay borrowed his brother's motorbike.'

In *na-* and *na?* the OTHER-referring vowel *a* is preceded by the consonant *n*, which is otherwise mainly employed as a prefix or infix (depending on the dialect) serving to nominalize verbs: *səlɔg* 'to sleep'→*sɛnlɔg* 'a sleeping' (phonemically, *slɔg*→*snlɔg*); *gəl* 'to sit'→*gɛlnəl* or *nɛlgəl* 'a sitting' (phonemically, *gəl*→*glnəl* or *nlgəl*); *golap* 'to carry on shoulder'→*gənolap* 'a carrying on shoulder' (phonemically, *golap*→*gnolap*); *jəro?* 'long'→*jɛnro?* 'length' (phonemically, *jro?*→*jnro?*); *cɛr* 'to pare'→*cənɛr* 'a knife' (phonemically, *cɛr*→*cnɛr*). Semantically, such nominals are more thing-like – more 'objective' – than the verbs from which they are derived. Thus, in the pronoun *na-* and the demonstrative *na?*, a degree of *a posteriori* iconicity is at play, reinforcing the iconic effect of the OTHER-referring vowel *a*.

6   Morphological iconicity

Syncretism is not restricted to the items just discussed, for it is also exhibited in the inflectional patterns of human nouns, verbs and adjectives, as illustrated in (7). The two features to note are (i) the 'incopyfixed' reduplicative pattern[17] and (ii) the infixed *-a-*. The incopyfixed pattern means 'plural' with adjectives (7a) and some human nouns (7b), and 'imperfective' with verbs (7c). The infix *-a-* means 'singular' (or, more strictly, 'entity-referring') with human nouns (7b), and 'middle voice' with verbs (7c) and (non-productively) with a substantial number of 'middle-voice' nouns:

(7)   a. *jəro?*   'long' (singular)
            je?ro?   'long' (plural)
        b. *taa?*   'sir' (title for an older man)
            tataa?   'old man'
            te?taa?   'old men'

---

[17] The label 'incopyfixation' is an invention of Matisoff (2003: 28). Other authors have referred to the same process as 'coda copy' (Kruspe 2004: 72; Burenhult 2005: 50), 'infixed reduplication' (Diffloth 1976a: 236), 'bare-consonant reduplication' (Sloan 1988; Hendricks 2001) or simply 'reduplication' (Benjamin 1976). Similar patterns of reduplication are widespread in the Aslian languages and elsewhere in the Mon-Khmer family. On present evidence, however, it is Temiar that exhibits the highest degree of regularity in this domain of morphology.

c. *ciib*   'go' (perfective)
    caciib   'go' (middle)
    cɛbciib   'go' (imperfective)

I discuss the inflectional morphology of human nouns no further here, as it raises complicated semantic issues. The rest of this section will concentrate on the 'aesthetic' components underlying the morphology of the Temiar verb – the feature that has occasioned most of the secondary discussion of Temiar grammar by other authors.[18] Temiar adjectives are effectively stative verbs, and – except for lacking the *-a-* infix – their reduplicative morphology relates transparently to that of the dynamic verbs.

6.1   Incopyfixation

The self-iconic term 'incopyfixation' refers to the reduplicative process in which a copy of the final consonant of the stem is infixed at an earlier position in the word: *sɔlɔg→sɛglɔg* 'to lie down' (phonemically, *slɔg→sglɔg*). In monosyllabic verbs the initial consonant is copied too, as the prefixed carrier of the incopyfixed final consonant: *gɔl→ gɛlgɔl* 'to sit' (phonemically, *gɔl→glgɔl*). This process applies also to the causative forms of the verb, marked with the *r*-containing affix *tr-* ~ *-r-*: *tɛrgɔl→tɔrɛlgɔl* (phonemically, *trgɔl→trlgɔl*), *sɛrlɔg→sɔrɛglɔg* (phonemically, *srlɔg→srglɔg*).[19] Tables 3.3 and 3.4 present the incopyfixed forms (labelled 'imperfective') for both monosyllabic and sesquisyllabic verbs. (Fully disyllabic verbs, such as *halab* 'to go downstream' or *golap* 'to carry on shoulder' do not undergo these inflectional changes in Temiar.)

In the incopyfixed forms (*sɛglɔg*, *gɛlgɔl*), therefore, the reduplication contains only elements derived from the verb stem itself, since the *-ɛ-* is wholly determined phonologically (Benjamin 1976: 144–145). The incopyfixed forms may thus be thought of as an expression of complete semantic verbiness, concerned with the event or process *in and of itself* as seen from the 'inside' (cf. Comrie 1978: 24). This fits well with their tendency to be durative, continuative or distributive in meaning. Incopyfixation therefore serves as the inflectional means of expressing the 'imperfective' aspect in Temiar (Tables 3.3 and 3.4). By contrast, the absence of any such inflection in the simple base form of the verb indicates the 'perfective' aspect.

---

[18] See especially McCarthy (1982), Gafos (1999: 75–107), Miyakoshi (2006), and Yap (2009). Note that the first three authors employed the invalid paradigm for the Temiar verb (Benjamin 1976: 169) that I have since corrected. In particular, the inflection that I originally characterized as marking the 'simulfactive mode' has been re-analysed as indicating the 'middle voice'.

[19] Incopyfixation should not be confused with full reduplication, which also occurs in Temiar: *ciib ciib* (two words) 'to keep on walking', as opposed to the incopyfixed imperfective form, *cɛbciib*, of the same verb. Both patterns are morphologically clearly iconic of their temporally 'extended' meanings.

Table 3.3 *Monosyllabic:* gəl *'to sit'*

VOICE	ASPECT		VERBAL NOUN
	Perfective	Imperfective	
Base	*gəl* 'sit' (completed act)	*glgəl* [gɛlgəl] 'sit' (incomplete act)	*glnəl* [gɛlnəl] ~ *nlgəl* [nɛlgəl] 'a sitting'
Middle		*gagəl* 'sit' (uncontrolledly, or all together at once)	*gnagəl* [gənagəl] 'a sitting' (uncontrolledly, or all together at once)
Causative	*trgəl* [tɛrgəl] 'set down' (completed act)	*trlgəl* [tərɛlgəl] 'set down' (incomplete act)	*trngəl* [tərɛngəl] 'a setting down'

Table 3.4 *Sesquisyllabic:* səlɔg *'to sleep' (also: 'lie down', 'marry')*

VOICE	ASPECT		VERBAL NOUN
	Perfective	Imperfective	
Base	*slɔg* [səlɔg] 'sleep' (completed act)	*sglɔg* [sɛglɔg] 'sleep' (incomplete act)	*snlɔg* [sɛnlɔg]; *snglɔg* [sənɛglɔg] 'a sleeping'
Middle		*salɔg* 'fall asleep' (uncontrolledly)	*snalɔg* [sənalɔg] 'a falling asleep'
Causative	*srlɔg* [sɛrlɔg] 'put s.o. to sleep' (completed act)	*srglɔg* [sərɛglɔg] 'put s.o. to sleep' (incomplete act)	*srnlɔg* [sərɛnlɔg] 'a putting (of s.o.) to sleep'

The aesthesis here is carried by a clear example of *a priori* iconicity. As Sapir remarked in a classic statement,

Nothing is more *natural* than the prevalence of reduplication, in other words, the repetition of all or part of the radical element. The process is generally employed, *with self-evident symbolism*, to indicate such concepts as distribution, plurality, repetition, customary activity, increase of size, added intensity, continuance. (Sapir 1921: 76; emphasis added.)

Given their relative semantic 'completeness', incopyfixed imperfective verbs do not require any further completion by the addition of participants or by embedding in any larger expression. For this reason, they usually serve as the neutral citation form: when asked for their word for 'sleep', for example, Temiars would usually say *sɛglɔg* rather than *səlɔg* or *salɔg*. The same semantic completeness allows incopyfixation to detransitivize verbs that are transitive in their unreduplicated perfective form: *ʔun-səluh ɲam* (3PL-shoot.blowgun.PFV animal) 'they blowgunned animals' (transitive), but *ʔun-sɛhluh* (3PL-shoot. blowgun.IPFV) 'they went blowgunning' (intransitive).

Nevertheless, the difference between the perfective and the imperfective is slight. Verbs sometimes appear consecutively within the same utterance in both forms with little discernible difference of meaning. In (8), for example, the perfective *kab* 'bite' occurs alongside the imperfective *reɲrec* 'devour' (from *rec*).[20] Perhaps this is just 'aesthetic' word-play, typical of Mon-Khmer languages more widely. Or perhaps the biting was seen as a punctiliar event, while the eating was imaged 'distributively' as more extended temporally:

(8)   *Na-ʔiid*   *ʔun-kah*   *kab*   *ʔəh,*   *ʔun-kah*   *reɲrec*   *ʔəh.*
      3SG-fear.PFV   3PL-perhaps   bite.PFV   3SG,   3PL-perhaps   devour.IPFV   3SG.
      'He feared they might bite [underline]perfective[/underline] him, they might devour [underline]imperfective[/underline] him.'

What then of the uninflected perfective forms, such as *gəl* (Table 3.2) and *səlɔg* (Table 3.3)? Here, the lack of reduplication is iconic of semantic incompleteness, indicating that the process is viewed *from the outside*, 'without regard to internal temporal consistency' (Comrie 1978: 12). In other words, the perfective normally has to be connected with something else for its meaning to be interpretable. Typically, the 'something else' is (i) a nominal, (ii) another verb, (iii) being embedded in discourse, or (iv) an inflection. Thus, unreduplicated perfective verbs in Temiar tend to be employed in

- simple imperatives, where 'you' is understood
- transitive or intransitive action expressions, linked with overt participants
- linking, reduced, discourse-continuity expressions, where they (i) lean on a following unstressed pronoun, as in *səˈlɔg weh* (sleep 3DU) 'they slept', or (ii) lean on a following modifier, as in *huj yəəl* (sup finish) 'having drunk (the soup)', or (iii) are linked to a repetition of the verb in a repetitive setting clause, such as *gəl ˈgəl weh* (sit sit 3DU) '[and so] they sat'
- in discourse, where a perfective verb standing alone may additionally serve as a means of taking up the story from where it last left off, as with *cap* 'to pack' in (4c).

The unreduplicated perfective form also serves as the stem to which the other participant-valency inflections are added. These are the middle-voice affix *-a-* (discussed below) and the causative-voice affix *ter-* ~ *bɛr-* ~ *-r-* (indicating extension of the causer's action to a causee). The morphology of the causative is discussed no further here, except to note that it can also be further inflected by incopyfixation to form the imperfective-causative, such as *trlgəl* [tərɛlgəl] from *trgəl* [tergəl] (Table 3.3) and *srglɔg* [səreglɔg] from *srlɔg* [serlɔg] (Table 3.4).[21]

---

[20] For the regular morphophonemic change involved in deriving *reɲrec* (instead of **recrec*) from *rec*, see Benjamin (1976: 143).

[21] See Benjamin (2012) for further discussion of the Temiar causative.

Similar, but not identical, patterns are found in some of the expressives, as discussed later.

The term 'incopyfixation' implies the view that Temiar morphology involves phonological *copying*; but this may not be the best way of approaching the question. In emphasizing meaning over phonology, the approach just presented accords with the alternative approach to reduplication advocated in the Morphological Doubling theory of Inkelas and Zoll (2005), who argue that the kind of reduplication exhibited by the Temiar imperfective is best thought of as the joining together of two 'sister' elements carrying the same meaning. On this view the incopyfixed Temiar imperfective would be a self-compound rather than a phonological copy, with each half of the compound sharing the same semantic features, together generating a new meaning ('imperfective') carried by the whole form. In other words, the reduplicative morphology of the Temiar imperfective exhibits a transparently *a priori* iconicity (as Sapir's comment too would indicate).

6.2   Infixation of -a-

The major productive function of infixed *-a-* 'SALIENT OTHER' is in forming the middle voice of verbs (Tables 3.3 and 3.4). This is closely paralleled by the appearance of *-a-* as a frozen infix in a large set of non-inflecting 'deponent' verbs and disyllabic ('middle-voice') nouns. As argued in detail elsewhere (Benjamin 2011a), the same semantic dimension underlies all of these occurrences of *-a-*, namely that the verbs and nouns in question indicate that the subject or entity is thought of as being simultaneously its own agent (or source) and patient. It is the embedded OTHER-referring open vowel *-a-* that symbolizes the incorporated patient.

6.2.1   Middle-voice verbs   There are at least three circumstances in which a Temiar speaker might choose to employ the middle voice:
- The action referred to by the verb is performed with reference to some *salient other*. This can apply to two kinds of activity: (i) those where the actors are thought of as working jointly in an 'all-together' mode, and (ii) symmetrically reciprocal actions.
- The *object* of the action or event is *incorporated within* the verb as part of its meaning (producing an 'unaccusative' verb). This carries with it the implication that the action or event has no external source. Prototypically, these would be (i) body-moves, (ii) events thought of as absolutive or mediopassive in character, or (iii) emotional, and hence relatively uncontrolled or undergone, actions or behaviours.
- Given its punctiliar character, the action or event referred to by the verb can be seen as a particular *determinate event* treated as a noteworthy object of comment – a 'proper verb', so to speak.

The following examples illustrate these various uses of the middle voice. First, two examples of 'salient other' middles. In (9), most of the story line's reported actions employ the 'all-together' middle-voice forms of the verb:[22]

(9)   *ʔun-maaʔ*   *ma-deek num-səlaay   rɛh,*   *kakeej   ha-jagok*
      3PL-return.PFV to-house from-swidden downstream, grate.MID ACC-maize,

      sasɛɛw   *ha-kayuuh,   sɔd   ha-sɔəh,*   *paʔɔɔl*
      scrape.clean.MID ACC-cassava, peel.PFV ACC-sweet.potato, cook.MID

      ha- cɔ̃s.
      ACC-bird.

      'They returned home from the swidden downstream, (together) grated the maize, (together) scraped the cassava clean, peeled the sweet potato, (together) cooked the bird.'

As illustrated in (10), reciprocal action is expressed by employing a dual pronoun together with *bar-* 'progressive' procliticized to the middle-voice form of the verb. This indicates that the two actors simultaneously serve as each other's patient:

(10) *Wɛ-bə-tatuuk.*
      3DU-PROG-fear.MID.
      'They are afraid of each other.'

The following three examples illustrate the unaccusative use of the middle voice. In (11), the middle-voice body-move verb *sasid* 'to (magically) transform oneself' occurs here (rather unusually) as an imperative, alongside its normal perfective form *sid*:[23]

(11) *'Jadiiʔ*   *la-ma-bərək,*   *sasid!',*   *wɛ-bɛʔbooʔ*
      'Become   EMP-to-seasonal.fruit,   transform.MID!',   3DU-woman.PL

      wɛ-tayɛs.   *Wɛ-sid*   *ʔə-lah.*
      3DU-point.   3DU-transform.PFV   3SG-EMP.

      '"Become seasonal fruits, transform yourselves!", the two women pointed. So the two men transformed.'

The absolute, medio-passive use of the middle voice with an inanimate subject to indicate a non-agentive spontaneous event is illustrated in (12a), contrasted with the equivalent transitive expression in (12b):

---

[22] Means (1998: 12) treats the *-a*-inflected form of the verb as indicating a 'plural' subject. This is incorrect: the *-a*-inflected form (my 'middle voice') occurs just as frequently in Temiar with singular subjects. Moreover, dynamic verbs carry no marking for grammatical number, while stative verbs (adjectives) indicate plurality by incopyfixation, not infixation of *-a-*.

[23] Note that *tayɛs* 'to point' in (11) is also a body-move verb; but it is a non-inflecting 'deponent' verb (next section) in which the middle-voice semantic is permanently marked by the *-a-* of the first syllable.

(12)   a. *Ɂɔɔk*   *na-kakoh.*
            Water   3SG-spill.MID.
            'The water spilled.' (Intransitive)

        b. *Na-koh*   *Ɂɔɔk.*
            3SG-spill.PFV   water.
            'She spilled water.' (Transitive)

In (13), the middle-voice form of the verb *doɁ* 'to run' serves to indicate the emotionally uncontrollable exasperation felt by the two brothers at the incessant crying of their young sister:

(13)   *Mɛn-kəlooɁ*   *Ɂi-Ɂun-bood*   *Ɂi-lah;*   *Ɂun-dadoɁ*   *yeh.*
        PL-elder.sibling 1SG-3PL-not.want 1SG-EMP; 3PL-run.MID 1SG.
        'My elder brothers couldn't stand me; they fled me.'

Examples of 'determinate-happening', 'proper verb' middles are relatively rare, especially when unassociated with 'all-together', reciprocal, absolutive or 'emotional' meanings. In (14), however, the middle-voice inflection of the second verb, *cacaaɁ* 'eat, consume', clearly indicates its noteworthy 'determinate happening' character at this point in the story. (The middle-voice inflection of the first verb, *taɁel* 'make', on the other hand, indicates an 'all-together' meaning.)

(14)   *JadiiɁ*   *habis*   *wɛ-taɁel,*   *jadiiɁ*   *Ɂat*   *na-cacaaɁ*
        Happen   finished   3DU-build.MID, happen   behold   3SG-eat.MID

        Ɂɔɔk   *mənuɁ*   *ma-Ɂalɨj.*
        water   big   to-Ɂalɨj.
        'And when they had both built [the fish-weir] together, a large amount of water suddenly consumed Ɂalɨj.'

6.2.2   Deponent verbs and middle-voice nouns   The infix *-a-* also occurs as the frozen non-productive marker of a middle-voice semantic in the class of verbs I label 'deponent' because they appear to have 'laid aside' (Latin: *deponere*) the meaning suggested by their 'middle' surface morphology, in favour of an ostensibly active meaning. Superficially, Temiar deponents appear to carry an active meaning, but closer examination shows that they indicate events or processes that are thought of as being simultaneously – and hence dialectically – their own source and undergoer. The same also applies to the entities indicated by the many Temiar nouns with *-a-* in the first syllable that I label 'middle-voice nouns'.[24] The main categories are:

---

[24] For a substantial listing of these words, see the Appendix (pp. 28–37) in Benjamin (2011a). The examples given here are new. For a close structural parallel to the Temiar middle-voice nouns see van Gijn's study (2010) of the connection between middle voice and ideophones in the Bolivian language Yurakaré.

(i) dynamic and stative verbs indicating conditions or circumstances that *the source simultaneously undergoes*; (ii) animals, as creatures that *move themselves through their own actions*; (iii) body parts, as organs that can be thought of as *both moving and being moved*; and (iv) certain physical objects and processes, thought of as being *simultaneously their own source and undergoer*.

Deponent verbs
> *haləəg* 'to laugh (in company)': because such laughing is catching, and therefore something both done and undergone
>
> *raceʔ* 'to grate': because the hand simultaneously does the grating and undergoes the resistance of the food
>
> *saluur* 'to faint': because it happens to and within the fainter

Middle-voice nouns
> *cadɛɛʔ* 'a small squirrel', *ʔalaay ~ʔalaaj* 'elephant': animals that move themselves
>
> *karɔɔl* 'knee': a body part, both moving and being moved

Despite containing the phonaestheme -*a*-, deponent verbs and middle-voice nouns are monomorphemic words of fixed form. But the -*a*- element also appears with the same 'undergoer' meaning in words that display a transparent inflectional and derivational history (Benjamin 2011a: 25). Deverbal nominalizations are formed in Temiar by inserting the infix -*n*-, but the resultant forms occur sometimes with and sometimes without an additional -*a*-. This depends on the presence or absence, respectively, of an implicitly 'middle-voice' 'undergoer' meaning, as in (15) and (16):

(15)   *sanɔɔʔ*   *sɛrnɔɔr*
        rot.MID.NMLZ   shave.IPFV.NMLZ
        'rotted remains of shavings'

These words are derived from *sɔɔʔ*, *sasɔɔʔ* 'to rot' and *sɔɔr*, *sɛrsɔɔr* 'to shave (wood)'. 'Shaving (wood)' is wholly active, but 'rotting' is something that the shavings undergo: hence the 'middle-voice' form *sanɔɔʔ*, rather than the otherwise expected **sənɔɔʔ*.

A particularly telling example occurs in (16). Here, the stative verb *jəroʔ*, *jɛʔroʔ* (but no **jaroʔ*) 'to be distant, long' has given rise to two distinct deverbal nominalizations: *jɛnroʔ* 'length' (as in *jɛnroʔ deek* 'the length of the house') and *jənaroʔ* 'distance travelled'. While both derivatives are formed with -*n*-, only the latter contains the 'middle-voice' infix -*a*-, in accordance with its 'undergoer' meaning:

(16)   *jənaroʔ*   *tɛʔ*   *ʔun-joog*   *naʔ*
         distant.NMLZ.MID   land   3PL-move.PFV   that
         'the distance of territory [through which] they moved'

7   Expressives

In a volume subtitled 'sound and meaning', the question of expressives inevitably arises. However, it seems that most of the sound–meaning symbolism in Temiar expressives is carried by *a posteriori* iconicity rather than by the direct employment of sound as such.[25] In other words, the iconic speech-sounds of Temiar are primarily a consequence of mental processes directed in the first instance at the motor activities of the speech organs.[26]

Expressives, which constitute a distinctive basic word-class parallel to verbs and nouns, are utterance-adjuncts that sum up in a word or two the feelings that are supposed to be aroused in the interlocutors' minds. They are therefore concerned as much with connotational as with denotational meaning, 'describing visual, auditory, olfactory, gustatory, haptic, emotional or other types of perceptions in relation to particular phenomena' (Tufvesson 2007: 53). Since they are voluntary additions to utterances that would still make sense without them, one can speak 'good' Temiar without ever using an expressive. But such speech would risk sounding uninvolved and unemotional.

In Temiar, the frequency of expressives varies from speaker to speaker. When telling stories, some speakers use them more than others – and some not at all. There is also some variation between valley populations in this regard, at least in the texts I collected. On the other hand, spontaneous conversation often includes more expressives than in story-telling. Temiars seem to be aware of the special character of expressives. For example, the expressive *kəlus!* 'the snapping off of a maize cob' was explained by one respondent as the *yaaj* or *cʉʉh* 'noise, sound' of the action. This was an *ad hoc*, non-standard characterization, however, and it should not be assumed that Temiars necessarily think of expressives only in aural terms.

Linguists mostly agree on the ideal-type criteria that characterize expressives: they are employed with their own special syntax; they cannot be negated; and they possess a distinct semantic function. Other criteria,

---

[25] This disregards such obviously onomatopoeic forms (which are not necessarily expressives) as *kɛeʔ kɛkɛɛk!* to describe badly performed drumbeats. But note that this too exhibits reduplicative morphology, although it breaks normal phonological rules – perhaps because it was intended to imply 'bad'.

[26] For the 'motor theory of speech perception' that lends support to this view, and which claims that both listeners and speakers model speech as articulations rather than sounds, see Liberman et al. (1967: 453) and Tsur (2006: 906, 914). Tsur's article contains an approving response to Diffloth's (1994) Mon-Khmer example of the dominance of articulatory gesture over sound in the expression of iconicity.

however, are recognized as less clear-cut, namely that expressives are sup-
posedly not derived from any other word-class and that they possess their
own morphology (cf. Diffloth 2001: 263). Indeed, in Temiar and other Aslian
languages the distinctiveness often wears thin. In particular, many Temiar
expressives display an obvious relation to similarly shaped verbs, and some
expressives could potentially also be analysed as adverbs (a word-class
not otherwise salient in the language). The following examples illustrate
some of the features just discussed; the expressives or expressive-like
forms are indicated by a postposed exclamation mark.

In (17), *Bəruj!* 'getting up and leaving!' (with its variants *bəraj, bəruj*) is an
example of an expressive occurring alongside its related verb (the latter here
displaying full reduplication):

(17) a. *Bəruj!* *ʔun-wɛʔ*   *bɛjruj*   *bɛjruj*   *yɔɔl.*
          Bəruj! 3PL-leave.PFV start.out.IPFV start.out.IPFV finish.PFV.
          '*Bəruj!* They set off and kept going until they stopped.'

The expressive *kəyɔɔb!* 'waking up!' in (18) was explicitly connected by my
respondent to the verb *kəyɔɔb, kɛbyɔɔb* 'to get up', *kɛryɔɔb* 'to get someone up'.
Here, it is its syntactic character as an adjunct to the verb phrase that indicates
the status of *kəyɔɔb!* as an expressive rather than as a verb:

(18)   *Kəyɔɔb!* *wɛ-wɔg.*
        Kəyɔɔb! 3DU-wake.up.PFV.
        '*Kəyɔɔb!* they woke up.'

In (19), *rənɛhduuh!* could perhaps also be interpreted as an adverb. Its
morphology is that of a verbal noun derived by *-n-* infixation from the incopyfixed imperfective of **rəduuh*. But I have failed to find any such verb in Temiar.

(19)   *Rənɛhduuh!* *wɛ-sɔlɔg.*
        Side-by-side! 3DU-sleep.PFV.
        'Side-by-side! they slept.'

Whether or not a verbal derivation can be traced, expressives often display a
verb-like morphology, but in shapes and combinations that are not found in verbs
proper. As examples (20)–(24) illustrate, these variously involve incopyfixation,
precopyfixation, postcopyposing, *-r-* insertion, and *-a-* insertion. This exemplifies
the sort of word game that Sidwell (2008: 256–257) and others have identified as
a frequent feature of the Mon-Khmer languages. Significantly, several of the
resultant patterns, if taken in their normal verbal sense, would indicate such
semantically impossible meanings as 'middle-causative' (i.e., simultaneous
valency-decrease and -increase). But, as already noted, reduplicative incopyfixation in itself carries various temporally linked meanings – durative, continuative,

distributive – and these carry over into those expressives that employ it. Thus, although the specific referential content may lack iconic expression, the *manner* of the process it refers to finds expression in the morphology. The same applies to those reduplicative processes that are found only in expressives but not verbs, namely precopyfixing and postcopyposing.[27]

The expressives listed in (20a) follow a marginally productive pattern, in which the syllable $C^i \varepsilon C^f$-is precopyfixed to a sesquisyllabic verb ($C^i \partial C^m V C^f$). Semantically, these fall at the adverbial end of the scale, but – unlike the verbs from which they are derived – they cannot be negated or take a syntactic subject.[28] In (20b), the same pattern occurs, but with no identifiable source-verb (*pəluuŋ).

(20) a. *rɛgrəweeg!* 'conspicuously upright', linked to *rəweeg*, *rɛgweeg* 'to stand erect'
          sɛdsəlood! 'unable to breathe', linked to the verb *səlood* 'to drown, be hard of breath'
          rɛɲrəŋaɲ! 'glowing, reddish colour (mahseer fish)', linked to *rəŋaɲ*, *rɛɲŋaɲ* 'to glow'
          cɛɲcəloɲ! 'the raising of a fish's fin', 'a raft shooting the rapids', 'a submarine diving', linked to *cəloɲ* (~*cələəɲ*) 'to produce a wash in the water'

      b. *Na-bəluh   lah,   pɛŋpəluuŋ!*
          3SG-pounce.PFV EMP, *pɛŋpəluuŋ!*
          'He pounced, *pɛŋpəluuŋ!*'

In (21), taken from a commercial pop-song recording sung in Temiar,[29] there is an almost Shakespearian play on the syllable *hɔj*, which by itself is the past-tense marker 'already'. But here, the singer plays with its possible derivative *bəhɔj* 'to fail to reach' through both plain (*bɛjbəhɔj*) and nominalized (*bɛnbəhɔj*) precopyfixation:

(21)   *Bəhɔj   bɛnbəhɔj!*   *ʔi-saar   beel   ha-jəroʔ*
       Out.of.reach out.of.reach.NMLZ! 1SG-follow.PFV when 2SG-distant

---

[27] Diffloth (1979: 58), in one of the key studies of phonic iconicity, puts this more generally:

Expressives are not a sort of 'pre-linguistic' form of speech, somehow half-way between mimicry and fully structured linguistic form. They are, in fact, at the other end of the spectrum, a sort of 'post-linguistic' stage where the structural elements necessary for prosaic language are deliberately re-arranged and exploited for their iconic properties, and used for aesthetic communication.

[28] Occasionally, this pattern is nevertheless used as an extended verb form, as in *tiiʔ na-sɛgsəlɔg* 'he's still sleeping', where the proclitic subject pronoun makes it clear that this is not an adjunctive expressive.

[29] From track 1, 'Cedet seniroi' (*cədut sənirɔy* 'remember echoes'), of the unnumbered audio CD *Bergoyang Bersama Kajol* (Sand Stream Enterprise, Pasir Puteh, Kelantan). A performance of this song by Kajol (real name, ʔaŋɛh Rəlɔg) can be viewed on www.youtube.com/watch?v=BiJ3B5oLqDY. The quoted verse appears at 0'50" into the song.

ma-yee²   *bəəh*   *hɔj*   *bɛjbəhɔj!*
to-1SG   father   PAST   out.of.reach!

'Out of reach, out of reach!, I follow behind when you are far away. Father (=lover) has passed out of reach.'

The less-productive pattern exhibited by the expressives in (22) is based on the use of incopyfixation and/or the infixation of *-r-* or *-ra-*, which in a real verb would mean 'causative' and (the impossible) 'causative-middle' respectively.[30] *Səregyɔɔg* and its variant *sərayɔɔg* refer to sounds that emanate from an unseen source, such as distant voices. Morphologically parallel to *sərayɔɔg* is *jəradɔɔŋ* (22b). The virtual source-verbs (**səyɔɔg* and **jədɔɔŋ*) of these forms seem not to occur:

(22)   a. *Na-koko²*   *səregyɔɔg!*   *səregyɔɔg!, kəjoɲ*   *lah*   *tiik*   *²əh.*
         3SG-crow.PFV   *səregyɔɔg!*   *səregyɔɔg!,* twitch.PFV EMP hand 3SG.
         'The bird crowed *səregyɔɔg! səregyɔɔg!* [unseen!] and [Ɂalʉj's] hand twitched.'

   b. *jəradɔɔŋ!* 'sound of struck bamboo'

A related pattern involves the further reduplicative morphemization of the final syllable of the stem as a separate postcopyposed word, as in (23). As with fully reduplicated verbs (17) or expressives (22a), this pattern seems to indicate a process or activity thought of as persistent or repetitious. In (23a), this pattern is applied, with little semantic contortion, to the adverb *gej* 'quick' by prefixing the non-productive 'adjectival' *lə-*, followed by incopyfixation and the post-copyposing of the morphemized root *gej*. In (23b), there is no identifiable source-verb (**cəhʉʉd*). But in (23c), the identifiable source-verbs combine reduplicative morphemization with the shared resultant element *kəra-*, which on *a posteriori* grounds could be thought of as an adversative (*kə-*) causative (*-r-*) middle-voice (*-a-*) form, with the semantically strange implication 'helplessly caused to undergo the effect of one's own actions'.

(23)   a. *lɛjgej gej* 'frequently' (cf. *gej, lɛjgej* 'quick')

   b. *²e-lo²*   *na-bɛrtook,*   *cərahʉd hʉd!?*
       Why   3SG-CAUS.knock.PFV,   *cərahʉd hʉd!?*
       'Why is she making that disturbing knocking, *cərahʉd hʉd*?'

   c. *kərahab hab!* 'lip-smacking' (cf. *kɛrhab* 'to eat noisily')
       kəralam lam! 'pitch blackness at night' (cf. *kəlam* 'darkness')

---

[30] Diffloth (1976b: 253) has identified *-ra-* in Semai as expressively indicating 'simultaneous plural'. This parallels the 'simulfactive, all-together' of the Temiar middle-voice formative *-a-* and the 'replicative' meaning of *-r-*, as discussed earlier.

In Temiar expressives, therefore, the various constitutive elements and morphological patterns just discussed serve as phonaesthemes, the meanings of which are symbolically condensed rather than explicitly referential. At least one question remains: given that the above examples all involve various forms of *a posteriori* iconicity, are there no instances in Temiar of expressives based on *a priori* iconicity? Does direct sound-symbolism never play a part? The following two examples show that it does indeed occur, albeit in qualified form.

In (24), the syllable *poŋ* directly echoes the sound of a bushknife on bamboo. Its extension to *poŋ papoŋ* (by morphemization combined with -*a*- infixation) to indicate repeated chopping illustrates Tufvesson's point (2011: 86) that 'through this type of form–meaning mapping, gradient relationships in the perceptual world receive gradient linguistic representations':

(24)   *Poŋ! na-bəhəd.   Poŋ papoŋ! ya²   deh,   naar yaaj*
        Poŋ! 3sG-chop.PFV. *Poŋ papoŋ!* PRSTV PRSTV, two   sound

        wɛ-kəyɔk   ²i-wɛ-bɛhbəəh.
        3DU-hear.PFV   NOM-3DU-male.PL.

        '*Poŋ!* she chopped. *Poŋpapoŋ!* The two brothers heard the sounds [made by two women].'

Finally, an example of an expressive that exhibits both onomatopoeic and oral-articulatory iconicity. The expressive *bə²ug!* in (25) has the phonemic patterning of an ordinary Temiar word. But it sounds like vomiting, and its enunciation requires the speaker to perform vomiting-like articulatory actions:

(25)   *Na-tuh,   bə²ug! na-ko².   Bə²ug! bəəh ²ə-na-ko²   hijɛ².*
        3sG-speak.PFV *bə²ug!* 3sG-vomit.PFV. *Bə²ug!* father 3sG-3sG-vomit.PFV also.
        'He spoke, *bə²ug!* he vomited. *Bə²ug!* his father also vomited.'

References

Becker, A. L. 1979. 'The figure a sentence makes: an interpretation of a Classical Malay sentence'. In Talmy Givón, (ed.), *Discourse and syntax*. New York: Academic Press, pp. 243–259.

Benjamin, Geoffrey. 1976. 'An outline of Temiar grammar'. In Philip N. Jenner, Laurence C. Thompson and Stanley Starosta (eds.), *Austroasiatic studies, part I*. Honolulu: University Press of Hawaii, pp. 129–187.

1993. 'Grammar and polity: the cultural and political background to Standard Malay'. In W. A. Foley. (ed.), *The role of theory in language description* [= Trends in Linguistics, Studies and Monographs 69]. Berlin: Mouton De Gruyter, pp. 341–392.

1994. 'Danger and dialectic in Temiar childhood'. In Josiane Massard-Vincent and Jeannine Koubi (eds.), *Enfants et sociétés d'Asie du Sud-est*. Paris: L'Harmattan, pp. 37–62.

2009. Affixes, Austronesian and iconicity in Malay. *Bijdragen tot de taal-, land- en volkenkunde* 165: 291–323.

2011a. 'Deponent verbs and middle-voice nouns in Temiar'. In Sophana Srichampa and Paul Sidwell (eds.), *Austroasiatic studies: papers from ICAAL4 (=Mon-Khmer studies, Special issue no. 2)*. Canberra: Pacific Linguistics E-8, pp. 11–37.

2011b. 'Egalitarianism and ranking in the Malay World'. In Kenneth Sillander and Thomas Gibson (eds.), *Anarchic solidarity: autonomy, equality and fellowship in Southeast Asia*. New Haven: Yale University Southeast Asia Studies, pp. 170–201.

2012. The Temiar causative (and related features). *Mon-Khmer studies* 41: 32–45.

Under review (2012). 'Irrealis in Temiar'.

Burenhult, Niclas. 2005. *A grammar of Jahai*. Canberra: Pacific Linguistics.

Comrie, Bernard. 1978. *Aspect*. Cambridge University Press.

Diffloth, Gérard. 1972. 'Notes on expressive meaning'. *Papers from the Eighth Regional Meeting, Chicago Linguistic Society*, pp. 439–447.

1994. 'i: big, a: small'. In Leanne Hinton, Johanna Nichols and John J. Ohala (eds), *Sound symbolism*, Cambridge University Press, pp. 107–114.

1976a. 'Minor-syllable vocalism in Senoic languages'. In Philip N. Jenner, Laurence C. Thompson, and Stanley Starosta (eds.), *Austroasiatic studies, part I*. Honolulu: University Press of Hawaii, pp. 229–247.

1976b. 'Expressives in Semai'. In Philip N. Jenner, Laurence C. Thompson and Stanley Starosta (eds.), *Austroasiatic studies, part I*. Honolulu: University Press of Hawaii, pp. 249–264.

1979. 'On expressive phonology and prosaic phonology in Mon-Khmer'. In Theraphan L. Thongkum et al. (eds.), *Studies in Tai and Mon-Khmer phonetics and phonology*. Bangkok: Chulalongkorn University Press, pp. 49–59.

2001. Les expressifs de Surin, et où cela conduit. *Bulletin de l'Ecole Française d'Extrême-Orient* 88: 261–269.

Gafos, Adamantios I. 1999. *The articulatory basis of locality in phonology*. New York: Garland.

Gell, Alfred. 1979. The Umeda language-poem. *Canberra anthropology* 2: 44–62.

Gellner, Ernest. 1989. *Plough, sword and book: the structure of human history*. Chicago University Press.

Harris, Roy. 1987. *The language machine*. London: Duckworth.

Hendricks, Sean. 2001. Bare-consonant reduplication without prosodic templates: expressive reduplication in Semai. *Journal of East Asian linguistics* 10: 287–306.

Inkelas, Sharon and Cheryl Zoll. 2005. *Reduplication: doubling in morphology*. Cambridge University Press.

Jakobson, Roman and Linda R. Waugh. 1979. *The sound shape of language*. Brighton: Harvester Press.

Kruspe, Nicole. 2004. *A grammar of Semelai*. Cambridge University Press.

Leach, Edmund R. 1971. 'More about "mama" and "papa"'. In Rodney Needham (ed.), *Rethinking kinship and marriage*. London: Tavistock, pp. 75–98.

Levinson, Stephen C. 2000. *Presumptive meanings: the theory of generalized conversational implicature*. Cambridge, MA: MIT Press.

Levinson, Stephen C. and Niclas Burenhult. 2008. Semplates: a new concept in lexical semantics? *Language* 85: 150–172.

Liberman, A. M. et al. 1967. Perception of the speech code. *Psychological review* 74: 431–461.

McCarthy, John. 1982. 'Prosodic templates, morphemic templates, and morphemic tiers'. In Harry van der Hulst and Norval Smith (eds.), *The structure of phonological representations (Part 1)*. Dordrecht: Foris, pp. 191–223.

Matisoff, James A. 2003. Aslian: Mon-Khmer of the Malay Peninsula. *Mon-Khmer studies* 33: 1–58.

Means, Nathalie. 1998. *Temiar–English, English–Temiar dictionary*. Edited by Gordon P. Means. St Paul: Hamline University Press.

Miyakoshi, Koichi. 2006. Aslian reduplication as the emergence of the unmarked. *Gengo Kenkyu* 129: 43–89. www3.nacos.com/lsj/modules/documents/LSJpapers/journals/129_miyakoshi.pdf.

Noone, H. D. 1949. The first fruits of the hill rice harvest among the Tĕmiar Sĕnoi of the Plus-Tĕmiar Aboriginal area. *Bulletin of the Raffles Museum, series B* 4: 5–7.

Polanyi, Michael. 1959. *The study of man*. University of Chicago Press.

Roseman, Marina. 1984. The social structuring of sound: the Temiar of Peninsular Malaysia. *Ethnomusicology* 28: 411–445.

Sapir, Edward. 1921. *Language: an introduction to the study of speech*. New York: Harcourt, Brace.

Shorto, H. L. 2006. *A Mon-Khmer comparative dictionary*. Canberra: Pacific Linguistics.

Sidwell, Paul. 2008. 'Issues in the morphological reconstruction of Proto-Mon-Khmer'. In Claire Bowern, Bethwyn Evans, and Luisa Miceli (eds.), *Morphology and language history: in honour of Harold Koch*. Amsterdam: John Benjamins, pp. 251–265.

Sloan, Kelly. 1988. 'Bare-consonant reduplication: implications for a prosodic theory of reduplication'. *Proceedings of the Eleventh West Coast Conference on Formal Linguistics*, Stanford: CSLI Publications, pp. 319–330.

Sperber, Dan. 1979. *Rethinking symbolism*. Cambridge University Press.

Tsur, Reuven. 2006. Size-sound symbolism revisited. *Journal of pragmatics* 38: 905–924.

Tufvesson, Sylvia. 2007. 'Expressives'. In Asifa Majid (ed.), *Field manual volume 10*. Nijmegen: Max Planck Institute for Psycholinguistics, pp. 53–58.

2011. Analogy-making in the Semai sensory world. *The senses and society* 6: 86–95.

Van Gijn, Rik. 2010. Middle voice and ideophones, a diachronic connection: the case of Yurakaré. *Studies in language* 34: 273–297.

Yap Ngee Thai. 2009. Non-exhaustive syllabification in Temiar. *JSEALS: Journal of the Southeast Asian Linguistics Society* 1: 267–282.

4   Decorative morphology in Khmer

John Haiman

1   Introduction[*]

It is a commonplace belief in the Western linguistic tradition that language exists for packaging information as clearly and as economically as possible. Major accounts of competing motivations of speakers and hearers (Gabelentz 1891) and of the distinction between utterance meaning and sentence meaning are predicated on the 'articulatory bottleneck' (Levinson 2000: 27–30), which makes it impossible to be both clear and economical at the same time. All of the resulting discussion tacitly implies that language has no other purpose than to transmit information. Yet, as we also know, language has a variety of non-referential functions (Bühler 1934): directive, expressive, and aesthetic. Beyond that, we account for a great deal of apparently useless 'junk discourse', for example, by invoking a phatic function (Malinowski 1923), which is so loosely defined as to be entirely vacuous. Speakers may, for example, repeat themselves:

(1)   We'll see, we'll see.

If all else fails (that is, if repetition is neither iconically nor aesthetically nor expressively nor directively motivated, see Haiman to appear), we attempt to account for such instances by desperately invoking a combination of plausible but untestable notions such as inertia (it is easier to repeat oneself than to say something new) and the fear of silence (which is unfriendly) to preserve the assumption that we have a reason for everything we do. Or we can admit defeat and acknowledge that the purpose of most discourse, like that of most DNA, is still unknown.

[*] An original draft of this paper was written and presented as a talk while I was a Visiting Fellow at the Institute for Evolutionary Anthropology, Max-Planck Institut, in Leipzig, 2003–4. It is a pleasure to express my gratitude to Bernard Comrie and the staff at EVA for their hospitality and friendship over this period, and to my audience for their reactions. Further heartfelt thanks to Philip Jenner, Tania Kuteva, David Gil, Bernhard Wälchli, and James Stanford for their expert comments on this final version.

Very well, discourse above the sentence level may be chock full of junk (a functionalist may answer) but at the sentence level, every morpheme pays its way by making a purely referential contribution. But does it? The evidence from many languages of Southeast Asia suggests that even this assertion may be false. My goal in Section 2 of this chapter is to focus on what looks like referential junk at the sentence level in the grammar of Khmer. I will argue that there is, most likely, a decorative motivation for much of the morphology of the language and that there are indeed parallels to this kind of morphology even in Western languages. But the most striking parallels with which we are likely to be familiar exist in the non-linguistic domains of art and ritual, briefly touched on in Section 3. I will raise some questions on the possible significance of decorative morphology in language in general, and why it should be so well attested in Southeast Asian languages like Khmer, and virtually unknown outside of this area in Section 4.

2   Decorative morphology in Khmer

The following survey will deal with decorative affixation and with decorative reduplication. The claim that these are 'decorative' is supported mainly by the acknowledgement that whatever else they are, they are not referential, and by the judgements of native speakers that the contribution they make to an utterance is not to its meaning but its elegance.

2.1   *Decorative affixation*

Consider the following snippet of dialogue between the leader of an anti-French resistance cell and one of his eager acolytes.

(2a)   Speaker A: – *kecka: jeu:ng ba:n samrac awh   haeuj*
                        matter   our   PST   ready   exhaust PFV
                        'Is our business/plot completely ready?'

(2b)   Speaker B: – *ba:t   ruac srac   awh   haeuj*
                        Yes ♂RESP PST   ready exhaust PFV
                        'Yes sir, it is completely ready.'

Speaker B is a 'yes-man', whose linguistic behaviour in this interchange is an enthusiastic Performance of the speech act of agreement with his boss. This is signalled from the first word he utters, *ba:t* 'very respectful "yes" from male speaker' and from the fact that his utterance is largely (but not entirely) the assertive counterpart to his boss's question. As we know from English, the yes-man can signal agreement through a variety of devices which include anaphoric reduction ('Me too'), and this is exemplified by the elision of the subject NP *kecka: jeu:ng* 'our business' in the passage above. Of greater interest to us here is the substitution of:

- *ruac* 'PST tense' for *ba:n* 'PST tense' and
- *srac* 'ready' for *samrac* 'ready'.

The first demonstrates that yes-man behaviour allows the sycophant to substitute a synonym for his model's words. As main verbs, *ba:n* 'come to have' and *ruac* 'escape' are not synonyms. They are synonyms only as serial verbs in a resultative construction, where they both function as verbs of accomplishment and signal that the act denoted in the preceding main verb was carried out. *Ba:n* is polysemous, and also functions as an auxiliary verb denoting past tense. Through polysemy copying (Heine and Kuteva 2005) *ruac* is also able to acquire this auxiliary function, although this is not, as of yet, a canonical meaning of this verb. While Heine and Kuteva (2005) deal with an interlanguage phenomenon, Khmer seems to exhibit polysemy copying within one language. Another term for this may be 'paradigmatic association': defined as words that are associated with other words through being partial synonyms are in a paradigm with these other words. Being in the same paradigm, they may borrow privileges of occurrence from each other.

The substitution of *srac* for *samrac* is equally complex. As it happens, Khmer derivational morphology includes a variety of prefixes and infixes. Speaker A's word *samrac* 'ready' can be parsed as *s-am-rac*. The infix *-Vm(n)-* is borderline productive, and has two major referential functions. Most frequently, it creates deverbal nominalizations:

(3)   *criang* 'sing' → *c-am-riang* 'song'

(4)   *thom* 'big' → *t-um-hom* 'size'

Less often, it creates transitive verbs from intransitives:

(5)   *slap* 'die' → *s-am-lap* 'kill'

(6)   *creah* 'fall' → *c-um-reah* 'drop'

Clearly, neither of these referential functions is performed in the interchange (2). Just as clearly, the substitution of *srac* for *samrac* is not anaphora. So what is the sycophant up to? A good hypothesis is that this is another case of synonym substitution: he is using *srac* as a synonym for *samrac*. In fact, while this example is particularly clear, it is by no means isolated. There are examples going back to Old Khmer of purely decorative infixation of *-am(n)-* . In an early inscription, *c-aN-pa:r* appears as a variant of *cpa:r* 'garden' (Lewitz 1976: 742). The modern language provides dozens of examples of the same phenomenon (Haiman and Ourn 2003).

Nor is *-am(n)-* the only meaningless infix. A native speaker of the Surin dialect of Khmer (spoken in the extreme north of Cambodia and in the border regions of Laos and Thailand) reports that in his own speech, it is possible to optionally insert a meaningless syllabic [r] between the initial consonants of any root (Prakorb 1992: 255). This is a most extraordinary statement for a native speaker to make about his native language. But other linguists studying Central or standard Khmer have come close to acknowledging the same possibility (compare Maspero 1915: 202; Gorgoniev 1966: 73; Jacob 1968: 179, 1976: 608; Pou 2004: 27 for the possibility of meaningless -*N*- insertion, and Pou 2004; Jenner 1969: 122–3 for meaningless -*rV*- insertion).

A plausible account for such infixation exists. Speakers who engage in it are hypercorrectly reinserting the rhyme portion of an initial unstressed syllable (= anacrusic) of bisyllabic words, which typically has the form *CVN*- or *CrV*-. Rules of erosion are forever eliding exactly these rhyme strings in casual speech (Haiman 1998a, 2003; Haiman and Ourn 2003). The following list gives some examples of the contrast between careful and colloquial pronunciations of the same word via loss of anacrusic -*VN*-.

Careful	>	Casual	
bambaek	>	pabaek	'destroy'
bampleu:h	>	papleu:h	'exaggerate'
bamra:m	>	pra:m	'prohibit'
bandeau	>	padaeu	'lead, make to walk'
banlae	>	palae	'vegetables'
banthaem	>	pathaem	'add'
banjcenj	>	pacenj	'emit'
bangho:	>	paho:	'irrigate'
bangkia	>	pakia	'saltwater shrimp'
bangkoap	>	pakoap	'order'
bang'uac	>	pa'uac	'window'
camnga:j	>	canga:j	'distance'
cangkeuh	>	cakeuh	'chopsticks'
cumngw:	>	cangw:	'illness'
damba:v	>	taba(:)v	'infection
dambo:k	>	tabo:k	'hillock'
dambo:l	>	tabo:l	'roof'
dambo:ng	>	tabo:ng	'first of all'
dambawl	>	tabawl	'two times two'
dambawn	>	tabawn	'region, zone'
dambaw:ng	>	tbaw:ng	'rattan, vine'
damnaeu	>	tanaeu	'trip'
dangha:l	>	taha:l	'fan'
dangkev	>	takev	'earthworm'
kamlang	>	kalang	'strength'
kanda:l	>	kada:l	'middle'
kanlaeng	>	kalaeng	'place'

samlap	> salap	'kill'
samngat	> sangat	'secret'
sam'a:t	> sa'a:t	'clean' (transitive, causative)
tungkec	> takec	'knock'
tumleak	> taleak	'drop'

It appears from these examples that only the final nasal is lost and that the change is *CVN* → *CV*. Note however that the initial consonant of the anacrusic syllable is devoiced in the casual pronunciation. The typologically more plausible mechanism for this devoicing is a rule that devoices consonants immediately before consonants, there being no rule that commonly devoices consonants at the beginning of open syllables. That is, of the two conjectured devoicing rules which could describe the changes 'b→p' and 'd →t', it is much more likely that the correct phonologically motivated rule takes the form of

(7)   'stop → devoiced/____ consonant'

rather than that of

(8)   'stop → devoiced/____ vowel'

Note also that the vowel quality of the initial syllable is not preserved: while the anacrusic vowel in careful speech may be either {a} or {u}, the anacrusic vowel in casual speech is invariably {a}. We are therefore more justified in positing a rule of anacrusis rhyme reduction that elides the underlying vowel and feeds (7) rather than a rule which preserves that vowel and which feeds (8). The vowel {a} (schwa in the practical orthography adopted here) is then inserted by a rule of anaptyxis, one of the most productive rules in Khmer phonology, as noted since Martini (1942–5), Henderson (1952), and Gorgoniev (1966):

(9) $\emptyset \rightarrow a/\# C$ ___ C

Erosion via a rule of -*rV*- deletion:

Careful	Casual	
kralee:k	> kalee:k	'cast one's eye on'
krama:	> kama:	'scarf, bandana'
kra'o:p	> ka'o:p	'fragrant'
pradap	> padap	'instrument, tool'
prado:c	> pado:c	'compare'
prahael	> pahael	'approximately'
prateah	> pateah	'run into, encounter'
pralwm	> palwm	'dawn'

Here, there is no unambiguous evidence that the elision rule applies to the whole string -*ra*- rather than to just the consonant [r]. The relatively weak argument that the former is the case rests on an appeal to functional unity. If the ultimate tendency of reduction rules is to convert bisyllables to monosyllables, then it is likely that it is *-ra-* which is elided. This argument is strengthened by the existence of a functionally related rule that deletes the entire anacrusic syllable as shown in the following examples:

(10)   robawh > bawh 'of'

(11)   babaw: > baw: 'rice porridge, gruel'

This argument is weakened, however, by other reduction rules such as the change r → l, which have no prosodic effect as shown in the following list.

rabam	> labam	'dancer'
rabang	> labang	'gate, shield, wall'
rabaj	> labaj	'form'
rabeh	> labeh	'peelings and rubble'
rabe:ng	> labe:ng	'tuberculosis'
rabiang	> labiang	'frontage road, alley'
rabiap	> labiap	'institution, method, practice'
rabo:c	> labo:c	'damage'
rabo:t	> labo:t ~ abo:t	'let go'

But we are left with a number of productive processes, which have a common prosodic effect: they convert bisyllabic words into monosyllables in casual speech. Crucially, they always do this when the initial anacrusic syllable has the form *CVN-*. While the rules of erosion reduce bisyllabic words to monosyllabic ones, hypercorrection either restores the original bisyllabics or mistakenly creates them from etymologically monosyllabic words. In fact, hypercorrection may even be responsible for the origin of such syllabic infixes in the first place (Haiman 1998a). But the end result of such behaviour is a proliferation of affixes in search of a meaning, among them *-VN-* and *-rV-*. In a handful of cases, they are recognized as such. Thus the standard dictionary recognizes *k-ra-sae* 'string' as an 'elegant' version of *ksae* (same meaning).

Why call this hypercorrect insertion an aesthetically motivated operation? We can say that partly, because 'elegance' is recognized as the motive for some of these alternations; and partly, because hypercorrection is not. That is, the restoration is not recognized as a careful pronunciation. Finally, partly because making the insertion creates a kind of symmetry in the vocabulary: all words undergoing the process conform to the same iambic template, as insertion applies only to monosyllables, and is therefore restricted to the creation of strictly bisyllables.

2.2   Decorative reduplication

Khmer has a large number of synonym compounds like our 'last and final'. Unlike English, where such compounds are restricted to a relatively small number of nouns ('let or hindrance'), verbs ('aid and abet'), and adjectives ('complete and utter'), Khmer ransacks its lexical resources to create such symmetrical compounds out of native and borrowed roots, and the resulting compounds include not only nouns, verbs, and adjectives, but also pairs of deictics, aspect markers, auxiliary verbs, prepositions, and conjunctions (Haiman 2011). Many of the resulting symmetrical compounds are alliterating words like *klec kli:* 'massage': these shade off into pairs of meaningful words + purely decorative *bo 'ri 'va: sap* 'servant words' which alliterate with the meaningful root. The expression *bo 'ri 'va: sap* (Neo-Sanskrit parivāra.sabda 'retinue word') derives from the Khmer grammatical tradition. All Khmer authorities concur on the important point that servant words are meaningless morphemes with a primarily euphonic function and are incapable of standing alone. 'A servant word is a sound which accompanies a base word in a compound, much like a retinue or entourage [accompanies a ruler] in order to make speech more pleasant to the listener's ear and also to qualify the original word' (Chun-Leuh 2007: 190). They may precede this root (as in *bampheut bamphej* 'scare'), or follow it (as in *lbej lba:nj* 'famous').

Khmer has an enormous vocabulary of such twin forms (Marchand 1960), which are formally much like our *helter-skelter*, or *jibber-jabber* (except that they alliterate, rather than rhyme with their partners). The mere existence of so many meaningless morphemes with no referential basis suggests an aesthetic or ludic motivation in the modern language. Still, one could suppose that the meaningless word is likely to have once been meaningful, much like the 'kith' in English 'kith and kin', in which case the alliteration is epiphenomenal. Indeed this was the default assumption of Ourn and Haiman (2000). More recently, we have come to change our opinion and now believe that a sizeable number, perhaps even the majority, of servant words are not the now semantically opaque holdovers from earlier lost synonyms that happened to alliterate, but rather creations out of whole cloth or non-synonyms which have been dragooned into servant status in order to provide symmetrical partners for meaningful words. While some servant words are clearly frozen former synonyms, there are at least four strategies by which such servant words can be produced in such a way that it is clear that their formal symmetry with their partner is an essential, rather than an incidental aspect of their nature.

2.2.1   Conscription strategy

They may be non-synonyms, which are 'conscripted' on the basis of their phonetic shape to serve as partners to the semantically relevant word in the compound (compare English 'loosey-goosey' and 'true blue'). In the examples below, the meaningful word is glossed in capitals, and the gloss of its semantically irrelevant conscripted partner is flagged with '?!'

(12a) *psah*   *psa:*   'heal'
       HEAL   market (?!)

(12b) *kliang*   *kliat*   'separate'
       unbalanced (?!)   SEPARATE

(12c) *lveung*   *lviaj*   'vast'
       VAST   slow (?!)

(12d) *kamlang*   *kamhaeng*   'force, energy'
       FORCE   yell (?!)

(12e) *samdej*   *samdav*   'speech style'
       SPEECH   towards (?!)

(12f) prakaw:t   pracia   'exact'
       EXACT   person (?!)

(12g) *tnak*   *tnaw:m*   'handle carefully'
       level (?!)   HANDLE GENTLY

(12h) *psaw:p*   *psa:j*   'disseminate, propagate,
                                                         spread'
       perception (?!)   SPREAD

(12i) *pranej*   *pranak*   'compassion'
       COMPASSION   nutcracker (?!)

(12j) *co:k*   *coam*   'drenched, soaked'
       WET   bruised (?!)

(12k) *rwang*   *ra:j*   'matter, affair'
       MATTER   clank (?!) (onomatopoeic word)

(12l) *ponma:n*   *pontae*   'but'
       how much (?!)   BUT

(12m) *ciat*   *cev*   'taste'
       TASTE   <crev 'deep'(?!)

(12n) *vu:m*   *veak*   'surprise'
       trumpeting of elephant (?!)   SURPRISE

(12o) *srango:t*   *srangat*   'downcast'
       SAD COUNTENANCE   dark green (?!)

(12p)	*ruac* FINISH	*roal* every (?!)	'perfective aspect marker'

(12q)	*samrac* READY, DECIDE	*samruac* sharpen (?!)	'finally'

2.2.2 *Procrustean adaptation strategy*

The servant words may be synonyms, which have undergone surgery (adding or subtracting phonetic material) to make them conform to their partners (compare English 'kit, cat, and ca-boodle'). In the examples below, the added bits are indicated in capitals:

(13a)	*PRA-hak* ? like	*prahael* approximately	'like, about, approximately'

(13b)	*mho:p* food	*M-ha:* ? food	'food'

(13c)	*d-AM-kom* gather	*damkaeung* carry up	'carry up; promote'

(13d)	*srango:t* sad	*s-RA-ngat* ? < quiet (or 'dark green')	'downcast, melancholy'

(13e)	*sangkawt* press down	*SANG-keun* grind, mill	'oppress, grind down'

(13f)	sranawh melancholy	s-RAN-aok < sad, cry	'sad'

(13g)	*DANG-ho:* ? <flow	*danghae* parade	'parade, procession'

Comparatively rarely, the Procrustean strategy involves reducing the adapting word by eliminating a chunk of it through the process of cutting it down to the size and shape of the main word. The eliminated chunk then becomes a plausible 'infix' as shown in example (14a) or a plausible 'prefix' as shown in example (14b):

(14a)	*sdok* IMMOBILE?	*sdeung* < *santheung* 'extend'	'stretched out unconscious'

(14b)	*anlauk* THINGS DIPPED	*anlae* < *banlae* 'vegetables'	'vegetables added to soup'

2.2.3 *Adam's rib strategy*

The servant words may be manufactured out of cognate accusatives of their partners. The cognate accusative consists of some light verb plus a nominalization of the targeted verb. The Adam's rib precedes its partner as shown in the copious examples that follow:

(15a)	*baek k-umn- wt*	*kwt*	'think'
	open thought	think	

(15b)	*mian c-amn-eh*	*ceh*	'know'
	have knowledge	know	

(15c)	*awh s-amn-aeuc*	*saeuc*	'laugh'
	exhaust laughter	laugh	

(15d)	*mian d-am-laj*	*tlaj*	'valuable'
	have value	valuable	

(15e)	*cia s-amn-aen*	saen	'make an offering'
	be offering	make offering	

(15f)	*praeu t-am-biat*	*tbiat*	'embrace, wrap one's arms around'
	use embrace	embrace	

(15g)	*leu:k k-amn-a:p*	*ka:p*	'write poetry'
	raise poem	write poetry	

(15h)	*mian c-umn-wa*	*cwa*	'believe'
	have belief	believe	

(15i)	*cia c-um-lo:h*	*clo:h*	'quarrel'
	be quarrel	quarrel	

(15j)	*cap k-amn-aeut*	*kaeut*	'be born'
	catch birth	be born	

2.2.4   Word splice and dice strategy Finally, servant words may be produced via a word game of constructed Spoonerisms in much the same way that English portmanteau words like *smog (*foke)* are constructed via rhyme swap from compounds like *sm-oke* plus *f-og*. The point of such rhyme swapping may be to show a hidden (sometimes nonsensical, sometimes rueful, and frequently obscene) 'subtext' to a conventional message. Thus Khmer speakers obscenely 'derive' the ethnonym of the Kui minority people from *kuj (kandeh)* (= Kui (+ *nonsense word)), which in turn 'derives' via this rhyme swap from the expression *k-eh kand-uj* which means 'scratch cunt' (Rongier 2005). Khmer grammarians are particularly enthusiastic about deriving a large number of servant words from this same game (Porisat 1972; Chun-Leuh 2007). In the examples shown in Table 4.1, the servant word that results from the rhyme swap is represented through capitalization.

Table 4.1 *Rhyme swapping in Khmer*

Common expression	Result of rhyme swapping		Resulting servant word
Ps- a: mian c- ao →	*ps- ao*	*mian c- a:* →	*psa: PSAO* 'market'
Market have thief	(nonsense)	have (nonsense)	market nonsense
J-om sr-aek →	*j-aek*	*sr-om* →	*jom JAEK* 'weep'
weep cry.out	(nonsense)	(nonsense)	weep nonsense
Rah-aek proh th-oj →	*rah-oj*	*proh th-aek* →	*rahaek RAHOJ* 'tear'
tear because soft	(nonsense)	because (nonsense)	
R-uk daoj co:l tantr-ian→	*r-ian daoj co:l tantr-uk* →		*RIAN ruk* 'invade'
invade by enter invade	(nonsense) by enter (nonsense)		

2.2.5 Servant words on the fringes of meaning In this section we illustrate the ubiquity of the decorative servant word phenomenon, and some of the issues that arise in making the claim that the decorative word is truly meaningless. We note the (inevitable) disputes that may arise among authorities as to whether a decorative compound is a single word like 'helter-skelter', a decorative compound like 'mish-mash', where only one word is meaningful, or a genuine compound like 'creepy-crawly', where indeed both words are meaningful. We note further that authorities may differ even in the case of unanimous agreement about the status of a compound, some speakers judging the first element to be the decorative partner, and others judging the second to be so. We note finally that since all such disputes are based on freewheeling etymologizing, a further area of disagreement may arise: a decorative partner to a prosaic word may be borderline meaningful, but this could mean either that it is on the point of entirely losing its original meaning (the presumable default assumption for most models of semantic change), or that it is on the point of acquiring a new one (see Haiman 2010). We begin with some unanimously shared judgements:

Sraoc sraw:p	sprinkle, irrigate (2nd DSW)
Srakek sraka:k	untidy, messy, dirty (faced) (1st DSW)
Sramee:k sramaw:k	stained all over (1st DSW)
Sramo:nj srama:nj	bushy (beard) (2nd DSW)
Sramo:m srama:m	ditto
Srangaeh srango:c	melancholy (1st DSW)
Srapec srapeu:l	confused, unclear (opp. *cbah*) (1st DSW)
Sravee: srava:	gather up, grab, reach for (1st DSW)
Sruac luac	pointed, pointy (2nd DSW)

In the last case, *luac* exists as an independent word meaning 'steal', but it is presumably clear to all observers that this meaning cannot possibly be relevant in the compound, and that *luac* has been conscripted for its rhyme (cf. Morgenstern 1964).

But disagreements arise in the following cases.

- The root *sra:k* 'diminish, fall off, reduce' is a well-established one in Khmer, and the source of the causative/nominalization *s-am-ra:k* 'relax(ation)'. The phrase *awt sra:k* 'lack falling off' means 'relentless, uninterrupted'. Now the symmetrical compound *sra:k sra:n* 'improve, relax, feel relief; subside' seems to be based on the first root, in which case the second morpheme is decorative (Chun-Leuh 2007), but my teacher Veasna Keat claims that it is the first root which is decorative. One possible reason for his assessment is that *sra:k* also occurs as an accompaniment to other roots, as in *sra:k srual* 'make peace', whose second element is the common word meaning 'easy'.

- The compound *sriav sra:nj* means 'feel feverish' and seems to consist of two meaningful words: *sriav* 'vertigo' and *sra:nj.* 'tingle, be asleep (like one's foot)'. But both authorities cited above agree that the second element of this compound is a meaningless decorative word. This could be because the second element no longer has this meaning, or has not yet fully acquired it.

- The compound *sroh srual* 'unanimously agree, be in harmony' seems to be a compound of *sroh* 'all together in unison' and *srual* 'easy': but for VK, the second element is a meaningless decorative element, while for C-L, the first element is. Since *srual* is a very common word, VK's response must be based on the judgement that its common meaning 'easy' plays no role in the compound, and that it is therefore an example of a conscripted servant word.

- The compound *srawh sra:j* 'clear, candid, unclouded' seems to be a compound of *srawh* 'fresh, beautiful, brightly coloured' and *sra:j* 'release, untie, solve, loose', but both cited authorities agree that the second element is a servant word.

- The compound *srak(a)ut srakum* 'serene, stately, calm, gentle, modest' seems to be a single word to VK. But for C-L, the first element is meaningful, and the second is a servant word. So, while decorative words are trembling on the verge of (losing or gaining) meaning, as suggested by the random sample of words considered above, it is also important to emphasize what such symmetrical structures arising from any of the four processes above do not mean.

- They do not mean plurality, duration, intensity, distributivity, iterativity, reciprocity, or any of the things reduplication iconically signals in most languages, and in fact these forms are formally distinguished from iconic reduplication in two ways. First, iconic reduplication is almost always a total reduplication: thus for example *cah cah* 'old + plural', while decorative reduplication is always partial (the servant word most often alliterating, less often assonant, least frequently rhyming with its model). Second iconic reduplication is subject to the iambic reduction rules, while decorative reduplication is not (see below*)*.

• They do not mean anything pejorative, like American schmo reduplication, or its congeners in a variety of languages (Stolz 2008).

• They do not even have the minimal meaning of emphasis: 'very', 'really', or 'truly'.

This last minimal meaning hypothesis (cf. Stanford 2007 on Sui) is a hard thing to challenge, since 'really' comes very close to being already meaningless. Nevertheless, I propose to challenge it. In support of my claim, I take note of a large number of collocationally restricted adverbial intensifiers (*vi'seh kun niam*, VKN) comparable to English 'hopping' in expressions like 'hopping mad'. All of them are glossed as synonyms of *nah* 'very'.

(16a)   *kra:h*   *kleuk*
        calloused   INTNS

(16b)   *khang*   *cralee:t*
        angry   INTNS

(16c)   *huj*   *tko:l*
        smoky   INTNS

(16d)   *ngungeut*   *clawp*
        dark   INTNS

(16e)   *reak*   *kamphael*
        shallow   INTNS

(16f)   *kdav*   *caeh*
        black   INTNS

(16g)   *haeum*   *pramaul*
        swell   INTNS

(16h)   *paong*   *kampleh*
        swell up   INTNS (applicable to bellies)

(16i)   *riav*   *kaklo:k*
        watery   INTNS (applicable to soups)

(16j)   *cu:*   *creah*
        sour   INTNS (applicable to taste)

The sheer number of these intensifiers raises suspicion. Why such a plethora of lexically restricted words, all meaning 'very', and where do they come from? If we are able to find etymologies for these words, we find that they frequently originated as near-synonyms of the words they now apparently intensify (Haiman 2011, Chapter 4). That is, expressions like many of the ones above originated as synonym compound pairs.

Bernhard Wälchli (pers. com.) has pointed out to me that there are lots of words for 'very' in even familiar languages like German, and so the situation in Khmer may not be so strikingly unusual – indeed he suggests that the real challenge is to find any languages with only one single word for this notion. Against this I draw attention to the fact that very often these intensifiers in Khmer do not originate as intensifiers at all, but as synonyms.

What chiefly distinguishes these present-day 'intensifiers' from totally mean-ingless servant words is that they happen to exhibit no formal symmetry with the words they modify. And it is this formal difference between erstwhile synonyms, which leads native speakers to characterize intensifiers as intensi-fiers, decorative words as purely decorative words. This suggests the following model of semantic change. Given a pair of conjoined synonyms 'A + B' which are unlike each other, and another pair 'A + Â' which are formally similar, if 'B' loses its original meaning, then it will be reinterpreted as an intensifier, but if 'Â' loses its meaning it will be reinterpreted as a decorative servant word of 'A'. That is, not only does Khmer exhibit a penchant for formal syntagmatic symmetry, it also exhibits a penchant for an iconic congruity between form and meaning: an asymmetric syntagm of erstwhile synonyms will receive an asymmetric interpretation, while a formally symmetric syntagm will be inter-preted as a decorative symmetrical compound.

2.3   *Iambicity versus symmetry*

Once created, any grammatical structure is prone to natural processes of change, including erosion. To ask the question 'How deeply is Khmer grammar com-mitted to the preservation of the symmetry of such compounds?' is to ask whether symmetrical compounds retain their symmetry in the face of grammat-ical processes, which would tend to destroy them. The major processes of erosion in Khmer are unquestionably the rules of anacrusic syllable reduction noted in Section 2.1, which are forever converting bisyllabic words into mono-syllables mostly through the loss of the rhyme portion of the anacrusic syllable, represented schematically as Figure 4.1.

Since the rule also applies to lexical compounds (e.g. *prambej* 'five three' becomes *pabej* 'eight') and two-word phrases (e.g. *muaj daw:ng* 'one time' becomes *madaw:ng*), one may suppose that symmetrical compounds are also exposed to them. What happens to decorative compounds? The short answer is

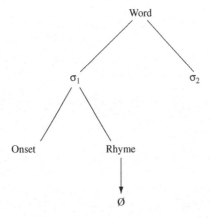

Figure 4.1 Anacrusic syllable reduction in Khmer

that symmetry trumps iambicity. When the symmetrical compound consists of two monosyllables, neither one is reduced as shown in the following list.

(17a)   *cha:v chee:v* (no reduction occurs)   'impatient'

(17b)   *ciat cev* (no reduction occurs)   'tasty'

(17c)   *ckoam ckau:ng* (no reduction occurs)   'out of joint'

(17d)   *cliav cla:t* (no reduction occurs)   'intelligent, cunning'

(17e)   *dac daoc* (no reduction occurs)   'ragged'

(17f)   *kliav klawm*   'flawless'

(17g)   *knan knoan*   'offended'

(17h)   *khwl kho:c*   'depraved'

(17i)   *kho: khev*   'violent'

(17j)   *lhae lhaeuj*   'alleviate'

(17k)   *pak paeuk*   'seesaw'

This is already a remarkable fact, given the fate of two-word phrases in general. In particular, it already distinguishes decorative from iconic reduplication. The latter is subject to the erosion rules, and so compounds like *psee:ng psee:ng* 'various' are reduced to prosodic iambs (Huffman 1970: 186 for Central Khmer; Jenner 1974 passim for Surin Khmer). The same process may have been originally responsible for a no-longer productive kind of iconic reduplication, whereby a root is preceded by a minimal unstressed prefix consisting of its initial consonant

Table 4.2 *Multi-reduction forms*

	Full form	Partial reduction	Total reduction
(18a)	damnae damneung→'information' (decorative)	tamnae tamnawng →	tanae tanawng
(18b)	damrae damrawng→'straighten' (decorative)	tamnae tamnawng →	tanae tanawng
(18c)	dam'ae dam'awk→'loiter' (decorative)	tam'ae tam'awk →	ta'awk
(18d)	bangkhia bangkheang →'prohibit' (decorative)	pakhia pakheang →	khia kheang
(18e)	papleh paplawh →'frivolous' (decorative)	aleh alawh→	leh lawh

and the default vowel schwa. Thus *teuk* 'water' yields the derived intensive form *tateuk* 'soaked' – which may, in the past, have been **teukteuk*. While it is intuitively plausible that reduplication is nothing but grammaticalized repetition, there is little hard diachronic evidence for such a process. For a rare exception, see Gil (2005) on the process in Riau Indonesian.

But more remarkable is the fate of conjoined iambic words, each of which may be subject to reduction. Does the first undergo more reduction than the second? The answer is that each element in such a pair undergoes exactly the same degree of reduction. This is particularly striking in the case of compounds each of whose members may undergo more than one degree of reduction. Among these are the examples in Table 4.2.

What is expressly forbidden (to take the last example as representative) is any asymmetric reduction as the following ungrammatical examples demonstrate.

(19a)   **papleh alawh*   (second conjunct partially reduced)

(19b)   **aleh paplawh*   (first conjunct partially reduced)

(19c)   **aleh lawh*   (first conjunct partially reduced, second conjunct totally reduced)

There are other rules besides those of anacrusic syllable reduction, which have the potential for disturbing the symmetry of paired compounds. Some of them are highly irregular, but it makes no difference since all of them are subjected to the same overarching constraint that symmetry must be preserved between decoratively paired conjuncts. Compare the coordinate structure constraint in syntax: movement out of one conjunct is forbidden, but across-the-board movement out of all conjuncts is acceptable (Ross 1967).

The upshot of this is that Khmer, an isolating language, is beginning to manifest a system of obligatory but non-referential grammatical agreement between symmetrically conjoined morphemes. This recalls the speculation of Ferguson and Barlow (1988: 17) that perhaps the original basis for even some referentially motivated inflectional agreement (cf. Sapir's 'relentless' *ill-orum bon-orum vir-orum*) may have been aesthetic.

3 Analogues to decorative morphology in non-linguistic realms

3.1 Art

A conventional distinction comparable to the one discussed in this essay is made between representational and purely decorative visual art. The former is referential, like the traditional Western conception of language, but decorative or ornamental art, as is well known, is at least as ancient as representative art (Boas 1928).

3.2 Ritual

In an earlier article (Haiman 1993), I used 'ritualization' as a cover term for reduction and standardization in language development. I now believe that this use of the term does violence to one of the remarkable and distinguishing features of non-linguistic ritual behaviour in general: its elaborateness relative to the everyday activity on which it is patterned. Ritual is characterized by a great deal of non-referential decorative 'galumphing' (Miller 1973), and the decorative morphology of Khmer should perhaps be compared with the useless but obscurely pleasing rigmarole of ceremonial clothing, dining, games, bureaucratic protocol, and other ritualized behaviour (Caillois 1958; Barthes 1983; Barry 1985; Haiman and Ourn 2009).

3.3 Music

All music is of course decorative in the sense that it is non-referential. Yet the distinction can be made between melody, which serves to advance the non-referential story and ornament, which serves to adorn it. Pure repetition, whether of a single note as in 'Ah vous dirais-je maman' or of a multi-note theme, as in almost every bar of the C minor prelude in the first book of Bach's *Well-Tempered Clavier*, is exactly analogous to the Khmer phenomenon of servant word repetition, it seems to me. Lundstrom discusses the decorative aspects of Khmui singing (this volume) and Williams (this volume) also points out the similarities in what could be considered overlaps between decorative elements in grammar and song text in Thai.

4 Back to language

4.1 Prosaic versus decorative language

Wilson (1975) following Tinbergen (1952) proposes that decorative galumphing is what first distinguishes many animal signals from practical goal-directed actions, and may thus be repeatedly implicated in the origin of language-like behaviour. If this speculation is correct, then the decorative morphology of Khmer and other languages of the region may not be a totally marginal geographically isolated fact. It may provide a window on the origin of language. The relationship between decorative language and prosaic or ordinary language:

decorative language = ordinary language + decorative galumphing

may be parallel to the relationship between the ritualized behaviour of language and the practical goal-oriented behaviour from which it may derive:

language = practical behaviour + decorative galumphing.

In both cases, galumphing is recognizable as purposeful but functionally unmotivated frills. The most common of these frills may be repetition.

4.2   Decorative language and grammaticalization

Does the presence of decorative morphology correlate with other characteristics of a language? Clearly, as attested by the existence and title of this volume, it seems to be a regional phenomenon, exuberantly attested in languages of Southeast Asia, but is it possible to say more? All of the languages of the area seem to be isolating languages; again a familiar fact, but it is not easy to see why this should be a relevant factor. I propose another correlation as a working hypothesis. As both Heine and Kuteva (2002, 2007) and Kuteva (2010) have pointed out, Southeast Asian languages offer a rich panoply of grammaticalization processes, with this striking 'anomaly': grammaticalization in their analysis does not include obligatorification (pace Jakobson 1959; Lehmann 1982, 1995), which Heine and Kuteva view as a last stage in the grammaticalization process, rather than one of its essential defining features. Thus, while Mandarin Chinese exhibits more than twenty of the grammaticalization processes catalogued in Heine and Kuteva (2002) (and Russian, a highly inflected language, only eight), Mandarin has virtually no grammatical categories that a Jakobsonian would recognize: if languages differ, as Jakobson put it, in what they must say (that is, in the categories that they have obligatorized), then Mandarin has no grammatical categories at all. And this is emphatically true in Khmer as well. A recurrent observation in the derivational morphology and morphosyntax of Khmer is that no grammatical category is obligatory (cf. Haiman 2011). The main verb *ba:n* 'come to have' does duty as a past tense preverbal auxiliary, but continues to be optional; the noun *ka:* 'matter, affair' does duty as a nominalizer, but continues to be optional; and so on for one grammatical category after another, including (as we have seen), the infix -*Vm(n)*- of Section 2.1. The same optionality characterizes the decorative servant words under discussion in

Section 2.2. Mandarin and Khmer and possibly other Southeast Asian languages may be characterized as resisting obligatorification of their meaningful morphology. Could this have anything to do with their penchant for decorative morphology?

The correlation that I predict is the following one. Only that morphology which has been emancipated from the prosaic function of making an obligatory referential contribution to a message is available to perform a decorative function at all. Once obligatorification has as it were 'kicked in' on a morphosyntactic construction, a purely decorative function becomes impossible. From the perspective of common sense, the observation that things can decorate only to the extent that they are not useful (or indeed are downright dysfunctional) is hardly novel. In his book on fashion, Barthes (1983) makes exactly the same point about the prosaic and semantic functions of clothing: one can wear clothing to stay warm and comfortable (the prosaic function), but also to make a statement (the semantic function). It is notable how Barthes on the genesis of semanticity in culture echoes Wilson (1975) on the genesis of semanticity in biology. Now, to wear one's keys on the left or right, or to dress in black, or to trail a bridal train that needs to be carried by a dozen attendant bridesmaids can, like Veblen's conspicuous consumption, serve as an advertisement. But it serves to advertise only because this choice has no practical benefits, and may in fact incur some costs. Consider for example high heels. Indeed, seen from the perspective of common sense, this observation is totally banal. So much so, in fact, that if this hypothesis is confirmed, it will do no more than reinforce a truism: almost by definition, what is decorative or ornamental is what you can do without. Nevertheless, since no one has attempted to link decorative morphology with grammaticalization before (and in fact the very existence of decorative morphology is still highly controversial in Western linguistics, and the idea that grammaticalization does not automatically entail obligatoriness is still very much a minority view), it is worthy of being spelled out here: Those languages with extensive decorative morphology may turn out to coincide exactly with or be a proper subset of those languages where grammaticalization is not (yet) the same as obligatorification. More generally, perhaps, languages with decorative morphology will be (a subset of) those, which in general resist obligatorification of any words, irrespective of their source.

One final observation: most linguistic discussion of words and affixes has always taken it for granted that language has a cognitive or referential function. The articles in this radical volume recognize a second, decorative function. I would like to go beyond this and propose not a dichotomy but a possible trichotomy of functions: cognitive, grammatical, and decorative. Grammatical morphology as traditionally conceived is meaningful, but has become semantically enfeebled through obligatorification. Like any ritual that is routinely observed, it has lost the prosaic function of providing news. In much the same way that a ritual meal like Thanksgiving dinner is not exclusively or even primarily about the prosaic function of staving off the pangs of hunger, so a grammaticalized structure like tense in English is not wholly or even primarily about transmitting information (Haiman 1998b). In fact, a number of radical observers (e.g. Dahl 2004; Gil 2009) have taken to calling all obligatory grammar – irrespective of its impeccably meaningful origins – essentially unnecessary for communication, and thus completely decorative or non-utilitarian. Decorative morphology of the sort described in this essay in contrast was and is not utilitarian at all, even in its origins. To continue with the Thanksgiving analogy, decorative morphology traces back its origins not to a prosaic meal, but to a ritual that was dreamed up for purely aesthetic reasons in the first place. There may be occasions when the two are nearly impossible to distinguish: a case in point is the apparent rise of obligatory alliterative agreement between symmetrical conjoined morphemes in Khmer discussed in Section 2.2.

The distinction between grammatical morphology and decorative morphology (both of which presumably originate from prosaic lexical morphology but in very different ways) is however illustrated by speakers who violate the contrastive rules and expectations of each. Someone who violates rules of grammar – say, Tarzan, or the Cookie Monster – is said to be talking ungrammatically. Someone who violates the expectations of decorative grammar, on the other hand, is – like Clint Eastwood – said to be a strong silent type if he's charismatic or colourless if he isn't. Admittedly, grammaticality and decoration are often thought of in the same way. Thus, being ungrammatical is often lumped together with being laconic (cf. the discussion of the cult of 'plain speaking' in Haiman 1998a). Indeed, in my discussion of the competing motivations of iambicity and symmetry, I claimed that alliteration in decorative agreement may be becoming obligatory, that is 'grammatical' precisely in the sense of Jakobson. But, to the extent that we can tell Tarzan apart from Clint Eastwood, it may still be useful to keep grammatical and decorative morphology distinct.

References

Barry, Dave. 1985. 'The rules'. In Dave Barry, *Dave Barry's greatest hits*. New York: Crown.

Barthes, Roland. 1983. *The fashion system*. New York: Farrar Straus Giroux.

Boas, Franz. 1928. *Primitive art*. Cambridge, MA: Harvard University Press.

Bühler, K. 1934. *Sprachtheorie: die Darstellungsfunktion der Sprache*. Jena: Fischer.

Caillois, R. 1958. *Le jeux et les hommes*. Paris: Gallimard.

Chun-Leuh. 2007. *Ve:jjakaw: kmae* [Khmer grammar]. Phnom Penh: Pon Caun and Tiang Ciat.

Dahl, O. 2004. *The growth and maintenance of linguistic complexity*. Amsterdam: John Benjamins.

Ferguson, Charles and Michael Barlow. 1988. 'Introduction'. In Michael Barlow and Charles Ferguson (eds.), *Agreement in natural languages*. Stanford: CSLI.

Gabelentz, G. Von der. 1891 [1969]. *Die Sprachwissenschaft*. Tübingen: Narr.

Gil, David. 2005. 'From repetition to reduplication in Riau Indonesian'. In B. Hurch (ed.), *Studies on reduplication*. (Empirical Approaches to Language Typology 28.) Mouton de Gruyter: Berlin, pp. 31–64.

2009. 'How much grammar does it take to sail a boat?' In Geoffrey Sampson, David Gil, and Peter Trudgill (eds.), *Language complexity as an evolving variable*. Oxford University Press, pp. 19–33.

Gorgoniev, Yu. 1966. *Grammatika Kxmerskogo jazyka*. Moskva: Nauka.

Haiman, John. 1993. 'Ritualization and the development of language'. In William Pagliuca (ed.), *Perspectives on grammaticalization*. Amsterdam: John Benjamins, pp. 3–28.

1998a. Possible origins of infixation in Khmer. *Studies in language* 22(3): 597–617.

1998b. *Talk is cheap*. London: Oxford University Press.

2003. 'Explaining infixation'. In John Moore and Maria Polisky (eds.), *The nature of explanation in linguistic theory*. Stanford: CSLI, pp. 105–120.

2010. The creation of new words. *Linguistics* 47: 549–72.

2011. *Cambodian: Khmer*. Amsterdam: John Benjamins.

To appear. 'Six motivations for repetition'. In Edith Moravcsik and Andrej Malcukov (eds.),*Competing motivations*. London: Oxford University Press.

Haiman, John and N. Ourn. 2003. Nouns, verbs, and syntactic backsliding in Khmer. *Studies in Language* 27(3): 505–528.

2009. 'Formulaic language in ritual (and everyday) speech'. In Roberta Corrigan et al. (eds.), *Formulaic language*, volume II. Amsterdam: John Benjamins, pp. 567–587.

Heine, B. and T. Kuteva. 2002. *World lexicon of grammaticalization*. Cambridge University Press.

2005. *Grammaticalization and language contact*. Cambridge University Press.

2007. *The genesis of grammar*. London: Oxford University Press.

Henderson, E. 1952. The main features of Cambodian pronunciation. *Bulletin of the School of Oriental and African Studies* 14: 149–174.

Huffman, Frank. 1970. *Contemporary Cambodian*. New Haven: Yale University Press.

Jacob, J. 1968. *Introduction to Cambodian*. London: Oxford University Press.

1976. 'Affixation in Middle Khmer, with Old Khmer and modern Khmer comparisons'. In Philip N. Jenner, Laurence C. Thompson, and Stanley Starosta (eds.), *Austroasiatic studies*, Part I. (Oceanic Linguistics Special Publications, No. 13.) Honolulu: University of Hawaii Press, pp. 591–623.

Jakobson, R. 1959. 'Boas' view of grammatical meaning'. In Roman Jakobson, *Selected writings*, volume 2. The Hague: Mouton, pp. 489–496.

Jenner, P. 1969. Affixation in modern Khmer. Unpublished PhD. University of Hawai'i.

1974. 'Observations on the Surin dialect of Khmer'. In N. D. Liem (ed.), *Southeast Asian linguistic studies*, volume I. Canberra: Australian National University, pp. 61–73.

Kuteva, Tania. 2010. 'Are there languages without grammar?' In Young-Se Kang, et al. (eds.), *Universal Grammar and individual languages* (SICOL-2010), E- publication for 2010 Seoul International Conference on Linguistics, 23–25 June, 2010, Korea University, Seoul: Hankookmunhwasa.

Lehmann, C. 1982. 'Universal and typological aspects of agreement'. In H. Seiler and F. J. Stachowiak (eds.), *Apprehension*, volume II. Tübingen: G. Narr, pp. 201–267.

1995. *Thoughts on grammaticalization*. Köln: Akup.

Levinson, S. 2000. *Implicit meanings*. Cambridge, MA: MIT Press.

Lewitz, S. 1976. 'The infix -b- in Khmer'. In Philip N. Jenner, Laurence C. Thompson, and Stanley Starosta (eds.), *Austroasiatic studies*, Part II. (Oceanic Linguistics Special Publications, No. 13.) Honolulu: University of Hawaii Press, pp. 741–760.

Malinowski, B. 1923. 'The problem of meaning in primitive languages'. In C. K. Ogden and I. A. Richards (eds.), *The meaning of meaning*. New York: Routledge and Kegan Paul, pp. 451–510.

Marchand, H. 1960. *The categories and types of present-day English word-formation*. Wiesbaden: Otto Harrassowitz.

Martini, F. 1942–5. Aperçu phonologique du cambodgien. *Bulletin de la Société de Linguistique de Paris* 42: 112–131.

Maspero, G. 1915. *Grammaire de la langue Khmere*. Paris: Imprimerie Nationale.

Miller, S. 1973. Ends, means, and galumphing. *American anthropologist* 75(1): 87–98.

Morgenstern, C. 1964. 'Das ästhetische Wiesel'. In *Christian Morgenstern, Christian Morgenstern's Galgenlieder*. Translated by Max Knight. Berkeley: University of California Press, pp. 18–19.

Ourn, N. and J. Haiman. 2000. Symmetrical compounds in Khmer. *Studies in language* 24(3): 483–517.

Pou, S. 2004. 'La dérivation en cambodgien modern'. In S. Pou (ed.), *Selected papers on Khmerology*. Phnom Penh: Reyum Publishing, pp. 22–41.

Prakorb, Phon-Ngam. 1992. The problem of aspirates in Central Khmer and Northern Khmer. *Mon-Khmer studies* 22: 251–256.

Rongier, J. 2005. *Parlons Kony*. Paris: L'Harmattan.

Ross, J. 1967. *Constraints on variables in syntax*. Cambridge, MA: MIT Press.

Sisovat, Porisat. 1972. *Bo'ri'va: sap knong phiasa: kmae* {Servant words in Khmer}. Phnom Penh: Privately printed.

Stanford, J. 2007. Sui adjective reduplication as poetic morphophonology. *Journal of East Asian linguistics* 16(2): 87–111.

Stolz, T. 2008. 'Total reduplication vs. echo-word formation in language contact situations'. In P. Siemund and N. Kintana (eds.), *Language contact and contact languages*. Amsterdam: John Benjamins, pp. 107–132.

Tinbergen, N. 1952. 'Derived' activities; their causation, biological significance, origin, and emancipation during evolution. *Quarterly review of biology* 27: 1–32.

Wilson, E. 1975. *Sociobiology*. Cambridge, MA: Harvard University Press.

5   Why is sound symbolism so common in Vietnamese?

Marc Brunelle and Lê Thị Xuyến

1   Introduction

Sound symbolism is found in all languages, but is usually treated as a marginal aspect of grammar. However, as illustrated in many contributions to this volume, it is particularly widespread in Southeast Asian languages. In this chapter, we will discuss the prevalence of sound symbolism in Vietnamese and establish a typology of its distribution (in Section 2) and propose mechanisms to account for the development, maintenance, and widespread use of sound symbolic expressions in that language (in Section 3).

1.1   Types of sound symbolism

Before we discuss the Vietnamese data, a brief typology of sound symbolism in the world's language is necessary. The proposed types of sound symbolism are not mutually exclusive, as some processes are difficult to fit into a single category.

The first type, *ideophones*, makes direct use of sound iconicity. It consists of *onomatopoeia*, but also of non-onomatopoeic words (known as *expressives* in the Southeast Asian literature) that are either predicates or modify predicates and have a sound symbolic component. The first formal definition of ideophones by Doke (1935), insists on these two criteria:

A vivid representation of an idea or sound. A word, often onomatopoeic, which describes a predicate, qualificative or adverb in respect to manner, colour, sound, smell, action, state or intensity. (Doke 1935: 118, cited in Voeltz and Kilian-Hatz 2001).

The Kedah Malay example in (1) illustrates the use of a non-onomatopoeic ideophone that describes a predicate with respect to manner.

(1)   bisui aku   sakit ɲut ɲut. (Collins 1979: 391)
       boil 1SG sick 'of steady sucking pain'
       'My boil is throbbing with pain.'

In many languages, ideophones are so iconic that they can have phonological properties that are not found in the rest of the lexicon (Klamer 2001; Newman

2001). This is not the case in Vietnamese, in which ideophones always follow regular phonotactics. Vietnamese ideophones are discussed in Section 2.2.

The second type of sound symbolic expressions consists in phonaes-themes (Firth 1930), i.e. phonemes or sequences of phonemes that denote a non-grammatical meaning that is not necessarily iconic and is often language-specific. For example, the words *snore, sniff, sneeze, snot, snout* all contain a phonaestheme *sn-* that is associated with the nose by English speakers, but that is not necessarily iconic to speakers of other languages. Interestingly, the boundary between phonaestheme and morpheme is not always clear (Nguyễn 1987–1988b; Waugh 1994). A morpheme with a totally arbitrary phonological structure can develop an iconic connotation. One could argue, for instance, that the suffix *-ette* has developed an association with smallness in the minds of English speakers (variation across speakers would not be surprising). Vietnamese phonaesthemes are discussed in Section 2.3.

The last type of sound symbolic pattern is less clearly defined. It includes regular morphological strategies in which phonological permutations *that are not entirely based on affixation* are systematically accompanied by a predict-able change in meaning (like reduplication, root templates, morphological metathesis, and morphological tone changes). Most of these processes do not involve sound symbolism per se, but they favour the creation of iconic sequences as they create sound alternations that are not strictly based on concatenation. In the case of Vietnamese, the best example of such a regular morphological sound symbolic process is reduplication, which is described in Section 2.1.

Finally, it has to be emphasized that these three types of sound symbolism are not mutually exclusive. Ideophones can contain phonesthemes, phonaes-themes can favour the selection or retention of certain types of ideophones, and phonological processes can create or be applied to ideophones or phonaesthemes.

1.2   Where does sound symbolism come from?

The three types of sound symbolism described in Section 1.1 are found to some degree in all languages, but one cannot help but notice their high frequency in Vietnamese and most Mainland Southeast Asian languages. Why is it so? There seems to be a tacit assumption in the literature that language attitudes and socio-cultural factors are mainly responsible for the frequency of sound symbolic expressions. While some cultures value sound symbolism and view it as a form of eloquence (Noss 2001; Nuckolls 1999), a weakening of sound symbol-ism is sometimes associated with modernization, urbanization, or westerniza-tion (Childs 2001; Malkiel 1994). However, it seems likely that structural factors that constrain or favour the development of iconicity are also involved. The diachronic development of iconicity in Vietnamese will be discussed in detail in Section 3, but a few general mechanisms that have been proposed to account for the development of sound symbolism in various languages must first be discussed.

The first mechanism is the imitation of non-linguistic sounds. Direct imitation of natural sounds (by whistling, for example) has little linguistic relevance. More interesting is the creation of onomatopoeia by applying constraints imposed by the speech tract and by the phonology of the imitator to non-linguistic sounds (Childs 1989). Iconic imitation of movements, shapes, or physical events is also possible, leading to the development of non-onomatopoeic ideophones. While ideophones often obey specific morphosyntactic constraints, they can also become full members of regular word classes (Bolinger 1940; Hutchison 1981; McGregor 2001). On the flipside, ideophones can also develop from non-iconic words through regular grammatical processes: Childs (1989) shows that ideophones can be created by reduplicating non-iconic verbs.

Natural associations between sound and meaning can also play a role in sound iconicity. Associations between low pitch and front vowels, on the one hand, and small size, on the other hand, are well established (Ultan 1978), although not necessarily universal (Diffloth 1994). A similar association between stops and spiky shapes and continuants and soft shapes is also well studied (Köhler 1929; Ramachandran and Hubbard 2001; Westbury 2004). Three types of explanations have been proposed for these associations. First, the ability to recognize the acoustic correlates of body size could have been genetically selected in vocalizing mammals (Morton 1994; Ohala 1983, 1994). This 'frequency code', linking high F_0 and F_2 with smallness, would explain why high pitch and front vowels are associated. The second type of explanation relates the size of the signified to the size of a supraglottal cavity (Diffloth 1976, 1994; Gregerson 1984). While most proponents of such an approach postulate universal associations between cavities and concepts, Diffloth (1994) raises the interesting possibility that these associations are learned and that different languages could associate different cavities or articulations with the same concepts. Lastly, it has been proposed that the synaesthetic relation between shape and continuancy be attributed to neurological interference between the areas of the brain responsible for visual and auditory processing (Ramachandran and Hubbard 2001; Westbury 2004).

It is clear, however, that acoustic or biological associations between sound and meaning cannot account for the existence of phonaesthemes, which extend far beyond universals. How does a network of words sharing both sound and meaning form in the lexicon? The first source is shared etymology (Vũ 1998). Two words derived from a common root are likely to share sound and meaning.

Besides words that are morphologically related synchronically, the common origin of two words sharing a phonaestheme can have been obscured by regular sound change. Another possible way of creating or reinforcing a phonaestheme is the semantic drift that can force phonologically similar words to take on similar meanings (Bolinger 1940, 1950). Bolinger (1940: 66–67) suggests that *glamour* has gradually taken on a meaning of 'visual appeal' by association with *glitter, glow, glory* and the like. Further, just as a phonaesthetic network can attract new members by forcing semantic drift, it can force them to undergo sound change (Hamano 1994; Joseph 1994; Malkiel 1994) or block regular sound change in its members (Kaufman 1994). These magnetic effects are even attested in loanwords (Joseph 1994; Rhodes 1994).

In the end, it seems that phonaesthetic networks emerge through the converging effect of several unrelated factors. We illustrate this with an example from Canadian French, in which a complex phonaestheme consisting of a sequence of labial and dental syllable onsets sharing the same voicing and manner of articulation seems to have emerged from different directions. The most typical example of thier phonaestheme is *minou*, a childish way of designating a kitten, attested as the root *min-* in Gallo-Romance (Picoche 1991). A related form *pitou* 'puppy', which is not attested in European French, is closely associated to it, and perhaps developed by analogy with *matou-mitou* (the latter only attested in France) 'unneutered cat' (ATILF 2004). These two words, which not only meet the basic labial-dental condition, but also share the vowel sequence [i-u], are at the core of a phonaesthetic network associated with childishness, lack of seriousness, or inadequacy. Close to the core, we find words that perfectly obey its formal requirements, like *vizou* 'bad aim' (from *viser*, 'to aim') and *bidou* 'money – childish' (unknown origin), but also words in which the phonological requirement on manner of articulation does not fully apply, like *bisou* [bizu] 'kiss – childish' and *pissou* 'coward – childish' (from English *pea soup*, a derogative term for French Canadians). Finally, the phonaestheme seems to have attracted words containing the labial-dental sequence, but non-templatic vowels, like *bazou* 'old car in bad condition', *bedon* 'belly – childish' and *piton* 'button – derogative or humorous'. What is important in this example is the apparently coincidental nature of phonaestheme formation, but also the fact that it can confer new semantic nuances to words that are originally unrelated to its members.

1.3   Previous studies of sound symbolism in Vietnamese

Sound symbolism has been described in a large number of Southeast Asian languages (Collins 1979; Diffloth 1976, 1994; Filbeck 1996; Gerner 2004, 2005; Gregerson 1984; Matisoff 1994; Wayland 1996, not mentioning a myriad of studies on reduplication). Further, parallels between Southeast Asian and African sound symbolic processes have been drawn by Watson (2001). Sound symbolism in Vietnamese has been studied extensively in the past. Along with discussions in traditional Vietnamese grammar (written in Classical Chinese or in *nôm*, the Vietnamese adaptation of Chinese characters), some sound symbolic expressions are listed in Alexandre de Rhodes' Vietnamese–Portuguese–Latin dictionary (1651). However, the first modern account in a Western language is found in Trương Vĩnh Ký's *Grammaire de la langue annamite* (Trương 1883). In a section entitled 'Locutions exprimant le super-latif, placés après l'adjectif', he shows how the morpheme *ngắt* [ŋat] can be added to some adjectives to form superlatives: *đắng ngắt* [ɗaŋ ŋat] 'very bitter', *vắng ngắt* [vaŋ ŋat] 'empty, deserted', *lạnh ngắt* [lajŋ ŋat] 'cold to the point of feeling throbbing pain'.

There have since been many accounts of sound symbolism in Vietnamese, written both in Vietnamese (Hồ 1976; Hoàng 1984; Lê 1985; Nguyễn 2001; Phi 1998; Vũ 1998) and in Western languages (Durand 1961; Emeneau 1951; Ngô 1984; Nguyễn 1990; Nguyễn and Ingram 2006; Nguyễn 1987–1988a, b; Thompson 1965; Vũ 2007). They will be discussed as needed in the relevant subsections of Section 2.

An important goal of the chapter consists in making the data discussed in previous sources available to a wider readership, by giving an overview of a wide range of Vietnamese sound symbolic processes and iconic word categories in a single English-language source. Major references on each type of sound symbolism will be given at the beginning of each subsection of Section 2. Our second goal is to propose explanations for the high prevalence of sound symbol-ism in Vietnamese, which we do in Section 3.

2   The typology of sound symbolism in Vietnamese

There are three major types of sound symbolic phenomena in Vietnamese: reduplication (2.1), ideophones (2.2), and phonaesthemes (2.3). These phenom-ena are not delimiting discrete classes. For instance, ideophones are usually similar to reduplicated forms and phonaesthemes can be found in reduplicative expressions.

Note that the IPA transcriptions given after each example follow the standard northern dialect. For lack of adequate symbols, tones are not rendered in these transcriptions. The six tones of Vietnamese vary across dialects, but the tones of the northern standard can roughly be described as follows (the vowel 'a' is just a dummy support for the tone diacritics): *á*: rising, *à*: low-falling, *ả*: low-falling slightly laryngealized, *ã*: high-rising with mid-glottalization, *ạ*: low with strong final glottalization, *a* (unmarked): high-level.

2.1   Reduplication

The rich system of reduplicative patterns of Vietnamese has long been a topic of investigation (Emeneau 1951; Ngô 1984; Nguyễn 1990; Phạm 2001, 2003; Thompson 1965). Although reduplicated forms are not necessarily iconic, reduplication plays an important role in the grammatical aesthetics of the language: according to Vũ (1991), 4,000 stative and non-stative verbs can undergo some form of reduplication. In this chapter, we limit ourselves to giving a few examples of common reduplicative patterns and show how they affect various syllable constituents.

The most basic form of reduplication is the full reduplication of adjectives, with an attenuative meaning. For instance, *đỏ* [dɔ] 'red' can be reduplicated as *đỏ đỏ* 'reddish'. However, a more common form of attenuative reduplication consists in copying all the segments of the base in a preposed reduplicant and to modify its tone. In this form of reduplication, the high register tones *a*, *á*, *ả* have to be replaced with the high-level tone *a*, while the low register tones *à*, *ạ*, *ã* have to be replaced with low tone *à*. Thus, high register *tím* [tim] 'purple' becomes *tim tím* 'purplish', whereas low register *nhẹ* [ɲɛ] 'light' becomes *nhè nhẹ* 'lightish'.

Other types of common if less productive, reduplicative patterns copy the onset and concatenate it to a fixed rhyme and a predictable tone. Intensive reduplication, for instance, copies the onset of an adjective in a postposed reduplicant and adjoins a rhyme [ɛ] to it, with the tone *ẻ* in the high register or *ẽ* in the low register. *Vui* [vuj] 'happy' thus becomes *vui vẻ* [vuj vɛ] 'very happy', while *mạnh* [maʲɲ] 'strong' becomes *mạnh mẽ* [maʲɲ mɛ] 'very strong'. In a few common reduplication types, rhyme changes can even be more radical. In attenuative reduplication, adjectives with checked syllables undergo change in both tones and codas. *Mát* [maːt] 'fresh' turns into *man mát* [maːn maːt] 'rather fresh' and *sạch* [saʲk] 'clean' becomes *sành sạch* [saʲɲ saʲk] 'rather clean'. The reduplication patterns just described do not create iconicity per se, but they introduce a form of sound alternation that is very characteristic in Vietnamese and, as we will see in Section 2.2, is maximally exploited by ideophones.

Interestingly, the reduplication patterns that copy rhymes and modify onsets tend to be less common and more lexicalized. An extreme example is *khéo* [xɛw] 'clever, skilful', which has a correspondent *khéo léo* [xɛw lɛw] 'very skilful': it looks reduplicated, but is the only attested word with a *kh-* [x] onset that has a *l-* reduplicant. In the end, this non-productive and non-systematic type of rhyme reduplication seems to obey some type of sound symbolism: neither its semantics nor its phonology are those of reduplicants, but it is aesthetically pleasing. The few onset-alternating reduplication templates that are found in more than one or two words are restricted to ideophones, like *tỉ mỉ* [ti mi] 'minute, detailed', *tủn mủn* [tun mun] 'obsessed with details', *tò mò* [tɔ mɔ] 'curious about other people's lives'. As neither of their two parts can be free-standing bases ('clear roots' in Phi 1998's terminology), these forms should be analysed as phonaesthetic (§2.3).

2.2   Ideophones and non-ideophonic onomatopeia

Although they are very common, Vietnamese ideophones have seldom been recognized as a class or systematically described (Nguyễn 1990: 46). They are typically described along with reduplicants (Emeneau 1951) and their semantic and syntactic functions are generally taken for granted.

The phonotactic structure of ideophones is identical to that of the rest of the lexicon. However, ideophones always look like reduplicants, without having any of their derivational semantics (they can be treated as 'false reduplicants' as in Phi 1998). From a syntactic point of view, ideophones behave like stative verbs (i.e. adjectives), in that they can modify nouns, or non-stative verbs or entire clauses, in which case they take an adverbial meaning. In (2), the ideophone *ù ù cạc cạc* [u u kaːk kaːk], which is derived from two onomatopoeia that respectively describe a low background noise and cackling, modifies the NP 'Mother Chấm'. In (3), by contrast, it modifies the VP 'to look for work'.

(2)   Mẹ Chấm . . . sợ chồng nhưng thương con, lại ù ù cạc cạc
       chẳng hiểu thời thế bây giờ các việc ấy ra làm sao, mỗi lúc bàn đến,
       bà lại rơm rớm nước mắt (Đào Vũ, cited in Hoàng 2007, p. 1673).

       'Mother Chấm, afraid of her husband but loving her children, was at loss, not
       understanding how these things work these days. Every time she mentioned
       them, her eyes got wet.'

(3)   Đi tìm   việc. . . ù ù cạc cạc (Việtbáo.vn, 10 February 2004)
       Go search work   confused
       'Job-searching . . . confusedly'

Most onomatopoeia belong to the class of ideophones, like *oàm oạp* [waːm waːp] 'of waves breaking on the shore', *hi hi* [hi hi] 'of high-pitched laughter', *phì phò* [fi fɔ] 'of panting'. However, some onomatopoeia that are not stative verbs and do not look like reduplicated forms have integrated non-ideophonic lexical categories. Among these, verbal onomatopoeia are the most common, like *khạc* [xaːk] 'to spit', *sịt* [sit] 'to spray, to sniff', *ợ* [ə] 'to belch'. Nouns, on the other hand, seem to be limited to names of animals, like *quạ* [kwaː] 'crow', *mèo* [mɛw] 'cat', *bò* [bɔ] 'cow'.

Besides onomatopoeia, Vietnamese ideophones also include a large number of expressions that either have a predicative function or modify a predicate in state, manner, intensity, etc. The examples given in (4) clearly illustrate that sound symbolism is far from being limited to the imitation of natural sounds and that iconicity is mostly language-specific.

(4)   Examples of non-onomatopoeic ideophones (non-exhaustive categories)

Colour/Light	*rực rỡ*	[zɨk zə]	'bright and intense'
	nhờ nhờ	[ɲə ɲə]	'faded'
Shape/State	*bầy nhầy*	[bəj ɲəj]	'slimy'
	thăm thẳm	[tʰam tʰam]	'deep'
Smell	*thum thủm*	[tʰum tʰum]	'pungent'
	hoăng hoắc	[hwaŋ hwak]	'of intense smell'
	lảo đảo	[la:w ɗa:w]	'stumbling because of intoxication'

Degrees of iconic gradation can be found in Vietnamese ideophones, although not as frequently and systematically as in other languages (Diffloth 1976; Gregerson 1984; Manduka-Durunze 2001). The simplest example, given in (5), consists of a set of onomatopoeic ideophones representing laughter, in which vowel quality is strongly associated to loudness while tone height roughly correlates with the pitch of the laughter (note that their tones and exact semantic nuances vary to some extent depending on speakers and dialects). These two types of iconicity could be attributed to the frequency code (Ohala 1983, 1994).

(5)   hi hi   'of neutral, generic laughter'

Soft	hí hí	'of high-pitched laughter'
	hi hí	'of medium-pitched laughter'
	hì hì	'of low-pitched forced laughter'
Medium	he hé (hé hé)	'high-pitched, not very classy laughter'
	hi hả	'high-pitched satisfied laughter'
	hề hề	'medium-pitched friendly laughter'
	hẹ hẹ (hè hẹ)	'very low-pitched discreet laughter'
Loud	hô hố	'high-pitched vulgar laughter'
	ha hả	'high-pitched natural laughter'

In the expressions in (6), the iconicity is also onomatopoeic: onset consonants symbolize the amount of noise made while chewing. This type of iconicity does not need to be attributed to universal factors as in (5): here, the sound imitation is transparent.

(6)

nhóp nhép	[ɲɔp ɲɛp]	'of chewing discreetly'
tóp tép	[tɔp tɛp]	'of chewing loudly'
chóp chép	[cɔp cɛp]	'of chewing very loudly'

However, there are also examples of apparently arbitrary iconicity, as in (7), where vowels and tones connote different degrees of loudness.

(7)

càu nhàu	[kaw ɲaw]	'to complain (mildly irritating)'
cằn nhằn	[kan ɲan]	'to complain (more irritating)'
cáu nháu	[kaw ɲaw]	'to complain (very irritating)'

To sum up, Vietnamese has a class of ideophones that are syntactically and phonologically well defined. Most onomatopoeia belong to it, although a small number of verbs and nouns also have onomatopoeic properties. The sound symbolic properties of ideophones mostly reside in the fact that they are false reduplicants, but iconicity is also occasionally attested, though not necessarily following universal tendencies (Diffloth 1994).

2.3   Phonaesthemes

Vietnamese phonaesthemes are well described in the literature (Cù 2001; Hồ 1976; Nguyễn 1987–1988a; Phi 1998; Vũ 1998). Aside from observations about the phonaesthemes found in demonstratives (Nguyễn 1990, 1992; Thompson 1965), there is also some discussion about whether phonaesthemes should be treated as morphemes or not (Nguyễn 1987–1988b and references therein).

As in many other Mainland Southeast Asian languages, the Vietnamese lexicon seems especially rich in phonaesthemes. A few basic examples are given in (8)–(11).

(8)   Rhyme -um[um]: grouped, put together

cụm	[kum]	'group'	*nhúm*	[ɲum]	'to grab with all the fingers'
chụm	[cum]	'to group'	*dúm*	[zum]	'to grab with all the fingers'
túm	[tum]	'to grab'	*xúm*	[sum]	'to gather up'
tụm	[tum]	'to gather up'	*chùm*	[cum]	'bunch'

Also with a loosely related meaning of 'put the lips together, holding something in the mouth by tightening the lips'.

hụm	[hum]	'gulp'	*chúm*	[cum]	'to tighten the lips'
ngụm	[ŋum]	'sip, mouthful'			

(9)   Rhyme -ep [ɛp]: to compress, to squeeze, to flatten

ép	[ɛp]	'to press, to crush'	*bẹp*	[ɓɛp]	'flattened'
dẹp	[zɛp]	'flat'	*lép*	[lɛp]	'flat'
kẹp	[kɛp]	'to pinch'	*khép*	[xɛp]	'to close gently'
nẹp	[nɛp]	'splint'	*nép*	[nɛp]	'to crouch'
ẹp	[ɛp]	'to deflate, to flatten'	*xẹp*	[sɛp]	'to flatten, to deflate'
hẹp	[hɛp]	'narrowly delimited, confined'			

(10)   Rhyme -eo [ɛw]: crooked, twisted, diagonal

queo	[kwɛw]	'crooked'	*vẹo*	[vɛw]	'crooked (body part)'
quẹo	[kwɛw]	'to turn'	*trẹo*	[cɛw]	'twisted (limb)'
chéo	[cɛw]	'diagonal'	*xéo*	[sɛw]	'diagonal'
khoèo	[xwɛw]	'crooked (limb)'	*ngoẹo*	[ŋwɛw]	'to bend (body part)'

đèo   [ɗɛw]   'mountain pass'   *eo*   [ɛw]   'waist, strait'
xẹo xẹo [sɛw sɛw] 'misaligned'

(11)   Rhyme -*ăt* [at]: to cut, to chop

cắt   [kat]   'to cut'   *gặt*   [gat]   'harvest with a sickle'
xắt   [sat]   'to cut'   *ngắt*   [ŋat]   'to pick'
tắt   [tat]   'to turn off'   *chặt*   [cat]   'to chop'
vặt   [vat]   'to pull out, tear off' *nhặt*   [ɲat]   'to pull out from stem'
                                                       (among other meanings)

Aside from these rhymes, phonaesthemes can also consist of two rhymes with variable onsets (12)–(13), or two onsets with variable rhymes (14)–(15).

(12)   Rhymes -*ất* -*ương* [-ət -ɨ°ŋ]: precarious, unstable

vất vưởng   [vət vɨ°ŋ]   'miserable and passive'
chất chưởng [cət cɨ°ŋ]   'unstable and elevated (of an object)'
khật khưỡng [xət xɨ°ŋ]   'intoxicated and stumbling'
ngật ngưỡng [ŋət ŋɨ°ŋ]   'very intoxicated and stumbling'

(13)   Rhymes -*ồn* -*ộn* [-on -on]: disorderly, not under control

ồn   [on]   'noisy'
bồn chồn   [bon con]   'anxious'
chộn rộn   [con ron]   'anguished'
lộn xộn   [lon xon]   'untidy'
cồn cộn   [kon kon]   'preoccupied'
ngồn ngộn   [ŋon ŋon]   'overflowing'

(14)   Rhymes *l*- *nh*- [l- ɲ-]: to talk (with negative connotations)

lải nhải   [laːj ɲaːj]   'to talk continuously'
lài nhài   [laːj ɲaːj]   'to ramble'
lẩm nhẩm   [ləm ɲəm]   'to mumble'
làu nhàu   [law ɲaw]   'to grumble'
lầu nhầu   [ləw ɲəw]   'to grumble'
lèo nhèo   [lɛw ɲɛw]   'to bother'
léo nhéo   [lɛw ɲɛw]   'to speak unclearly (because of distance)'
lè nhè   [lɛ ɲɛ]   'inarticulate because of intoxication'
lí nhí   [li ɲi]   'to mutter'
lảm nhảm   [laːm ɲaːm]   'to be incoherent'

(15)   Rhymes *b*- *nh*- [ɓ- ɲ-]: shapeless (with many more variants of words related to meat)

bạc nhạc   [ɓaːk ɲaːk]   'half lean, half fat (of meat)'
bạng nhạng [ɓaːŋ ɲaːŋ]   'half lean, half fat (of meat)'
bèo nhèo   [ɓɛw ɲɛw]   'no longer fresh (of meat)'

bầy nhầy	[ɓəj ɲəj]	'slimy' (also bậy nhậy)
bùng nhùng	[ɓuŋm ɲuŋm]	'loose, not fitted (of clothes)'
bắng nhắng	[ɓaŋ ɲaŋ]	'not serious'
bét nhè	[ɓɛt ɲɛ]	'very inebriated
		or exhausted after having too much fun'

Disyllabic phonaesthemes are often found in ideophonic false reduplicants (false in the sense that they do not have a base). However, reduplicants with a base are also found. In (14), *lí nhí* and *làm nhàm* seem derived from *nhí* 'little' and *nhàm* 'non-sensical'. Similarly, in (15), *bùng nhùng*, *bét nhè*, and *bắng nhắng* seem derived from *bùng* 'shapeless', *bét* 'to be last', and *nhắng* 'behaving ridiculously'. This means that phonaesthemes can be composed of regular monosyllabic words and compounds, but also of reduplicated forms and ideophones. As such, they are blind to word categories and seem to emerge whenever there is a convergence of sound and meaning.

3   Reasons explaining the high prevalence of sound symbolism in Vietnamese

As the phenomena and processes described in Section 2 illustrate, sound symbolism is very prevalent in Vietnamese (as in other Mainland Southeast Asia languages). What are the factors explaining this state of affairs?

A first element is that, as in many other speech communities, linguistic creativity, and more specifically sound symbolism, is highly valued (Noss 2001; Nuckolls 1999). In Vietnamese, reduplication and ideophones are considered eloquent and witty. Good talkers are expected to use them frequently (along with word games: see Macken and Nguyễn 2006) and they are considered an essential part of any stylish prose or poetry. In fact, ideophones and reduplicated forms are explicitly taught to pupils in literature and Vietnamese courses throughout primary and secondary education. Contrary to what is suggested for other language communities (Childs 2001; Malkiel 1994), urbanization, modernization, and contact with Western languages do not seem to threaten sound symbolism in Vietnamese. In fact, sound symbolism is perceived as sophisticated and educated. Vietnamese speakers often cite it as a characteristic of their language that makes it more *phong phú* 'rich' than Western languages.

However, besides social factors, a number of linguistic factors favour the use and maintenance of sound symbolic phenomena in Vietnamese. The prevalence of ideophones is relatively easy to explain. First, although derivational markers like *tiền* [tiᵉn] 'pre-' and *hoá* [hwa] '-ation' (Nguyễn 1990) are gaining ground in the learned lexicon, Vietnamese has no affixation per se. Morphology seems to be limited to compounding and reduplication processes that equally affect the various lexical categories. For this reason, onomatopoeia and other ideophones can easily be integrated into the regular lexicon. Moreover, the fact that the phonotactics of Vietnamese ideophones are not different from that of the rest of the lexicon facilitates this integration. Second, the large proportion of the lexicon that is composed of reduplicated forms, be they derived productively or fossilized, makes the repetition of onsets, rhymes, or tones in disyllabic words familiar to speakers, and creates templates of sound alternations that can easily be used for coining new ideophones. Third, it is likely that many disyllabic words that now sound like ideophones were originally regular compounds whose bases were lost altogether. The surviving reduplicated forms, which are not derivable from a base, would have been reinterpreted as ideophonic 'false reduplicants'. For example, Phi (1998) mentions the false reduplicant *lấm lét* [ləm lɛt] 'to look slyly', in which the original base *lét* [lɛt] 'to glance' has now disappeared. As a result, the [l] onsets are now easily reinterpreted as sound symbolic, despite their non-iconic source. This example also raises the possibility, which is difficult to evaluate, that the frequency of ideophonic words in the lexicon, combined with a cultural bias, favours their selection and preservation at the expense of non-ideophonic words.

The high frequency of phonaesthemes in Vietnamese is more difficult to explain. The first type of explanations is not language-specific and is likely to play the same role in Vietnamese as in other languages. First, words can simultaneously share a string of phonemes by coincidence or because they have a common origin. For instance, the words *lạt* [laːt] and *nhạt* [ɲaːt] 'bland, insipid', which are in free variation in Hà Nội Vietnamese, both derive from Middle Vietnamese **mlạt* (Gregerson 1969; Vũ 1998). Second, words sharing strings of phonemes can attract one another semantically. For example, the word *lúm* [lum] 'dimple' originally has nothing to do with the phonaestheme [-um] 'grouped, assembled', exemplified in (8), yet native speakers sense that it contains the idea of a grouping of tissues or muscles. A last general characteristic of phonaesthemes could be that they reinforce the stability of the words that contain them: perhaps they are replaced at a slower rate than non-phonaesthetic words.

There are also a few language-specific factors that might account for the prevalence of phonaesthemes in Vietnamese. A first important factor in the development of phonaesthemes is that Proto-Việt-Mường, the ancestor of Vietnamese, was sesquisyllabic (it allowed a light syllable before the main final syllable) and had complex onsets. A crucial point is that some sesquisyllables and onset consonants were derivational morphemes. Ferlus (1982), for example, reconstructs a nominal infix -r-. Thus, the original forms of the first part of the compound *xum họp* [sum] 'reunite' and the word *chùm* [cum] 'group' would have been **tʃum* and **tʃrum*, respectively. The onset **tʃ* then became [s], and **tʃrum* took its modern form *chùm* through a sequence of cluster simplification and of voicing and tone changes. Another example is a Proto-Việt-Mường instrumental infix -rn- that accounts for correspondences with modern words sharing a rhyme, but whose onsets differ in nasality, like *đắp* [ɗap] 'to cover' and *nắp* [nap] 'lid' (Ferlus 1977). These examples illustrate the fact that the process of monosyllabization that took place between Proto-Việt-Mường and Old Vietnamese, along with the process of cluster simplification that ensued, already contained the seeds of phonaestheme formation, an observation already made by Vũ (1998). A second language explanation for the high frequency of phonaesthemes is that monosyllabic languages have a relatively small number of possible words. As pointed out in Vũ (1998), Vietnamese only has 6,000 possible monosyllables. However, if we exclude the tones that do not seem to prevent phonaesthetic resemblance, we are left with only 1,000 to 2,000 possible monosyllables. With such a small number of possible roots, it is not surprising that many words would share both sound and meaning out of pure chance. If we combine the effects of common etymology, loss of affixation, and chance similarities, it is not surprising that Vietnamese (like other monosyllabic languages of Southeast Asia) has far more phonaesthemes than Western European languages.

4 Conclusion

Vietnamese, like its neighbours, makes widespread use of sound symbolic expressions. While sound symbolism is mostly expressed through the use of language-specific reduplicated forms, ideophones similar to reduplicated forms, and phonaesthemes, there is little evidence of an exceptional reliance on direct iconicity in the language. It seems that in Vietnamese, as in most languages, iconicity is primarily learned: as they acquire the language, speakers learn to attribute sound symbolic values to arbitrary phonological forms.

The strong cultural association between eloquence and sound symbolic expressions explains in large part their prevalence in the language. However, we argue that structural factors, synchronic or diachronic, also play a role. First, the central role of reduplication in Vietnamese favours the development of ideophones. Second, the monosyllabic structure of the language explains the frequency of phonaesthemes, both for synchronic and diachronic reasons.

References

ATILF (Analyse et traitement informatique de la langue française). (2004).'Le Trésor de la Langue Française informatisé'. Retrieved 2010–11–08, from http://atilf.atilf.fr/.
Bolinger, Dwight L. 1940. Word affinities. *American speech* 15(1): 62–75.
1950. Rime, assonance, and morpheme analysis. *Word* 6(2): 117–136.

Childs, G. Tucker. 1989. Where do ideophones come from? *Studies in the linguistic sciences* 19(2): 55–76.

2001. 'Research on ideophones, whither hence? The need for a social theory of ideophones'. In F. K. E. Voeltz and C. Kilian-Hatz (eds.), *Ideophones*. Amsterdam, John Benjamins, pp. 63–74.

Collins, James T. 1979. 'Expressives in Kedah Malay'. In Đ. L. Nguyễn (ed.), *Southeast Asian linguistic studies vol. 4. Pacific linguistics*. Canberra: Australian National University Press, pp. 379–406.

Cù, Đình Tú. 2001. *Phong cách học và đặc điểm tu từ tiếng Việt*. Hà Nội: Nhà Xuất Bản Giáo Dục.

Difloth, Gérard. 1976. Expressives in Semai. *Oceanic linguistics special publications* 13: Austroasiatic Studies Part I: Honolulu: University of Hawaii Press, pp. 249–264.

1994. 'i: big, a: small'. In L. Hinton, J. Nichols, and J. Ohala (eds.), *Sound symbolism*. Cambridge University Press, pp. 107–114.

Doke, Clement Martyn. 1935. *Bantu linguistic terminology*. London: Longmans, Green and Company.

Durand, Maurice. 1961. Les impressifs en vietnamien: étude préliminaire. *Bulletin de la Société des Études Indochinoises* 36(1): 7–50.

Emeneau, Murray. 1951. *Studies in Vietnamese (Annamese) grammar*. Berkeley: University of California Press.

Ferlus, Michel. 1977. L'infixe instrumental rn en khamou et sa trace en vietnamien. *Cahiers de linguistique – Asie orientale* 2(2): 51–55.

1982. Spirantisation des obstruantes médiales et formation du système consonantique du vietnamien. *Cahiers de linguistique – Asie orientale* 11: 83–106.

Filbeck, David. 1996. Couplet and duplication in Mal. *Mon-Khmer studies* 26: 91–106.

Firth, Raymond. 1930. *Speech*. London: Benn's Sixpenny Library.

Gerner, Matthias. 2004. Expressives in Kam (Dong): a study in sign typology (part I). *Cahiers de linguistique – Asie orientale* 33(2): 159–202.

2005. Expressives in Kam (Dong): a study in sign typology (part II). *Cahiers de linguistique – Asie orientale* 34(1): 25–67.

Gregerson, Kenneth. 1969. A study of Middle Vietnamese phonology. *Bulletin de la Société des études indochinoises* 44: 133–193.

1984. Pharynx symbolism and Rengao phonology. *Lingua* 62: 209–238.

Hamano, Shoko. 1994. 'Palatalization in Japanese sound symbolism'. In L. Hinton, J. Nichols, and J. Ohala (eds.), *Sound symbolism*. Cambridge University Press, pp. 148–160.

Hồ, Lê. 1976. *Vấn đề cấu tạo từ của tiếng Việt hiện đại*. Hà Nội: Nhà Xuất Bản Khoa Học Xã Hội.

Hoàng, Cao Cương. 1984. Nhận xét về một số đặc điểm các từ láy đôi tiếng Việt. *Ngôn Ngữ* 4: 29–36.

Hoàng, Phê. 2007. *Từ Điển Tiếng Việt*. Đà Nẵng: Nhà xuất bản Đà Nẵng.

Hutchison, John P. 1981. 'Kanuri word formation and the structure of the lexicon'. In *Nilo-Saharan: Proceedings of the First Nilo-Saharan Linguistics Colloquium*. Dordrecht: Foris, pp. 217–239.

Joseph, Brian D. 1994. 'Modern Greek ts: beyond sound symbolism'. In L. Hinton, J. Nichols, and J. Ohala (eds.), *Sound symbolism*. Cambridge University Press, pp. 222–236.

Kaufman, Terrence. 1994. 'Symbolism and change in the sound system of Huastec'. In L. Hinton, J. Nichols, and J. Ohala (eds.), *Sound symbolism*. Cambridge University Press, pp. 63–75.

Klamer, Marian. 2001. 'Expressives and iconicity in the lexicon'. In E. F. K. Voeltz and C. Kilian-Hatz (eds.), *Ideophones*. Amsterdam: John Benjamins, pp. 165–182.

Köhler, Wilhelm. 1929. *Gestalt psychology*. New York: Liveright.

Lê, Văn Siêu. 1985. *Văn minh Việt Nam*. Paris: Đông Nam Á.

Macken, Marlys A. and Thị Hành Nguyễn. 2006. Nói Lái and the structure of the syllable. *Linguistics of the Tibeto-Burman area* 29(2): 1–61.

Malkiel, Yacov. 1994. 'Regular sound development, phonosymbolic orchestration, disambiguation of homonyms'. In L. Hinton, J. Nichols, and J. Ohala (eds.), *Sound symbolism*. Cambridge University Press, pp. 207–221.

Manduka-Durunze, Omen N. 2001. 'Phonosemantic hierarchies'. In E. F. K. Voeltz and C. Kilian-Hatz (eds.), *Ideophones*. Amsterdam: John Benjamins, pp. 193–204.

Matisoff, James. 1994. 'Tone, intonation, and sound symbolism in Lahu: loading the syllable canon'. In L. Hinton, J. Nichols, and J. Ohala (eds.), *Sound symbolism*. Cambridge University Press, pp. 115–129.

McGregor, William. 2001. 'Ideophones as the source for verbs in Northern Australian languages'. In E. F. K. Voeltz and C. Kilian-Hatz (eds.), *Ideophones*. Amsterdam: John Benjamins, pp. 205–222.

Morton, Eugene S. 1994. 'Sound symbolism and its role in non-human vertebrate communication'. In L. Hinton, J. Nichols, and J. Ohala (eds.), *Sound symbolism*. Cambridge University Press, pp. 348–365.

Newman, Paul. 2001. 'Are ideophones really as weird and extra-systematic as linguists make them out to be?' In E. F. K. Voeltz and C. Kilian-Hatz (eds.), *Ideophones*. Amsterdam: John Benjamins, pp. 251–258.

Ngô, Thanh Nhàn. 1984. The syllabeme and patterns of word formation in Vietnamese. Doctoral dissertation, New York University.

Nguyễn, Đại Bằng. 2001. *Khuôn vần tiếng Việt và sự sáng tạo từ*. Hà Nội: Nhà xuất bản Văn hoá Thông tin.

Nguyễn, Đình-Hoà. 1990. *Vietnamese*. Amsterdam: John Benjamins.

Nguyễn, Phú Phong. 1992. Vietnamese demonstratives revisited. *Mon-Khmer studies* 20: 127–136.

Nguyễn, Thị Anh Thư' and John Ingram. 2006. 'Reduplication and word stress in Vietnamese'. In P. Warren and C. I. Watson (eds.), *Proceedings of the 11th Australian International Conference on Speech Science & Technology*. University of Auckland Press, pp. 187–192.

Nguyễn, Thiện Giáp. 1987–1988a. La Phénomène de quasi-synonymie en vietnamien. *Cahiers d'Études vietnamiennes*: 19–25.

———. 1987–1988b. A propos des morphèmes subsyllabiques en Vietnamien. *Cahiers d'Études vietnamiennes* 9: 27–36.

Noss, Philip A. 2001. 'Ideas, phones and Gbaya verbal art'. In E. F. K. Voeltz and C. Kilian-Hatz (eds.), *Ideophones*. Amsterdam: John Benjamins, pp. 259–270.

Nuckolls, Janis B. 1999. The case for sound symbolism. *Annual review of anthropology* 28: 225–252.

Ohala, John. 1983. Cross-language use of pitch: an ethological view. *Phonetica* 40: 1–18.

1994. 'The frequency code underlies the sound-symbolic use of voice pitch'. In L. Hinton, J. Nichols, and J. Ohala (eds.), *Sound symbolism*. Cambridge University Press, pp. 325–347.

Phạm, Andrea Hoà. 2001. Vietnamese tone: tone is not pitch. Ph.D., Linguistics, University of Toronto.

2003. *Vietnamese tones: a new analysis*. New York: Routledge.

Phi, Tuyết Hinh. 1998. Từ láy không rõ thanh tố gốc và vấn đề biểu trưng ngữ âm trong từ biểu tượng tiếng Việt. *Ngôn Ngữ* (1): 35–73.

Picoche, Jacqueline. 1991. *Dictionnaire étymologique du français*. Paris: Robert.

Ramachandran, V.S. and E. M. Hubbard. 2001. Synaesthesia – a window into perception, thought and language. *Journal of consciousness studies* 8: 3–34.

Rhodes, Richard. 1994. 'Aural images'. In L. Hinton, J. Nichols, and J. Ohala (eds.), *Sound symbolism*. Cambridge University Press, pp. 276–292.

Thompson, Laurence. 1965. *Vietnamese reference grammar*. Seattle: University of Washington Press.

Trương, Vĩnh Ký. 1883. *Grammaire de la Langue Annamite*. Saigon: C. Guillaud et Martinon.

Ultan, Russel. 1978. 'A typological view of metathesis'. In J. Greenberg (ed.),*Universals of human language, 2 phonology*. Stanford University Press, pp. 403–442.

Voeltz, F. K. Erhard and Christa Kilian-Hatz. 2001. 'Introduction'. In F. K. E. Voeltz and C. Kilian-Hatz (eds.), *Ideophones*. Amsterdam: John Benjamins, pp. 1–8.

Vũ, Đức Nghiệu. 1998. *Các mức độ tương đồng và tách biệt của một hiện tượng tượng tự (paronymy) trong tiếng Việt*. Hà Nội: Trung tâm khoa học xã hội và nhân văn quốc gia.

Vũ, Sonny X. 2007. 'A unified analysis of some Vietnamese reduplication forms'. In M. Alves, P. Sidwell, and D. Gil (eds.), *SEALS VIII: Papers from the 8th meeting of the Southeast Asian Linguistics Society (1998)*. Canberra: The Australian National University, pp. 165–191.

Vũ, Thế Thạch. 1991. *Consonant copying and tone harmony in Vietnamese reduplicatives*. Papers from the First Annual Meeting of the Southeast Asian Linguistics Society, University of Arizona, Program for Southeast Asian Studies.

Watson, Richard L. 2001. 'A comparison of some Southeast Asian ideophones with some African ideophones'. In F. K. E. Voeltz and C. Kilian-Hatz (eds.), *Ideophones*. Amsterdam: John Benjamins, pp. 385–406.

Waugh, Linda R. 1994. Degrees of iconicity in the lexicon. *Journal of pragmatics* 22: 55–70.

Wayland, Ratree. 1996. Lao expressives. *Mon-Khmer studies* 26: 217–231.

Westbury, Chris. 2004. Implicit sound symbolism in lexical access: evidence from an interference task. *Brain and language* 93: 10–19.

6   Grammatical aesthetics in Wa

Justin Watkins

1   Introduction

The tendency for Southeast Asian languages to use linguistic structures to encode expressiveness has been noted as an areal characteristic since the 1960s. Such linguistic structures have been referred to using a broad range of terms, among them Haas's (1964) 'elaborate expressions', Henderson's (1965) 'phonaesthetic words' and Diffloth's (1972) 'expressives'. This chapter examines the capacity of the Wa language to use aesthetically motivated constructions in this context.

Simply put, most languages in the Southeast Asian linguistic area make use of expressives in Diffloth's (1972) sense or of ideophones (Voeltz and Kilian-Hatz 2001). In his study of expressives in Mon-Khmer, Diffloth (1979) discusses the degree to which iconicity is pervasive in the morphosyntax of Southeast Asian languages. Of course this dimension of language is by no means confined to Southeast Asia, and there is an ongoing need for cross-linguistic studies, especially cross-regional studies joining communities of linguists who do not often get together, if any universal understanding of the linguistic encoding of expressiveness is to emerge. One valuable contribution is the collection of papers edited by Voeltz and Kilian-Hatz (2001) which demonstrate the common ground between Africanists' 'ideophones' and the 'expressives' of linguists elsewhere: indeed, it seems often to be simply the diversity of terminology as much as anything else which may hinder meaningful cross-linguistic comparison of aesthetically motivated and expressive elements in human language.

Gérard Diffloth was among the first linguists to apply rigorous linguistic scrutiny to expressive constructions and their role within grammar, and indeed one of the most enjoyable aspects of preparing this chapter has been the opportunity to revisit his pioneering publications (1972, 1976, 1979) on expressive language and linguistic aesthetics in Semai, Surin Khmer, and other Southeast Asian languages. In later work, Diffloth (2001: 268) hints that the failure of descriptive linguistics to account fully for the expressive structures prevalent in Southeast Asian languages such as Surin Khmer may have unlimited significance for our understanding of the underpinnings of human language:

Would it be better to simply ignore expressives? It would be convenient, but to do so would be to close our eyes to a fundamental fact: human language presents two over-lapping architectures, namely the prosaic structure and the expressive structure. During the course of the evolution of our capacity for language, which of these two structures arose relying on the other? And why would there be two structures instead of just one? Expressives in Surin, and in other Asian languages, give us reason to question the monogenesis of human language. (Diffloth 2001: 268, translated)

Diffloth's claims are not trivial; they are a cool reminder of the value of devoting our full attention to the richness and diversity of linguistic constructions with an expressive function or systemic aesthetic dimension while we still can. They abound most in formal and ritual registers of languages which are often as endangered as the social systems and spiritual practices which sustain them become, in some cases reaching the point of moribund near-extinction before being even partially documented and understood. Examples studied elsewhere in Southeast Asia are the ritual language of Kachin kinship systems (Sadan and Robinne 2007; Sadan in press) and ritual languages in Eastern Indonesia (Fox 1988).

The uncertain, or unstudied, status of expressive and aesthetic language is a problem faced by any linguist, descriptive or theoretical, who wishes to grapple with expressives: they are fleeting, spontaneous, complex, and hard to pin down, and therefore often unnoticed, underemphasized, or ignored completely. The fact that grammatical aesthetics tend not to be approached with due academic rigour and indeed are often omitted from descriptive grammars is unacceptable to Diffloth. Writing on Khmer, he (Diffloth 2001: 263, translated) argues that 'expressives constitute a basic syntactic category in Khmer, on the same tier as nouns and verbs ..., in that expressives are not derived from another category, have their own morphological properties, and have a distinct semantic function'.

Much is generally made of the fact that expressives and ideophones are what distinguishes the poetic from the prosaic in speech, or transforms linguistic drabness into nuanced colour in language. Without deploying the aesthetic dimension, Southeast Asian languages may seem flat and contourless. On the other hand, European languages are most likely to encode the functional equivalent of expressives and ideophones with prosody and intonation – without which they are *literally* flat and contourless.

Considering the functions of prosody and intonation, then, is one way of trying to gain some perspective on the functions of grammatical aesthetics in Southeast Asian languages like Wa. Gussenhoven (2004: 50) considers whether intonation is part of the grammar or whether it is a separate expressive system overlaid on the linguistic structure, and finds that intonation serves both purposes. As part of linguistic structure, intonation has grammatical functions such as the indication of stress, focus, and the formation of questions, while as part of an expressive system, intonation has quasi-iconic features: pitch rises when we want to sound excited, or stays down when we sound depressed.

This dual purpose led Bolinger (1978) to refer to intonation as a 'half-tamed savage'; Gussenhoven draws a clear line between the 'savage' expressive half of intonation and the 'tamed' grammatical half. The 'tame' half of intonation functions neatly and systematically within a grammar and is squarely part of language. If we consider the aesthetic dimension of Southeast Asian grammars in the same way, it is not surprising to find that it too has a dual function, comprising clearly defined 'tame' grammatical functions such as semantic intensification or fine semantic distinctions on the one hand, and on the other a 'savage' expressive function which serves to make language more colourful, rich, interesting, and, just perhaps, more beautiful.

The case of expressive systems in Southeast Asian languages challenges the implication that certain functions within grammar are basic or fundamental, and that expressive systems are secondary or at best only partly linguistic. The extent to which expressive and aesthetically motivated language is ordinarily prevalent in Wa is difficult to quantify. The data presented in this chapter are certainly evident in the published linguistic descriptions of Wa and in corpus of the written Wa sources assembled to compile a Wa dictionary (Watkins in press). One shortcoming of this study is that it is unable to refer to spontaneous Wa speech, though there is every indication that expressive forms occur as frequently as in other Southeast Asian languages. In Khmer, for example, 'an alert listener can catch them on the wing, several times a day, in spontaneous conversation in Khmer' Diffloth (2001: 263).

2   Wa and Wa speakers

Wa is spoken in a corridor of land between the Salween and Mekong rivers; an area which straddles the south-western Chinese province of Yúnnán, the Shan States of north-eastern Burma, and Northern Thailand.

Speaker numbers cannot be known exactly in such a geographically remote, ethnically diverse, and politically disparate area, but the figure of just under 1.2 million speakers arrived at in the SIL Ethnologue (Lewis 2009) seems realistic. This total is for speakers of all varieties of Wa, including Paraok, the variety described here, as well as other varieties. About two-thirds of Wa speakers are in Burma and one-third in China.

The Wa languages make up the Waic section of the Palaungic or Palaung-Wa branch of Northern Mon-Khmer (Ferlus 1974; Diffloth 1980). The sub-categorization of dialects within Waic languages is confusing as some forty

Waic languages are known to exist. Diffloth's (1980) reconstruction of Proto-Waic gives the fullest account of the subcategorization of Waic, and the language situation is further described in Watkins (2002) and Lewis (2009).

Wa speakers live interspersed with speakers of many other languages. The status of Wa as a viable language is threatened by the encroachment of Chinese, and to a lesser extent also Burmese. The Wa lexicon, in particular, is subject to a high rate of attrition from borrowed Chinese vocabulary. In the experience of the author, speakers of other languages rarely learn Wa, sometimes even in mixed marriages, while Wa speakers are typically multi-lingual. In a straw-poll sample of Wa speakers recorded for a field study (Watkins 2002) in the late 1990s, all were able to speak Chinese or Burmese to some degree if they had lived in China or Burma, or in several cases both. Those who had settled in Thailand also spoke at least some Thai. About half of the group spoke Lahu and about half of those who lived or had lived in the Shan State spoke Shan. A quarter spoke five or more languages.

3   Vowel alternations in Wa

The account of grammatical aesthetics presented here starts with vowel alter-nations, which are one of the basic building blocks in the formation of ideo-phones. Writing about expressives in Bahnar, Diffloth (1994) challenges the idea that some kind of universal sound symbolism is in force linking vowel height to semantic correlates indicating dimension or proximity, however attractive and convenient the explanatory power of such a linguistic universal might be. Persuasive though much of the evidence might seem (e.g. Sereno 1994), such correlations are simply commonly observed, Diffloth reasons, rather than universal.

Nonetheless, deixis in Wa makes use of vowel alternations. A conventional two-way proximal–distal contrast is indicated by alternating /i/ and /a/ to indicate proximity and distance, respectively, as shown in Table 6.1.

Vowel alternations are also found in the Wa pronoun system. There are four pairs of dual and plural pronouns where the vowel in the dual pronoun contrasts with a more open vowel in the plural pronoun. For the two pairs of pronouns

Table 6.1 *Proximal–Distal vowel contrasts*

	proximal /i/	distal /a/
'this ~ that'	ʔin	ʔan
'like this ~ like that'	nin	nan
'here ~ there'	din	dan

Table 6.2 *Extentives*

Stative verb			Extentive	
tiɲ	'big'	>	*diɲ*	'this big'
laŋ	'long'	>	*glaŋ*	'this long'
lʰaoŋ	'high'	>	*gʰlaoŋ*	'this high'
rauʔ	'deep'	>	*grauʔ*	'this deep'
rʰuŋ	'long (time)'	>	*gʰruŋ*	'for this long'
hun	'many'	>	*gʰun*	'this many'
haoh	'much'	>	*gʰaoh*	'this much'

Table 6.3 *Augmented extentives*

Stative verb			Extentive			Augmented extentive	
tiɲ	'big'	>	*diɲ*	'this big'	>	*duaiɲ ~ duɲ*	'this big!'
laŋ	'long'	>	*glaŋ*	'this long'	>	*glaŋ ~ glɔiɲ ~ gluɲ*	'this long!'
lʰaoŋ	'high'	>	*gʰlaoŋ*	'this high'	>	*gʰliaoŋ ~ gʰlioŋ*	'this high!'

where the addressee is included (1st person inclusive and 2nd person), the dual–plural vowel alternation is /a/ ~ /e/; for the two pairs of pronouns where the addressee is not referred to (1st person exclusive and 3rd person) the vowels are /ɛ/ ~ /i/. Data are given in Table 6.2.

	dual /a/	plural /e/
1st person inclusive	*ʔaʔ*	*ʔeʔ*
2nd person	*paʔ*	*peʔ*

	dual /ɛ/	plural /i/
1st person exclusive	*yɛʔ*	*yiʔ*
3rd person	*kɛʔ*	*kiʔ*

Here, the sound symbolism in force seems harder to account for: duality–plurality are represented by an alternation between relatively lower (/a/ /ɛ/) and higher (/i/ /e/) vowels.

A third kind of interplay between sound and semantics is found in Wa 'extentives'. This class of words, described as 量代词 *liángdàicí* ('quantitative pronouns') by Zhāo et al. (1998: 218–221), is akin to the extentive verbs of Lahu (Matisoff 1973a: 117–118, 1994: 122). Extentives are derived from stative verbs by prefixation of the kind which is shown in Table 6.2.

Once formed, vowel alternation may be further deployed to indicate that the extent of the quality described is being encountered to an increased, surprising, contrastive, or enhanced degree as shown by the examples in Table 6.3.

The three types of vowel alternation in this section all have clearly definable grammatical correlates; in the case of the augmented extentives there is additionally an expressive dimension.

4   Extending monosyllables

In this section, we see how monosyllabic morphemes in Wa may be extended by the addition of prefixes or presyllables like Henderson's (1952: 15–151) 'extensile' monosyllable. In doing so, they conform to the iambic stress-pattern and 'sesquisyllabic' (Matisoff 1973b) word-shape prevalent in Mon-Khmer and further afield in Southeast Asian languages.

The first kind of extension is an alliterative partial reduplication. In Table 6.4 the initial consonant of monosyllabic stative verbs is used to form a pre-syllable with the vowel [u] in the register of the source syllable, with the semantic function of augmenting or intensifying the meaning of the verb and at the same time rendering the description more expressive, colourful, or engaging. The dual-function extension cannot be separated into discrete morphemes: the semantic function and the expressive function are woven inseparably into the grammatical fabric of the language.

If the root morpheme is a transitive verb, the effect of adding the pre-syllable has a predictable reiterative meaning: '. . .back and forth' or '. . . repeatedly', as in Table 6.5.

In some cases we see a mixed pattern. There are a number of alternative forms of the word 'scatter' as shown in (1).

Table 6.4 *Alliterative partial reduplication*

Root			pre-syllable + root	
lạn	'wet'	>	*lut lạn*	'soaking, drenched'
siah	'thin'	>	*su siah*	'trivial, insignificant'
yịh	'fluffy'	>	*yụ yịh*	'dishevelled'
sɛt>	'tight'	>	*sut sɛt*	'packed, thronging'

Table 6.5 *Reiteratives*

pạc	'scrape, rake'	>	*put pạc*	'rake back and forth'
pạm	'bump, knock'	>	*pụ pạm*	'knock about, knock back and forth'
gɔk	'bent'	>	*gu gɔk*	'winding back and forth'
kliən	'twist'	>	*ku kliən ~ klu kliən*	'twist repeatedly'
dịc	'trample'	>	*dụ dịc*	'trample repeatedly'

(1)   *pu praŋ ~ pru praŋ ~ puŋ praŋ ~ pruŋ praŋ*
        'scatter, disperse'

The forms *pru* and *pruŋ praŋ* seem to be stable in the lexicon, both meaning 'scatter'. The variation in (1) may be a rightward extension of *pru* by the addition of a chiming syllable (see Section 5.1 below) or else *pu praŋ* may be seen as a reduced form of *pruŋ praŋ*, the first syllable reducing and losing stress so the word acquires the sesquisyllabic word-shape. Which form is unmarked and which derived is neither here nor there, but fairly clearly *pu praŋ* and *pru praŋ* conform to the expressive pre-syllable pattern with the meaning 'back and forth' seen in Table 6.5. For Enfield (2005), reduplication with vowel mutation in the repeated syllable (such as *pruŋ praŋ*) is a basic category of elaborative morphology in Southeast Asian languages.

In a similar vein, *gɔk* 'bent' (2) may be doubly extended.

(2)   *gɔk > gu gɔk > gu gɔk gu gek*
        'bent' > 'winding back and forth repeatedly'

The semantic function of doing so is to express intensification and reiteration of the action described, but the way it is done also serves an expressive function, since the speaker can choose how colourfully to express the winding quality of whatever is being described by choosing the degree of elaboration of the root morpheme *gɔk*.

In common with other Mon-Khmer languages and in the Mainland Southeast Asian linguistic area generally, Wa has rich lexical resources to describe the way that objects move or the ways in which they may be manipulated. The process of augmenting or extending monosyllables described above allows verbs of motion and manipulation to be fine-tuned semantically while allowing scope for an expressive dimension to bring to life the verbal depiction of the action being described.

5   Compounding in Wa: general principles

The Wa lexicon makes extensive use of compounding. Morphemes may combine in many ways to form complex polymorphemic lexemes which are more than the sum of their component parts, in the way that in English 'black' and 'bird' combine to form the word 'blackbird' to indicate a specific species of bird, rather than just a bird which is black in colour. Examples in Wa are the words for 'school' and 'bus station' shown in (3)

(3a)   *ɲiɛʔ*   + *ʔah*   + *lɑi*   > *ɲiɛʔ ʔah lɑi*
        'house' + 'read' + 'text' > 'school'

(3b)   *du̟*   + *pɑuŋ* + *lɔ li̤* > *du̟ pɑuŋ lɔ li̤*
        place   + rest   + bus   > 'bus station'

Often in Wa, however, aesthetically motivated elements are added which contribute nothing new semantically and have no identifiable syntactic or semantic function, but which make an expressive contribution, as in (4).

(4)   *krạuŋ kʰrai*
       clothes + clothes > 'clothing, things, goods, possessions'

The additional element is a synonym or near-synonym, and the effect of adding it makes the expression sound and feel richer: in this case there is no systematic semantic intensification or augmentation of the unadorned monosyllabic morpheme. Haiman and Ourn (2009) use the term 'non-referential bulking' to refer to the use of pairs of parallel expressions instead of single expressions in their analysis of Khmer.

5.1   Compounds with an aesthetic component: X + X* chime

The expressive riches of Wa come further to the fore when non-referential doublets such as (4) additionally involve some kind of chiming sound symmetry or partial rhyming. We shall describe these doublets generally as consisting of a base morpheme X which is bulked by being paired with an expressive chiming partner-word X* which shares the initial (and sometimes also the final) consonant but has a contrasting vowel. The X* element is a quasi-bound form, apparently semantically synonymous with X but not normally occurring independently of X except in poetic or ritual contexts. Examples are given in (5).

(5a)   *rʰɔm*   heart   >   *rʰɔm.rʰi*   heart.heart*

(5b)   *prɛʔ*   food   >   *prɛʔ prụm*   food.food*

(5c)   *ɲʰu*   weeds   >   *ɲʰu. ɲʰɔk*   weeds.weeds*

(5d)   *lʰut*   deaf   >   *lʰụtlʰɔ*   deaf.deaf*

(5e)   *ŋɛʔ*   itch   >   *ŋɛʔŋɔɲ*   itch.itch*

(5f)   *mʰɔm*   good   >   *mʰɔm.mʰiam*   good.good*

(5g)   *s.bịt*   miserly   >   *s.bịt s.bịtan*   miserly.miserly*

The unmarked source lexeme X may be followed (6a) or preceded (6b) by the chiming syllable X*.

(6a)   *kloŋ*   >   *kloŋ kloc*
        'interrogate, question'

(6b)   *s.kạoŋ* >   *s.kạoŋ s.kịat*
        'cold'

Table 6.6 *Trisyllabic intensives*

Stative verb			XYY-Enhanced form	
lɯŋ	'black'	→	*lɯŋ lị̈ lị̈*	'jet black'
pạɲ	'white'	→	*pạɲ cạt cạt*	'white and fair'
ʔɔn	'soft'	→	*ʔɔn tʰɔi tʰɔi*	'soft and fluffy'
kian	'hard'	→	*kian gɯc gɯc*	'rock hard'
kịan	'heavy'	→	*kian lụ lụ*	'heavy and unwieldy'
pụ	'thick'	→	*pụ lụk lụk*	'very thick'

6 Trisyllabic XYY patterns

As is common in other Southeast Asian languages, stative verbs, in particular colour terms as in Table 6.6, can be semantically intensified or expressively enhanced with adverbials, themselves reduplicated, similar to the Burmese 'colour expressives' described by Wheatley (this volume).

While these forms have an aesthetic element in their distinctive rhythm, these XYY forms have a semantic intensifying function, so the function is not purely expressive. Note that these adverbials do not rhyme or chime with the base word. They are bound forms which do not occur as independent morphemes.

7 Four-syllable patterns

Next, we come to four-syllable patterns. The four-syllable phrase is a pattern observed and frequently described as an 'elaborate expression' in Mainland Southeast Asian languages (e.g. Haas 1964 for Thai, Matisoff 1973a for Lahu) and as *sìzìgé* 四字格 in Chinese. The degree of internal rhyme, chime, and phonological parallelism within four-syllable phrases may vary. At one end of the scale is (7c), a four-syllable phrase for 'body', expanded from monosyllable (7a) and bisyllabic (7b), in which there is a semantic connection between the four component nouns but no sound symmetry or phonological repetition.

(7a) *kaɯʔ* body 'body'

(7b) *kaɯʔ.hak* body.skin 'body'

(7c) *kaɯʔ.hak.nẹʔ.nʰam* body.skin.flesh.blood 'body'

The X + X* chiming doublets in (6) above can be used as a base form to make up various kinds of four-syllable phrases. We find examples such as (8) where the only connection between the four nouns is semantic.

(8)   *krạuŋ kʰrai*   *dai*   *tɕah*
    clothes clothes*   skirt   shirt
    'clothing, clothes'

Further examples in (9) have internal syntactic symmetry [(verb-object)(verb-object)].

Aesthetically speaking, the examples in (9) illustrate two rhyme patterns, very commonly observed in Wa, namely (9a) ABAC and (9b) ABBC, which will be described more fully later.

(9a)   *krạuŋ*   *tɕuup*   *kratuuŋ*   *sɔm*
    clothes   wear   clothes   use
    'clothing'

(9b)   *krạuŋ*   *tɕuup*   *ʔuup*   *sɔm*
    clothes   wear   rice   eat
    'food and clothing'

7.1   pa X pa X* *extensions*

The Wa relativizer (REL) *pa* is one of very few purely functional morphemes used productively in the derivation of nominalized forms, a process which can make abstract nouns from stative verbs. These have the form *pa X pa Y* (where X and Y are synonyms) as in (10a) and (10b) or *pa X pa X** from an X + X* chiming doublet, as in (10c) and (10d).

(10a)   *pa*   *rạuh*   *pa*   *suu*
     REL   upright   REL   straight
     'righteousness' < 'that which is upright and straight'

(10b)   *pa*   *sac*   *pa*   *sɔŋ*
     REL   pitiful   REL   bitter
     'truth' < 'that which exists'

(10c)   *pa*   *mɔh*   *pa*   *mɛh*
     REL   exist   REL   exist*
     'truth' < 'that which exists'

(10d)   *pa*   *mʰɔm*   *pa*   *mʰiam*
     REL   good   REL   good*
     'goodness' < 'that which is good'

The phrases (10c) and (10d) are examples of the highly productive pattern AXAX*, coined by making the two elements of an X + X* chiming doublet the second and fourth of an expressive four-syllable phrase in which the first and third items are the same. The element A in such formulations is by no means rescricted to functional morphemes like the relativizer *pa*; indeed, for any AX can be expanded, if desired, to AXAX* if an X* chiming match can be found for X. Further examples of such forms are given in (11) below.

(11a) *gạuʔ*   *rʰɔm*   *gạuʔ*   *rʰi*
      happy   heart   happy   heart*
      'happy'

(11b) *loh*   *rʰɔm*   *loh*   *rʰi*
      change   heart   change   heart*
      'start afresh'

(11c) *soŋ*   *rʰɔm*   *soŋ*   *rʰi*
      bitter   heart   bitter   heart*
      'enraged'

(11d) *yụh*   *prɛʔ*   *yụh*   *prụm*
      make   food   make   food*
      'cook food'

(11e) *ŋɔ*   *prɛʔ*   *ŋɔ*   *prụm*
      leftovers   food   leftovers   food*
      'leftovers'

(11a–c) are examples of 'psycho-collocational expressions' similar to those described by Vittrant (this volume).

7.2   *AXAY forms*

Along the same lines as the expansion of X+X* doublets to AXAX*, Wa can extend compounds X and Y to form elaborate AXAY forms, where X and Y are synonyms, two elements of an established XY bare or two semantically related words. Here the aesthetic dimension lies in the symmetry of the construction rather than in rhyme, chime or alliteration. In (12) the compound is *taiʔ cạoŋ* 'hand leg', a compound used to form expressions referring to the body.

(12a) *sauʔ*   *taiʔ*   *sauʔ*   *cạoŋ*
      sick   hand   sick   leg
      'unwell'

(12b) *pʰai*   *taiʔ*   *pʰai*   *cạoŋ*
      fast   hand   fast   leg
      'nimble, agile'

(12c) *tịn*   *taịʔ*   *laŋ*   *cạoŋ*
      big   hand   long   leg
      'adult, grown up'

In (13) *brɛʔ* 'thief' is extended with the Tai loan *lak* instead of a chiming partner-syllable. The formation of doublets (and from them four-syllable elaborate expressions) with loans from Tai conveys an impression of loftiness similar to that conveyed by the formation of X + X* doublets.

(13a)   *pṵi*   *brɛʔ*   *pṵi*   *lak*
      person   thief   person   thief.TAI
      'thief'

(13b)   *pɑ̰oʔ*   *brɛʔ*   *pɑ̰oʔ*   *lak*
      partner   thief   partner   thief.TAI
      'partner in crime'

(13c)   *pɔn*   *brɛʔ*   *pɔn*   *lak*
      get   thief   get   thief.TAI
      'acquire by dishonest means'

Many AXAX* and AXAY formulations such as those seen above can also appear in the less elaborate form AXX* (Xiāo and Wáng 1994: 227); following this pattern, the examples in (13) would appear as the data in (14)

(14a)   *pṵi*   *brɛʔ*   *lak*
      person   thief   thief.TAI
      'thief'

(14b)   *pɑ̰oʔ*   *brɛʔ*   *lak*
      partner   thief   thief.TAI
      'partner in crime'

(14c)   *pɑ̰n*   *brɛʔ*   *lak*
      get   thief   thief.TAI
      'steal'

The processes we have described above are productive in the language. The array of rhythmically pleasing, symmetrical, rhyming or chiming patterns allows Wa speakers a great deal of scope for creativity and flexibility of expression. In addition, there is often a rich lexical pool from which to select the second element in XX* or XY compounds, allowing for further expressive and semantic fine-tuning. For instance, the three compounds in (15) all mean 'neighbour' – and more besides these are probably possible. They can all be used to form four-syllable expressions of the AXAY form in (16).

(15a)   *s.juun*   *plɔk*
      friend   plot of land
      'neighbour'

(15b) *pɑoʔ*   *ɲʰɔm*
       partner   neighbourhood
       'neighbour'

(15c) *pɑoʔ*   *plɔk*
       friend neighbourhood
       'neighbour'

(16a) *pɑoʔ*   *plɔk*   *pɑoʔ*   *ɲʰɔm*
       friend   neighbourhood   friend   plot of land
       'neighbour'

(16b) *s.juun*   *plɔk*   *s.jʰɔk*   *ɲiɛʔ*
       close by   neighbourhood   pile up   house
       'next door neighbour'

In (16b) a different third element in the construction, no longer synonymous with the first element, introduces an internal rhyme which is especially characteristic in Wa, described at greater length in Section 8 below.

8   ABBC rhyme patterns

The rhyme pattern ABBC is a template which can be used to bind together a wide range of linguistic forms in Wa, including four-syllable elaborate expressions, idioms, saying, and proverbs. Examples are given in (17) below.

(17a) *pɑu*   *ŋʰoʔ*   *goʔ*   *kɔi*
       guard   rice.plant watch.over   millet
       'tend crops'

(17b) *pɑuh*   *ʔia*   *cia*   *plai*
       slaughter chicken infuse   rice.beer
       'celebrate, hold a festival'

(17c) *taʔ*   *yɛʔ*   *mɛʔ*   *kuɲ*
       Grandfather grandmother   mother   father
       'forefathers and elders'

(17d) *krɑuŋ*   *kʰrai*   *dai*   *tɕah*
       clothes   clothes   skirt   shirt
       'clothing, clothes'

(17e) *krɑuŋ*   *tɕuip*   *ʔuip*   *sɔm*
       clothes   wear   rice   eat
       'food and clothing'

(17f) *ʔuip sɔm rɔm   ɲɑuʔ*
       rice   eat   water drink
       'food and drink'

(17g)   pot   bʰɔŋ   pʰɔŋ   ɲɛʔ
     break   ladder   destroy   house
     'destitute and homeless'

The phrases in (17) are not formed by productive processes but rather are stable in the lexicon, being multiply bound together by the internal rhyme, by internal syntactic symmetry, and by the shared semantic theme. Aesthetically motivated forms like these exist solely to allow the humdrum to be rendered expressively.

9   Proverbs with an internal ABBC-type rhyme pattern

This final section presents a generous selection of Wa proverbs, drawn chiefly from Wáng et al. (1992) and Xiāo and Wáng (1994). The former is a rich resource comprising several thousand Wa proverbs and sayings. The tiny, but broadly representative, examples presented here all have a central rhyme, which straddles the divide between two syntactically symmetrical constituents. They can thus be thought of as an elaboration of the ABBC pattern described above, though the material either side of the two central rhyming syllables may vary greatly in quantity and syntactical complexity. Often the syntax of the two halves of the whole phrase is symmetrical in structure, a phenomenon referred to by Xiāo and Wáng (1994) in Chinese as 骈俪 *piánlì*, which can be translated as 'aesthetic parallelism'. This form of syntactic counterpoint bears a certain similarity to Chinese 对联 *duìlián* 'antithetical couplets'. Wa sayings and proverbs may deal with subject matter which is either lofty or earthy, and historical or legendary allusions are commonly found. The examples here represent just a glimpse into the creative potential of the form. These are, unfortunately, presented out of context, but in many cases it is reasonably clear how a metaphorical or figurative interpretation might be arrived at from the literal meaning.

(18a)   soŋ   mɔh   prɛʔ,   nɛʔ   mɔh   kɑɲ
     bitter   is   food,   sour   is   work
     'Food [through] bitterness, work [done with] effort.' [describes something hard to obtain]

(18b)   ʔup   mai   s.bʰɔm,   rɔm   mai   s.dap
     rice   with   famine,   water   with   frost
     'Food in time of famine; water during a hard frost.' [something extremely precious or valuable]

(18c)   kʰaoʔ   koi   num,   rɔm   koi   tɑoh.
     tree   have   trunk,   water   have   source
     'Every tree has a trunk; all water has a source.'

(18d)   *pạn   dauı?   ŋạc,   lạc   dauı?   grụan.*
        rest   place   fragrant   enter   place   hunting-hide
        'Rest in a fragrant place, enter a hunter's hide.' [describes the joys of hunting]

(18e)   *suı   nɔh   yuıt,   pruıt   nɔh   grai.*
        splash   it   extinguished,   smother   it   gone
        'Sprinkle it out, extinguish it till it's gone.' [a saying to ward off fire]

(18f)   *klεh   tit?   vǫŋ,   luŋ   tị?   bǫk.*
        play   one   period,   act diligently   one   time
        'Be romantic for a while, make a true effort once.' [said between a courting
        man and woman]

The examples in (18), and the longer examples in (19), have two syntactically
symmetrical halves. The penultimate element in each half is identical and the
last item in the first half rhymes with the first item in the second.

(19a)   *haok   kao?   ?ɔm   goi,   lǫi   rɔm   ?ɔm   kʰiat.*
        climb   tree   like   lizard,   swim   water   like   frog
        'Climb like a lizard, swim like a frog.' [describes physical agility]

(19b)   *koc prại?   vε?   nε?,   lʰε? prại?   vε?   s.ŋịan.*
        clear weather   bring   beans,   rain weather bring   gourd
        'Beans in fine weather, gourds in rainy weather.'

The examples presented thus far have illustrated the aesthetic structures, sym-
metries, rhymes, and chimes, which underpin the expressive realm of the Wa
language. The examples which remain are a sample of the themes for
which these proverbs and sayings are the vehicle of expression: human qualities
and behaviour (20), Wa social history, the interactions with the charactistics
of the neighbouring ethnic nationalities, and geography in the Wa-speaking
area (21).

(20a)   *puk rạo   ?o?   pai   liŋ,   gliŋ rɔm   klɔŋ haok   blạoŋ.*
        bend frond   bamboo   quick   wheel,   spin water   river ascend slope
        'Bend bamboo fronds into a wheel and can spin river water up a slope.'
        [describes dexterity and skilfulness]

(20b)   *nɔk   kạɲ   gạɲ   yʰaok.*
        nod   head   bend   ear
        'Nod the head but bend the ear.' [describes nodding so as to appear to be
        listening attentively when one is not actually listening]

(20c)   *gʰrɤh   lǫi siaŋ,   tịaŋ   lǫi mụ.*
        Jump.over   [name of mountain]   cross.over [name of mountain]
        'Jump over Mount Laixiang, cross over Mount Moeknu.' [describes a long
        journey]

(21a) *vạʔ kut   lut   bl̦ɔŋ,   vạʔ lạt lɔŋ   gɔt.*
Wa remain wrong direction,   Wa extend follow mountain. pass
'The Wa Who Remained took the wrong path, the Wa Who Strode
Forth followed the mountain passes.'
[describes the history of the settlement pattern of different clan-groups of
Wa: one in the area around Kengtung and Möng Yang [modern-day Shan
State in Burma], one in the Lancang-Cangyuan area [in Yunnan province,
China]]

(21b) *yaoŋ   rutŋ   sac   dɔ,   sai   sɔ   kɔ   prạiʔ*
Yaong Rung   drill skull-post, Sai So start new.land
'The Yaong Rung clan chiselled out the skull posts and the Sai So clan
opened new land to cultivation.' [describes clans inhabiting new areas]

(21c) *glup   kah   cu.yi   mạn,   plạn   kah   cu.yi   siam.*
defeat by   knowledge Burmese, worn by   knowledge Shan.
'Defeated by the cunning of the Burmans, worn out by the cunning of the
Shan.'

(21d) *kọn   dɔʔ   hɔʔ,   krɔʔ   tɔʔ   siam.*
deputy. headman   give   Chinese, chief.headman give   Shan
'The deputy headman appointed by the Han Chinese, the chief headman
appointed by the Shan.' [a Wa saying reflecting the political situation of the
early twentieth century]

(21e) *kʰɔŋ   mịan   taŋ,   saŋ   mạn   don.*
beast   Lahu   carry, elephant Burmese   carry
'The Lahus' beasts of burden tote and the Burmans' elephants carry.' [a
saying describing cooperation among different ethnic groups]

(21f) *plạuŋ   s.naʔ   giah,   rịah   s.naʔ   hɔʔ*
sprout   among   thatchgrass root among   Chinese
'Sprout in the middle of flat thatchgrass, put down roots among the Chinese.'
[describes something difficult to do]

(21g) *tọŋ mụn   ŋɔi,   yaoŋ sɔi   rot.*
Tong Mun   scabies   Yaong Soi   spots
'The Tong Mun villagers have scabies and Yaong Soi villagers have
spots.' [describes the venereal and other infectious diseases brought to the
Cangyuan/Yaongsoi area by outside traders and soldiers]

(21h) *bịh   mọc   gọŋ,   prɔŋ   nʰɔŋ   prạiʔ.*
chant spirit mountain appease lake   local.place
'Pray to the spirit of the mountain, appease the [spirit of the] local lake.'
[refers to Wa animist beliefs and their connections with the natural world]

(21i) *pịaŋ   pʰa cao,   lạo   kʰun   mɤŋ*
worship   Buddha   report   official   country

'Worship the Buddha, report to the officials of the realm.' [describes the need to fit in with the prevailing belief systems of the people among whom the Wa live, the Buddhist Burmese/Shan and bureaucratic Chinese officialdom]

The last three examples in (22) deal with universal matters of love and sex, the final two in a delightfully direct and earthy way.

(22a)   *puɲ   kuɲ   nat   ʔah   baŋ.baŋ,   gʰraŋ   mɛʔ   loʔ   ʔah*
        shoot father gun   say   bang.bang! scold   mother words say
        kʰlaok.kʰlaok
        cluck.cluck!
        'Father fires the gun with a bang-bang, Mother is quick to scold with a cluck-cluck.' [describes parental disapproval of their child's choice of partner]

(22b)   *tɔʔ   ŋɛʔ   krǎc,   tɔʔ   ŋac   te.*
        give   itch   scratch   give   fragrant   fuck
        'If it itches, scratch it; if it smells good, fuck it.'

(22c)   *ŋǎc   mɔ̌h   te,   tɛ   mɔ̌h   pɤt.*
        fragrant   is   fuck,   sweet   is   fuck
        'Fragrance is having sex, sweetness is making love.'

10   Conclusion

This chapter has presented an overview of the aesthetically noteworthy structures and patterns found in Wa, encountered principally while foraging through a corpus of printed material in Wa for the purposes of compiling a dictionary (Watkins in press). It has not been possible to investigate the detail of the contexts, registers, or domains of language in which expressive features of Wa are prominent, and especially regrettably no spoken material is considered here. Nonetheless, the properties described show Wa to be typical of the languages of Mainland Southeast Asia. It is clear that the structural templates and the expressive dimension they convey are a core feature of the grammar, which is hard to describe adequately in the absence of an established descriptive framework. Until such a framework exists, we can only delight in the elaborate, expressive euphony of Wa and enjoy it as we find it.

References

Bolinger, Dwight. 1978. 'Intonation across languages'. In J. Greenberg (ed.), *Universals of human language. Vol II: phonology.* Palo Alto: Stanford University Press, pp. 471–524.
Diffloth, G. 1972. Notes on expressive meanings. *Chicago linguistic society* 8: 440–447.
        1976. Expressives in Semai. *Oceanic linguistics special publications* 13: 249–264.

1979. 'Expressive phonology and prosaic phonology in Mon-Khmer'. In T. L. Thongkum et al. (eds.), *Studies in Tai and Mon-Khmer phonetics and phonology in honor of Eugenie J. A. Henderson*. Bangkok: Chulalongkorn University Press, pp. 49–59.

1980. *The Wa languages*. Berkeley: Department of Linguistics, University of California.

1994. 'i:big, a: small.' In L. Hinton, J. Nichols, and J. Ohala (eds.), *Sound symbolism*. Cambridge University Press, pp. 107–114.

2001. Les expressifs de Surin, et ou cela conduit. *Bulletin de l'Ecole Française d'Extrême-Orient* 88.

Enfield, Nick J. 2005. Areal linguistics and Mainland Southeast Asia. *Annual review anthropology* 34: 181–206.

Ferlus, Michel. 1974. Les langues du groupe austroasiatique-nord. *Asie du sud-est et monde insulindien* (ASEMI) V(I): 39–68.

Fox, James (ed.). 1988. *To speak in pairs: essays on the ritual languages of Eastern Indonesia*. Cambridge Studies in Oral and Literate Culture. Cambridge University Press.

Gussenhoven, Carlos. 2004. *The phonology of tone and intonation*. Cambridge University Press.

Haas, Mary R. 1964. *Thai–English student's dictionary*. Stanford University Press.

Haiman, John and Noeurng Ourn. 2009. 'Decorative symmetry in ritual (and everyday) language'. In Roberta Corrigan, Edith A. Moravcsik, Hamid Ouali and Kathleen M. Wheatley (eds.). *Formulaic language*. Amsterdam: John Benjamins.

Henderson, Eugénie J. A. 1952. The main features of Cambodian pronunciation. *Bulletin of the School of Oriental and African Studies* 14: 149–174.

1965. The topography of certain phonetic and morphological characteristics of Southeast Asian languages. *Lingua* 15: 400–434.

Lewis, M. Paul (ed.). 2009. *Ethnologue: languages of the world*, sixteenth edition. Dallas, TX: SIL International.

Matisoff, James A. 1973a. *The grammar of Lahu*. Berkeley/Los Angeles: University of California Press.

1973b. 'Tonogenesis in South East Asia'. In Larry Hyman (ed.), *Consonant types and tone*. Southern California Occasional Papers in Linguistics No. 1., pp. 71–95.

1994. 'Tone, intonation, and sound symbolism in Lahu: loading the syllable canon'. In L. Hinton, J. Nichols, and J. Ohala (eds.), *Sound symbolism*, Cambridge University Press, pp. 115–129.

Sadan, Mandy. (in press). *Being and becoming Kachin*. London: British Academy and Oxford University Press.

Sadan, Mandy and Francois Robinne, eds. 2007. *Social dynamics in the highlands of South East Asia: reconsidering 'Political Systems of Highland Burma' by E. R. Leach. (Handbook of Oriental Studies. Section 3 Southeast Asia; 18).* Leiden: Brill.

Sereno, Joan A. 1994. 'Phonosyntactics'. In L. Hinton, J. Nichols, and J. Ohala (eds.) *Sound symbolism*. Cambridge University Press, pp. 263–275.

Voeltz, E. F. K, and C. Kilian-Hatz (eds.). 2001. *Ideophones. Papers presented at the 1st International Symposium on Ideophones, Jan. 1999, St. Augustin.* Amsterdam: John Benjamins.

Wáng Jīngliú 王敬骝, Chén Xiāngmù 陈相目, Xiāo Yùfēn 肖玉芬, and Wěi Ānxiáng 魏安祥. 1992. *Loux Gāb Vax* (佤语熟语汇释). Kunming: Yunnan Minzu Chubanshe.

Watkins, Justin. 2002. *The phonetics of Wa: experimental phonetics, phonology, orthography and sociolinguistics.* Canberra: Pacific Linguistics, The Australian National University.

   (ed.) (in press). *Wa–Burmese–Chinese–English dictionary.* Leiden: Brill.

Zhāo Àishè 赵岩社 and Zhāo Fúhé 赵福和 1998 佤语语法 *Nbēen loux graī Vāx [A grammar of Wa].* Kunming: Yunnan Minzu chubanshe.

7 Beautifying techniques in Kammu vocal genres

Håkan Lundström

1 Introduction

Singing occupies a central place in Kammu culture. There are several kinds of songs for various situations. Especially important is the singing that takes place in social situations where people engage in alternating singing, which means that songs will demand a reply in singing. This kind of singing is organized in a mono-melodic system, meaning that all singing that takes place in a given situation may be done by use of the same melody template. There are different melody templates for different situations.

When a pre-existing orally transmitted poem, *trnəəm*, is being combined with the melody template of a vocal genre the singer re-creates the song while singing, *təəm*. The poem itself is often very rich in rhymes and expressives and usually by the principles of parallelism. In the process of singing the singer may develop the poem by combining different poems, by adding words and lines and by also reduplicating syllables of the song text. There is a thin line between poetic singing and eloquent speech, and by using the term vocal genre rather than 'song' it is easier to recognize a continuum that spans from daily speech via polite speech, prayer, recitation, and chant to song.

The poetic contents of the *trnəəm* have been analysed in some detail by Lundström (2010) and Lundström and Tayanin (2006). In this chapter the documentation and analysis will be broadened by comparison to other vocal genres with the aim to study the beautifying techniques in the verbal expressions and possible principles behind their uses. The majority of the material used for this chapter stems from the Kammu research team at Lund University. Unless otherwise indicated in the text, all of the songs and recitations in this paper were performed by Damrong Tayanin (Kàm Ràw, 1938–2011), who grew up in the village Rmcùal in the Yùan area in northern Laos.

Kammu (ISO 639–3:kjg and also written as Khmu) is an Austroasiatic language belonging to the Mon-Khmer subfamily. Kammu is one of the main members of the Khmuic branch of Mon-Khmer and its speakers are found mainly in mountainous regions of northern Vietnam, Laos, Thailand, Burma, and parts of southwestern China.

The tradition under study here is part of the cultural heritage of the Yùan Kammu of northern Laos. The Yùan dialect of the Kammu language is a tone language with one high (´) and one low (`) tone. Words are made up of full syllables and half syllables, meaning a syllable with a very short, almost inaudible vowel after a consonant ('kn' has a short ə-sound: 'kᵊn') (Svantesson 1983). In music performances these semisyllables are treated as full syllables and the short vowel given normal length. Sung poetry is therefore syllabic and the poetry basically syllable-counting, whereas the word appears to be the basic unit in spoken rhymes.

Reduplication plays an important role in common speech as well as in poetry and the use of expressives is abundant (see Svantesson 1983: 84–85, 115 ff.). An essential technique that can be found in most vocal genres – if not all – is what may be referred to as grammatical parallelism or lexical parallelism, i.e. a word (or words) is replaced by a synonym or by another word of the same kind. In its basic form it may be only one sentence that is repeated with only a few words exchanged, often built on the same rhythm as shown in the song calling for rain.[1]

(1)   Kláaŋ ká,   əə,   kláaŋ ká,
       Egret,   oh,   egret,
                    ɔ̀ɔr   cùur   ɔ̀m   sr -   lòoy
                    bring down water scoop

       ⇓   ⇓
       Kɔ̀ɔn róoy, əə,   kɔ̀ɔn róoy,
       child spirit, oh,   child spirit
                                   ⇓
                    ɔ̀ɔr   cùur   ɔ̀m   k -   mà
                    bring down water rain
       'Egret, oh, egret!
       Bring down scoops of water!
       Spirit-child, oh, spirit-child!
       Bring down showers of rain!'

Lines of five and seven syllables usually dominate the structure of Kammu poetry. While it is not self-evident where a poetic line starts and ends in Kammu poetry, the method employed here is based on breathing pauses and rhythm in a number of song templates.

---

[1] The following conventions are used in this chapter: *Italics*, **bold italics**, Italics , **bold italics** indicate rhyme (final syllable rhyme); underlining indicates vocalic or consonantal rhyme; and ⇓between two lines indicates a substituted word in the phrases.

In example (2) each line is composed of a five-syllable sequence. One word is substituted and the last word of the first line rhymes with the first word(s) of the second line, which I refer to as a chain rhyme.

(2)   Klók,   klók   ò   tèŋ   *nə̀əŋ*
        Klók   klók   I   well   know
        'The klók, klók, I know it well.'
                          ⇓
        Klə́əŋ,   klə́əŋ   ò   tèŋ   mèc
        Klə́əŋ,   klə́əŋ   I   well   hear
        'The klə́əŋ, klə́əŋ, I hear it well.'

This is a spoken saying depicting what the bear says when it finds out that people are preparing bamboo instruments to scare off bears and other animals that may bother people working in the fields and the growing rice.

2   The *trnə̀əm* sung poems

Rhyme and sound-play are important creative elements of the genre of sung poems known as *trnə̀əm*. Example (3) belongs to the traditional drum feast when a male person of more than 60 years of age was presented a drum as a sign of his high status. It will be noted that the expressives (*exp looks* and *exp sounds* respectively) are three-syllable words consisting of one full syllable repeated with a 'semi'-syllable in the middle.

(3)   *trnə̀əm*, sung poem

(a)   tm -   pír   ŋàk -   kn -   ŋàk   crì   k -   táaŋ
        turtle   dove   *exp looks*   nodding   ficus   glade

(b)   tm -   pír   ŋàk -   kn -   ŋàk   crì   c -   lə́ɔŋ
        turtle   dove   *exp looks*   nodding   ficus   riverbank

(c)   kr -   làk   crír -   tn -   crír   kàaŋ   tr -   tì
        slit drum   *exp sound*   rumble   house   centre

(d)   kr -   làk   crír -   tn -   crír   tòoŋ   tr -   tì
        slit drum   *exp sound*   rumble   part of   centre
                                                                 village

'The turtle dove nods and coos in the fig tree in the glade.
The turtle dove nods and coos in the fig tree by the river.
The slit drum rolls and rumbles in the central house of the village.
The slit drum rolls and rumbles in the central part of the village.'

Most songs can be said to have a central sentence, i.e. the sentence that in a concrete way explains the contents of the song, in this case 'The slit drum rolls and rumbles in the central house of the village.' Through a combination of rhyme-pattern, rhyme-words, and parallelism a singer can 'reconstruct' a song from the central sentence. The singer must know the rhyme-words, which in this case are cross-rhymes:

(4)   kr -   *làk*   *crír* - tn -   *crír* |*kaaŋ*| tr - |*tì*|
        tm -   *pír*   *ŋàk* - kn -   *ŋàk* |*crì*| k - |*táaŋ*|

Then by use of parallelism and substitution, i.e. replacing one word with a synonym or a word of the same class – in this case house/part of village – another line can be deduced and rhymed:

(5)   kr -   *làk*   *crír* - tn -   *crír*   kàaŋ   tr - |*tì*|
                                        ⇓
        tm -   *pír*   *ŋàk* - kn -   *ŋàk* |*crì*| c - |*lɔ́ɔŋ*|

In this way a poem, *trnə̀əm*, can be created going backwards from a central sentence. This is basically how it works and this also explains why the first parts of songs are often difficult to understand, whereas the contents become clear (or clearer) in the latter parts. This creates beauty and suspense.

3   Tales

Repetitions and parallelism are more common in orally transmitted tales than in daily speech as shown by these excerpts (6) from 'The water buffalo tinkling with frogs' told by Mr. Léeŋ (Lindell et al. 1998: 124–126, 162–164).

(6)   làə   ɔ̀or   yɔ̀   tèe   yɔ̀h   **héɛl,**
        and   lead   together   go   weed,
               héɛl túh   pháay...
               weed   fallow cotton...
               héɛl ɔ̀or   kɔ̀ɔn   tee,
               Weed   lead   child   own,
               héɛl ré   nì.
               weed   field   that.
        Kɔ́ɔn mə̀h,
        Child   be,
               Kɔ́ɔn núm.
        child   young.
        'and they went together to *weed*,
               weed a second year fallow with cotton...
               She *weeded*, took her child along
               to *weed* the field.
        The *child* was
               a young *child*.'

It will also be noted that there is a good deal of consonant rhymes and vowel rhymes (examples underlined).

(7) Wàay ni   héɛt yɔh   oo,   thúuk sát,
     After that   call go   oh,   every animal
           thúuk snít nèey *phìɨn phí phóp kii*
           every kind on   earth   this
           thúuk snít sìt,
           every kind animal
     yɔh   àn   lòoc.
     go   let   finish.
           Yɔh   *téɛŋ   kàaŋ   knì* oo.
           Go   build house   that oh.

'After that they called one another, every animal,
   all kinds that are on the earth,
   every kind of animal.
Went there to the very last one.
They went to build that house.'

4   Children's songs

The difference between tales and songs may sometimes only be the fact that repetition or parallelism in a song is regular so as to create a strophic whole. The following song consists only of vocables and a sentence that is repeated. However, the form is quite settled – even though in singing the song may continue.

In a traditional Kammu village on a mountain slope the fields will be located higher up on the mountainside some distance from the village. The youngest children, younger than about seven years of age, would not be allowed to go with their parents to work in the fields. At the end of the day children would go a short way along the path leading from the village to the fields to wait for their parents to return. This is when this song would be sung.

(8)   léel   lée léel lél   yòŋ   ò   lée léel lél
                               father my
                               ⇓
       léel   lée léel lél   mà   ò   lée léel lél
                               mother my
       yòŋ   ò   yèt   tàa   ré
       father my   stay at   field
       ⇓
       mà   ò   yèt   tàa   ré
       mother my   stay at   field

léel	lée		léel	lél	mà	ò		lée	léel	lél l
					mother	my				

⇓

léel	lée		léel	lél	yòŋ	ò		lée	léel	lél
					father	my				

'Leel lee leel lel, my father, lee lee lel
Leel lee leel lel, my mother, lee lee lel
My father stays in the field
My mother stays in the field
Leel lee leel lel, my mother, lee lee lel
Leel lee leel lel, my father, lee lee lel.'

5   Prayers

Prayers in Kammu culture are normally spoken or recited (cf. Tayanin 2006: 123). The prayer that appears here as example (9) is for a bronze drum when it is to be used on the occasion of a funeral. The sentences or phrases are grouped in pairs, as is often the case, using rhyme in the first two lines and then substitution of words.

(9)	əə	khɔ́ɔŋ	nàay	*háaŋ,*	
	oh	thing	mister	merchant	
	r -	*màaŋ*	tr -	làh	
	wealth		infect		
	ùun	kə̀ə	klɔ́ɔc,		
	let	it	safe		
	ùun	kə̀ə	ŋàr		
	let	it	calm		
	ùun	cùm,			
	let	well			
	ùun	yèen			
	let	well [?]			

'Oh, thing of Mister merchant,
    infect us with wealth.
Let us be safe,
    let us be calm.
Let us be well,
    let us be good.'

Before sowing, a field that has been fallow for several years must be burnt and the following prayer may be used as the master of ceremonies plants a certain plant that symbolizes safety.

(10)   əə,   kìt   ré,
       Oh,   start field,
              Kìt   pràay   kìi.
              start falling trap this.
       ùun   kə̀ə   là   ŋɔ́,
       Let   it   good rice,
                           kɔ̀h   cít
                           without   grass
       Là   yɔ̀ɔ   k -   mà,
       Good   with   rain,
                     há   yɔ̀ɔ   pr-   lìa
                     burn   with   fire
       ŋɔ́   là   tàa   ré,
       rice   good   on   field,
                     k-   né   wàt   tàa pràay
                     rat   caught in   trap
       Là   lɔ̀h,
       Well   body,
              krɔ̀h   tòh
              peel off dirt
'Oh, starting the new field,
       starting the falling traps.
Let it be full with rice,
       free from grass.
Good from rain,
       burnt by fire,
The rice good on the field,
       the rats caught in the traps.
May we be healthy,
       may impurity peel off.'

The structure of these rhyme sequences may be called chain rhymes because they function to link lines together. This pattern occurs in all Kammu poetic genres and is common throughout many verbally artistic genres in Mainland Southeast Asia ethnolinguistic groups. In this prayer the phrases are linked together two by two. In other cases whole sections of several lines can be linked together in this way.

6   Indirect speech

Indirect speech, *trñɔɔl*, is a joking exchange of words according to a pre-set pattern and with certain rhymes. They are spoken in a manner similar to prayers and particularly used by young people. The first speaker will *cɔ̀ɔl*, i.e. praise or flatter the other party, who in turn will reply belittling him or herself. The communication continues with the first speaker reassuring the initial statement.

(11) *Trñɔɔl*, joking words between a boy (♂) and a girl (♀).

(♂) əə,   pàa   kàay plìa   mə́h   láak - lə́n
      oh,   you   indeed beauty what   extremely
      'Oh, you are really extremely beautiful.'

(♀) cɔ́ɔl   *cák*,   sn - *tàk*   lá   t -   *làa*,
      praise poke   form a cone   leaf thin bamboo,
      mèc   tèe   *kràa*,
      know   yourself white-skinned
      tèe   plìa   kàay,
      yourself   beautiful   then
      cɔ́ɔl   ì   kòn cə̀
      praise me   person ugly
                       kòn yíaŋ
                       person black.
      'Praise and poke, make a cone of a bamboo leaf.
      You know that you yourself
      are handsome and fair,
      still you praise me who
      am ugly and black.'

(♂) oo,   lía   nì   kə̀ə cə̀ə *kláay*,
      oh,   more than that will too much;
      wáay nì   kə̀ə cə̀ə klàat.
      After that it   will pass.
      'Oh, more beauty than yours would be too much.
      More beauty than yours would be unthinkable.'

7   Sayings, proverbs, and terms of address

There are sentences or rhymes that may be used in common speech. Some are basically built on grammatical parallelism as the following, which could be uttered or sung to the man who was about to receive a wooden drum at a ceremony the following day.

(12) 'Saying' in anticipation of a gift of wooden drum.
      tɨm   tɨm   ɨɨk   cə̀ə *maa* mɨɨ   ɨɨn,
      IDEO   drum   will come   tomorrow
      ɨa   sŋ-   ɨa   *laal laal* cə̀ə   *maa* mɨɨ   ɨɨn.
      IDEO   gongs and cymbals   will   come   tomorrow
      'The sound of the drum will arrive tomorrow,
      The sound of gongs and cymbals will arrive tomorrow.'

A closer look will reveal, however that there are several vowel (ɨ, a) and consonant (t, l) rhymes that serve to tie the sentences together. Many proverbs are artfully rhymed, by means of a pivot-rhyme, i.e. they consist of two parts that are linked together by a rhyme. They can vary in length and while the first part always seems to end with the rhyme word, the rhyme of the second part can be anywhere from the 1st to the 4th word (Lindell 1988). Example (13) shows how this is accomplished in a Kammu proverb.

(13)   wàar   ñìir   *lá,*   *kmà*   ñìir   pùŋ
         sunny slip   leaf,   rain   slip   mud
         'When it is sunny, you slip on leaves; when it is rainy, you slip on mud.'

The proverbs have a natural place in somewhat formal language and a whole set of proverbs belong to the marriage ceremony as do a number of songs. Also riddles, which belong to the funeral ceremonies, make use of pivot-rhyme in the first line (see Tayanin 2006: 155–157). The sung poems, *trnəəm*, may be combined with words of address when performed in certain social situations. These are set rhymes normally combining pivot-rhymes with more complex rhymes (Lundström and Tayanin 2006). In some cases all words of the first part are mirrored by rhyme-words in the second part, a chiasmus.

(14)   Words of address to friends with chiasmus rhyme.
         ùul |*hɔɔm*| *trɔ̀*   *yɔ̀* |*prɔɔm*| *tùul*
         fire-wood [?]   bind   torch, friends good   old
         'Torches bound together; good old friends.'

These words of address differ from proverbs, however, in that when performed the two parts are spread out in the sung poem, *trnəəm*, normally so that the first part ends the first stanza and the second part ends the second stanza (Lundström 2010). On hearing the performance the rhymes are thus separated by several lines of poetry.

Returning to the *trnəəm* that was quoted at the beginning of this chapter, the lines that are separated in performance will look different when juxtaposed with each other as shown in example (15).

(15)   Line 1 of example (3) juxtaposed to demonstrate rhyme structure.

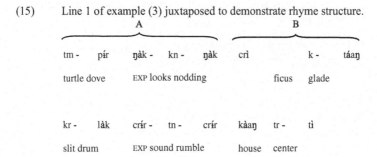

	A				B		
tm -	pír	ŋàk -	kn -	ŋàk	crì	k -	táaŋ
turtle dove		EXP looks nodding				ficus	glade
kr -	làk	crír -	tn -	crír	kàaŋ	tr -	tì
slit drum		EXP sound rumble			house	center	

When separated into two parts the rhyme of the latter part (B) comes out as a developed pivot-rhyme like in the words of address:

(B)   *crì*   k - *táaŋ*, *kàaŋ*   tr - *tì*
       ficus   glade,   house centre

Similarly the first part (A) shows similar characteristics:

(A)   tm - *pír* *ŋàk* - kn - *ŋàk*, kr - *làk* *crír* - tn - *crír*
       turtle dove EXP looks nodding slit drum EXP sound rumble

The cross-rhymes of the sung poems, *trnə̀əm*, can thus be seen as advanced variants of the pivot-rhyme. Actually this also goes for the chain-rhyme exemplified in the prayer, example (6) quoted above:

        khɔ́ɔŋ nàay *háaŋ*,   r -   *màaŋ* tr - làh
        thing mister merchant, wealth   infect

8   Magic formulas

The magic formulas used by shamans are called *krùu*. Generally speaking they are longer than prayers and they are chanted rather than spoken, usually the speed increases during the course of the chant and it also becomes quieter thus gradually turning more monotonous. The magic formulas normally make much use of pivot-rhymes in the form of chain-rhymes so that several lines are tied together in this way. This pattern is usually interrupted by two or more phrases or sentences organized according to grammatical parallelism. In the following excerpt rhymes are in italics and parallel lines with an indent. These formulas contain many Lao words.

(16)   *Krùu ɔ́ɔy*, calling spirits from a sick person.

   (a) àk   àk   λʌy
       ak   ak   oh

   (b) kùu   mɛ̀ɛn mɔ́ɔ   càaŋ   *cɔ̀ɔy*
       I   am   shaman master help

   (c) kùu   cə̀ə ɔ́ɔy   phíi *hàay*,
       I   will call out spirit evil

   (d) kùu   cə̀ə *phàay*   phíi *sía*, hrm.
       I   will chase out spirit tiger [cough]

   (e)   *mìa* yə̀ə phíi, *mìa*   yə̀ə
            go away   spirits, go away

(f)   *mìa*   yàam kùu   wàa   **dáay.**
        go away   call I   speak [politely]

(g) **pháay** yə̀ə phíi,   **pháay**   yə̀ə
    run away,   spirits, run away

(h) **phàay** yàam kùu wàa   *díi,*   hrm.
    go   call I   speak nicely [cough]

(i) prìaŋ   *díi* pìan   pə́əŋ **lèɛw,**
    people nice   for you like   indeed

(j) nàaŋ   **Kéɛw** ɔ̀ɔk   màa   kín.
    Miss   Kéɛw   come out   come eat

(k)   níi yə̀ə àay   Khóŋ- khɔ́ɔt
        run away mister Khongkhoot,
                    ⇓

(l)   níi yə̀ə àay   Khót- mìaŋ,   hrm.
        run away   mister Khotmiang. [cough]

(m) mìŋ   bɔ́ɔ   'yáan kùu rìi...
    you   not   afraid me   away...
'Ak ak eey,
I am a shaman who can help people,
I will call out the evil spirits,
I will chase away the tiger spirits,
        Go away, spirits, go away,
        Go while I'm telling you politely.
Run away, spirits, run away,
Leave while I'm telling you nicely.
People have made good food for you,
Miss Keew come out and eat.
        Run away Mister Khongkhoot,
        Run away Mister Khotmuong.
Aren't you scared . . .'

9   Vocal genres and beautifying techniques

When the different vocal genres are ordered on a scale spanning from 'speech' to 'song' it becomes evident that there is no sharp boundary between the two. One may rather think in terms of degrees or levels or modes of speech – or degrees or levels or modes of song for that matter. Seeger arrived at the following descriptions of the two extremes and an intermediary mode (Seeger

1987: 51). Seeger studied the Suyá people in Amazonas and his conclusions are here adapted – or generalized – so as to be relevant to Kammu practice:

> Speech Priority of text over melody;
> Text and melody determined by speaker;
> Increasing formalization in public performances.

> Intermediary Relative priority of relatively fixed texts over relatively established melodies.

> Song Priority of melody over text;
> Time, text and melody fixed.

In its main outline this also holds for Kammu practice. Apart from the vocal genres mentioned in this chapter also the following are included in Figure 7.1 (Lundstrom 2010: 34–35, 47–70).

> Ceremonial Songs belonging to certain ceremonies verbally similar to
> songs   prayers but with distinct individual melodies.

> *Hrlìi* Vocal genre for *trnə̀əm* with set melody template built almost totally on word tones.

> *Hrwə̀,* Vocal genres for *trnə̀əm* with set melody template built on a specific
> *Húuwə̀* melodic motif.

> *Yàam* Vocal genre for *trnə̀əm* with set melody template built on a specific melodic motif.

It must be considered, of course, that the listing of these vocal genres on a scale from speech to song should be seen as a suggestion. Despite some over-lapping and other inconsistencies it, however, provides an overview that in turn corresponds to the beautifying techniques.

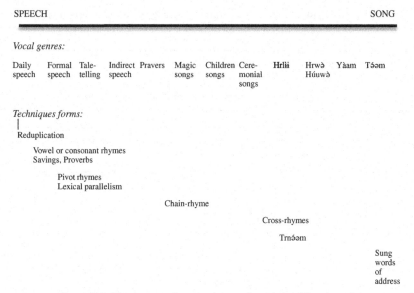

Figure 7.1 Vocal genres in a continuum from 'speech' to 'song'

10   Conclusion

As has been demonstrated in this chapter one may see a continuity within the beautifying techniques studied here that makes it possible to list them from simple to complex. In this chain the one to the right may be seen as a special case of the preceding one.

Reduplication ⇒ Lexical parallelism ⇒ Pivot-rhyme ⇒ Chain-rhyme ⇒ Cross-rhyme

It should be taken into account that there may be other beautifying methods that are not included here. It should also be noted that the different vocal genres are characterized also by a number of other traits that together define them like meaning, situation, function etc. When those techniques under study here are juxtaposed with the vocal genres the general picture is that the complexity of the beautifying techniques increases when moving from speech to song.

Mixed techniques in a song

Moving from left to right in Figure 7.1 means that new techniques are added. For example, the cross-rhymes seem to be rare in prayers. On the other hand some prayers have cross-rhymes, but they hardly occur for example in tales (unless another vocal genre is quoted in a tale, which happens).

Cross-rhymes are mainly found in the sung poems *trnə̀əm*. This does not mean that they consist only of cross-rhymes. On the contrary, some build on simpler rhyme patterns altogether, but all of the techniques mentioned in the table are present in the *trnə̀əm* as a genre. Which one is the dominating one varies from case to case. What this analysis is showing is that the farther to the right we move on this scale the wider variety of techniques can be used.

Example (17) has cross-rhymes and substituted words. In the end a sentence is added and repeated with substitution of words. This is rather common in *trnə̀əm*. The song is a polite song of depreciation when visiting somebody and there is a singing situation. The central sentence, which summarizes its meaning is, 'Anyone who hears, don't listen!' ('speaking' is often synonymous with 'singing').

(17)   A *trnə̀əm* for depreciating one's own singing and make excuse for making a visit.

(a)	mɔ̀	*pén*	táa	km -	*tèc*				
	anyone	cut	not	completely					
(b)	àay	mɔ̀h	*lɔ̀ən*	òm	*Lo̠*	lm -	*pùut*	pr -	lùŋ
	I	am	catfish	stream	name	step		ember	
(c)	mɔ̀	*pén*	táa	km -	tèc				
	anyone	cut	not	completely					
(d)	àay	mɔ̀h	*lɔ̀ən*	òm	*Lo̠*	lm -	*pùut*	pr -	lìa
	I	am	catfish	stream	name	step		fire	
(e)	mɔ̀	*mèc*	táa	km -	ñèŋ				
	anyone	hear	not	listen					
(f)	àay	mɔ̀h	*plò*	s -	*tɔ̀ən*	lm -	pɔ̀ɔŋ	kt -	*súut*
	I	am	dumb	half-way		talk		talk without pause	
(g)	m̀	*mèc*	táa	km -	ñèŋ				
	anyone	hear	not	listen					
			⇓					⇓	
(h)	àay	mɔ̀h	béey	s -	*tɔ̀ən*	lm -	pɔ̀ɔŋ	pn -	lía
	I	am	stupid	half-way		talk		talk very much	
(i)	pɔ́ɔ	nɔ̀əŋ	pŋ -	kà	priaŋ				
	not	know	shy		other people				
			⇓						
(j)	pɔ́ɔ	nɔ̀əŋ	pk -	síik	priaŋ				
	not	know	disturb		other people				

'Anyone who cuts, don't cut through!
I am a River Ló catfish, stepping on embers.
Anyone who cuts, don't cut through!
I am a River Ló catfish, stepping on fire.
Anyone who hears, don't listen!
I am half dumb, speaking ceaselessly.
Anyone who hears, don't listen!
I am half stupid, speaking incessantly.
I don't have the sense to show respect,
I don't have the sense not to disturb.'

References

Lindell, Kristina. 1988. 'Rhyme-pivot sayings in northern Kammu'. In Leif Littrup (ed.), *Analecta Hafniensia: 25 years of East Asian studies in Copenhagen*. London: Curzon Press, pp. 88–99.

Lindell, Kristina, Jan-Öjvind Swahn, and Damrong Tayanin. 1998. *Folk tales from Kammu VI: a teller's last tales*. Richmond: Curzon Press.

Lundström, Håkan. 2010. *I will send my song. Kammu vocal genres in the singing of Kam Raw*. Copenhagen: NIAS Press.

Lundström, Håkan and Damrong Tayanin. 2006. *Kammu songs: the songs of Kam Raw*. Copenhagen: NIAS Press.

Seeger, Anthony. 1987. *Why Suyá sing: a musical anthropology of an Amazonian people*. Cambridge University Press.

Svantesson, Jan-Olof. 1983. *Kammu phonology and morphology*. Lund: Liber Förlag/ Gleerup.

Tayanin, Damrong. 2006. *Where do our souls go after death? Kammu traditions, rituals and ceremonies*. Kristina Lindell (ed.) and Arthur Holmer (assoc. ed.). Privately published.

Part II

Tai-Kadai

8 Proverbs, proverbial elaboration, and poetic development in the Tai languages

Thomas John Hudak

1 Introduction

Proverbs and short, pithy sayings can be found throughout the Tai language family, a family that extends from southern China in the north to the Malay peninsula in the south, and from the island of Hainan in the east to Myanmar and Assam in the west. These proverbs can be as short as one line linked internally by alliteration and rhyme such as the following Red Tai example (DeGeorge 1927: 912).[1]

(1)   kay² say² kay² katak¹
        chicken-lay-egg-chicken-crow
        'It's the chicken with eggs that crows.'

Most frequently, they occur as couplets linked together by rhyme (*pɔɔ⁴* and *cɔɔ⁴*) as in this Muong Yong Lue example (Hudak 1996: 1339).[2]

(2)   ciʔ⁵ liʔ⁵ baw² pɔɔ⁴
        not smart-not-enough
        cɔɔ⁴ lɔɔ⁴ baw² thuuk²
        character-not-correct
        'If one is not smart enough,
        one's character is inappropriate.'

In other cases, a couplet may be linked solely by parallel syntactic structures as in the following Hsi Paw Shan example (Hudak 1994: 709–710).[3]

(3)   soy³ kan¹ kin¹ sɔŋ² vaan¹
        help-each other-eat-therefore-sweet
        soy³ kan¹ haam¹ sɔŋ² maw¹

---

[1] Approximate Red Tai tones include: 1 – rising; 2 – low; 3 – falling; 4 – mid; 5 – high-falling; 6 – high-rising.
[2] Muong Yong Lue tones include: 1 – high-rising; 2 – low-rising; 3 – low level, glottalized; 4 – mid, with slight rise and fall; 5 – mid; 6 – falling, glottalized.
[3] Hsi Paw Shan tones include: 1 – low-rising; 2 – low-falling; 3 – mid-falling, glottalized; 4 – high; 5 – high-falling, glottalized.

help-each other-carry-therefore-light
'Help each other and eat, then it's tasty.
Help each other and carry, then it's light.'

Less frequently, three line sets occur as in this Bouyei proverb (Snyder 2000: 69). The Bouyei orthography has been converted to a phonetic transcription.[4]

(4)   çeu^6 pɔɔ^6 kuk^5
generation-father-tiger
çeu^6 luk^3 ɲen^1
generation-child-wildcat
çeu^6 laaŋ^1 tuu^2 tɕii^6 sɛn^3
generation-after-classifier-yellow weasel
'The father's generation is like a tiger.
The son's generation is like a wildcat.
Those to come are like a yellow weasel.'
(i.e., later generation will not be as good as the former without teaching or training)

Each of the above examples embodies characteristics that define and appear in more formal poetic compositions in the Tai languages: identical syllable number, alliteration, rhyme, and parallel syntactic strings. Each of these devices also plays a part in the construction of larger texts. Two similar compositions, a collection of maxims from Red Tai and one from Siamese, exemplify how these devices contribute to such a construction.

Red Tai, a member of the Tai language family and closely related to White and Black Tai, is spoken in northwestern Vietnam and in contiguous parts of Laos. A frequent question addresses the place of origin of Red Tai speakers. Gedney (1964: 4) notes that many Red Tai speakers refer to their place of origin as *muaŋ^4 lɛɛŋ^1* (Red Town) in northern Vietnam while others claim that they originated in the area of the Red River. He notes further that the Red Town theory is supported by the texts collected by the missionary J. B. DeGeorge in Yên Khương (*muaŋ^4 lɛɛŋ^1*) in Thanh Hoa province in the early part of the twentieth century. In a series of publications in the journal *Anthropos*, DeGeorge provided extensive examples of folktales and legends (1921–22, 1923–24, 1925) as well as proverbs and maxims (1927, 1928). While there are problems with DeGeorge's transcriptions (see appendix for comments), his collection of proverbs and maxims is important because it provides a window on the techniques and types of oral literature found in Tai dialects other than those found in Siamese and Lao. In particular, the Red Tai material

---

[4] Bouyei tones include: 1 – low-rising; 2 – low-falling; 3 – mid level (same as tone 8 on checked syllables); 4 – high-falling; 5 – high-rising (same as tone 7 on checked syllables); 6 – high level.

demonstrates the striking use of parallelism in various forms that has come to be associated with literary examples in Tai dialects.

In his 1927 'Proverbes, maxims et sentences Tays', DeGeorge records 112 different maxims ranging from one line to couplets of two and sets of three lines. Separate from these maxims is a collection from 1928 of 69 more proverbs plus, in a separate entry, 71 counsels of advice that have been transcribed 'faithfully' (*fidèlement*) from the notebook of a Red Tai noble by the name of Phia Nam (*phia³ naam⁴*) or Lương-Văn-Ky (p. 609).[5] While there is no written evidence to substantiate the claim, it seems reasonable to assume that these 71 maxims form a single continuous text. First and foremost, they are an oral form that has been converted to a written form, probably to serve as a permanent source of reference located in one place. Because they belong to a notable of the village who traditionally looks out for the welfare of the village, one can also surmise that they are used for instructional purposes, advice, and counsel as to how one is to live (or rule) so as to maintain a smooth functioning society. Their grouping together further suggests that they might be used as a single, continuous text or as a source for individual proverbs suited to a particular problem or occasion. Second and most importantly, unlike the other 182 proverbs, these 71 are linked to one another phonologically, syntactically, and semantically. In other words, they complete a single interlocking text that can function as a unique composition.

2   The text as a whole

In their most general form, these Red Tai proverbs are written in a series of lines ranging from four to six syllables connected by occasional rhyme. This template corresponds to the Siamese verse form known as *raay³*. While Siamese has a number of different forms (*raay³ boo¹raan¹*, *raay³ su²phaap³*, *raay³ dan³*, *raay³ yaaw¹*), the basic template consists of a series of five-syllable lines (*wak⁴*) connected by a rhyme between the end syllable of one line with one of the first three syllables of the following line.[6] The addition of tonal requirements (*raay³ su²phaap³* and *raay³ dan³*) as well as syllable type (*raay³ boo¹raan¹*) and syllable number (*raay³ yaaw¹*) account for the different varieties in Siamese.

The simplest and oldest form appears to be *raay³ yaaw¹*, which allows any number of syllables per line, although five to six syllables and six to eight appear to be the favoured sequences. In addition, rhyme may occur, but is not required, between the final syllable of a line, known as *soŋ²*, and any syllable in the next, known as *rap⁴*, as long as the syllables are not one and the same.

---

[5] See the appendix for the complete text and a note on the transcription used.
[6] Thai tones: 1 – mid; 2 – low; 3 – falling; 4 – high; 5 – rising.

Moreover, unlike other verse forms, identical tones between syllables need not be followed. It is this type of verse type used in the Red Tai text. The following sequence from the text (lines /5–8/) has sequences of eight, five, six, and six syllables per line respectively:[7]

/5/   pen^1 khun^1 pen^1 naay^4, h𝑟𝑟^3 hak^6 luuk^6 muu^4 (eight syllables)
        be-noble-be-chief-make-love-child-group
        'If you're a chief, then love your subordinates.'

/6/   pen^{1}puu^2, h𝑟𝑟^3 hak^6 laan^1 (five syllables)
        be-grandfather-make-love-grandchildren
        'If you're a grandfather, then love your grandchildren.'

/7/   pen^1 kwaan^3, h𝑟𝑟^3 hak^6 luuk^6 baan^3 (six syllables)
        be-mandarin-make-love-child-village
        'If you're a ruler, then love your people.'

/8/   pen^1 caw^6, h𝑟𝑟^3 tat^1 hit^6 khɔɔŋ^4 (six syllables)
        be-prince-make-establish-customs
        'If you're a prince, then lay down traditions.'

This series also exhibits the non-required rhyme sequences between lines: *muu^4* in line /5/ with *puu^2* in line /6/; *laan^1* in line /6/ with *kwaan^3* in line /7/; but no rhyme between lines /7/ and /8/. The seventy-one-line text, then, consists of a series of lines that range from five to eight syllables connected by intermittent rhyme. Semantically, the text is a series of wise counsels used by an elder for instructional purposes.

3   The internal structure of the text

The seventy-one lines of counsel can be divided into sections that are semantically parallel. This parallelism is highlighted by a repeated syntactic frame that contributes to the isolation of a particular section (Matisoff 1991: 18). There are roughly five separate sections.

3.1   *Appropriate actions in appropriate places (lines /1–30/)*

Each line in this section begins with an implied if-clause with no corresponding morph in the Red Tai followed by *h𝑟𝑟^3* 'make, do': (if) xxxxx, *h𝑟𝑟^3* xxxxx.

/1/   yaak^2 khap^1, h𝑟𝑟^3 yɛɛŋ^4 tii^5 muan^5
        want-sing-do-aim-place-merry
        'If you want to sing, then seek out a merry place.'

---

[7] Examples that refer to 'lines' of the extended text are in slanted brackets to disambiguate them from other linguistic examples that appear in parentheses.

/12/   pen^1 caa^6, hɰɰ^3 hian^4 sut^1
be-stupid-do-study-end
'If one is stupid, then study thoroughly.'

This section is further divided into subsections based upon the initial word that begins the line as shown in the examples following.

(if) *puan^1* xxxxx, *hɰɰ^3* xxxxx (lines /3–4/).
/3/   puan^1 thii^2, hɰɰ^3 thii^2 lɛɛn^5
others-stingy-do-stingy-return
'If others are stingy, then be stingy in return.'

(if) *pen^1* xxxxx, *hɰɰ^3* xxxxx (lines /5–8/)
/6/   pen^1 puu^2, hɰɰ^3 hak^6 laan^1
be-grandfather-do-love-grandchildren
'If you're a grandfather, then love your grandchildren.'

(if) *yaak^2* xxxxx, *hɰɰ^3* xxxxx (lines /1–2/, /19–29/)
/24/   yaak^2 khaw^3 huam^5, hɰɰ^3 hian^4 hit^6 khɔɔŋ^4
want-enter-together-do-study-customs
'If you want to live with others, then study their traditions.'

3.2   *How to maintain proper decorum (lines /31–40/)*

Each line in this section begins with *ɲaa^4* 'don't': *ɲaa^4* xxxxx. The opening maxim, number 31, however, is slightly longer, beginning with an if-clause which is then followed by the syntactic pattern that begins with *ɲaa^4*. In some respects this slight break with the syntactic pattern in the following lines announces a new topic for that section, with the following nine lines completing the meaning. To complete the linkage, this line is connected to the next by the rhyme between *lɰɰ^4* in line /31/ and *khɰɰ^3* in line /32/:

/31/   yaak^2 ʔet^1 kun^4, ɲaa^4 ciaw^5 phuu^3 lɰɰ^4
want-do-person-don't-incline-person-any
'If you want to be a man, then don't follow just anyone.'

/32/   ɲaa^4 yuu^2 khɰɰ^3 phuu^3 thɔy^2
don't-be-near-person-deceitful
'Don't go near deceitful people.'

Following these introductory lines, the syntactic pattern becomes regular in the next eight lines:

ɲaa^4 xxxxx

/35/   ɲaa^4 luuum^4 phuu^3 thaw^3
don't-forget-person-old
'Don't forget the aged.'

/36/   ɲaa^4 kaw^1 kun^4 baap^2
don't-scratch-person-sin
'Don't associate with sinners.'

/37/   ɲaa^4 tɯɯ^1 haap^2 lɯa^1 hɛɛŋ^4
don't-carry-load-exceed-strength
'Don't carry loads that exceed your strength.'

/38/   ɲaa^4 kɛɛ^5 kun^4 dii^1
don't-reproach-person-good
'Don't reproach good people.'

3.3   How to avoid inappropriate actions (lines /41–49/)

The initial clause of the line begins with an implied 'if' and ends with *bɔɔ^2 kuan^4* plus a verb 'not appropriate to do something'. The concluding clause follows with *ɲaa^4* 'don't' and the repeated verb: (if) xxxxx, *bɔɔ^2 kuan^4* verb, *ɲaa^4* verb:

(if) xxxxx, *bɔɔ^2 kuan^4* verb, *ɲaa^4* verb
/43/   khwaay^4 yuu^2 thuun^5, bɔɔ^2 kuan^1 khaay^1, ɲaa^4 khaay^1
buffalo-be at-under the house-not-appropriate-sell-don't-sell
'If it's not appropriate to sell the buffalo under the house, then don't sell it.'

/49/   hɤɤ^3 bɔɔ^2 kuan^4 ʔaw^1, ɲaa^4 ʔaw^1
give-not-appropriate-take-don't-take
'If it's not appropriate to take something given, then don't take it.'

3.4   How to benefit in given situations (/lines 50–59/)

Each line begins with an implied if-clause which is then followed by *hɤɤ^3* 'do, make': (if) xxxxx, *hɤɤ^3* xxxxx:

(if) xxxxx, *hɤɤ^3* xxxxx
/52/   baan^3 mii^4 baaw^2, hɤɤ^3 hak^6 pɔɔ^5 mɛɛ^5 phuu^3 saaw^1
village-have-young men-do-love-parents-young woman
'If a village has young men, then become skilled with young girl's parents.'

/53/   yaam^4 naaw^1, hɤɤ^3 hak^6 huk^2
period-cold-do-love-weave
'If it's the cold season, then learn to love weaving.'

As in Section 3.1, subgroups are formed depending upon the initial word following the implied 'if':

(if) *baan^3* xxxxx, *hɤɤ^3* xxxxx (/50–52/)
/51/   baan^3 mii^4 sɯa^1, hɤɤ^3 hak^6 caaŋ^5 haaw^2
village-have-tiger-do-love-skill-trap
'If a village has tigers, then become skilled with traps.'

Maxims 54–59 also form a subgroup in which the implied 'if' is followed by the verb hak^6 'love' and then $caŋ^2$ 'then': (if) hak^6 xxxxx, $caŋ^2$ xxxxx:

(if) hak^6 xxxxx, $caŋ^2$ xxxxx
/58/   hak^6 kham^4 luaŋ^1, caŋ^2 mii^4 ?an^4 sɤɤ^4 tay^5
love-gold-yellow-then-have-thing-put-bag
'If you love gold, then you have something to put in your bag.'

3.5   *Dangers to the village or individual (lines /60–71/)*

Each line begins with the perceived enemy (a noun) and then concludes with the assertion that it is an enemy ($kɔɔ^2$ sak^1): xxxxx, $kɔɔ^2$ sak^1:

xxxxx, $kɔɔ^2$ sak^1
/60/   khaw^3 yuu^2 yia^5, kɔɔ^2 sak^1
rice-be at-granary-then-enemy
'Rice in the granary is an enemy.'

/70/   ɲaa^4 ?ɔɔk^2 bɔɔ^2, kɔɔ^2 sak^1
rice field-go out-spring-then-enemy
'A rice field with a spring is an enemy.'

4   Parallelism within syntactic strings

As noted above the entire text can be divided into five sections, with the general syntactic parallelism highlighting each section of semantic parallelism. Within each of these syntactic strings there is a corresponding repetition of the same classes of phrases and words.

Section 3.1. The basic syntactic string is (if) xxxxx, $hɤɤ^3$ xxxxx. Following the implied 'if' a verb or noun sets a condition followed by $hɤɤ^3$, a verb, and frequently an object.

Section 3.2. The basic syntactic string here is $ɲaa^4$ xxxxx. Following the negative imperative marker is a verb and most often an object.

Section 3.3. The basic syntactic string is (if) xxxxx, $bɔɔ^2$ $kuan^4$ + verb, $ɲaa^4$ + verb. Following the implied 'if' is a noun and verb most often, then the negative phrase $bɔɔ^2$ $kuan^4$ + verb, the negative imperative with the same verb.

Section 3.4. The basic syntactic string is (if) xxxxx, $hɤɤ^3$ xxxxx. Following the implied 'if' is a noun, verb, and object, then $hɤɤ^3$, a verb, and an object.

Section 3.5. The basic syntactic string is xxxxx, $kɔɔ^2$ sak^1. Most frequently there is a noun, verb, and noun followed by $kɔɔ^2$ sak^1.

5   Siamese proverbs

Turning to Siamese, one finds a similar collection of maxims that reveals how to live in harmony and happiness, *The maxims of Phra Ruang* (in Thai

Su²phaa¹sit² Phra?⁴ Ruaŋ³). The dating and identity of the author of this collection remains problematic with a number of theories circulating. Probably the most common theory is based upon the linguistic and lexical similarities of the collection to the Ramkhamhaeng Inscription. Coupled with that is the traditional belief that King Ramkhamhaeng (1279–98) actually met and taught his subjects using these maxims. These two claims combined suggest that King Ramkhamhaeng is the actual author. A second theory holds Phya Lithai (1346–74) to be the author. This theory arises from Phya Lithai's authorship of the Buddhist cosmology *Three worlds according to King Ruang*, translated by Frank E. Reynolds and Mani B. Reynolds (1982). Both of these theories attribute the composition to the Sukhothai Period (1240–1438). Other claims hold that the work is a far more recent composition, one made during the Ratanakosin era (1782–present) by Prince Paramanuchit Chinorot (1790–1853). Finally there are those who believe that no single author existed and that the collection was compiled over a period of time by a number of different individuals.

Dating and authorship aside, the text represents a more rigorous phonological arrangement of maxims. The maxims fall into a section 174 lines long, not including a nine-line introduction and a ten-line coda, with nearly every line exactly five syllables in length. In lines of more than five syllables (six and seven syllables, for example), the extra syllables are primarily short and easily elided in a recitation, for example, *pra²* in the following:

(33)   yaa² pra²maat² thaan³ phuu³ dii¹   (six syllables with one short syllable)
don't-demean-elder-person-good
'Don't belittle nobles.'

On the other hand, without fail, every line is connected by a rhyme between the last syllable of the line with one of the first three syllables of the next line. In the following, *tɔɔp³* and *chɔɔp³* complete the couplet:

(54)   thii³ phit² chuay³ tɯan¹ tɔɔp³ (five syllables)
that-error-help-advise-answer
'To those in error, offer advice.'

(55)   thii³ chɔɔp³ chuay³ yok⁴ yɔɔ¹ (five syllables)
that-like-help-praise
'To those in favour, offer praise.'

Syllable number and rhyme appear to be the dominant parallel features that determine the construction of the entire text. Unlike the Red Tai text, the topics are not arranged in semantically parallel sections. Thus maxims dealing with behaviour toward royalty, for example, can be found in several different places. Other topics include respect toward one's elders, loyalty toward the king and court, friendship, relations with others, everyday life, and ways to protect oneself. This haphazard arrangement of content could be attributed to the need to rhyme one line (one proverb) with another, assuming that the proverbs functioned as single lines of advice that were later combined into a continuous text whether by King Ramkhamhaeng or by a later author. While certain lines are syntactically parallel, there is no clear division of sections based on syntax.

6   Conclusion

Syllable number, rhyme, and parallel syntactic strings dominate single lines (i.e. proverbs) as well as longer compositions created from those lines. In the Red Tai text, all three devices are employed whereas in the Siamese only two. Because both of these texts can be used as a single composition or separated into individual lines (both cases used for teaching purposes), one would like to surmise that the devices that united them into a single unit could and would be used in other compositions in which the overall meaning would extend beyond the individual line or couplet. In fact this is the case. In a 1992 study of a Black Tai (Tai Dam) origin myth, Hartmann demonstrates that the text is also dependent upon the devices discerned in the Red Tai and Siamese proverbs. At the same time, he mentions a collection of Black Tai proverbs compiled by Ha Văn Năm (1978) in which the proverbs favour the rhymed couplet in lines of five to seven syllables (Hartmann 1992: 270). Snyder's study of the Northern Tai Bouyei proverbs also demonstrates the preference for the rhymed couplet. The conclusion reached, then, suggests that proverbs, and their elaborated structural components, are one of the paramount influences, and even the potential source, of the more formal poetic compositions that occur throughout the Tai language family. The rhymed couplet certainly appears to be the basis of verse forms, with the Red Tai and Siamese examples showing that when combined into larger units the same devices contribute to the construction of the overall composition.

7   Appendix: Red Tai text

For his Red Tai data, DeGeorge used the transcription system used by Guignard in his 1912 *Dictionnaire Laotien–Français*. Here that system has been changed, with a few modifications, to a phonetic system based on Mary Haas's (1964) Thai dictionary. As for DeGeorge's data, Gedney (1964: 4) notes that the Red Tai 'is accurately recorded for the most part, but for many words there is an occasional inconsistency in the marking of tones'. There are also occasional inconsistencies in the spelling. At this point, there is no way of knowing the sources for these inconsistencies, whether they are printing errors, transcription errors, or the result of dialect mixtures. In other cases, the *breve*, indicating a short vowel, had to be eliminated because of other diacritics above that vowel. Because this study has dealt with text building and not lexical phonetics, no attempt has been made to correct those inconsistencies, and they appear here as they do in the original publication. Commas within each line, added by DeGeorge, separate the natural speech groups of two and three syllables into which Tai languages tend to fall.[8]

1.   yaak² khap¹, hɤɤ³ yɛɛŋ⁴ tii⁵ muan⁵
        want-sing-do-aim-place-merry
        If you want to sing, then seek out a merry place.

2.   yaak² pay¹ buan⁴, hɤɤ³ tuuu¹ haap² bɛɛm¹ baw¹
        want-go-trade-do-carry-load-basket-light
        If you want to trade, then carry light baskets.

3.   puuan¹ thii², hɤɤ³ thii² lɛɛn⁵
        others-stingy-do-stingy-return
        With the stingy, be stingy in return.

4.   puuan¹ pɛɛn⁴, hɤɤ³ pɛɛn⁴ tɔɔ²
        others-generous-do-generous-toward
        With the generous, be generous in return.

5.   pen¹ khun¹ pen¹ naay⁴, hɤɤ³ hak⁶ luuk⁶ muu⁴
        be-noble-be-chief-do-love-child-group
        If you're a chief, then love your subordinates.

6.   pen¹ puu², hɤɤ³ hak⁶ laan¹
        be-grandfather-do-love-grandchildren
        If you're a grandfather, then love your grandchildren.

7.   pen¹ kwaan³, hɤɤ³ hak⁶ luuk⁶ baan³
        be-ruler-do-love-child-village
        If you're a ruler, then love your people.

8.   pen¹ caw⁶, hɤɤ³ tat¹ hiit⁶ khɔɔŋ⁴
        be-prince-do-establish-customs
        If you're a prince, then lay down traditions

9.   yaak² huu⁶, ɲaa⁴ kaaw⁴ khwaam⁴ khɛɛŋ¹
        want-know-don't-argue-speech-hard
        If you want to know something, then don't dispute what's said.

---

[8] Approximate Red Tai tones include: 1 – rising; 2 – low; 3 – falling; 4 – mid; 5 – high-falling; 6 – high-rising.

10.   tii^5 phit^1, h$\gamma\gamma^3$ ʔɔɔn^2 khwaam^4 baw^6
      place-error-do-soft-speech-speak
      When there's an error, use sweet speech.

11.   tii^5 mɔɔŋ^4, h$\gamma\gamma^3$ khat^4 sii^4
      place-sad-do-resist-guard
      Wherever there's sadness, resist it.

12.   pen^1 caa^6, h$\gamma\gamma^3$ hian^4 sut^1
      be-stupid-do-study-end
      If stupid, then study thoroughly.

13.   haap^2 cii^4 luut^2, h$\gamma\gamma^3$ hiit^4 pɛɛŋ^1
      load-about to-slip-do-make-fix
      If the load is about to slip, then adjust it.

14.   kin^1 kɛɛŋ^1 hɔɔn^6, h$\gamma\gamma^3$ hiit^4 paw^2
      eat-soup-hot-do-make-blow
      If the soup is hot, then blow on it.

15.   hua^{1}c$\gamma\gamma^1$ maw^4, h$\gamma\gamma^3$ hiit^4 haay^4
      heart-drunk-do-make-lay on the back
      If you're disturbed, then lie on your back.

16.   m$\gamma\gamma^3$ ci^2 taay^1, h$\gamma\gamma^3$ huu^6 bɯaŋ^1
      when-about to-die-do-know-inform
      When you're about to die, then inform your heirs.

17.   khua^1 tii^5 bɯaŋ^3, h$\gamma\gamma^3$ hiit^4 say^4
      bridge-place-sink-do-make-repair
      If the bridge sags, then repair it.

18.   m$\gamma\gamma^1$ luuk^6 pay^1, ɲaa^4 caa^1 tɔɔ^5 khwaam^4 lɛɛn^4
      when-child-go out-don't-intend-toward-speech-return
      When a child goes out, don't plan to go with them.

19.   yaak^2 nɔɔn^4 tɛɛm^1, h$\gamma\gamma^3$ mii^4 khwaam^4 caa^1
      want-sleep-?-do-have-speech-intend
      If you want to sleep, then ask permission.

20.   yaak^2 mii^4 ʔok^1, h$\gamma\gamma^3$ man^2 phaw^4 caw^6
      want-have-chest-do-firm-serve-prince
      If you want dignity, then loyally serve your prince.

21.   yaak^2 kin^1 khaw^3, h$\gamma\gamma^3$ man^2 thaam^1 thiam^4 hay^5 naa^4
      want-eat-rice-do-firm-diligent-dry field-rice field
      If you want to eat, then diligently work the fields.

22.   yaak^2 mii^4 paa^1, h$\gamma\gamma^3$ thaam^1 thiam^4 kɔɔŋ^1 huum^6
      want-have-fish-do-diligently-thing-cover
      If you want fish, then diligently set traps.

23. yaak^2 pay^1 liin^3, hɤɤ^3 thaam^1 tii^5 hak^6
    want-go-play-do-ask-place-love
    If you want to play, then seek a place you love.

24. yaak^2 khaw^3 huam^5, hɤɤ^3 hian^4 hiit^6 khɔɔŋ^4
    want-enter-together-do-study-customs
    If you want to live with others, then study their traditions.

25. yaak^2 ʔet^1 bun^1, hɤɤ^3 pɛɛŋ^1 hɯan^4 khɤɤ^3 vat^1
    want-make-merit-do-repair-house-near-temple
    If you want to make merit, then build houses near a temple.

26. yaak^2 khaa^3 sat^1, hɤɤ^3 pɛɛŋ^1 hɯan^4 khɤɤ^3 paa^2
    want-kill-animal-do-repair-house-near-forest
    If you want to hunt, then build houses near the forest.

27. yaak^2 khuuy^2 maa^6, hɤɤ^3 phaŋ^4 khwaam^4 phuu^3 thaw^3
    want-ride-horse-do-listen-speech-old man
    If you want to ride horses, then listen to the old men.

28. yaak^2 kin^{1}law^3, hɤɤ^3 caa^1 tɛɛ^2 khwaam^4 law^3
    want-drink-liquor-do-intend-only-speech-liquor
    If you want to drink wine, then just do that.

29. yaak^2 khaw^3 nɔɔn^4, hɤɤ^3 caa^1 tɛɛ^2 khwaam^4 nɔɔn^4
    want-enter-sleep-do-intend-only-speech-sleep
    If you want to sleep, then just do that.

30. khwaam^4 lɤɤ^4 dii^1 ŋaam^4, saŋ^2 sɔɔn^1 luuk^6 mia^4
    speech-which-good-beautiful-do-teach-child-wife
    With language that is appropriate, teach your children and wife.

31. yaak^2 ʔet^1 kun^4, ɲaa^4 ciaw^5 phuu^3 lɤɤ^4
    want-do-person-don't-incline-person-any
    If you want to be a man, then don't follow just anyone.

32. ɲaa^4 yuu^2 khɤɤ^3 phuu^3 thɔy^2
    don't-be-near-person-deceitful
    Don't go near deceitful people.

33. ɲaa^4 yam^5 khan^4 naa^4
    don't-tread-dikes-rice field
    Don't trample the dikes in the rice field.

34. ɲaa^4 khwaa^4 phaa^1 tuu^2
    don't-close-door
    Don't close the door.

35. ɲaa^4 lɯɯm^4 phuu^3 thaw^3
    don't-forget-old person
    Don't forget the aged.

36.   ɲaa⁴ kaw¹ kun⁴ baap²
        don't-scratch-person-sin
        Don't associate with sinners.

37.   ɲaa⁴ tɯɯ¹ haap² lɯa¹ hɛɛŋ⁴
        don't-carry-load-exceed-strength
        Don't carry loads that exceed your strength.

38.   ɲaa⁴ kɛɛ⁵ kun⁴ dii¹
        don't-reproach-good people
        Don't reproach good people.

39.   ɲaa⁴ tii¹ kun⁴ khun²
        don't-hit-person-merit
        Don't injure the virtuous.

40.   ɲaa⁴ han² thot⁶ thuɯɯŋ¹ khiiŋ⁴ too⁴
        don't-attribute-punishment-reach-body-self
        Don't punish yourself.

41.   kay² yuu² lɔɔk⁶, bɔɔ² kuan⁴ khaa³, ɲaa⁴ khaa³
        chicken-be-not-appropriate-kill-don't-kill
        If it's not appropriate to kill the chicken in the henhouse, then don't kill it.

42.   maa⁶ yuu² huuŋ⁵ too⁴, bɔɔ² kuan⁴ khaay¹, ɲaa⁴ khaay¹
        horse-be-stable-self-not-appropriate-sell-don't-sell
        If it's not appropriate to sell the horse in the stable, then don't sell it.

43.   khwaay⁴ yuu² thuun⁵, bɔɔ² kuan⁴ khaay¹, ɲaa⁴ khaay¹
        buffalo-be-under the house-not-appropriate-sell-don't-sell
        If it's not appropriate to sell the buffalo under the house, then don't sell it.

44.   hin¹ khwaay¹ pɯan¹, bɔɔ² kuan⁴ khaa³, ɲaa⁴ khaa³
        see-buffalo-other-not-appropriate-kill-don't-kill
        If it's not appropriate to kill another's buffalo, then don't kill it.

45.   hiŋ⁴ bɔɔ² kuan⁴ nan⁴, ɲaa⁴ nan⁴
        bell-not-appropriate-shake-don't-shake
        If it's not appropriate to ring the bell, then don't ring it.

46.   khan⁴ bɔɔ² kuan⁴ kaw¹, ɲaa⁴ kaw¹
        itch-not-appropriate-scratch-don't-scratch
        If it's not appropriate to scratch an itch, then don't scratch it.

47.   hen¹ naa³ pɯan¹, bɔɔ² kuan⁴ ɲiŋ⁴, ɲaa⁴ ɲiŋ⁴
        see-crossbow-other-not-appropriate-shoot-don't-shoot
        If it's not appropriate to shoot another's crossbow, then don't shoot it.

48.   naw⁵ bɔɔ² kuan⁴ khɤɤ³, ɲaa⁴ khɤɤ³
        rotten-not-appropriate-near-don't-near
        If it's not appropriate to go near something rotten, then don't go near it.

49. hɤɤ³ bɔɔ² kuan⁴ ʔaw¹, ɲaa⁴ ʔaw¹
     give-not-appropriate-take-don't-take
     If it's not appropriate to take something given, then don't take it.

50. baan³ too⁴ yuu² khɤɤ³ taa⁵, hɤɤ³ hak⁶ caaŋ⁵ hɯa⁴
     village-self-be-near-river-do-love-skill-boat
     If your village is near a river, become skilled with boats.

51. baan³ mii⁴ sɯa¹, hɤɤ³ hak⁶ caaŋ⁵ haaw²
     village-have-tiger-do-love-skill-trap
     If a village has tigers, become skilled with traps.

52. baan³ mii⁴ baaw², hɤɤ³ hak⁶ pɔɔ⁵ mɛɛ⁵ phuu³ saaw¹
     village-have-young men-do-love-parents-young girl
     If a village has young men, become skilled with young girl's parents.

53. yaam⁴ naaw¹, hɤɤ³ hak⁶ huk²
     time period-cold-do-love-weave
     If it's the cold season, then learn to love weaving.

54. hak⁶ phaay⁴ hak⁶ ʔaay¹, khaay¹ laay¹ caŋ² mii⁴ khwaam⁴ caa¹
     love-cotton-love-father-sell-much-then-have-speech-intention
     If you love cotton, love the father and sell much, then you can aspire.
     hak⁶ loŋ⁴taa¹ caŋ² day³ khɯn⁴ kaa⁵
     love-father-in-law-then-get-return-price
     If you love your father-in-law, then the bride price is returned.

55. hak⁶ pɔɔ⁵ puu² mɛɛ⁵ yaa⁵, caŋ² day³ sɯɯp² khaw³ tɛɛn⁴ muun⁴
     love-husband's father-husband's mother-then-get-they-?-heritage
     If you love your husband's parents, then you'll gain their property.

56. hak⁶ puun¹ puu⁴, caŋ² mii⁴ ʔan⁴ kap¹ maak²
     love-lime-betel-then-have-thing-with-areca nut
     If you love lime and betel, then you have something for areca nuts

57. hak⁶ phuu³ caaŋ⁵ paak² caaŋ⁵ baw⁶, caŋ² mii⁴ phuu³ khut⁶ khwaam⁴ mɯaŋ⁴
     love-person-skill-speak-skill-speak-then-have-person-think-affair-city
     If you love a skilled speaker, then you have someone to consider the city's
     affairs.

58. hak⁶ kham⁴ lɯaŋ¹, caŋ² mii⁴ ʔan⁴ sɤɤ⁴ tay⁵
     love-gold-yellow-then-have-thing-put-bag
     If you love gold, then you have something to put in your bag.

59. hak⁶ pay⁵ nɔy⁶, caŋ² mii⁴ phuu³ tɯɯ¹ haap² nam⁴ laŋ¹ khɔy³ laay¹
     love-freeman-little-then-have-person-carry-load-follow-behind-slave-many
     If you love commoners, then you'll have someone to carry loads and many
     slaves.

60. khaw^3 yuu^2 yia^5, kɔɔ^2 sak^1
rice-be-granary-then-enemy
Rice in the granary is an enemy.

61. kay^2 yuu^2 law^6, kɔɔ^2 sak^1
chicken-be-coop-then-enemy
Chickens in a coop are an enemy.

62. mia^4 nɔɔn^4 saaŋ^3, kɔɔ^2 sak^1
wife-sleep-side-then-enemy
A wife sleeping on her side is an enemy.

63. caaŋ^6 yuu^2 huuŋ^4, kɔɔ^2 sak^1
elephant-be-stable-then-enemy
Elephants in the stable are an enemy.

64. pen^1 phuuŋ^5 yuu^2 huam^5 baan^3, kɔɔ^2 sak^1
have disease-leprosy-be-together-village-then-enemy
Lepers together in the village are enemies.

65. khii^3 caan^6 yuu^2 huam^5 huɯan^4, kɔɔ^2 sak^1
lazy-be-together-house-then-enemy
Lazy people together in a house are enemies.

66. taa^1 luɯan^3 huam^5, kɔɔ^2 sak^1
eye-blur-together-then-enemy
Those with the evil eye are enemies.

67. phuu^3 thaw^3 mii^4 mia^4 saaw^1, kɔɔ^2 sak^1
old men-have-wife-young girl-then-enemy
Old men with young wives are enemies.

68. fay^4 sum^1 vay^6, kɔɔ^2 sak^1
fire-burn-keep-then-enemy
An ignored burning fire is an enemy.

69. hay^5 huam^5 ʔet^1, kɔɔ^2 sak^1
field-together-one-then-enemy
A field worked with others is an enemy.

70. naa^4 ʔɔɔk^2 bɔɔ^2, kɔɔ^2 sak^1
rice field-go out-spring-then-enemy
A ricefield with a spring is an enemy.

71. phuu^3 haay^6 sɔɔ^3 khɔɔt^4 sia^1, kɔɔ^2 sak^1
person-evil-dispute-lose-then-enemy
Evil men quarreling are enemies.

150   *Thomas John Hudak*

References

Bhamorabutr, A. 1985. *King Ruang's maxims.* Bangkok: Department of Corrections Press.

DeGeorge, J. B. 1921–1922. Légendes des Tay, Annam. *Anthropos* 16–17: 109–146, 633–656.

1923–1924. Légendes des Tay, Annam. *Anthropos* 18–19: 40–68.

1925. Légendes des Tay, Annam. *Anthropos* 20: 496–515, 952–980.

1927. Proverbes, maxims et sentences Tays. *Anthropos* 22: 911–932.

1928. Proverbes, maxims et sentences Tays. *Anthropos* 23: 596–616.

Gedney, W. J. 1964. A comparative sketch of White, Black, and Red Tai. *The social science review* 14: 1–47.

Guignard, T. 1912. *Dictionnaire Laotien–Français.* Hong Kong: Imprimerie Nazareth.

Ha Văn Năm. 1978. *Thai proverbs* (In Vietnamese). Hanoi.

Haas, M.R. 1964. *Thai–English student's dictionary.* Stanford University Press.

Hartmann, J. F. 1992. 'Tai Dam poetics and Proto-Tai tone categories'. In C. J. Compton and J. F. Hartmann (eds.), *Papers on Tai languages, linguistics, and literatures.* DeKalb, IL: Center for Southeast Asian Studies, Northern Illinois University Press, pp. 262–277.

Hudak, T. J. 1994. *William J. Gedney's Southwestern Tai dialects: glossaries, texts, and translations.* Ann Arbor, MI: Michigan Papers on South and Southeast Asia, The University of Michigan.

1996. *William J. Gedney's The Lue Language: glossary, texts, and translations.* Ann Arbor, MI: Michigan Papers on South and Southeast Asia, The University of Michigan.

Matisoff, J. 1991. Syntactic parallelism and morphological elaboration in Lahu religious poetry, unpublished paper, University of California, Berkeley.

Reynolds, F. E and M. B. Reynolds. 1982. *Three worlds according to King Ruang: a Thai Buddhist cosmology.* Berkeley: Berkeley Buddhist Studies Series, University of California Press.

Snyder, D. 2000. 'Folk wisdom in Bouyei proverbs and songs'. In S. Burusphat (ed.), *Proceedings: the international conference on Tai studies, July 29–31, 1998.* Bangkok, Thailand: Institute of Language and Culture for Rural Development, Mahidol University, pp. 61–87.

9   Lexicalized poetry in Sui

James N. Stanford

1   Introduction*

This study investigates 'lexicalized poetry' in Sui, a Tai-Kadai language of southwest China. Sui adjective modifiers have strikingly aesthetic patterns of rhyme and alliteration that are neither fully predictable nor productive. Stanford (2007a–b) provided a lexicon and morphophonological analysis of these modifiers, using data from a single Sui speaker in order to focus the formal analysis. The present study expands the fieldwork investigation into cross-dialectal variation and discourse, thereby gaining a wider perspective on the range and role of this aesthetic feature of Sui. After all, Jakobson (1960) suggested that poetic effects occur in everyday speech in all languages. The present study shows that Jakobson's notion can be taken one step further: some languages, like Sui, have systematic poetic effects embedded within the lexicon itself.

Sui word-specific adjective intensifiers have complex patterns of partial reduplication, rhyme, and alliteration that are neither fully predictable nor productive. A few examples are provided in (1).[1] (Tones are represented with superscript numbers, as discussed in Section 3.1.)

(1) xom^3 'sour'   → $xom^3 tom^4$ 'very sour'
        $pj\varepsilon k^7$ 'dirty'   → $pj\varepsilon k^7 lj\varepsilon k^7$ 'very dirty'
        $\kappa o\eta^5$ 'young'   → $\kappa o\eta^5 \kappa\varepsilon w^3$ 'very young'
        za^3 'light'   → $za^3 zu^1$ 'very light'

Sui adjective intensifiers are 'word-specific' in the sense that a root has a unique intensifying affix, which is not attested elsewhere in the language, except for occasional phonological coincidences. Stanford provides a lexicon of Sui adjective intensifiers (2007b) and uses Optimality Theory to analyse morphophonological patterns (2007a). In particular, he finds a tendency for

---

* I would like to thank the Sui people for their kind assistance in this project. Thanks also to Jerold Edmondson, Dennis Preston, John Haiman, Yen-Hwei Lin, Grover Hudson, David Dwyer, David Peterson, and Tim Pulju.
[1] Sui also has a few generic intensifying expressions such as εo^3 'very' that can be used with any root adjective, such as $\kappa o\eta^5$ 'young' → $\kappa o\eta^5 \varepsilon o^3$ 'very young.'

coronal onsets in the partially reduplicated intensifiers, as well as a set of statistically significant tendencies for tonal correspondences between roots and intensifiers. Those prior studies focused on a single Sui speaker in order to simplify and narrow the analysis. The present study expands into dialect variation and discourse, considering the phenomenon from a wider perspective to gain a fuller grasp on the range and roles of these aesthetic devices. The results show that this Sui phenomenon may be viewed as 'lexicalized poetry'.

The remainder of the chapter is organized as follows. First, Section 2 discusses overall notions of poetry and lexicon, and provides discourse examples. Section 3 outlines the poetic patterns of Sui adjective intensifiers. Section 4 analyses intensifiers in four different Sui dialects, finding consistent poetic patterns despite variability in the specific intensifiers used in different dialects. Conclusions are given in Section 5.

2   Poetry, lexicon, and discourse

2.1   A false dichotomy

In traditional analyses, poetry and lexicon are often treated as two separate subjects. For example, when reading Tennyson's 'The Eagle', a literary analyst might discuss how Tennyson artfully used English lexical resources to compose an original poem filled with an aesthetic blend of alliteration, rhyme, assonance, metrics, imagery and affect:[2]

> The Eagle
> He clasps the crag with crooked hands;
> Close to the sun in lonely lands,
> Ring'd with the azure world, he stands.
>
> The wrinkled sea beneath him crawls;
> He watches from his mountain walls,
> And like a thunderbolt he falls.

In writing 'The Eagle', Tennyson creatively and agentively selected individual words from his mental lexicon and composed them into phrases and stanzas. It goes without saying that the poem itself did not exist until Tennyson wilfully composed it. Presumably, Tennyson is the first person who ever formed this particular sequence of words.

But can poetry also exist within the memorized lexicon of a language, such that every child naturally acquires it through the normal process of first-language acquisition? Of course, many well-known poems, lyrics, and popular

---

[2] 'The Eagle' by Alfred, Lord Tennyson, in Millgate (1963).

phrases enter a speaker's lexicon during childhood language acquisition and later. Most English speakers, for example, can easily complete the line 'Mary had a little lamb whose fleece was white as snow, and everywhere that Mary went _____.' Likewise, some of Tennyson's famous lines have entered the lexicon of English through frequent usage, such as 'Theirs not to reason why, Theirs but to do and die'[3] (or various alternations of that famous line). Similarly, Jakobson observes that poetic devices are commonly found within 'ordinary' speech, showing that poetic effects are not limited to the field of poetry:

A girl used to talk about "the horrible Harry."
"Why *horrible*? ...Why not *dreadful, terrible, frightful, disgusting*?"
[The girl replied], "I don't know why but *horrible* fits him better." (1960[1999: 57])

Speakers of all languages occasionally use such poetic devices in their everyday speech, and Jakobson and Waugh therefore suggest that 'both aspects of language, the ordinary and the poetic, are two copresent and coacting universals familiar to the human being from his first linguistic steps' (1979 [2002: 225]; cf. Haiman, this volume).

2.2   Lexicalized poetry in Sui

Evidence from Sui suggests that Jakobson and Wardhaugh's notion can be taken one step further. Not only is it the case that poetic devices are found in everyday speech in all languages, but certain languages have extensive poetic effects *systematically embedded within the lexicon*. For these languages, large and systematic sectors of the lexicon have 'poetic' patterns, e.g. Sui adjective intensifiers. As observed above, speakers of all languages have items like *Mary had a little lamb* as part of their memorized, readily accessible resources (lexicon), and some of those sequences include rhyme and other poetic devices. Moreover, English and other languages have a number of 'twin forms' like *jibber jabber* and *helter skelter* (Haiman, this volume). Yet *jibber jabber* and *Mary had a little lamb* are not a systematic part of the language; such features are usually not centred around any particular word classes, nor do they have a high degree of systematicity, patterned phonology, or frequent usage. By contrast, Sui and other languages in this volume have extensive, patterned systems of intensification and elaboration that may be viewed as lexicalized poetry. As Yip explains it, 'Humans have both an aptitude and a taste for creating repetitive sequences, and they may use this skill in a variety of ways that are more or less part of the core grammar of the language' (1999, quoted in Stanford 2007a).

---

[3] Tennyson, 'The Charge of the Light Brigade' in Millgate (1963).

2.3   *Sui intensifiers in discourse*

Sui adjective intensifiers are a frequent and vibrant part of daily discourse, commonly observed in everyday conversation as well as in traditional story telling. The following excerpts are taken from free narratives of a 20-year-old Sui woman as she told anecdotes from her own life experiences. Note how she uses intensifiers in moments requiring emphasis or to add affect. Intensifiers are shown in boldface.[4]

Story Excerpt (1)

a. ...jɯ   ai   kʰaːk   li fe   **ʔdaːi ʔdeu**
   each CLF diligent do make good-INT
   ...Everyone was careful to make everything very nice (laugh)

b. tsa   pjen   ʔnaŋ ti ai laːusə   ɕiŋ   Wu man tɔn kʰaːk li tɔ
   that finish have one CLF teacher surname – 3SG most careful do more
   Now there was a teacher named Wu. He got ready even more thoroughly than the rest. (laugh)

c. jinwei pʰinsə   man njʊt **ʔɣaːiɲaːi** pjam ku   man pu tjang   tifei me suk ha
   because usually 3SG beard long-INT hair   head 3SG also long.time some NEG wash NEG
   Because he usually wore a long beard, and he also hadn't washed his hair for a while. (laugh)

Story Excerpt (2)

a. ...hoŋ pɔ ka man tei   man paːi hoŋ pɔ   ʔban tsa, qɔ hei   ʔnjam ljeu
   let bull PL 3SG take 3SG go   let bull time that just almost dark   PFV
   ...When the people taking care of the bull took it to pasture, it was almost dark.

b. pɔ tsa qɔ tiet paːi **ʔdi ʔdiu** tʰaːu kang tsje...tsa hoŋ pɔ ka man me tsjak ʔniŋ ha
   bull that just along go far-INT search grass eat then let bull PL 3SG NEG careful look NEG
   The bull wandered far away looking for grass to eat... And the people taking care of the bull were not watching carefully.

c. tau ʔban ʔnjam pu   tʰaːu   **tjaŋ njaŋ**   pu tʰaːu me ʔdei tɔ   pɔ tsa...
   until time dark   also search long.time-INT also search NEG COMP CLF bull that
   When it got dark, they searched for a long time and still couldn't find the bull.

---

[4] Tones are omitted for simplicity here.

d. ni   ai   man qɔ ju ʔdei faːi   nu ʔbaːn   tɔŋ paːi tʰaːu tɔ   pɔ
   mother 1SG 3g   just call COMP brother child village together go search CLF
   tsa
   bull that
   My mother and the others called everyone in the village to go help search for that bull.

e. liu   saːn   paːi   tʰaːu   **ɕen ɕui**
   expend night   go   search exhausted-INT
   They searched all through the night, really exhausted.

Story Excerpt (3)

a. …ni   ai   ⁿdɔ man fan 'a! Wei, nja heɲu kʊtku   paːi le?'
   mother 1SG see him say -   -   2SG why   cut.hair go PRT
   …My mother saw him and said, 'Ah! Wei, why did you shave your head!?'

b. ni   ai ʁaːu loŋ   qɔ   **njit njɔ**
   mother 1SG inside stomach just cold-INT
   My mother's heart froze.

c. man sə   'heɲu he tsa? ɣɔsi   ailaːu man me   njaːu ha!'
   3SG think how do that maybe parent 3SG   NEG at NEG
   She thought, 'Why would he do that? Maybe one of his parents has died!'

3   Morphophonology of Sui adjective intensifiers

3.1   Language background

The Sui people are an indigenous ethnic minority in Guizhou province, China. A member of the Tai-Kadai language family (Edmondson et al. 2004; Edmondson and Solnit 1988; Zhang 1980; Li 1948, 1965; Zeng and Yao 1996), Sui is a largely monosyllabic, isolating, tonal language with approximately 300,000 speakers (Bradley 2007: 179). The present study is based on fieldwork in Sandu Sui Autonomous County in southeast Guizhou, widely considered the heart of Sui culture.

Table 9.1 shows tones for the Lu clan (Zhonghe region), using Chao's (1930) 1–5 pitch scale, e.g., 13=low rising, 33=mid level, 53=high falling, etc. The tone numbering system (Tones 1–8) follows the traditional tone notation used in areal comparative work (e.g. Zhang 1980; Zeng and Yao 1996; Edmondson and Solnit 1988). Checked syllables (i.e. syllables with -p, -t, -k codas), are typically analysed as either long (L) or short (S).

Fieldwork on Sui intensifiers was conducted by the author in Guizhou province during 1999–2003 and during a return fieldtrip in 2004. Stanford (2007a–b) provides a lexicon of about 400 intensifiers from a single speaker

Table 9.1 *Sui tones in the Zhonghe region*

Tone numbers	Tone 1	Tone 2	Tone 3	Tone 4	Tone 5	Tone 6	Tone 7S	Tone 7L	Tone 8S	Tone 8L
Tone pitch values	13	31	33	53	35	24	55	35	32	31

and analyses patterns in a formal phonological framework. Other work on Sui intensifiers includes Wei (1999) and Feng (2008).

3.2   A question of terminology

As with many other languages of Mainland Southeast Asia discussed in this volume and other work (e.g. Thompson 1965; Peterson 2010; Ratliff 1992; Haiman and Ourn 2009; Yu, Snyder, and Snyder 1994), Sui has a set of 'aesthetic expressions' that show rhyming and alliterative patterns. Similar or related phenomena have been variously described as 'word-specific intensifiers' (Yu, Snyder, and Synder 1994), 'echo words', 'chameleon affixes', 'expressives', and 'ideophones' (Williams, this volume), 'elaborate expressions' (Peterson 2010; Matisoff 1973, 2003: 210), and 'twin forms' (Marchand 1960, cited in Haiman 2011; Ourn and Haiman 2001). For Sui, it seems that 'word-specific intensifier' may be the most appropriate term. Unlike ideophones, Sui intensifiers are not necessarily sound symbolic. The Sui expressions also differ from Diffloth's (1976) 'expressives' in Semai, which focus on sensory perception and have a syntactic category of their own. Moreover, since the Sui expressions have the primary function of adjective intensification, it seems that a more general term like 'elaborate expression' is less appropriate than 'word-specific intensifier'.

3.3   Description of Sui adjective intensifiers

Sui intensifiers may be subdivided into a Rhyming Class, Alliterative Class, and an Irregular Class.
• The Rhyming Class
In the Rhyming Class, the intensifier shares the rhyme of the root but not its onset. A set of examples is given in (2) below.[5] Note: superscripts represent tone numbers (section 3.1).

(2)   a. $ʁɑːt^7$ 'agile'   → $ʁɑːt^7 tɕɑːt^8$ 'very agile'
        b. $ʔmɛj^5$ 'selfish'   → $ʔmɛj^5 tɛj^1$ 'very selfish'
                                                                    (often referring to a child)

---

[5] Additional examples for each intensifier class are provided in Stanford (2007a), and the entire lexicon is printed in Stanford (2007b).

c. fɑːɲ^3 'wide'   → fɑːɲ^3 lʲɑːɲ^2 'very wide'
d. tom^1 'dull'   → tom^1 ʔnom^1 'very dull'
e. ^{m}bu^3 'bulging'   → ^{m}bu^3 tɕʰu^5 'very bulging'
f. ʔnəm^1 'dark/black' → ʔnəm^1 fəm^2 'very dark/black'
g. lap^7 'garrulous'   → lap^7 tap^8 'very garrulous'
h. pʲɛːk^7 'dirty'   → pjɛːk^7 lʲɛːk^7 'very dirty'
i. ɱow^1 'crude, rash' → ɱow^1 low^1 'very crude/rash'
j ^{m}bʲa^3 'blurry'   → ^{m}bʲa^3 tɕa^4 'very blurry'

                                                (from Stanford 2007a)

• The Alliterative Class
Intensifiers in the Alliterative Class share the same onset as the root but have a different rhyme as shown in the next group of examples.

(3)   a. ʁaːt^7 'agile'   → ʁaːt^7 ʁow^1 'very agile'
       b. ʔmɛj^5 'selfish'   → ʔmɛj^5 ʔmʊːt^7 'very selfish'
                                                (general usage)
       c. çu^1 'green'   → çu^1 ciŋ^5 'very green'
       d. tɕʰoŋ^5 'spicy'   → tɕʰoŋ^5 tɕʰat^7 'very spicy'
       e. za^3 'light'   → za^3 zu^1 'very light/
                                                casual' (attitude)
       f. za^3 'light'   → za^3 zeŋ^3 'very light' (weight)
       g. qəm^1 'bitter'   → qəm^1 qe^5 'very bitter'
       h. ça^1 'sharp'   → ça^{1}çɛn^1 'very sharp'
       i ʁəm^1 'muddled'   → ʁəw^1 ʁoj^1 'very muddled'
                                                (from Stanford 2007a)

• The Irregular Class
In the third class of intensifiers, the Irregular Class, intensifiers do not bear any phonological resemblance to the root. Nonetheless, these intensifiers are 'word-specific': they are associated with a single root and are not attested elsewhere in the lexicon. Examples are given in (4).

(4)   a. pi^2 'fat'   → pi^2 ɲəŋ^2 'very fat'
       b. xom^3 'sour'   → xom^3 pʲaːt^7 'very sour'
       c. xɑːn^3 'red'   → xɑːn^3 səŋ^1 'very red'
       d. kʰiŋ^3 'brown'   → kʰiŋ^3 ^{n}di^2 'very brown'
       e. ʔɣɑk^7 'wet'   → ʔɣɑk^7 ʔbət^7 'very wet'

• Three-syllable expressions
While most intensifiers are monosyllables affixed to the root, there is a subset of polysyllabic expressions exemplified in (5).

(5)   xɑːn^3 'red'
       xɑːn^3 tʲaːn^2 'very red'
       xɑːn^3 tʲaːn^2 lʲaːn^2 'extremely red'
       xɑːn^3 tʲaːn^2 lʲaːn^2 sʲaːn^2 'really, really red'

• Productivity and predictability
There is no productive, predictable pattern governing Sui word-specific inten-
sifiers. When tested with nonce roots, speakers were unable to form intensifiers.
Moreover, it is not possible to predict whether an intensifier of a given root will
be a member of the Rhyming Class, Alliterative Class, or the Irregular Class.
In fact, some roots have intensifiers drawn from more than one class, e.g. (6).
In such cases, the speaker's choice depends on subtle semantic and pragmatic
contrasts.

(6)   ?mɛj^5 'selfish'   →   ?mɛj^5 tɛj^1 'very selfish' (often referring to
                                                   a child)
                           →   ?mɛj^5 ?mʊːt^7 'very selfish' (general usage)
       ?nəm^1 'dark/black' →   ?nəm^1 ?nɛj^1 'very dark/black'
                                                   (most commonly used form,
                                                   e.g. dark clothes)
                           →   ?nəm^1 ?nʊt^7 'very dark/black' (higher
                                                   level of intensity than
                                                   ?nəm^1 ?nɛj^1)
                           →   ?nəm^1 fəm^2 'very dark/black'
                                                   (especially referring
                                                   to a group of dark
                                                   objects, such as a group
                                                   of dark clouds)
                                                   (from Stanford 2007a)

• The Emergence of The Unmarked (TETU, McCarthy and Prince 1994)
Despite the lack of full predictability, broad morphophonological patterns are
clearly evident. Among the Rhyming Class, 88% of the intensifiers have
coronal onsets (7). Stanford (2007a) suggests that this unmarked place of
articulation is an example of McCarthy and Prince's (1994) The Emergence
of The Unmarked (TETU).

(7)   Examples of coronal onsets in the Rhyming Class
       a. vɑːŋ^1 'tall'   → vɑːŋ^1 tɕɑːŋ^2 'very tall''
       b. fɑːŋ^3 'wide'   → fɑːŋ^3 ɬʲɑːŋ^2 'very wide'
       c. ?bɑj^3 'crooked'   → ?bɑj^3 tʲɑj^4 'very crooked'
       d. ^{m}bu^3 'protruding' → ^{m}bu^3 tɕʰu^5 'very protruding'
       e. ^{m}bʲɑ^3 'blurry'   → ^{m}bʲɑ^3 tɕɑ^4 'very blurry'
       f. ?mɛj^5 'stingy'   → ?mɛj^5 tɛj^1 'very stingy'
       g. xom^3 'sour'   → xom^3 tom^4 'very sour'
       h. qɔn^4 'short'   → qɔn^4 ?nʲɔn^3 'very short'
       i. mət^7 'tight'   → mət^7 tɕət^8 'very tight'
       j. pən^1 'stupid'   → pən^1 ?nən^1 'very stupid'
       k. xɔ^3 'poor'   → xɔ^3 ɬʲɔ^4 'very poor'

                                                   (Stanford 2007a)

• Identity avoidance

Full reduplication is very rare among Sui adjective intensifiers. Instead, the intensifier usually has a different onset or rhyme or tone. Furthermore, in three-syllable intensifiers in the Rhyming Class, TETU effects are combined with identity avoidance (cf. Stanford 2007a; cf. Yip 1998; Hicks Kennard 2004). Sui intensifier onsets tend to be coronals, yet they also tend to avoid sharing the same sonority and voice features of adjacent syllable onsets (8).

(8)

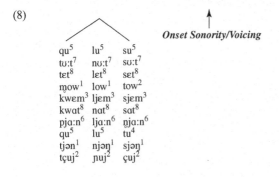

Onset Sonority/Voicing

qu⁵	lu⁵	su⁵
tʊːt⁷	nʊːt⁷	sʊːt⁷
tɛt⁸	lɛt⁸	sɛt⁸
m̥ow¹	low¹	tow²
kwɛm³	ljɛm³	sjɛm³
kwɑt⁸	nɑt⁸	sɑt⁸
pjɑːn⁶	ljɑːn⁶	ɲjɑːn⁶
qu⁵	lu⁵	tu⁴
tjən¹	njəŋ¹	sjəŋ¹
tɕuj²	ɲuj²	ɕuj²

4   Comparison of intensifiers across four different clan dialects

The description of Sui intensifiers in Section 3 is based on a single speaker (Lu clan), making it possible for the analyst to narrowly focus on the patterns within that speaker's set of intensifiers. The tradeoff in that analytical choice, however, is a lack of perspective on the scope and range of variation possible within Sui. In the absence of written historical records,[6] a comparative approach is an effective way to explore this phenomenon more deeply. Therefore, the present section compares Sui intensifiers across four different clan dialects. The clan dialects in the Sui region studied here are mutually intelligible, but there is a significant amount of phonological and lexical variation between dialects (Stanford 2008a–b). What types of variation may be found in adjective intensifiers in these different dialects?

Rural Sui people strictly practise clan exogamy, and wives move permanently to the husband's village at the time of marriage. Sui villages have intensive inter-clan contact as a result of these patrilocal customs, but clan dialects remain distinct. For example, Stanford (2008a–b, 2009) finds that in-married Sui women maintain the dialect features of their original home village even after decades in the husband's village.

---

[6] There is no Sui writing system in active use. An ancient system of Chinese-based characters is used ritualistically by shamans. Chinese scholars created a Roman Alphabet-based writing system for Sui, but most speakers have not been trained in that script (Zhou 2003: 133–136).

Adjective intensifiers were collected from (1) a Lu clan member from Zhonge, (2) a Wei clan member from Miaocao, (3) a Pan clan member from Sandong, and (4) a Yang clan member from Xiyang. These regions represent a total linear distance of about 25 kilometres (Stanford 2011).

The results show significant dialect variation. For example, 23% of the intensifiers collected in the study were not attested by the Lu clan speaker. On the other hand, the overall morphophonological patterns are very consistent across all four dialects, as described below.

4.1   The Lu clan

The Lu clan speaker provided 407 total intensifiers, and the intensifiers have a distribution of 63% Alliterative, 31% Rhyming, and 6% Irregular.

First, consider the results for the Alliterative Class. A tonal distribution is provided in Table 9.2, where the horizontal dimension represents the tone of the root. The vertical dimension represents the tone of the intensifier. For example, the adjective root ʁoŋ^5 'young' has an intensifier ʁɛw^3, creating the intensified form ʁoŋ^5 ʁɛw^3 'very young'. In the table, this is counted as one instance of Tone 5 in the root and Tone 3 in the intensifier.

In Table 9.2, note that there is a tendency for roots with odd-numbered tones (Tones 1, 3, 5, 7) to have intensifiers with odd-numbered tones. Likewise, roots with even-numbered tones (Tones 2, 4, 6, 8) tend to have intensifiers with even-numbered tones. The tone numbering system used in areal linguistics (i.e. the even and odd numbering of the tones) is designed to reflect a historical tone split between voiced and voiceless onsets (Edmondson and Solnit 1988).

Table 9.2 *Lu clan alliterative class (Stanford 2007a)*

Intensifier → Root ↓	Tone 1	Tone 3	Tone 5	Tone 7	Tone 2	Tone 4	Tone 6	Tone 8
Tone 1	26	10	9	11	0	0	0	0
Tone 3	21	14	5	12	1	1	0	0
Tone 5	27	17	6	15	0	2	0	0
Tone 7	15	9	2	8	1	0	0	0
Tone 2	1	0	0	0	4	0	0	9
Tone 4	0	1	0	1	1	1	0	2
Tone 6	1	1	0	0	6	1	1	4
Tone 8	0	0	0	0	3	2	0	1

Table 9.3 *Historical tone split*

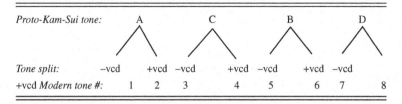

Proto-Kam-Sui tone:	A		C		B		D	
Tone split:	−vcd	+vcd	−vcd	+vcd	−vcd	+vcd	−vcd	+vcd
Modern tone #:	1	2	3	4	5	6	7	8

Table 9.4 *Lu clan rhyming class (Stanford 2007a)*

Intensifier → Root ↓	Tone 1	Tone 3	Tone 5	Tone 7	Tone 2	Tone 4	Tone 6	Tone 8
Tone 1	14	0	0	0	6	0	0	0
Tone 3	1	5	2	0	1	15	0	0
Tone 5	2	0	17	0	0	2	0	0
Tone 7	0	0	0	17	0	0	0	12
Tone 2	1	0	0	0	8	0	0	0
Tone 4	0	1	2	0	1	1	0	0
Tone 6	0	0	0	0	0	0	6	0
Tone 8	0	0	0	0	0	0	0	13

As Table 9.3 shows, Proto-Kam-Sui had four basic tones, while there are now eight tones in the modern languages. Although there are no historical records to trace the origins of Sui intensifiers, there is clearly a tendency for roots and intensifiers to share the same 'branch' of the historical tone split – either the voiceless (odd numbered) side or the voiced (even numbered) side. A chi-squared test of the data in Table 9.2 shows that this tendency is statistically significant (chi-squared = 181.9, p ≤ 0.001).

Now consider the Rhyming Class in the Lu clan. In Table 9.4, shaded cells along the major diagonal illustrate the fact that rhyming intensifiers often share the tone of the root adjective. In this table, cells with five or more tokens are highlighted with shading. The secondary, smaller diagonal in the upper right quadrant shows that intensifiers sometimes share a tone pairing that reflects the proto-forms of Table 9.3. For example, proto-tone A split into tones 1 and 2, and it turns out that modern adjective roots with Tone 1 often have intensifiers with Tone 2. The same effect is seen with tones 3–4 and tones 7–8.

Table 9.5 *Wei clan rhyming class*

Intensifier → Root ↓	Tone 1	Tone 3	Tone 5	Tone 7	Tone 2	Tone 4	Tone 6	Tone 8
Tone 1	11	1	0	0	3	0	0	0
Tone 3	1	2	1	0	2	10	0	0
Tone 5	2	0	13	0	0	2	0	0
Tone 7	0	0	0	10	0	0	0	11
Tone 2	0	0	0	0	12	1	1	0
Tone 4	0	1	0	0	1	1	0	0
Tone 6	0	0	0	0	2	0	2	0
Tone 8	0	0	0	0	0	0	0	5

In addition to the tone patterns described above, the Lu clan's Rhyming Class also has a tendency for coronal onsets in the intensifiers (recall from Section 3.3 that this may be attributed to The Emergence of The Unmarked, McCarthy and Prince 1994; cf. Stanford 2007a).

4.2   The Wei clan

The Wei clan speaker provided 332 total intensifiers, and the intensifiers were distributed as 63% Alliterative, 27% Rhyming, and 10% Irregular. As with the Lu clan, the Wei clan speaker's Alliterative Class has a significant tendency for the tones of the root and intensifier to be both odd, or both even (chi-squared=191.194, p < 0.0001). The Rhyming Class has the same overall pattern as the Lu clan, but it is slightly less consistent in tones. As Table 9.5 shows, the Wei clan speaker has 5 of 8 cells along the main diagonal, and 2 of 4 in the secondary region (compare with the Lu clan above, which has 7 out of 8 cells in the main diagonal, and 3 of 4 in the secondary region).

4.3   The Pan clan

Some 196 intensifiers were elicited from the Pan clan speaker: 65% of the intensifiers were in the Alliterative Class, 22% in the Rhyming Class, and 13% Irregular. There is a statistically significant tendency for the tone of the root and intensifier to be both odd or both even (chi-squared=121.899, p < 0.0001). The

Rhyming Class shows the same overall pattern as Lu, but there are only 5 of 8 cells along the main diagonal, and 2 of 4 in the secondary region.

4.4   The Yang clan

The Yang clan speaker provided 355 intensifiers: 66% in the Alliterative Class, 27% in the Rhyming Class, and 7% in the Irregular Class. As with the other clans, this speaker's lexicon shows a statistically significant tendency for the tone of the root and intensifier to share the same side of the historical tone split: even or odd (chi-squared=182.66, $p < 0.0001$). The Rhyming Class had 5 of 8 cells along the main diagonal, and 2 of 4 in the secondary region.

4.5   Intensifiers shared across all four clans

In the last step of the dialect analysis, shared intensifiers were examined among the four dialects: the four dialects overlapped in 185 intensifiers. In this shared set, the intensifiers were distributed as 74% Alliterative Class, 17% Rhyming Class, and 9% Irregular. As with the individual dialects, there was a significant tendency for the tones of the root and intensifier to be both odd or both even (chi-squared=94.987, $p < 0.0001$). The Rhyming Class had 3 of 8 cells along the main diagonal, and 2 of 4 in the secondary region.

5   Conclusions

5.1   Summary of the cross-dialectal study

The results of the cross-dialectal study suggest significant variability among individual intensifiers among the four dialects. On the other hand, all four clans shared the same overall patterns:
1. Similar percentages of Rhyming, Alliterative, and Irregular Classes. A pairwise test of proportions showed no significant differences between the four clans in these proportions.
2. For the Alliterative Class, all four clan-lects have a significant tendency for the root's tone to be on the same side of the tone split as the base (both even or both odd).
3. For the Rhyming Class, the following two tendencies were shared among the four clans: either the tone of the root is the same as the intensifier, or the root and intensifier share the same proto-tone (tone pairs 1–2 or 3–4 or 7–8).
4. The Emergence of The Unmarked (TETU): rhyming intensifiers usually have coronal onsets.
5. Identity avoidance: full reduplication is very rare. Instead, the intensifier usually differs in rhyme or onset or tone.

5.2   New intensifiers for the future?

Sui intensifiers are not productive in the traditional sense. When nonce adjective roots are presented, speakers are not able to produce corresponding intensifiers. Yet speakers can recognize the typical patterns of well-formed intensifiers, even across dialects. Example (9) illustrates this point, listing intensifiers elicited for the word *qu lu* 'round'.

(9)   a. qu lu   'round'
       b. qu lu su   'very round'
       c. qu lu tu   'very round'
       d. qu lu tu təŋ   'very very round'

Forms (9a–c) were attested in all four clans, but (9d) was only attested by the Wei clan speaker. Yet when (9d) was produced for the Lu clan speaker, he immediately responded positively and said, 'It's good Sui!' – even though he had never heard this variant before. He was then overheard producing (9d) many times that day in his village with obvious aesthetic enjoyment. This anecdote suggests a sense of aesthetic appreciation and cross-dialectal consensus in the range of possible poetic devices, much like a person appreciates the creativity and patterns found in a newly composed poem. What particular aspects of (9d) may have appealed to the Lu clan speaker? Note that (9d) includes both rhyme *and* alliteration: (9d) interweaves three rhyming syllables (*qu lu tu*) with two alliterative syllables (*tu təŋ*). Perhaps this complex expression is perceived as a 'playful galumph' (Haiman and Ourn 2009, citing Miller 1973; Haiman, this volume), an extension of (9c) created by analogy with the overall poetic patterns of existing intensifiers across the lexicon.

Sui intensifiers could conceivably be viewed as fossils from some earlier, fully productive era or eras, but the sheer scope of variety (especially in the alliterative class) seems instead to suggest an active, creative process of analogy and poetry, not rigid phonological rules. Such an analysis would be consistent with Bybee's (2001: 13) view that frequently occurring patterns are judged more acceptable than less frequently occurring patterns.

In fact, some Sui consultants speculated that new intensifiers may be continuing to emerge, especially when Sui story-tellers and singers occasionally 'embellish' their words for stylistic effect. Although adjective intensifiers are common in everyday language, consultants suggested that intensifiers are especially frequent in story-telling and song lyrics. As listeners hear such new forms, they may gradually incorporate them into their own lexicons for daily usage. In this way, Sui intensifiers exemplify a mutually influencing relationship between language and human agency: verbal art influences and is influenced by the lexicon, while the lexicon influences and is influenced by verbal art (Figure 9.1).

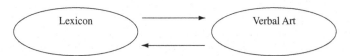

Figure 9.1 The mutually influencing relationship of verbal art and the lexicon

5.3   Final thoughts

Jakobson argues that a sense of the poetic is commonly observable in everyday speech, and it is clear that Sui supports this notion. In addition, however, Sui and other languages in this volume have extensive, systematic features that can be viewed as 'lexicalized poetry'. Analysis of Sui intensifiers in cross-dialectal variation and discourse shows a set of aesthetic patterns of rhyme and alliteration in disyllabic expressions and polysyllabic expressions, and statistically significant but not fully predictable patterns in tones and onsets. Sui word-specific adjective intensifiers are a vibrant, systematic, aesthetic feature of daily speech. In this way, verbal art constructs and is constructed by the lexicon, and the lexicon constructs and is constructed by verbal art.

References

Bradley, David. 2007. 'East and Southeast Asia'. In R. E. Asher and C. J. Moseley (eds.), *Atlas of the world's languages* (second edition). London: Routledge.
Bybee, Joan. 2001. *Phonology and language use*. Cambridge University Press.
Chao, Y. R. 1930. A system of tone letters. *La Maitre phonetique* 45: 24–27.
Diffloth, Gérard. 1976. 'Expressives in Semai'. In Philip N. Jenner, Laurence C. Thompson, and Stanley Starosta (eds.) *Austroasiatic studies*, Part I. (Oceanic Linguistics Special Publications, No. 13.) Honolulu: University of Hawaii Press, pp. 249–264.
Edmondson, Jerold A. and David B. Solnit (eds.). 1988. *Comparative Kadai: linguistic studies beyond Tai*. Dallas, TX: SIL.
Edmondson, Jerold A., John H. Esling, Jimmy G. Harris and James Wei. 2004. A phonetic study of Sui consonants and tones. *Mon-Khmer studies* 34: 47–66.
Feng, Ying. 2008. *Shuiyu fuyinci yanjiu [Research of sui reduplicative expressions]*. Beijing: Zhonghua Shuju.
Haiman, John. 2011. Six motives for repetition. Ms.
Haiman, John and Noeurng Ourn. 2009. 'Decorative symmetry in ritual (and everyday) language'. In Roberta Corrigan, Edith A. Moravcsik, Hamid Ouali and Kathleen M. Wheatley (eds.), *Formulaic language*. Amsterdam: John Benjamins, pp. 567–588.
Hicks Kennard, Catherine. 2004. Copy but don't repeat: The conflict of dissimilation and reduplication in the Tawala durative. *Phonology* 21(3): 303–23.
Jakobson, Roman. 1960. 'Closing statement: linguistics and poetics'. In T. A. Sebook (ed.), *Style in language*. Cambridge, MA: MIT Press, pp. 350–377.
Jakobson, Roman and Linda Waugh. 1979. *The sound shape of language*. Bloomington: Indiana University Press.

Li, Fang Kuei. 1948. The distribution of initials and tones in the Sui language. *Language* 24: 160–67.

1965. The Tai and Kam-Sui languages. *Lingua* 14: 148–79.

Matisoff, James A. 1973. *The grammar of Lahu*. Berkeley: University of California Press.

2003. 'Lahu'. In Graham Thurgood and Randy LaPolla (eds.), *The Sino-Tibetan languages*. London: Routledge, pp. 208–220.

McCarthy, John and Alan Prince. 1994. The emergence of the unmarked: Optimality in prosodic morphology. *NELS 24, Proceedings of the 24th Conference of the Northeast Linguistics Society*. Amherst, MA: GLSA, University of Massachusetts, pp. 333–379.

Miller, Stephen. 1973. Ends, means, and galumphing. *American anthropologist* 75(1): 87–98.

Millgate, Michael. 1963. *Tennyson: selected poems*. Oxford University Press.

Ourn, Noeurng and John Haiman. 2001. Symmetrical compounds in Khmer. *Studies in language* 24(1): 483–514.

Peterson, David A. 2010. Khumi elaborate expressions. *Himalayan linguistics* 9(1): 81–100.

Ratliff, Martha. 1992. *Meaningful tone: a study of tonal morphology in compounds, form classes, and expressive phrases in White Hmong*. Northern Illinois University Center for Southeast Asian Studies, Report No. 27.

Stanford, James. N. 2007a. Sui adjective reduplication as poetic morphophonology. *Journal of East Asian linguistics* 16(2): 87–111.

2007b. Lexicon and description of Sui adjective intensifiers. *Linguistic discovery* 5(1): 1–27.

2008a. Child dialect acquisition: new perspectives on parent/peer influence. *Journal of sociolinguistics* 12(5): 567–96.

2008b. A sociotonetic analysis of Sui dialect contact. *Language variation and change* 20(3): 409–450.

2009. 'Eating the food of our place': Sociolinguistic loyalties in multidialectal Sui villages. *Language in society* 38(3): 287–310.

2011. Rice paddies, clans, and dialect geography in rural China: a 50-year real-time comparison of regional dialect variation in the indigenous Sui language. Ms.

Thompson, Laurence. 1965. *A Vietnamese grammar*. Seattle: University of Washington Press.

Wei, Xuechun. 1999. Shuiyu xingrongci houzhui yanjiu [Research of Sui language adjective suffixes]. *Shuijiaxue yanjiu* 3: 221–25. Guizhou, China: Guizhou Province Sui Association.

Yip, Moira. 1998. 'Identity avoidance in phonology and morphology'. In Steven G. Lapointe, Diane K. Brentari, and Patrick M. Farrell (eds.), *Morphology and its relation to phonology and syntax*. Stanford, CA: CSLI, pp. 216–246.

1999. Reduplication as alliteration and rhyme. *Glot International* 4(8): 1–7.

Yu, J., Wil Snyder, and Donna Snyder. 1994. 'Two initial grammatical discoveries in the Fucun speech of Libo Buyi'. In Stuart Milliken (ed.), *SIL occasional papers on the minority languages of China*, Vol. 1. Hong Kong: SIL, pp. 1–11.

Zeng, Xiaoyu and Fuxiang Yao. 1996. *Han–Shui cidian [Chinese–Sui dictionary]*. Chengdu: Sichuan Minorities Publishing.

Zhang, Junru. 1980. *Shuiyu jianzhi [A sketch of the Sui language]*. Beijing: Minorities Press.

Zhou, Minglang. 2003. *Multilingualism in China: the politics of writing reforms for minority languages 1949–2002*. Berlin: Mouton de Gruyter.

10   Attitudes towards aesthetic aspects of Thai grammar

Wilaiwan Khanittanan

1   Introduction[*]

As chapters in this volume establish, throughout Mainland Southeast Asia reduplicative compounds, elaborative expressions, and similar repetitive constructions are widespread and form an important part of what can be called the aesthetics of grammar. Such constructions are well represented in Thai with early linguistic analyses by Haas (1942, 1946, 1964) followed by many subsequent studies.[1] Since those works focus primarily on structural patterns and different types occurring in Thai, I will focus my chapter on questions of productivity and attitude. The two primary purposes of this chapter are to: (i) demonstrate that such forms are a distinct kind of vocabulary in Thai and that new members of the class are still being created in present-day Thai by rhyming and reduplicating; and (ii) report results of a survey examining the attitudes of Thai speakers to several kinds of these forms, with emphasis on speakers' feelings of appropriateness of usage in different situations or genres. This enables more general considerations of how Thai speakers feel about linguistic aesthetic evaluation and how this may relate to sociolinguistic variables.

In his paper entitled 'Tai Aesthetics', Hudak calls attention to the Thai term *phay-rɔ́ʔ*, which he explains as meaning 'sweet, melodious, musical, harmonious, worth listening to' (Hudak 2008: 404). Hudak notes *phay-rɔ́ʔ* is often applied in Thai to describe 'highly esteemed and valued poetry'. His study, citing earlier work of Gedney, goes on to illustrate various repetitive or elaborative patterns considered to have such *phay-rɔ́ʔ* properties. Hudak's study raises several questions, but I will take up only two of those here. In contexts other than poetry or classical literature, do all of these constructions necessarily retain the same positive associations? Do qualifications or other conditions need

---

[*] I am deeply grateful to Dr Anthony Diller for his kind suggestions and encouragement throughout. Although he read and provided suggestions on a draft of this chapter, all the mistakes remain my own. The data presented in this chapter were collected by questionnaire from 100 native Thai speakers.

[1] Hudak (2008) provides a listing of these references.

to be considered? In the following sections I attempt to provide answers to these questions.

2   Reduplicative compounds and elaborative expressions

Reduplicative compounds form a large category of vocabulary and phrasal units in Thai grammar. In fact, there are more reduplicative compounds and similar expressions than there are non-reduplicative ones in the language. This is so because reduplication, which can involve a variety of syntactic phrasal patterns, is an active language process that is widely used in daily spoken Thai. Virtually all verbs, including adjectival modifiers and adverbs, in Thai can be reduplicated in more than one way to form new words and expressions. Even though not all nouns can be reduplicated, there are still a large number of noun reduplicative constructions. Non-reduplicative compounds cannot be created as easily and numerously. For example, *khít* 'to think' can be reduplicated and/ or turned into elaborate expressions by different rules.

(1)   chán   *khít-khít*   lέεw   kɔ̌ɔ   plìan-cay
       1SG   think-think   already   then   change mind
       'I thought it over and then changed my mind.'

(2)   chán   *khít-khít-khít*   lέεw   kɔ̌ɔ   plìan-cay
       1SG   think-think-think   already   then   change mind
       'I thought it over and over again and then I changed my mind.'

(3)   chán   *khít-*   pay-   *khít-*   maa   lέεw   kɔ̌ɔ   plìan-cay
       1SG   think-   go-   think-   come   already   then   change mind.
       'I thought it over (back and forth; again and again) and then I changed my mind.'

(4)   chán *khít-* lέεw *-khít-ʔìik*   lέεw kɔ̌ɔ plìan-cay
       1SG   think-then -think-again   already   then change mind.
       'I thought it over again and again and then I changed (my) mind.'

(5)   mây-*khít*   mây-*khét*   ʔa-ray   lέεw
       not-think   not-think   what   any
       '(I'm) not thinking about anything any more.'

(6)   mây-*khít-* mây- *khət*   ʔa-ray   lέεw
       not-think -not-think   what   any
       '(I'm) not thinking about anything any more.'

(7)   mây-*khóŋ-* mây- *khít*   ʔa-ray   lέεw
       not-think -not-think   what   any
       '(I'm) not thinking about anything any more.'

A quick glance at a Thai dictionary will reveal that there are a large number of reduplicative compounds and elaborative expressions for every consonant sound listed in the dictionary. A very brief sampling includes the following:

(8)	phɔɔ – phiaŋ	'to be sufficient'
(9)	prɛɛ – pruan	'to change; to fluctuate'
(10)	thát – thaan	'to oppose'
(11)	tìt – tɔ̀ɔ	'to be in touch'
(12)	chák – cháa	'to be slow'
(13)	càt – cɛɛŋ	'to arrange, to organize'
(14)	khrêŋ – khrát	'to be strict'
(15)	kè? – kà?	'to be obstructive'
(16)	bɔ̀ɔk – baan	'to be cheerful'
(17)	dɯ̀ɯ – dâan	'to be obstinate'
(18)	mûŋ – mǎay	'to have a definite purpose'
(19)	nɔ̂ɔp – nɔ́ɔm	'to show respect'
(20)	ŋɔ̂ɔk – ŋaam	'to grow, to develop'
(21)	?òp – ?ùn	'to be warm'
(22)	fùk – fǒn	'to practise'
(23)	sáp – sɔ́ɔn	'complicated'
(24)	hɯ̀at–hǎay	'to disappear gradually'
(25)	wiŋ – wɔɔn	'to implore; to beseech'
(26)	yók – yɔ̂ŋ	'to praise'
(27)	rûat – rew	'to be fast'
(28)	lóm – láaŋ	'to over throw'
(29)	kin khâaw kin plaa eat rice eat fish	'to have a meal'
(30)	klay hǔu klay taa far ear far eye	'to be far from'
(31)	khàat tòk bòk phrɔ̂ŋ torn fall dry not full	'to be deficient'

There is a significant difference between the forms listed (1) through (7) and those listed (8) through (31). Unlike the reduplicatives of *khít* 'to think' shown in examples (1) through (7), all of the examples in (8) through (31) can be found in standard dictionaries of the Thai language. Those in (1) to (7) result from the application of different types of aesthetic grammatical rules, through which speakers create new words and expressions all the time.

Developing a comprehensive inventory or lexicon of aesthetic expressions in Thai would be next to impossible and it would certainly contain far more derivatives than would a dictionary that catalogued only the basic word forms. Aesthetic expressions, especially those involving alliteration and vocalic rhyming, are constantly being created to capture meanings in context by individual Thai speakers. Not unlike slang forms, which are also created by individuals or social groups, aesthetic expressions may later become lexicalized as words or phrases in common use and so become listed in dictionaries, such as those in (8) through (31). Should a dictionary of reduplicative compounds and elaborative expressions be compiled, it would certainly contain more items than a Thai dictionary cataloguing only basic word forms. However, a complete dictionary of this kind probably could not be filed because of reduplication, especially involving alliteration and vocalic rhyme.

3   **Repetitive and elaborative patterns in language:**
       developmental aspects

All great Thai poems are remembered first by their sound play – rhyming, alliterations, and tone placements. Discussions of how good or how *phay-rɔ́ʔ* a poem is always centre around the topic of how effectively the sounds used in the poem express emotions or sensibilities relevant to the poem. This might include: the noise of waterfalls, animal cries, furious thunderclaps, or the wailing of a person in agony. Narrative content in a poem is almost always secondary to its euphony. Rhyming, alliterations, and elaborate patterns are indispensable instruments of what Thai speakers evaluate as good poems.

Those instruments – including rhyming, alliterations, and elaborate patterns – happen to be used constantly and widely in conversational Thai as well. Unlike poems, the primary function in conversation is not to sound melodious and musical. Content or meaning is more important than sounds. *Phay-rɔ́ʔ*, or 'aesthetic value' is secondary and the sonic resources – alliterations and elaborate patterns – acquire new sociolinguistic or pragmatic functions. These include specifying (i) the mood of the speaker, (ii) the relationship between listener and speaker, and (iii) the level of formality. Thus linguistic forms and processes associated with 'aesthetic value' in poetry receive a different set of interpretations when they appear in conversational discourse.

Alliteration, rhyming, and elaborative patterns have been used in the spoken language as well as in prose from ancient times. The Ram Khamhaeng Inscription or the First Thai Inscription, of 1292 AD which is considered *phay-rɔ́ʔ* – or sweet, melodious, and musical – is full of alliteration, rhyming, and elaborative patterns, as shown in examples (32) through (34).[2]

(32)　　*nay náam mii* plaa　　　*nay naa　mii* khâaw
　　　　in　water there is fish　　in　field there is rice
　　　　'There are fish in the water.'　'There is rice in the field.'

(33)　　phûan cuuŋ wua **pay kháa**　　kh**ìi máa　pay khǎay**
　　　　they　lead cows go trade　　ride horse go　trade
　　　　'People bring cows to trade.'　'(They) ride horses to trade.'

(34)　　*khray càk khrây* kháa cháaŋ kháa　　　*khray càk khrây* kháa máa kháa
　　　　who　will want　trade elephants trade　　who　will want　trade horses trade
　　　　'Whoever wants to trade horses may do so.'　'Whoever wants to trade elephants
　　　　　　　　　　　　　　　　　　　　　　　　may do so.'

There is no evidence for a clear distinction between formal and informal Thai at the time of this inscription. What was used in early written Thai presumably must have been used in the spoken language too. At that time very few people knew how to read or write any language known to be used in the community. There were no schools for ordinary people. Later however as Thai society became stratified, linguistic distinctions between written and spoken forms of Thai became important in daily life. In this way Thai came to reflect linguistic ideologies of nearby peoples such as the Khmers and Chams. With this development, differences emerged between formal more literary and informal more conversational types of Thai. Owing in part to its politico-religious foundational ideology, the literary written language was considered sacred and formal.

Over time, poetic genres that were associated with literary Thai became more codified, with some types of repetitive structure, such as alliteration and internal rhyme, subject to conventions or rules (Gedney 1989). During the nineteenth and twentieth centuries written Thai underwent many shifts (Khanittanan 1987; Diller 1993). These included both the setting of norms and the elaboration of a wide variety of styles that were felt to be appropriate for different situations. Some styles were especially affected by Western models or other modernizing tendencies (Khanittanan 1979). One kind of innovation promoted a more 'autonomous' type of Thai: more generalizing, abstract, and impersonal (Khanittanan 1988). In this more autonomous type of Thai, the emotional impact associated with the traditional *phay-rɔ́ʔ* (sweet, melodious, and musical) expressions considered above would be less appropriate and would generally be

---

[2] For more detail see Diller (1991).

avoided. Instead, other features would be characteristic, such as complex syntactic structures and the heavy use of abstract nominalizations, also common in Western scientific, technical, and bureaucratic discourse.

4   Repetitive and elaborative patterns in the language of daily life

These considerations introduce a degree of complexity into how Thai speakers react to or evaluate linguistic material with *phay-rɔ́ʔ* expressions in different types of written and spoken Thai. Even the term *phay-rɔ́ʔ* itself may be applied and evaluated differently by speakers. For instance, if repetition, alliteration, etc., occur in a passage of written Thai where such constructions are not considered appropriate, will speakers still assess them as *phay-rɔ́ʔ*? When questioned, it seems that some will still use the term *phay-rɔ́ʔ* to refer to this material, but others will not apply the term when situations or contexts seem inappropriate to them.

In fact, some Thai writers are good at exploiting *phay-rɔ́ʔ* expressions and similar material to create special effects. In journalism, for example, news writers often vary a more colloquial style for (large print) headlines and a more autonomous style for the factual reporting of the following (small print) detailed story (Khanittanan 2007). Thai speakers feel that this variation is appropriate. In this way, the more personal and aesthetically appealing type of Thai, admitting *phay-rɔ́ʔ* expressions, alternates with impersonal narrative that strives to seem more objective and impersonal. In the latter type, *phay-rɔ́ʔ* expressions would be found more sparingly or not at all.

5   Present use of repetitive or elaborative patterns as stand-alone titles

The usage of repetitive or elaborative patterns in headlines mentioned above is part of a wider phenomenon. Although these expressions are strongly associated with spoken and informal language, at present they are regularly and widely used in many situations that are associated with more formal language, both spoken and written. It is noteworthy that since elaborative patterns mostly occur as compounds, they are suitable for functioning as stand-alone units. This means that they may not necessarily be directly linked linguistically with the rest of the text or other main body material to which they are attached, e.g. as in newspaper headlines. Such usages of elaborative patterns are popular in naming books, foundations, television and radio programmes, movie titles, advertisements, and in mottos. For example:

5.1   *Television programmes*

(35)   *khàaw lâa maa rew*   '*Quick, Late News*'

(36)   *càp khàaw maa khuy*   '*Talk about News*'

(37)   *khàaw khôn khon khàaw cháaw*   '*Stir, Heavy Morning News*'

(38)   *rûaŋ dèn yen níi*   '*Conspicuous Stories this Evening*'

(39)   *yùu dii kin dii*   '*Live Well Eat Well*' (a health programme)

(40)   *din dam náam chûm*   '*Black Soil Moist with Water*'
                                               (an agricultural programme)

5.2   **Books**

Of the fifty-three books her Royal Highness Princess Sirindhorn has published about the countries she has officially visited, eighteen titles show internal rhyme and alliteration.
For example:

(41)   khâaw **thay** **pay** yîi-pùn
        rice   Thai go   Japan
        '*Thai rice goes to Japan.*'

(42)   bəə-**lin** **sîn** kam-phɛɛŋ
        Berlin   end   wall
        '*Berlin without the wall.*'

(43)   bə̀ŋ bɔ̀ɔ than   bə̀ŋ bɔ̀ɔ mòt
        see not in time see not all
        '*Not all seen in time.*'

On the other hand, none of the academic works surveyed uses any of the elaborative patterns. Instead, the nominalizing prefix /kaan-/ seems to be the prominent first morpheme of many such titles. There are six uses of /kaan-/ out of twenty-eight Thai titles. This difference supports the importance of genres mentioned above in speakers' sensibilities about appropriateness or not of elaborative expressions; in this case, travel accounts versus academic writing.

6   **Questionnaire survey results**

To explore further reactions of Thai speakers to usages like those noted above, a questionnaire was prepared and administered to 100 respondents. (For this limited survey, respondents were well-educated native speakers from several locations within Thailand.) In one item, respondents were asked to choose the titles of two books. One was a book about the development of the Thai language, the other about a tour/survey of the forest along the Dongrak Ranges. There were three title choices for each book: one with internal rhyme, one using semiformal prose, one with technical/academic terminology. The results of the survey are enumerated as follows:

(1) For the book about Thai language development, the technical-terminology title, *Wí-wát-tha-naa-kaan phaa-săa-thay*, 'Development of Thai', received the most votes, with little variation; and (2) for the book on the Dongrak Ranges, equal votes were received between titles with internal rhyme and technical terminology (geography).

The difference in (2) responses could be interpreted as showing that people decide first if the book is academic/formal or not. If they take the book to be formal content-wise, they tend to choose the title with technical terminology. If they think it is not a formal/academic book, but an informal travel account, etc., then they prefer the title with internal rhyme. Note that for (1), the genre is obviously technical and academic, so there is no basis for a difference in interpretation.

Similarly, a questionnaire item relating to an actual Police Department campaign confirmed general aspects of this analysis. On Saint Valentine's Day there was a campaign to have policemen check on teenagers in hotels on Valentine's night. A name for the campaign was constructed with internal rhyme *săay-trùat sam-rùat rák*, ('Police exploring love'). Respondents were asked to select or reject this name, and provide a reason. The number of people voting for and against was about the same. Among those voting for the name with internal rhyme, some cited as a reason that the rhyme makes the serious situation light. Others chose the rhyme because they felt that it sounds *phay-rɔ́ʔ*. Those rejecting the name did not share these reactions, showing that attitudes regarding appropriateness depend on interpretation and are still in a state of some flux.

7   Conventionalization and lexicalization

Apart from informal conversation and titles considered above, repetitive or elaborative patterns seem to be ingrained in the language both at the vocabulary and phrasal levels. When genre and content are felt to be appropriate, these constructions are found in newspaper columns, books, chapters of books, and in all kinds of advertisements, including those in general elections and lower-level elections. More than 90% of the seventy-seven provinces' mottos in Thailand are expressed through repetitive and elaborative patterns. As items such as those listed in examples (46) through (56) become conventionalized in general usage, they become good candidates for inclusion in dictionaries.

(44)   sǔay – sǔay
         'good'

(45)   sùt – sǔay
         'most beautiful'

(46)   chon – chán
         'social class'

(47)   mòk – mét
         'a hidden agenda'

(48)   ʔɯm – khrɯm
         'an unclear (of situation)'

(49)   nɯ̀p – nàp
         'sticky, stingy'

(50)   priâŋ – prâaŋ
         'all of a sudden'

(51)   rɔ̂ɔp – rúa
         'around, about'

(52)   chiw-chiw
         'nice and easy'

(53)   hɯɯ – haa
         'rumoured'

(54)   wàa – wûn
         'confused; unable to decide'

(55)   tua – kuu – khɔ̌ɔŋ – kuu
         'I; ego'

(56)   chɯ̂ɯn – chɔ̂ɔp
         'admire'

8   Conclusion

Alliteration, rhyming, and elaborate patterns or the qualities of being *phay-rɔ́ʔ*, sweet, melodious musical, and harmonious have been important in Thai classical poetry and these features still play a significant role in spoken Thai. Many principles that create these expressions remain highly productive, with new items being produced by speakers all the time. Their aesthetic qualities are highly valued and sought after to induce appreciation and attention. However, based on the questionnaire data, it appears that in conversation and in prose the qualities of being sweet and melodious are associated with something being crafted rather than being entirely natural. Hence, they are especially suitable for advertisements, political campaigns, and similar non-formal genres. They are avoided in more formal discourse, such as academic writing. Thai has thus developed rather complex pragmatic functions and weighting associated with aesthetic aspects of the language. In particular, one should avoid oversimplifying Thai sociolinguistics.

References

Diller, Anthony. 1991. 'Consonant mergers and Inscription One'. In James Chamberlain (ed.), *The Ram Khamhaeng controversy.* Bangkok: Siam Society, pp. 161–192.
——— 1993. 'Diglossic grammaticality in Thai'. In William A. Foley (ed.), *The role of theory in language description.* Berlin: Mouton de Gruyter, pp. 393–420.
Gedney, William J. 1989. 'Siamese verse forms in historical perspective'. In Robert Bickner, John Hartmann, Thomas John Hudak, and Patcharin Peyasantiwong (eds.), *Selected papers on comparative Tai studies. Michigan papers on South and Southeast Asia 29, Center for South and Southeast Asian Studies.* Ann Arbor: University of Michigan Press, pp. 489–544.
Haas, Mary R. 1942. Types of reduplication in Thai (with some comparisons and contrasts taken from English). *Studies in linguistics* 1(4): 1–6.
——— 1946. Techniques of intensifying in Thai. *Word* 2: 127–30.
——— 1964. *Thai–English student's dictionary.* Palo Alto: Stanford University Press.
Hudak, Thomas John. 2008. 'Tai aesthetics'. In Anthony Diller, Jerold A. Edmondson, and Yongxian Luo (eds.), *The Tai-Kadai languages.* London: Routledge, pp. 404–414.
Khanittanan, Wilaiwan. 1979. 'How much is English influencing the language of educated Bangkok Thais?' In Nguyen Dang Liem (ed.), *Southeast Asian linguistic studies, volume 4.* Pacific Linguistics C-49. Canberra: Australian National University, pp. 55–59.
——— 1987. 'Some aspects of linguistic change in the language usage of King Rama IV, Rama V and Rama VI'. In Ann Buller (compiler), *Proceedings of the International Conference on Thai Studies, volume 3.* Canberra: Australian National University, pp. 55–70.
——— 1988. 'Thai written discourse: a change to a more autonomous style?' In C. Bamroongraks, et al. (eds.), *The International Symposium on Language and Linguistics.* Bangkok, Thailand: Thammasat University, pp. 120–128.
——— 2007. Language of the news media in Thailand. *International journal of the sociology of language* 186: 29–42.

Part III

Hmong-Mien

11　White Hmong reduplicative expressives

Martha Ratliff

1　Introduction

The lexical category of expressives (or ideophones) is well represented in both Asian and African languages (for Asian languages, see the pioneering work of Diffloth 1972, 1976, 1979; as well as Klamer 2001, 2002; Svantesson 2003; and contributors to this volume). The Hmong language of the Hmong-Mien (Miao-Yao) language family of southern China and northern Southeast Asia is an especially good example of an expressives-rich Asian language. I have published preliminary studies of these words (1986, 2010 [1992]), but the occasion of this book on the aesthetics of grammar has given me an opportunity to examine these words once more, and to offer a new analysis of them. My earlier publications addressed the iconicity of the tone patterns in these reduplicative expressives, but I can now offer preliminary observations on the iconicity of pattern choice, consonant choice, and vowel choice as well. I am also eager to share this data with those who are interested in the aesthetics of grammar more generally; Hmong provides an excellent case study for those who wish to propose universals of aesthetic language on the basis of a large cross-linguistic study.

Expressives in Hmong and other languages constitute a distinct lexical category; they are not nouns, verbs, adjectives, or adverbs. Some languages such as Korean, Semai, and Hmong are rich in these words, while some languages such as English have only a handful of lexicalized expressives. In expressive-rich languages, speakers of average creativity can produce new exemplars on the spot, and hearers know how to interpret them: according to one Semai speaker "we just fire them" (Diffloth 1979: 56). In languages with only a few lexicalized expressives, speakers of average creativity tend not to produce new ones – they are inherited from speakers from past generations, just like all other words, and they do not constitute a separate lexical category. Examples of inherited expressive-like words in English are the adjective *itsy-bitsy* (~ *itty-bitty*) and the noun/verb *flim-flam*. Both are listed in dictionaries; both are assigned to regular lexical categories; and their first published uses are noted by lexicographers (the *American Heritage Dictionary* reports that *flim-flam* first appeared in 1538).

True expressives, on the other hand, in the languages that have them, constitute an open class; given the well-understood rules of expressive formation in each language, new expressives can be produced easily. They are not regular words that participate in the formation of statements, questions, orders, or requests; they are comments on the passing scene. They thus are closer to elaborated exclamations than they are to any other type of word. They reflect the speaker's perception of the essence of an object or event: its sound, its movement, its persistence, its visibility, or the feelings it evokes. They may seem to be surprisingly specific, as this Hmong example:

(1)   /cì cɔ̀/ used of a group of monkeys coming toward you through the trees, but not very fast[1]

but if enough associations for each expressive are collected, it is possible to approach an understanding of its deeper meaning. Each expressive can be used to refer to a theoretically limitless number of experiences that share 'a cluster of elementary sensations' (Diffloth 1976: 257):

(2)   /njû njǎ/ used of whining, of an insincere smile, of a turtle's walk, of the bittersweet feeling of missing someone – so, of something that is two things, or goes two ways, at once.

In Hmong reduplicative expressives, the base is not a morpheme that can be used in isolation, nor does it belong to a lexical category, nor does it have referential meaning; thus, the bases /cɔ̀/ and /njǎ/ above do not 'mean' anything (although they may be accidentally homophonous with prosaic words in the language: /cɔ̀/, for example, means 'treadmill' in Hmong). The meaning of the expressive is rather derived from the listener's interpretation of the interplay of pattern, tone, consonant, and vowel choice across the two syllables.

Hmong was until the twentieth century an unwritten language,[2] and is characterized by a variety of different types of aesthetic language. In addition to the verbal elaboration of experience captured by these reduplicative expressives, there are complex forms of language used for funerals and shamanistic ritual, and an intricate form of poetry, reminiscent of the oral epic poetry of Western cultures, that is delivered in a half-sung, half-chanted style. These expressives come to mind first in connection with the topic of the aesthetics of grammar, however, because they are part of everyday language, not /pâ lụ/ or

---

[1] The data in this chapter was collected by the author primarily from Hmong immigrants who had just arrived in the United States in the 1980s, but also from published dictionaries and literacy materials. The more detailed associations, and all multiple associations, come directly from native speakers who were describing when they might use a particular expressive.

[2] A number of scripts were developed by both outsiders and the Hmong themselves in the twentieth century, the most successful of which has been a romanized script developed by missionary linguists in the 1950s, but literacy has never been widespread.

'flowery language' reserved for special occasions. Their nature is both 'purely aesthetic', because their function is to encapsulate sensory and emotional experience, and "purely grammatical", because their formation is strictly governed by rules that are part of the grammar.

The invariant components of the expressive (described in Section 2 below) serve simply to identify the utterance as an expressive. Against this predictable background, the listener's attention is drawn to those elements of the expressive that are variable: the choice of one of the two expressive types (or templates), the choice of base syllable tone, the choice of alliterating syllable onset, and the choice of base syllable vowel. After first explaining how speakers build expressives according to the rules of the grammar, how these reduplicative expressions differ from regular reduplication, and how expressives are used, I will present what I have been able to observe about iconic sound/meaning relationships involving each of the four variable components of the Hmong reduplicative expressive.

2 Expressive reduplication vs. regular reduplication in Hmong

Hmong reduplicative expressives are composed of a base syllable on the right and a reduplicant syllable on the left. The reduplicant is largely, but not entirely, predictable. Here are some examples:

Type A

(3) /kị kụa/   of a mouse running across an empty box

(4) /ĭ à/   of a mute person trying to talk

(5) /nkăɯ nkŭa/ of the sudden movement of a snake's tongue

(6) /ntʃî ntʃîa/ of the sound of pushing/pulling bolt on an M-16

Type B

(7) /nʈhû nʈho/   of making inopportune pauses in speech

(8) /nû nụa/   of the movement of a wild animal through the undergrowth

(9) /lû làɯ/   of a big, continuous, humming sound, such as an electric generator, or a person speaking without expression, but not without feeling; of complaining to oneself; of doing something without liking it

(10) /nʈû nʈì/   of nodding while sleeping, or of the way a horse walks, raising and lowering his head at each step; to walk right along, with application

The rules for creating a reduplicative expressive in Hmong are strict:

1. The reduplicant must have the same initial consonant or consonant cluster as the base, and a different vowel from the base.
2. The reduplicant vowel is limited to one of the following: /i/, /aɯ/, /u/.

Type A: If the reduplicant tone is the same as the tone of the base, the reduplicant vowel must be /i/ or /aɯ/.

Type B: If the reduplicant tone is different from the tone of the base, it must be a high falling tone, and the reduplicant vowel must be /u/.

Hmong expressive reduplication is to be distinguished from regular reduplication in Hmong on both semantic and formal grounds. In regular reduplication the base also appears on the right, but this is where the similarity ends. Here the base is a prosaic word of the language, and can be of any lexical category, whereas in a reduplicative expressive, the base is not a morpheme that can be used in isolation, nor does it belong to a lexical category, nor does it have referential meaning. The function of regular reduplication is the familiar one of augmentation or intensification: /ʒoŋ ʒoŋ/ 'good good' is simply 'very good' and /khĭa khĭa/ 'run run' is simply 'run and run'. Formally, the reduplicant is either a copy of the base or a phonologically reduced copy of the base, with a reduced vowel and an indiscernible tone. These simple reduplications are part of a larger suite of techniques available to 'bulk up' monosyllabic morphemes for purposes of enriching communication: these other techniques include compounding that does not seem to be semantically motivated (/me njʉa/ 'child', literally 'small-little'), four-syllable coordinative constructions (/cua dâ cua dú/ 'storm', literally 'wind-yellow-wind-black'), and insertion of an intensifying morpheme in the middle of a regular reduplication for further augmentation (/lɔ̂/ 'big', /lɔ̂ lɔ̂/ 'very big', /lɔ̂ tʃì lɔ̂/ 'extremely big').

There are, however, interesting cases of lexicalization that fall between expressive reduplication and regular reduplication in formal terms. In these cases the word either retains (if originally expressive) or assumes (if originally non-expressive) some of the formal properties of expressives. One such lexicalization follows expressive formation rules perfectly: the noun /npû npạ̈/ 'butterfly'. Others deviate from the expressive rules slightly, but are not regular reduplications, either: /npâu npạ̈/, a variant for 'butterfly' (cf. /npâu/ 'moth'), /khâu khạ̈/ 'shell', and /vɔ̂ vòŋ/ 'circle'. In these three nouns, the reduplicant vowel is not /u/, although the tone on the first syllable is falling, and in the case of 'shell' the base and reduplicant vowels are not different.

In terms of use, reduplicative expressives are not embedded within the propositional structure of sentences. They are not subjects, topics, modifiers, or predicates. If used with a sentence, they are adjunct to the sentence as a whole. They are frequently introduced by a word that indicates the sense being engaged by the expressive, e.g. something 'sounds' or 'cries' this way, or something 'falls', 'drips', or 'moves' this way.

3   Iconicity of template choice

The rules of expressive formation given above describe two templates: Type A expressives comprise two syllables bearing the same tone and Type B expressives comprise two syllables bearing different tones, the first of which is high falling. In my sample of 183 expressives the two types are equally well represented, with 94, or 51%, of Type A, and 89, or 49%, of Type B; clearly neither one of these two expressive templates is dominant. This raises the question: on a given occasion, what motivates the speaker to choose one type of expressive over the other? Does either one, or both, have an iconic function that makes it better suited to what he or she wants to say?

I noticed one correlation between expressive type and meaning, although it is not perfect. For 75 of the 94 Type A 'same tone' expressives, a clear majority, I was given only onomatopoeic associations. The following are examples of expressives of this type: /nplhí nplhéŋ/ 'the sound of a pin coming out of a hand grenade'; /mî mê/ 'the sound of mosquitoes buzzing by your ear'; /plĭ plŏn/ 'the sound of an empty bottle submerged in water filling up'; /dì dàɯ/ 'the sound of many people walking on a surface of twigs, rock, and soil'; /dị dụ/ 'the sound of a thick liquid like corn mash boiling (thick, ponderous bubbles)'.

On the other hand, for more than half of the 89 Type B 'different tone' expressives, a majority, I was given either non-onomatopoeic associations (invoking senses other than the auditory) or affective associations only, for example: /hnyû hnyía/ 'to do something against one's own wishes to please another'; /hlû hlŭa/ 'to drag the feet, delay in taking action'; /tʃhû tʃhàɯ/ 'to keep on coming, so that one cannot see the end of their coming'; /txû txǫŋ/ 'to be always eating'; / dû dǫ/ 'to walk at a good clip'.

However, there are numerous exceptions to each rough generalization, and there are also several expressives for which I was given both an auditory association and another sensory or emotional association; this indicates to me that Hmong expressives are indeed abstract in essence, since they can cross sense/emotion borders. For example, one expressive given in Section 2 above, /lû làɯ/, is used both of sounds (of an electric generator; of a person speaking without expression) and of attitudes (of complaining to oneself, of doing something without liking it). Nonetheless, not only do these generalizations work fairly well, it is possible to propose a reason for it: in Type A expressives, the sound of the repeated tone is more salient because it is heard twice. A low-level tone repeated twice, for example, makes a droning sound, and is therefore better suited to represent droning noises that the speaker hears. The iconic functions of some tonal patterns are presented in Section 4 below.

A serious challenge to this hypothesis, however, comes from five pairs of expressives in my sample that differ only in template. The base is the same in the members of each pair, but two reduplicants, following the Type A/B distinction, exist for each base:

(11)   nʈàɯ nʈì (A) / nʈû nʈì (B)
   A: manner of (a human) walking, with application (Bertrais 1979: *nris*)
   B: manner of (a human) walking, with application; manner of a horse walk-
       ing, with head raising and lowering at each step (Bertrais 1979: *nris*);
       manner of nodding while sleeping (Heimbach 1979: 179)

(12)   nkhì nkhòŋ (A) / nkhû nkhòŋ (B)
   A: sound of hollow things (Heimbach 1979: 156); sound of head bumping
       against something or sound of chewing bones (Bertrais 1979: *nkhis*)
   B: sound of chopping soft wood (Heimbach 1979: 478), sound of chopping
       on dead or hollow tree with an ax; sound of a dog gnawing a bone;
       appearance of an old person walking with a bent back (field notes)

(13)   pị pọŋ (A) / pû pọŋ (B)
   A: tottering walk of a fat man (Vwj et al. 1983: 29); sound of running feet
       hitting the earth (Bertrais 1979: *poog*); sound of bomb impact (field
       notes)
   B: tottering walk of a fat man (Vwj et al. 1983: 29)

(14)   khǎw khǔa (A) / khû khǔa (B)
   A: of doing something energetically and steadily (i.e., running) (Vwj et al.
       1983: 100)
   B: of doing something in a deliberate, slow manner (i.e., a chicken scratching
       for worms) (Vwj et al. 1983: 92)

(15)   hǎɯ hǔa (A) / hû hǔa (B)
   A: sound of animals growling, ready to bite (Heimbach 1979: 479); sound of
       human panting; manner of nervous, tense pacing (field notes)
   B: sound of open mouth panting, purring from within throat (here, of a turtle)
       (Vwj et al. 1983: 51)

Since the meanings of the members of each pair are so close, these expressives appear to be meaningful bases to which a second syllable, apparently arbitrarily of Type A or Type B, has been added. This suggests that further study is needed to determine the lexical status of these particular bases. It also calls for a new experiment, one in which speakers are asked to give associations for new expressives created with other bases that exist in the data, to see whether or not the Type A structure is indeed more readily accepted if the expressive is onomatopoeic. These five pairs of words throw doubt on the outcome of such an experiment.

4   Iconicity of tone choice

There are seven major tones in White Hmong:[3] high level (á), high falling (â), mid rising (ǎ), mid level (a), low level (à), breathy/falling (a̤), and creaky/low (a̰). Generalizations about the iconicity of tone choice were originally presented in Ratliff 1986 and Ratliff 2010, and are repeated briefly here.

The Type A 'same tone' expressives in my sample make use of five of these seven tones, all but the mid level tone and the creaky/low tone. The absence of expressives with two of the seven tones may represent accidental gaps, or may be explained by the facts that (1) the mid level tone is less distinctive than the other tones (it is hard to exaggerate and exploit the features of a tone that lacks features!) and (2) the creaky/low tone is short, and creakiness may be difficult to either produce or hear on both syllables in quick succession.[4] Of the remaining five tones, I can make rough generalizations about the iconic values of three of them, although there are counter-examples to these generalizations as well:

falling-falling: energetic, fast, short sights and sounds (many, high, close)
    e.g., popcorn popping, chicks chirping, bullets whizzing, fish
    wriggling
low level-low level: continuous, flat sights and sounds
    e.g., loud droning, speaking in a monotone, the view of a long line of
    people
breathy-breathy: low-pitched, echoic, hollow, airy sounds (big)
    e.g., thunder, a bomb impact, a great flapping of wings, a strong wind

The Type B 'different tone' expressives in my sample involve all six tones other than the high falling tone of the first syllable (the second syllable cannot bear this tone since by definition the two tones must be different). The only Type B expressive whose iconic value I could discern was the falling–rising tone combination. These expressives have double orientation associations: the conjunction of separate sounds, movements, and attitudes. This is understandable given the mirror-image shapes of the falling and rising tone contours. For example: to almost remember, then forget again; of rising from and falling back into unconsciousness; the sound of weaving on a loom; an insincere smile; the sound of whining; the sound of a creaky door.

---

[3] There is also one minor falling-rising tone that does not play a role in the expressives in my sample.

[4] In a tone identification task, native speakers sometimes confused the low level and creaky/low tone (Andruski and Ratliff 2000).

5   Iconicity of consonant choice

The choice of consonant in certain expressives is almost trivially iconic, given particular real-world associations. Clearing the throat or coughing is represented by an aspirated uvular stop, air whizzing past is represented by labiodental fricatives (both /f/ and /v/), and lightning is represented with an aspirated retroflex stop (which is the exact sound I use when I imitate a lightning crash, even though English has no retroflex stops). These meaning/consonant connections are interpretable in one direction only, however; given a particular event, it is possible to guess which consonant might be used, but given a particular consonant, it is difficult, if not impossible, to predict the association the speaker has in mind.

One clear and novel iconic relationship holds between zero-initial, h-initial, and ŋ-initial expressives and a range of meanings having to do with an open mouth: laughing, panting, growling, crying, hiccupping, vomiting, and unintelligible speech. Of course, with either no consonant or an h-initial, no closure is made in the mouth at all, and with an ŋ-initial, the only closure is at the very back of the mouth, leaving the front of the mouth open. These expressives are: /i̠ a̠ɯ/ 'wild pigs open-mouthed gobbling and growling'; /î â/ or /ŋî ŋâ/ 'babies crying'; /î âɯ/ or /î ău/ 'hiccupping'; /i à/ 'the speech of a mute person'; /i ùi/ 'speaking in a monotone'; /û i̠a/ 'to vomit without ceasing'; /hî hâ/ 'laughing or crying'; /hì hùa/ 'laughing'; /hău hŭa/ 'growling or panting'; /hû hŭa/ 'purring or panting (from within the throat)'.

Another novel relationship holds between the lateral liquid /l/ and length: all five of the expressives in my sample with a simple lateral initial also have a base syllable with a low-level tone. It may be that the relatively long sonorant /l/ is chosen to highlight and exaggerate the inherent length of the low-level tone. This combination in turn is used in association with the idea of a prolonged sound or activity in most of these expressives: /lì lòŋ/ 'loud droning, bees buzzing'; /lû làɯ/ 'a big, continuous, humming sound', 'to speak without expression', 'sound of continual complaining to oneself'; /lû lè/ 'the sound of a vacuum cleaner, bees, an airplane'; /lû lìa/ 'a manner of flying (of a butterfly)'; /lû lùa/ 'of a lethargic feeling', 'of wandering'.

6   Iconicity of vowel choice

The contribution of vowels to the sound picture of the expressive is difficult to ascertain. There are a few patterns: for example, all six expressives having to do with lengths of bamboo clapping together, rolling and hitting each other, or popping/bursting in a fire contain an /o/, perhaps because the rounded vowel invokes the hollowness of the bamboo stem. Then a few expressives seem to follow the universal tendency to use high, front vowels for small or slight referents: /cû cĭ/ 'chicks cheeping'; /ntû ntĭ/ 'rats eating'; /ntshû ntshĭ/ 'to cry gently'; /plû plĭ/ 'dying coals, which make little red lights'.

I also observed a correlation between a tone/rhyme combination – /u/ or /oŋ/ with a breathy tone – and a deep and heavy sound: for example, /dị dụ/ 'boiling of a thick liquid like corn mash'; /qị qụ/ 'a growling stomach'; /pị pọŋ/ 'a bomb impact'; /tị tọŋ/ 'heavy footsteps'; /vị vọŋ/ 'a stampeding herd'. It is interesting that the vowel /o/ by itself without the final nasal does not participate in this association; the final nasal appears to give the syllable the extra weight it needs to convey the impression of heaviness.

An interesting question about vowel iconicity is raised by the variation in the Type A reduplicant form between /i/ and /aɯ/. I expected the difference not to be a simple matter of free variation; it seemed reasonable to think that the choice between the monophthong and the diphthong would be governed by iconic considerations. But I did not discover an iconic motive in the choice between the two, but rather a formal motive for some of them: if the vowel of the base is /i/ and the vowels of the two syllables must be different, then speakers must choose /aɯ/ for the vowel of the reduplicant in a Type A expressive. This accounts for the fact that all expressives with /i/ in the base are either Type B or are Type A with /aɯ/ in the reduplicant. Otherwise, no pattern was detected.

7 Conclusion

It is possible to analyse a Hmong reduplicative expressive as an interlocking set of iconic values that serves the communicative needs of the occasion especially well. I believe speakers must interweave such values both when building and when interpreting new expressives. Thus the components of /vị vọŋ/ 'a stampeding herd' would be

1. Type A: onomatopoeic
2. breathy tone/breathy tone: low-pitched, echoic, hollow, airy sounds (big)
3. /v/: whizzing air
4. /oŋ/: deep and heavy

... an appropriate comment on the passing of a thundering herd of animals.

Beyond the analysis of the structure of these aesthetic expressions, a study of how they are used in day-to-day life is yet to be undertaken. Such a study can only be carried out in a Hmong community in Southeast Asia. Younger bilingual Hmong Americans do not use expressives, and all with whom I have talked in recent years are unaware of their existence. Expressives are part of the oral artistry of the Hmong people, and all of these oral skills have taken only one generation to start disappearing in immigrant communities in the West. This raises the larger, and perhaps historical, question of why some human languages appear to have a well-developed lexical category of this type, others do not, and yet others can lose these words so easily. Does mere literacy eliminate the need for these expressions, or is the loss of such a rich and subtle form of communication due to a more complex set of pressures?

References

Andruski, Jean and Martha Ratliff. 2000. Phonation types in production of phonological tone: the case of Green Mong. *Journal of the international phonetic association* 30: 37–61.
Bertrais, Yves. 1979 [1964]. *Dictionnaire hmong-français*. Bangkok: Sangwan Surasarang.
Diffloth, Gérard. 1972. 'Notes on expressive meaning'. *Papers from the Eighth Regional Meeting of the Chicago Linguistics Society*. Chicago Linguistics Society, pp. 440–447.
    1976. 'Expressives in Semai'. In Philip N. Jenner, Laurence C. Thompson, and Stanley Starosta (eds.), *Austroasiatic studies*, Part I. (Oceanic Linguistics Special Publications, No. 13.) Honolulu: University of Hawaii Press, pp. 249–264.
    1979. 'Expressive phonology and prosaic phonology'. In Theraphan L. Thongkum, V. Panupong, P. Kullavanijaya, and M. R. K. Tingsabadh (eds.), *Studies in Tai and Mon-Khmer phonetics and phonology in honor of Eugenie J. A. Henderson*. Bangkok: Chulalongkorn University Press, pp. 49–59.
Heimbach, Ernest E. 1979. *White Hmong–English dictionary*, revised edition. Linguistics Series 4, Data Paper 75. Ithaca: Cornell University Southeast Asia Program, Department of Asian Studies.
Klamer, Marian. 2001. 'Expressives and iconicity in the lexicon'. In Erhard Voeltz and Christa Kilian-Hatz (eds.), *Ideophones*. Amsterdam: John Benjamins, pp. 165–181.
    2002. Semantically motivated lexical patterns: a study of Dutch and Kambera expressives. *Language* 78: 258–286.
Ratliff, Martha. 1986. 'Two-word expressives in White Hmong'. In Glenn L. Hendricks, Bruce T. Downing, and Amos S. Deinard (eds.), *The Hmong in transition*. New York: Center for Migration Studies, pp. 219–236.
    2010 [1992]. *Meaningful tone: a study of tonal morphology in compounds, form classes, and expressive phrases in White Hmong*. DeKalb, Illinois: Northern Illinois University Press. Originally published by Northern Illinois University Center for Southeast Asian Studies.
Svantesson, Jan-Olof and Damrong Tayanin. 2003. 'Sound symbolism in Kammu expressives'. In M. J. Solé, D. Recasens, and J. Romero (eds.), *Proceedings of the 15th International Congress of Phonetic Sciences*. Barcelona: Casual Productions, pp. 2689–2692.
Vwj Tsawb, et al. 1983. *Phau qhia nyeem ntawv Hmoob Dawb [White Hmong literacy primer]*. Washington, DC: Center for Applied Linguistics.

Part IV

Austronesian

12   The aesthetics of Jarai echo morphology

Jeffrey P. Williams and Lap M. Siu

1   Introduction*

Grammatical resources that include articulatory contrasts and patterning, word formation, euphony, and cultural poetics are all employed to distinguish highly refined and nuanced meanings in Jarai discourse. The ideology of grammatical aesthetics of Jarai is condensed – at least partially – into utterance (1).

(1)   Tai anai (.) ta   kiăng ñu pơ-hiăp   hay¹   biă
       like this   1PL   want   3   CAUS-speech ECHO (VN) better
       'We like for our speech to sound better.'

This portion of narrative discourse gives the Jarai perspective on euphony, even to the extent of employing a grammatically aesthetic form *hai biă*. Example (2) provides a more complex set of forms demonstrating the intricate use of a multiplicity of grammatical resources to express an intensity of feeling.

(2)   Nư djik-djăk khăk-kơčah kơ   kâo
       3   criticize   hack-spit   DAT 1
       'S/he is very critical of me.'

Example (2) demonstrates the functioning of echo word formation as well as a type of compounding that creates derivatives that are analogous to what are referred to as 'four-syllable expressions' in the literature on Southeast Asian linguistics.² The English gloss, although an appropriate translation, is not able to convey the depth and complexity of what is being expressed by vocalic alternation in the predicate 'criticize' and the addition of the adverbial

* Research for this paper was supported by a Texas Tech University Research Enhancement Fund award to Williams in 2009–10. Our thanks go out to the Montagnard community in Raleigh, North Carolina for hospitality, kindness, generosity, and their keen interest in preserving their indigenous languages.

¹ This is a borrowing from Vietnamese, although it is considered the meaningless portion of the echo formation involving the Jarai root *biă*.
² It is clear that this collocation does not have four syllables; however, the process and overall semantic force is identical to what is described as such for other non-Austronesian languages (Tai-Kadai, Mon-Khmer, etc.) of the region.

intensifier, which is a compound of two verbs referring to the expulsion of sputum and mucus.

The Austronesian languages of Mainland Southeast Asia have typically suffered from under-representation in discussions of the areal features and areal linguistic landscape of the region.[3] Also, being the latest of the linguistic arrivals to the region, the Austronesian representatives are often seen as the recipients of change, not as the innovators and it is clear from an examination of Jarai morphology that there are striking parallels with the Mon-Khmer languages as well as with some Tai languages. The purpose of our chapter is not to pursue the contact history of Jarai aesthetic morphology, but instead to document and categorize this important area of Jarai grammar.

2   The linguistic position of Jarai

Jarai belongs to the Chamic subgroup of the Malayo-Polynesian branch of the far-flung Austronesian language family. The proto-Cham ethnolinguistic group arrived onto coastal Vietnam from Borneo in the first or second century BCE (Edmondson and Gregerson 2007). Jarai, along with Êđê (or Rhade), Haroi, and Bih (see Nguyen 2009 and this volume) form the Highland Chamic branch of Cham. The generally agreed upon story in regards to the distribution of the Highland Chamic speakers is that they spread westward from the coastal areas with the defeats of the Cham Empire in AD 982 and in AD 1471 by Vietnamese kingdoms.[4] Movements of portions of this larger Chamic-speaking group created a linguistic intrusion in the pre-existing Mon-Khmer (Bahnar) territory. This intrusion separated the South Bahnaric group from the rest of Bahnar (Sidwell 2007).

The Jarai language has over 317,000 speakers in Vietnam, the traditional homeland of the Jarai, as well as unnumbered speakers in the Montagnard diaspora including Canada, Australia, and the United States. In Jarai traditional territories of the Central Highlands of Vietnam (primarily in Pleiku and Kontum Provinces), there were at least seven different dialects spoken; however, these dialect distinctions have been rapidly degrading through subgroup intermarriages and other external social pressures.

The data that we rely upon in our paper comes primarily from Jarai speakers in the United States, although most of this population acquired the language while growing up in Vietnam, and while there are differences in the frequency

---

[3] Thurgood (1999), however, is the glaring counter argument here.

[4] One argument against this hypothesis is that the Highland Chamic languages show no lexical evidence of the kind of religious hierarchy and social organization that was clearly present in the Cham Empire. An unsupported yet possible explanation is that more than one group of migrants came from insular Southeast Asia to the shores of the mainland.

of usage of many of these forms and their derivative processes, we do not examine the social factors underlying those changes here.

3 Jarai phonology, prosodics, and phonotactics

3.1 Jarai phonetics and phonology

The phonetics and phonology of Jarai have yet to be fully described in a consistent and coherent fashion, in spite of the fact that data on the language has played an important role in reconstructing proto-Cham (cf. Thurgood 1999). Some selected features of the Jarai sound system are:

i. distinctive vowel length as in [blan] 'to sleep with one's eyelids partially open' and [bla:n] 'moon';
ii. an implosive stop series ([ɓ] and [ɗ]);
iii. reduction and elision of vowels in minor syllables, which can result in complex onsets in major syllables; and
iv. a register system similar to that found in Mon-Khmer with examples such as [pʰaʔ] 'chisel' and [pʰa] 'thigh'.[5]

Phonetic features and metrical structure are heavily employed in the aesthetic component of Jarai grammar. The features of the sound system are resources for the aesthetic qualities of Jarai grammar.

3.2 Jarai orthography

The Jarai language has an orthography that was developed by French-speaking Catholic missionaries in the early twentieth century. This orthography is based on the existing system that had been developed for Vietnamese some time earlier. In this chapter, we employ the Jarai writing system and the following transliteration table can be used to convert Jarai orthography to phonetic equivalencies.

i	=	[i]
ê	=	[e]
e	=	[ɛ]
ư	=	[ɨ]
ơ, â	=	[ə]
a	=	[a]
u	=	[u]
ô	=	[o]

---

[5] Jarai orthography partially represents this contrast by the presence of 'h' after vowels in breathy register and a 'breve' over the vowel in tense register.

o = [ɔ]
˘ = HIGH or TENSE register (glottal stop – laryngealization)
p = [p]
t = [t]
č = [tʃ]
k = [k]
ph = [pʰ]
th = [tʰ]
kh = [kʰ]
b = [b]
d = [d]
g = [g]
j = [j]
ɓ = [ɓ]
ɗ = [ɗ]
dj = [ʔc]
m = [m]
n = [n]
ñ = [ɲ]
ng = [ŋ]
w = [w]
l = [l]
r = [r]
y = [y]
s = [ʃ]
h = [h]

3.3   Register

Jarai like the other Highland Chamic languages has a register system, which contrasts breathy syllables with tense ones. Register is incompletely denoted in the orthography in which breathy syllables usually have a final 'h' and tense syllables have a breve over the vowel.

(3a)   *pă*

(3b)   *pah*

This system is undoubtedly due, yet not fully attributed, to contact with Bahnar and other Mon-Khmer languages where register is pervasive given that such a system is not found in other Malayo-Polynesian languages.

3.4   Syllables

Jarai, like other Chamic languages, demonstrates a tendency towards monosyllabic roots that are derived historically from disyllabic sources. In some forms, Proto-Malayo-Polynesian disyllabic forms lose the vowel of the first syllable, forming complex onsets in the remaining monosyllable as mentioned previously. In the majority of forms however, the PMP vowel is reduced to schwa as in examples (4) through (6), forming sesquisyllabic words (cf. Matisoff 1973a).

(4)   hơdip   [hə.díp̚]   'to live'

(5)   pơhiap   [pə.hyáp̚]   'to talk or speak'

(6)   rơkơi   [rə.kói]   'husband'

Cho and King's (2005: 187) characteristics of semisyllables that include the sesquisyllabic forms easily incorporate the evidence from Jarai as well as the rest of the Chamic family. In their account, a semisyllable is defined as:
a. having no nucleus;
b. having no coda;
c. having no stress/accent/tone;
d. having well-formed onset clusters; and
e. being restricted to morpheme peripheral positions.
Cho and King's typological casting encompasses the Jarai data very well. Minor syllables in sesquisyllabic words do not participate in reduplication or echo formations in Jarai. I have chosen to represent these and their relationship to what is sometimes referred to as the 'major' syllable of the word as shown in (7).

(7)

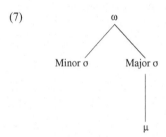

From a moraic perspective, we can state that reduplication and echo word formation are sensitive to weight.

4   Jarai morphosyntax

Some of the features of Jarai morphosyntax have raised speculation that the language might have experienced creolization during its sociolinguistic history (see Grant 2007). It is beyond the purview of our chapter to delve into these speculations, so we reserve our comments to the basic structural features of the grammar.

Jarai is a configurational language with SVO word order in transitive clauses. Questions are marked with an utterance final interrogative marker and there is no change in word order. The language possesses a complex and culturally linked numeral classifer system, although not all nouns participate.[6]

(8a)   Ñu   nao   pơ   sang   hră   sa   čô   ñu
       3   go   PREP house book one CLF 3
       'He goes to school by himself.'

(8b)   Ñu   mă   sa   drơi   abêk
       3   catch one CLF   tadpole
       'He caught a tadpole.'

By any account, the inflectional morphology of Jarai is minimal. There are only a couple of bound morphemes in the language, and the most frequently occurring – the causative prefix *pơ-* – is a clear borrowing from Mon-Khmer.[7] Although it appears to combine with another form *rơ-* to create a reciprocal construction, the reciprocal is *pơrơ-*.[8]

(9a)   taih   'to hit'

(9b)   pơ-taih   'to cause someone to hit'

(9c)   pơrơ-taih 'to hit each other repeatedly; to fight'

There is no inherent number distinction in nouns in Jarai and nouns without a numeral (and classifer) can be interpreted as either being singular or plural. Specification of number in Jarai discourse does not occur very often. Tense and aspect are marked only through free morphemes that typically convey other meanings in other contexts.

4.1   Reduplication

Being genetically Austronesian, Jarai makes broad use of reduplication and the language possesses a highly productive system of reduplication. Reduplication in Jarai is always complete in the sense that an entire prosodic consitituent is copied. There are no partial reduplicative forms, if one eliminates prefixes from consideration. These forms are invariably roots, excluding semisyllables, as shown in a handful of examples as follows.

(10a)   dhĕt   'movement of an object back and forth'

---

[6] One notable example is *atăô* 'ghost', which is not countable. There is a homonym *atăô*, meaning 'corpse' that is countable and takes a numeral classifier.
[7] A free morpheme *pơ* is the locative preposition in Jarai, as in *Ñu truh pơ hma ñu*, 'He arrived at his field.'
[8] The reciprocal is typically shortened to [pə] in fast speech. Disambiguation occurs through context.

(10b)   đhĕt đhĕt   'describing the motion of a (i) stick in the water; (ii) fish;
                     (iii) bird; or a pig's tail'

(11a)   ding   'sound of thunder'

(11b)   ding ding   'sound of intense thunder'

In opposition for what is claimed for Vietnamese by Brunelle and Lê Thị Xuyến (this volume), Jarai speakers do not consider reduplicative constructions to be aesthetic.

5   Aesthetic processes in Jarai grammar

In manners akin to what is found and described for so many of the languages of Mainland Southeast Asia, the grammar of Jarai is impressive with resources to convey qualities of the senses, emotions, movements, and the like. These resources are also operational with nominal roots to shade meanings. And not unlike the other languages described within the covers of this volume, Jarai relies heavily on aspects of the phonological system including metrical structure to accomplish this conveyance. In Jarai, this way of speaking is called *toloi pơtŭh*, which means roughly 'rhyming speech'.[9] It is a highly valued socio-linguistic resource that is highlighted in other genres beyond conversational discourse, such as sung poetry, verbal duelling, and veiled public critique.

5.1   Echo word morphology

Echo word morphology has been the subject of considerable attention in prosodic theories of phonology and morphology (see McCarthy and Prince 1996). In opposition to accounts which seek either to collapse echo word morphology into reduplicative constructions (cf. Alderete et al. 1999) or to marginalize it as a special type of morphology that exists outside grammar (Pullum and Rawlins 2007), we respect a tack that is steered by native speakers' grammatical knowledge, both as observed in fieldwork with the Jarai language and through one of the author's intuitions.[10] What we present here is broad descriptive information on a core aesthetic aspect of Jarai native speaker competency. It is, unfortunately, an aspect of Jarai grammar that is eroding due to cultural changes both in Vietnam and in the Jarai diaspora. What drives the machinery of echo morphology is the speaker's intent to convey highly

---

[9] The glosses for the name of the genre break down to *toloi* that functions as a nominalizer and *pơ-* is the causative prefix attached to the verbal root *tŭh* that means 'to rhyme'.

[10] Cf. Hyman 2006, 'Phonological theory and field work: is the gap widening?' Paper presented at the Fourteenth Manchester Phonology Meeting, Manchester, England, 25–27 May.

nuanced meaning through the use of prosodic and phonetic devices in the grammar.

Echo word morphology involves a systematic change in the copied portion of a collocative form constructed from a root morpheme. The systematic changes – grammaticalized – involve both changes in onsets, nuclei, and codas in major syllables in Jarai. Example (12) shows onset replacement in a left-headed construction.

(12)   čim   →   čim brim
        'bird/s'   bird ECHO 'a grouping of different species of birds'

In this example the branching nature of the onset is maintained.

Echo formation is also used productively with other nominals to create a mass grouping of all types, on par with *čim brim*, as shown in (13).

(13a)   arŏng   →   arŏng arot[11]
        'insect/s'   insect ECHO 'all kinds of insects'

(13b)   ôh   arŏng arot   bŏng podia kāō biă   abih
        EXCL insect ECHO eat   rice   1   almost COMPL
        'Oh my, insects have eaten almost all of my rice crop.'

There can be significant variation within a single formal echo construction, meaning that many roots can have two or more echo collocations as shown in (14a). In examples (14b) and (14c), the meanings of the two collocations are identical. The choice of echoant is determined purely on aesthetic grounds.

(14a)   lŭk ⎰   lŭk   lăk
                ⎱   lŭk   pŭk

(14b)   lŭk lăk
        mix ECHO 'mix'

(14c)   lŭk pŭk
        mix ECHO 'mix'

---

[11] The initial 'a' in 'arot' is deleted in normal speech, so the form follows the rule that only major syllables participate in echo formation and weight is preserved.

(14d)   kaō lŭk lăk   abih bang anŏ bŏng anai hrŏm
         1   mix ECHO   all   DET eat this together
         'I eat all of my food mixed together.'

(14e)   kaō pohiăp lŭk lăk   dua thlāō toloi po-   hiăp
         1   speak mix ECHO two three NMLZ CAUS- speak
         'I speak a combination of two or three languages.'

Example (14e) shows that the same *lŭk lăk* echo formation that is used in (14d) to describe the mixing of food can also be used to describe speech, but in this case it specifically refers to code-switching or code-mixing between Jarai and other languages, especially Vietnamese, English, and Ede.[12]

Prefixes and other grammatical morphemes can occur with echo collocations in Jarai. The most common bound morpheme that occurs in some echo collocations is the causative prefix *po-*. Its occurence with both members of the formation is variable and we cannot comment on exactly what parameters govern the variation. Examples (15a) through (15c) provide some typical, illustrative cases.

(15a)   rodah rodong   → po-   rodah rodong
         clear ECHO   CAUS   clear ECHO
         'very clear'   'to make something very clear'

(15b)   rung   rang   → po-   rung po-   rang
         ECHO   troubles, confusion CAUS ECHO CAUS troubles, confusion
         'problems'   'to create problems for someone else'

(15c)   grĭ   grăn   → po - grĭ   po -   grăn
         dirty ECHO   CAUS dirty CAUS   ECHO
         'extremely dirty'   'to make something very dirty'

5.2   Types of echo formation in Jarai

5.2.1   Left-headed echo formations   These echo formations are the most commonly used in vernacular Jarai. In each echo form, the root is the left-most member of the formation. The echoant appears to the right of the root.

(16a)   păl
         ROOT 'wrap around something as of a string or a rope or a vine'

(16b)   păl   wăl
         ROOT ECHO 'run around, specifically as when a child runs around his/her
                    parents' legs'

---

[12] This style of speaking is called *lŭk lăk toloi pohiăp* in Jarai.

(17a)   nêt
ROOT   'very thin, in describing string that is worn'

(17b)   nêt   nêo
ROOT   ECHO   'describing a piece of string that has worn through and about
to break'

(17c)   trĕ   rɔmô   anai   [nêt   nêo]   biă   tɔi   laih
string   this   [very thin   ECHO]   almost   break   EMP
'This string has worn through and is about to break.'

They are also frequently employed in specialized genres such as *tɔloi pɔtuh*.[13]
In these forms, the left member of the collocation is the root and it is the only
portion that carries intrinsic semantic value. The echoant is always the right
member. As can be seen, both rhyme and alliteration function as resources for
the change in the echoant.

(18)   rɯng   →   rɯng   rang
'farmland'   ROOT   ECHO
'forest'

(19)   glêh   →   glêh   glan
'tired'   ROOT   ECHO
'complaining, whining'

(20)   rɔmuăn   →   rɔmuăn   rɔmĕ
'flexible'   ROOT   ECHO
'very weak and flexible'

(21)   arŏng   →   arŏng   arot
'insects'   ROOT   ECHO
'all kinds of insects'

(22)   ôh   arŏng   arot   bŏng   pɔdai   kāō   biă   abih
EMP   insects   ECHO   eat   rice   1   almost   COMPL
'All of the insects have almost eaten all of my rice crop.'

5.2.2   Right-headed echo formations   In these echo formations, the root is the
right member of the collocation and is the only form with independent meaning.
The left member is echoant (on par with reduplicant) in these constructions and
carries no independent meaning. Likewise, native speakers cannot use these
forms independently nor can they assign them a partial meaning within an echo

---

[13]   The poetics of *tɔloi pɔtuh* involve a complex rhyme and alliteration schema that link prosodic
phrases together in a text. Equally complex are the principles of semantic relationships between
words, reduplicative forms, and echo forms that govern the narrative cohesion in the texts.

collocation. In general, these collocations carry the meaning of generality, plurality, emphasis, as well as a melodic connotation – in that they are more pleasing to the listener than the non-echoed forms.

(23)   hơng   'empty'
         heng   hơng
         ECHO   empty   'empty'

(24a)   djư   'hesitate'
         djưng   djư[14]
         ECHO   hesitate 'hesitate'

(24b)   ih   mă   yơh   anăm   [djưng djư]   ôh
         2   get EMPH NEG   [ECHO   hesitate] EMPH
         'Feel free to get anything.'

(24c)   huă   yơh   anăm   [djưng djư]   ôh   hŏ
         eat   EMPH NEG   ECHO   hesitate EMPH EMPH
         'Go ahead and eat – don't wait.'

5.2.3   Idiosyncratic echo formations   These echo collocations do not easily fit in any other type and they typically are used in negative constructions in Jarai.

(25)   ơu   honĭng   bu   rơming
         NEG homesick NEG ECHO
         'not homesick'

(26)   bu   hưp   bu   ham
         NEG ECHO NEG greedy
         'not greedy'

As can be seen in these examples, the forms can be either left or right-headed. Further research will be needed to determine the full extent of these forms but our impression is that they are very limited.

5.2.4   Discourse, genres, and echo words   The masterful usage of echo collocations is the hallmark of certain genres in Jarai. While all speech has the potential to be beautiful, genres such as *tơloi pơtuh* are defined by such beauty. This genre of Jarai spoken and sung language involves the creative use of echo collocations and the structure of Jarai meter, rhyme, and alliteration.
    Here is an example of a sung text performed in a duet:

---

[14] Vietnamese has a very similar echo collocation, *do dự*.

(27)   A: ơ   ⌈ goʼyut ⌉   kao mŏʼng hlâo   la   dih   lah

    B: ơ   ⌊ goʼyâo ⌋   kao mŏʼng đưm   la   dih   lah

    A: EMP   ⌈ friend ⌉   1   from   before   VCBL   over there   VCBL

    B: EMP   ⌊ ECHO ⌋   1   from   ancient   VCBL   over there   VCBL

    A: 'Oh my old friend from far away.'
    B: 'Oh my old friend from far away.'

In this example, the echo collocation is deconcatenated with each person singing one part of it, which demands a high level of grammatical comprehension and semantic interpretation on the part of the listener.

In the poetics of *tơloi pơtuh*, left-headed echo collocations can be separated, becoming non-contiguous. In (28a) taken from a text of a *tơloi pơtuh* that is used to exorcise a malevolent spirit, the discontinuity is evident. Example (28b) shows an aesthetic compound not based on echo formation.

(28a)   đuaĭ   yang   drĭ

      leave   spirit   ECHO
      'Leave spirit!'

(28b)   đuaĭ   yang   drang

      leave   spirit   violent
      'Leave violent spirit!'

Example (29) provides another lyric from Jarai sung poetry in which the echo collocation is also discontiguous, showing the pervasiveness of parallelism in the text.

(29)   dĭt   kơ   rung   dưng   kơ   rang
      VCBL   PREP   ROOT   VCBL   PREP   ECHO

5.3   Two-syllable expressions

Haas (1964) and Matisoff (1973b) have brought considerable attention to elaborate expressions and four-syllable expressions in the grammars of Southeast Asian languages. The general forms are A–B–A–C or A–B–C–B. Elaborate expressions, broadly defined by Haas, would include the echo word formations in Jarai discussed in the previous sections.

In Jarai, four-syllable expressions of the type described by Haas and Matisoff do not exist. Instead, we find two-syllable expressions in which independent forms are conjoined for both semantic and aesthetic qualities. These forms are not echo forms although there are general principles of rhyme and alliteration that govern the conjunction of forms that might lead a language learner or fieldworker to believe that they are. Contrary to what is the case for echo collocations, each member of the compound (not collocation) carries its own meaning.

(30)   soh   'wrong'
        sat   'ugly'
        soh sat   'a wrong doing, or a sin for Christianized Jarai'

(31)   hɯp   'intense desire'
        ham   'greedy'
        hɯp ham   'to be extremely greedy'

(32)   mɔak   'pleasing' (ADJ)
        mɔai   'plenty' (ADV)
        mɔak mɔai 'to have enough to please'

(33a)   ngui   'play'
        ngor   'tease, joke with'
        ngui ngor 'to enjoy someone's company'

(33b)   kaō   ngui ngor   hăng   sang   anŏ   gŏyut kaō
        1   play tease   PREP   house   DET   friend 1
        'I am hanging out with my friend's family.'

5.4   Fossilized aesthetic compounds

Jarai also evidences compound expressions that are completely unanalysable in terms of the meanings of the apparent constituents since there are no independent meanings. The meaning resides in the complete aesthetic compound. We analyse these as fossilized aesthetic compounds. The forms appear on the surface to be echo formations due to the alliterative or rhyming aspects that bind the collocation and create its pleasing sound effect. It is only at the semantic level that these forms are distinguished from non-echo collocations. We provide some examples as follows.

(34)   suh sah[15]   'to be moved emotionally'

(35a)   hel hol   'lonely'

(35b)   kaō   dŏ   *hel hol*   hɔjan   kaō
         1   stay   lonely   alone   1
         'I remain alone and lonely.'

Interestingly, *hel hol* can be replaced with *heng hŏng*, which is an echo word collocation, as shown in (36).

(36)   kaō   dŏ   *heng hŏng*   hɔjan   kaō
         1   stay   lonely   alone   1
         'I remain alone and lonely.'

(37a)   ngek ngŏk
         'describes something with the shape of a human head that is bobbing, or flopping around; instability'

(37b)   kaō   buh   akŏ   ñu   ngek ngŏk   gah ngô   jɔlah   ia
         1   see   head   3   bobbing   PREP   tongue   water
         'I see his head bobbing above the water.'

(38a)   glĕk glŏk
         'describes the movement of a loosely attached object'

(38b)   tɔgai   ñu   glĕk   glŏk
         tooth   3   wiggle
         'His tooth is loose and wiggling.'

6   Conclusion

The Jarai language is endowed with grammatical processes that permit speakers to convey emotions, states, commentary, and observations, and we have not ventured into all aspects of the grammatical aesthetics in the language here. One difference between Jarai and other non-Austronesian languages in Southeast Asia is the high degree of multiple aesthetic forms for a singular lexical item in echo word formation.

Grammatical aesthetics in Jarai also sheds insight into sociolinguistic aspects of code-switching and code-mixing as shown in (39).

(39)   kaō   pɔhiăp   lŭk   lăk   tɔloi   jarai   hang   tɔloi   yuan
         1   speak   mix   ECHO   NMLZ   Jarai   PREP   NMLZ   Vietnamese
         'I speak mixed Jarai and Vietnamese language.'

---

[15] This example has an analogue in Vietnamese, *xuc động.*

In this utterance, *lŭk lăk toloi jarai hang toloi yuan* is a complex noun phrase that is headed by an echo word collocation. Unfortunately for future research into the aesthetics of Jarai grammar, the impacts of cultural change on language structure and use are profound. In the transnational Jarai communities in North America, refugee communities have grown in which extensive language contact is the norm. In these contact environments, patterns of aesthetically motivated speaking are being replaced by sociolinguistic behaviour that reflects a new Montagnard-American identity.[16] This new identity, based on being American, involves a shift to English as well as shifting to a new Montagnard language, based on the use of Êđê and Jarai. While this new variety is wholly Chamic, it lacks the aesthetic properties of either input language.

References

Alderete, John, Jill Beckman, Laura Benua, Amalia Gnanadesikan, John J. McCarthy, and Suzanne Urbanczyk. 1999. Reduplication with fixed segmentism. *Linguistic inquiry* 30: 327–364.

Cho, Young-mee Yu and Tracy Holloway King. 2005. 'Semisyllables and universal syllabification.' In Caroline Féry and Ruben van de Vijver (eds.), *The syllable in optimality theory*. Cambridge University Press, pp. 183–212.

Edmondson, Jerold A. and Kenneth J. Gregerson. 2007. The languages of Vietnam: mosaics and expansions. *Language and linguistics compass* 1/6: 727–749.

Grant, Anthony. 2007. 'Admixture and after: the Chamic languages and the creole prototype'. In Umberto Ansaldo, Stephen Matthews, and Lisa Lim (eds.), *Deconstructing creole*. Amsterdam: John Benjamins, pp. 109–139.

Haas, Mary. 1964. *Thai–English student's dictionary*. Palo Alto: Stanford University Press.

Matisoff, James. 1973a. 'Tonogenesis in Southeast Asia'. In Larry Hyman (ed.), *Consonant types and tone*. University of Southern California Occasional Papers in Linguistics 1: 73–95.

1973b. *The grammar of Lahu*. Berkeley: University of California.

McCarthy, John J. and Alan S. Prince. 1996. *Prosodic morphology 1986*. http://ruccs. rutgers.edu/pub/papers/pm86all.pdf

Nguyen, T. 2009. Some basic constructions in Bih (compared to Ede). Presented at the 19th Southeast Asian Languages Conference. National University of Social Sciences and Humanities, Ho Chi Minh City, Vietnam, May 2009.

Pullum, Geoffrey and Kyle Rawlins. 2007. Argument or no argument? *Linguistics and philosophy* 30: 277–287.

---

[16] Montagnard is a term used for indigenous peoples of the Central Highlands of Vietnam, which includes the Jarai as well as other Chamic peoples and Mon-Khmer groups in the area.

Sidwell, Paul. 2007. 'The Mon-Khmer substrate in Chamic: Chamic, Bahnaric and Katuic contact'. In Ratree Wayland et al. (eds.), *SEALS XII Papers from the 12th Annual Meeting of the Southeast Asian Linguistics Society (2002)*. Canberra: The Australian National University, pp. 113–128.

Thurgood, Graham. 1999. *From ancient Cham to modern dialects: two thousand years of language contact and change*. Honolulu: University of Hawaii Press.

13 Expressive forms in Bih: a Highland Chamic language of Vietnam

Tam Nguyen

1 Introduction[*]

Mainland Southeast Asia is justly acknowledged as a linguistic area where many of the languages are rich in grammatical resources to convey sensations and perceptions as well as emotions (Diffloth 1979). One of the most recognized of these resources is the special class of words termed 'expressives' by Diffloth (1972). Due to their rich and textured iconicity as well as their widespread occurrence, expressives have become an important area of research for scholars working on the languages of Mainland Southeast Asia (Diffloth 1979, 1994; Enfield 2005, 2007; Kruspe 2004; Matisoff 2001; Thompson 1987; as well as the contributors to the present volume).

Data presented in this chapter from Bih, a previously undescribed Austronesian language of Vietnam, provides new examples of expressives, further advancing arguments for this class as a defining feature of Mainland Southeast Asian languages. There are approximately 500 Bih speakers living in the Krong Ana district of Daklak Province of the Socialist Republic of Vietnam. Daklak Province, in the Southern Highlands region of the country, is also home to other Chamic speaking peoples, including the Rhade/Êđê (hereafter Êđê), and to a lesser extent, the Jarai. The Chamic languages are a major branch of the Malayo-Chamic subgroup of Austronesian (Thurgood 1999). The Highland Chamic languages include Bih, Êđê, Bih's closest linguistic relative, and Jarai.

Because of the similarities of the two Bih and Êđê cultures and languages, even though little evidence had been presented, Bih was thought to be an Êđê dialect (Maitre 1912; Đoan 1998) until the publication of this author's field research in 2009 (Nguyen 2009a, 2009b).

This chapter will provide an analysis of Bih expressive forms. Following Diffloth (1972), I use the term 'expressive' to refer to an iconic word class defined by its distinct phonological and semantic properties, and not to refer to a

---

[*] The main source of data on Bih for this chapter is derived from about fifty oral texts, mostly on the topics of culture and beliefs, provided by ten consultants of the Bih Documentation Project; a two-year project (2008–2010) that was funded by HRELP at the School of Oriental and African Studies.

group of onomatopoeic forms. I will explore Bih expressives by describing the phonology of the class, including the full reduplication in monosyllabic roots and other patterns in which only a portion of the root is changed. In the class of Bih expressives analysed here, forms include a base or root morpheme and a reduplicant whose phonological form is either identical with the base (e.g., full reduplication) or only partly identical with the base (e.g., partial reduplication). Diffloth (1994) has proposed that expressives are created by phonic elements available within the phonological system of the language where there is a relation between the iconic system of the language and the semantic properties of the expressive, which means that reduplication with iconicity contributes to the inventory and distribution of the class of expressives.

2   The phonology of Bih

In this section I will describe the Bih phonological system since it plays a vital role in the formation of expressives. Tables 13.1, 13.2, and 13.3 show the

Table 13.1 *Bih consonants*

	Labial	Labial-dental	Alveolar	Palatal	Velar	Glottal
Plain stops	p b		t d	č j	k g	(unmarked)
Aspirated stops	ph		th	čh	kh	
Implosives	ɓ		ɗ	dj		
Nasals	m		n	ñ	ng	
Fricatives			s			h
Approximants		w			y	
Rhotics			r			
Lateral approximant			l			

Table 13.2 *Consonant clusters*

Plain stop + lateral	pl bl			kl gl
Plain stop + approximant	pr br	tr dr	čr	kr gr
Palatal + approximant			djr	
Nasal + approximant		nr		
Fricative + approximant		sr		

Table 13.3 *Bih vowels*

	Front	Centre	Back
Close	i	ɯ	u
Close-mid	ê	ơ	ô
Open-mid	e	â	o
Open		ă/a	

orthographic symbols of Bih arranged according to their articulatory properties. The orthography for the Bih language has been influenced considerably by the social and linguistic relationships between Bih and Êđê. In fact, Bih orthography is based on the Êđê system, including the shared phonemic feature that vowel initial words have the initial glottal stop unrealized in the orthography.

All of these consonants are allowed as the onset of a monosyllable. However, as mentioned above, Bih words can be composed of a sesquisyllable. The relations between initial consonants in the sesquisyllable and the main syllable restrict the number of consonants occurring in these two positions. Therefore, of the consonantal segments listed in Table 13.1, Bih only permits /p/, /t/, /k/, /m/, /r/, and unmarked glottal stop as onsets in sesquisyllables. Additionally, only twelve consonants – /p/, /t/, /k/, /č/, -unmarked glottal stop, /m/, /n/, /ng/, /r/, /l/, /s/, and /h/ – can occur as codas in a main syllable. All three aspirated stops are only in the initial position of main syllables.

Of the clusters listed in Table 13.2, the sequences /pl/, /bl/, /kl/, /gl/, /pr/, /br/, /tr/, /dr/, and /kr/ are all inherited clusters from Proto-Chamic while the other clusters were borrowed by Bih after Proto-Chamic had broken into different languages (Thurgood 1999).

As for vowels, Bih has four vowels /i/, /u/, /a/ and /ə/ that can occur respectively in both pre-syllable and main syllable. This inherited Proto-Chamic feature marks Bih as the only Chamic in Mainland Southeast Asia having the four-way distinction of vowels in pre-syllabic position.[1] In addition, Bih also has a distinction of vowel length in which each vowel has its corresponding short and long versions. In Bih orthography, the short version is marked by the symbol '˘' above the vowel. Bih also has six diphthongs /ei/, /âo/, /ao/, /ui/, /ia/, and /ua/ and three triphthongs, /iêu/, /uai/, and /uay/.

Bih words may be up to three syllables in length, although the most common ones are monosyllabic with a 'sesquisyllable' in which a canonical word consists of a reduced 'pre-tonic' and a main 'tonic' syllable (Matisoff 1973).

---

[1] Thurgood (1999) indicates that Acehnese, a Chamic language of Sumatra also has this distinction.

This phonotactic feature is also typical of the non-Austronesian languages of Mainland Southeast Asia (Matisoff 1973). Examples (1) and (2) show the main syllable types in Bih.

(1)   CVCCV or CVCC/CCV

(2)   CVC/CV

3   Bih reduplication

3.1   Complete reduplication

Complete reduplication in Bih involves expressives in which a reduplicant is reduplicated from a base that sometimes synchronically has no lexical meaning (as example (6)). If a base lacks meaning, this raises the fundamental question how to determine the base and the reduplicant. However, in Bih complete reduplication, mainly the base form is the one that receives high intonation and it is used to create partial reduplication as well as shown in examples (3) and (4) where *djeh* and *mʉt* are the bases and they are also the bases in their partial reduplications in (5a) and (5b). As for examples like (6) where the base cannot be determined (by the consultants), we can't find its partial reduplication either (more data needed for further conclusion on this).

(3)   'djeh djeh[2]   'doing something not seriously'

(4)   'mʉt mʉt   'doing something very slowly'

As shown in example (5a–b), considering *djeh djeh*, the base is the first occurrence of the form *djeh* – the leftmost member of the collocation – and the one that carries high intonation. It is also the one used to create a partial reduplication *djeh djut* where the rhyme of the base, *-eh*, is replaced by *-ut*, and in *mʉt mač*, the rhyme of the base, *-ʉt*, is replaced by *-ač*.

(5a)   'djeh djut   'describing bad manners'

(5b)   'mʉt mač   'doing things without a serious attention'

(6)   'wah wah   'doing something the same and the same'

Monosyllabic roots are the only forms that participate in complete reduplication. None of the complete reduplication in the data so far is from disyllabic forms. It is necessary to mention here that in Bih, disyllable words are not common, except those created by the two morphological prefixes: a verbal

---

[2] The diacritic ' indicates high intonation on the base.

causative *pa-* and a formative *ma-* that can be added into any Bih word, for example, *padjŏ* ('make it right') and *mamang* ('nothing'). However, none of the disyllabic roots with either of these prefixes is reduplicated completely, but rather they reduplicate partly with the pattern exactly the same as that of partial reduplication from a monosyllabic root. In other words, for disyllabic roots having a prefix either *pa-* or *ma-*,[3] the root is the constituent on which the phonological pattern of an expressive is based, and not the morphological prefix. For example, from *mamang*, a partial reduplication *mamung mamang* ('doing nothing') can be formed. There is also a partial reduplication *mung mang*, which has the same meaning and distribution as *mamung mamang*.[4] Both *mamung mamang* and *mung mang* exhibit the same partial phonological change regardless of the fact that the previous one has a prefix in a root and the other does not. In other words, the point here is whether or not the prefix exists in a word, the phonological rhythm of the main root will decide the pattern of an expressive, but not the prefix if one exists. This helps to determine that, in Bih, reduplication is a phonological characteristic of expressives but not a morphological means for deriving expressives from already existing lexicon.

3.2   Partial reduplication

Partial reduplication describes expressives in which only a certain portion of the main root is changed. As mentioned in Section 1, only monosyllabic root reduplication is explained. Included in this section are partial reduplications which have either peak or onset or coda or rhyme in the base different from that of the reduplicant.

3.2.1   Peak changes
The expressive forms that belong to this group are those in which initial consonant/consonant clusters and final consonant of the root (the first word in the examples below) and the reduplicant are the same while the main vowel between them are different. Below are examples for this type of partial reduplication.

(7a)   arblĕ arblŏ: 'describing lands with too much water'

(7b)   brwâp brwɔp: 'describing place with a lot of moving people'

(7c)   nik nak: 'describing things having its original history'

(7d)   pŭk păk: 'describing too much talk'

---

[3] These are some of the only productive prefixes in the language.

[4] Jarai exhibits similar variation in these sorts of expressives, which Williams and Siu refer to as echo formations. A cognate *ma-* prefix can also be either present or absent in the forms without impacting the meaning.

(7e)   rlung rlưng: 'describing things moving side by side in water'

(7f)   trpĭm trpŭm: 'describing things shorter than their expected size'

(7g)   tadŭt tadăt: 'describing hesitation in speaking'

As shown in examples (7a–g), the initial consonant or consonant clusters and the final consonant in the base are repeated respectively in the reduplicant. Laurence Thompson (1987) refers to these types of reduplicative changes as 'chiming' in Vietnamese. The only portion of the root changed is the peak, which does not require any phonological changing rules for its vowel such as high/low or front/back. The vowels of the root and the reduplicant could be the same high as in *arƀlĕ arƀlŏ* or the same position as back vowels in *rlung rlưng*, but they could be from different groups of vowels as in *ƀrwâp ƀrwɔp* and *nik nak*. In addition, these vowel changes don't carry any difference in meaning either. In other words, the changed phonological patterns for vowels between the root and the reduplicant are unpredictable. Also, the onset consonants or onset consonant clusters distributed to this group vary: any consonant or consonant clusters allowed in an onset position could occur in the reduplicant as far as a whole expressive carries its iconicity, the main characteristic of expressives. In other words, there is no restriction on the nature or quality of the initial consonant of the base. However, as for final consonants, this group mainly has final stops even though it also allows some final nasals.

3.2.2   Onset changes   This group of expressives is created by reduplicating the root rhyme and changing the onset consonant/consonant cluster in the reduplicant. There is no onset-changed condition between the root and the reduplicant: it could be from a single consonant in the base to a consonant cluster in the reduplicant or vice versa. Examples *hŏk krdŏk* and *tŭt trlŭt*, (8a) and (8b) respectively, show how the initial consonant of the base, which is a single consonant, changed into any initial consonant cluster of the reduplicant.[5] On the other hand, *tloh inoh* and *ƀhĭt-lĭt* demonstrates the converse whereby the onset of the base is a cluster while that of the reduplication is a single consonant. Example (8e), *kriêp mliêp*, demonstrates another case in which the base *kriêp* and the reduplicant both have an onset consonant cluster, *ml-*, which is not very common for this type of reduplication and also the cluster '*ml-*' itself is irregular in Bih.

(8a)   hŏk krdŏk: 'describing a very happy feeling'

(8b)   tŭt trlŭt: 'describing trees/plants without leaves because they all fell off'

(8c)   tloh inoh: 'describing things in a large number'

---

[5] Thompson refers to these forms as rhyming reduplications in Vietnamese.

(8d)   b̓hĭt-lĭt: 'describing things very tiny'

(8e)   kriêp mliêp: 'very quiet'

(8f)   b̓iă riă: 'describing things coming very shortly'

(8g)   nɯih kɯih: 'describing things easy to do'

3.2.3   Coda changes   As the name itself 'coda changes' indicates, the only element changed in the reduplicant in comparing to the base in this group is the final consonant as in examples (9a–c).

(9a)   lah lañ: 'very lazy'

(9b)   kruh krun: 'describing an action happening frequently'

(9c)   jhăk jhăr: 'describing things in a large quantity'

As indicated in Section 2, Bih has twelve consonants which can be in the coda but not all of these twelve consonants can occur in a coda-changed reduplication group. In Bih expressives, the most common coda replacements are the voiceless glottal fricative /-h/ or alveolar/palatal nasal /-n/ or /ñ/. This type of expressive formation is not as pervasive in Bih as is the class of rhyme replacements, where both the final consonant and preceding vowel are altered.

3.2.4   Rhyme changes   Rhyme changes are the most productive pattern of the partial reduplication. In Bih, it is common to see more closed syllables with a rhyme changed than open syllables as shown in (10).

(10a)   arlăn arlet: 'always'
(10b)   arleh rluăt: 'describing things not smooth (as clay, mortar, dough)'
(10c)   brañ brô: 'describing a very bright light as sun'
(10d)   găt gĭn: 'describing things in a very big size'
(10e)   gɔ̆ gɔi: 'things everywhere'
(10f)   grɯ̆ grɯm: 'describing things very dirty'
(10g)   lič lek: 'doing something again and again'
(10h)   moh măl: 'lucky'
(10i)   mprŭč mpruĭ: 'describing things with splayed ends'
(10j)   rhô rhêč: 'describing things in a very long length'
(10k)   rɔ̆ ruôm: 'embarrassing'

4   The semantics of Bih expressives

One common characteristic of the semantics of expressives is the fact that expressives could be used to describe an iconic event/situation as a whole in a form of a single lexical item, which would otherwise be expressed by an independent clause or phrase in languages without expressives. Equally, because expressives describe sensory perceptions such as visual, smell, taste, and feelings, one expressive can be used in various situations: it could be used to describe an event as a 'cluster of elementary sensations' (Diffloth 1976: 257) or to express one particular sense in that 'cluster'. Thus, with the same expressive, one speaker may use it to describe a visual situation, another may use it as a feeling expressive, and it could also be used in reference to an aural perception. These various meanings and attributions are all acceptable among speakers as far as the meanings of that expressive share a common core. This situation is found with *awung awăng*, which could be interpreted as a whole of sensations in terms of all feelings and actions that alcohol can cause after a person drinks too much, or as a specific sense in 'describing feelings of a person, who drank a lot of alcohol, feels excited in doing something he wants', or as in 'describing feeling unstable of a person who is drunk or sick'. It equally can be used to describe a visual-based expression of 'a walk from a person who is either drunk or sick, whose one foot is on this side but the other could be on the other side'. The point here is each speaker may find one sensation he wants to convey through the use of an expressive, but which others use for other sensations. This generalization holds as far as they all agree that sensations they want to describe all exist in that expressive. The more people agree on its meaning, the more frequent that expressive is used and accepted.

Another example is from the use of *pujip pujap*. This expressive is used to describe any situation in which things are out of their regular expectation. For example, a package of salt is normally sold for a thousand *đồng* – the national currency of Vietnam. In one situation that I observed, packages of salt were being sold for five or even six thousand *đồng*. In the speaker's mind, it was unbelievably expensive, and beyond her expectations. Thus, that whole event is expressed by *pujip pujap*. Another context where *pujip pujap* is used is the situation in which people whittle bamboo to make sticks for their weaving. After they get what they want, they continue to whittle bamboo to make sticks even though they may really not know what these sticks could be eventually used for. Bih speakers refer to this activity of doing things for a non-specific purpose as *pujip pujap*. *Pujip pujap* can also be used to describe the case where people are engaged in moulding clay pieces together to form cooking pans, but it turns out that the clay is too dry and the object falls apart into small pieces. The whole event and its constituent processes is *pujip pujap*.

Another common characteristic of expressives is that meanings of certain expressives co-occur with some specific verbs even though expressives themselves do not co-occur with those verbs. For example, *rep čhep* is an expressive describing an itch that affects the whole body.

(11a)   rep čhep asei   prlei kâo
         itchy   body body 1
         'My body is itchy.'

Although its meaning is associated with itchiness, it does not occur in other contexts elsewhere, or even with the verb that means 'itchy' *ktăl*. A similar example is found in *paliă palia*. *Paliă palia* is used to describe non-endless actions, commonly for walking.

(11b)   paliă palia   ñu
         Walk   3
         'He walks for a while.'

It is often used in sentences describing a non-endless walking without the occurrence of the verb 'walk' *nao*. In other words, expressives can and do, within a certain degree, stand for themselves and do not modify other words.

5   Conclusion

As in other Mainland Southeast Asian languages, expressives in Bih constitute an anomalous class with respect to the descriptive categories that we apply to other linguistic forms. They are derived by phonological alternation, but unlike typical morphophonological processes, they are unconstrained and have a greater freedom to combine sound units that are available in the language.

Syntactically, expressives mostly function as independent clauses[6] by themselves (such as the case of examples 11a–b) even though they may have the function of an adjective or an adverb. And semantically, they are associated with impressionistic, emotive, or 'expressive' values quite unlike the more easily definable semantics associated with even abstract nouns and verbs.

From a typological point of view, it is interesting to observe how Bih, originally not a Mainland Southeast Asian language, adapts the two common phonological and semantic features of expressives like other languages in this area (such as Srê, Sêmai Khasi (Diffloth 1976) and Bahnar (Banker 1964). From a historical point of view, more data on expressives from other surrounding languages in the region, in particular Mnông, a Mon-Khmer language which is thought to have had significant influence on Bih, is needed to help determine whether or not the divergence between Bih and Êđê expressives may be explained by the degree of language contact and change.

References

Banker, E. 1964. Bahnar reduplication. *Mon-Khmer studies* 1: 119–134.
Diffloth, G. 1972. Notes on expressive meanings. *Chicago linguistic society* 8: 440–447.
      1976. Expressives in Semai. *Oceanic linguistics special publications* 13: 249–264.

---

[6] Thanks to Gérard Diffloth for bringing this to my attention.

1979. 'Expressive phonology and prosaic phonology in Mon-Khmer'. In T. L. Thongkum et al. (eds.), *Studies in Tai and Mon-Khmer phonetics and phonology in honor of Eugenie J A. Henderson*. Bangkok: Chulalongkorn University Press, pp. 49–59.

1994. 'i:big, a: small'. In L. Hinton, J. Nichols, and J. Ohala (eds.), *Sound symbolism*. New York: Cambridge University Press, pp. 107–114.

Doàn, V. P. 1998. *Từ vựng các phương ngữ Êđê = lexique des Dialects Êđê*. Thành phõ Hõ Chí Minh: Nhà xuãt bản Thành phõ Hõ Chí Minh.

Enfield, N. J. 2005. Areal linguistics and Mainland Southeast Asia. *Annual review of anthropology* 34: 181–206.

2007. *A grammar of Lao*. New York: Mouton de Gruyter.

Hoàng, V. H., Q. N. Hà, V. K. Nguyen, and Viện ngôn ngữ học. 1998. *Từ tieng Viet: hình thái, cấu trúc, từ láy, từ ghép, chuyen loai*. [Hà Nội]: Nhà xuất bản Khoa học xã hội.

Hoàng, V. H. and Viện ngôn ngữ hotc. 1998. *Tù điển tù láy tiếng Viet*. [Hà Nôi]: Nhà xuất bản Khoa học xã hôi.

Kruspe, N. 2004. *A grammar of Semelai*. Cambridge University Press.

Maitre, Henri. 1912. *Les jungles moi: Mission Henri Maitre (1909–1911), Indochine Sud-centrale*. Paris: Larose.

Matisoff, James. 1973. *The grammar of Lahu*. University of California Publications in Linguistics, No. 75. Berkeley: University of California Press.

2001. 'Genetic versus contact relationship: prosodic diffusability in South-East Asian languages'. In Alexandrea Y. Aikhenvald and R. M. W. Dixon (eds.), *Areal diffusion and genetic inheritance: problems in comparative linguistics*. Oxford University Press, pp. 291–327.

Nguyen, T. 2009a. Some basic constructions in Bih (compared to Ede). Presented at the 19th Southeast Asian Languages Conference. National University of Social Sciences and Humanities at Ho Chi Minh City, Vietnam, May 2009.

2009b. Bih phonology. Presented at the 42nd International Conference on Sino-Tibetan Languages and Linguistics. Payap University, Chiangmai, Thailand. November 2009.

Thompson, L. C. 1987. *A Vietnamese reference grammar*. Honolulu: University of Hawaii Press.

Thurgood, G. 1999. *From ancient Cham to modern dialects: two thousand years of language contact and change*. Honolulu: University of Hawaii Press.

Part V

Tibeto-Burman

14 Aesthetic aspects of Khumi grammar

David A. Peterson

1 Introduction

Khumi is a Tibeto-Burman language (Kuki-Chin branch) with two mutually intelligible dialects spoken by around 2,000 individuals in southeastern Bangladesh. There are other Khumi varieties spoken just over the border in Burma by much larger populations. This chapter is based primarily on a large text corpus assembled for the northern dialect.

As a language on the border between South and Southeast Asia, Khumi potentially has two major areal pulls on it. However, in terms of the devices and strategies speakers have for providing their audience with an aesthetically pleasing experience, the language falls squarely within the realm of Southeast Asia. While I will not argue that Khumi is unique in terms of an overabundance of prototypically reduplicative and sound symbolic aesthetic elements, the relative importance of such devices in Southeast Asian languages is undeniable, and Khumi is no exception. I do not think it is necessary to argue for a specifically aesthetic component of grammar based on this observation, but I will attempt to demonstrate that the elements of grammar most clearly related to aesthetics in Khumi show significant formal and functional overlap, and can in some sense be viewed as all arising from similar motivations.

I will consider in some detail three main elements of Khumi grammar which speakers consistently appear to regard as contributing to aesthetically satisfying speech. First, I will look at verbal classifiers, which have reduplicative and sound symbolic aspects typical of the aesthetic elements the chapters in this volume focus on. Ultimately, however, I will suggest that this device is more crucial to word-formation than simply playing a stylistic role. Next, I will discuss elaborate expressions; these differ in certain formal respects from those found in other languages of the area, but are used in a functionally similar way to the elaborate expressions seen elsewhere. I will then turn to Khumi's mimetic lexicon. It will be seen that there are frequent points of convergence between these otherwise independent devices. Finally, I will briefly look at a preference for parallel structures more generally in Khumi narrative, and conclude with an assessment of the extent to which the main elements considered form a coherent grammatical subsystem by virtue of their overlap.

2   Verbal classifiers

Khumi actually has fairly limited *numeral* classifier phenomena compared to other Southeast Asian languages. Numeral classifiers are few in number, and they are often omitted in natural discourse. However, the language makes up for its lack of numeral classifiers by its development of a separate classificatory type of phenomenon: the verbal classifier.[1]

Khumi's verbal classifiers form a discrete class of bound postverbal elements containing around 100-paired members.[2] Some simple examples showing how verbal classifiers are used are given in (1–2).[3]

(1)   co^5 deng^3-mab'lö^1 h'ni^3 k'say^5 tlängm^3 apë^1='ë^{10}
       rice   pound-ANT   this   elephant   suddenly   move=SEQ

       h'nay^3 h'ni^3 areng^6 c'niw^3 co^5 deng^3=nö^3=a^1
       thus   this   king.GEN   daughter   rice   pound=NMLZ=LOC

       ciw^1-ka^1=vöyng^1=bo^3
       step.on-AUGVCL=UNFORTUNATELY=REAL

       'When they were pounding rice, this elephant suddenly moved and thus stepped on and killed this king's daughters, who were pounding rice.' (33.31)

(2)   tuydu^3=a^1 tuy^1-'ung^4 t'pång^4=b'lö^1=bo^3
       stream=LOC   water.gourd   carry=SEQ=REAL

       biw^{10} töng^4=b'lö^1 cë^4-kö^1=te^5 ca^1=vuy^3=te^5
       hut   arrive-SEQ   beat-DIMVCL=EVID   eat=PFV=EVID

---

[1]   For a detailed account of verbal classifiers in Khumi, see Peterson 2008. This section reviews the main findings of that study and offers several new observations.

[2]   There may actually be a far larger number of these. Exhaustive testing for the potential of specific predicates to co-occur with verbal classifiers has so far not been possible, and it is unlikely that all of them have been identified.

[3]   Superscript numerals indicate tones (1–5 are lexically distinct tones; higher numbers (6 and above) indicate tone variants found in particular tonal combinations, or as markers of high-frequency morphosyntactic categories which may be given a tonal rather than a segmental instantiation, e.g., 'genitive', 'negative', 'irrealis', and 'locative'). A full discussion of Khumi tonal alternations is not possible here; see Peterson (to appear) for further details. The data does not include the details of all alternations: only alternations related to tonal instantiation of morphosyntactic categories are included. Other formatives are cited with their underlying tone. Several Khumi vowel phonemes are indicated here by means of umlauts, including *ë*, an unrounded front vowel intermediate between [i] and [e], *ä*, which is [æ], *ü*, close to [ɣ], and *ö*, which represents a vowel slightly higher than [ɔ]. I use *å* to indicate [ɔ]. For consonants, the only unexpected convention is the use of *y* rather than *j* for a palatal glide. ' indicates the short pre-syllable of a sesquisyllabic structure. Numbers following examples indicate location of the data in the text corpus.

lu⁴=lö¹   c'pay¹¹-thång¹¹   biwng³-hä¹=te⁵
head=TOP   granary-stick.LOC   plant-DIMVCL=EVID

'He carried a gourd of water from the stream, and when he arrived at the field hut, he beat him [his son] with a stick, ate him, and planted his head on one of the bamboos sticking up from the rim of the granary.' (3.14)

The first example occurs in a narrative where an elephant has been disturbed by a bat flying into its ear, and in its uncontrolled movements, it accidentally steps on a king's daughters and kills them. In the second (also narrative) example, a man who has turned into an ogre kills one of his young sons. In (1), the element *-ka¹* indicates that one of the participants in the scene, the king's daughters in this case, is relatively large (or perhaps that there is more than one person involved); *-ka¹* is an augmentative verbal classifier. If the speaker had instead selected the corresponding diminutive verbal classifier, *-kö¹*, he would have been commenting on the relatively small size of a participant, as in (2), where the classificatory element reflects the small size of the child.

In and of itself, this phenomenon does not appear to have any particular aesthetic effect. However, there are at least two respects in which the verbal classifier phenomenon is relevant for our consideration.

First, all classifiers have either a fully reduplicated or a quasi-reduplicative extended form, though the speakers in (1) and (2) chose not to use them here. Thus, insofar as reduplicative structures are taken to be an essential aspect of the Southeast Asian aesthetic gestalt, verbal classifiers are of potential interest. Some text instances with reduplicated classifiers, which otherwise might be monosyllabic, are seen in (3) and (4). The context for the first example is a traditional story in which a widower and his son receive a magical piece of deer meat; while they are off in the fields at work, it turns into a woman, does all their housework for them, and then turns back into a piece of deer meat. In this sentence, they discover what is going on and capture the piece of deer meat while it is in human form. Note the fully reduplicated form of the verbal classifier associated with *p'tiw²* 'catch', *-räng¹räng¹*, which elsewhere in the corpus is simply *-räng¹*.

(3)   am-p'cew²-täng³=b'lö¹=bo³   düng⁵   pa¹¹-nüng²kha⁴=b'lö¹
        MID-skewer-again=SEQ=REAL   night second   time=SEQ

        biw¹-'ang¹ thewng³   may¹¹thu¹t'käng¹¹   amhë⁴-thüng³   kha⁴
        rice-curry cook   hearth.LOC   move.around-WHILE time

        p'tiw²-räng¹räng¹=te⁵ h'ni³   s'khi⁴=ya¹ s'khi⁴-mÅy¹-ceng¹=a¹
        catch-DIMVCL=EVID this   deer=LOC deer-meat-portion=LOC

        'It got back on the stick again, and the next afternoon, when it was moving around at the hearth, cooking food, they caught it, this deer, this portion of deer meat.' (5.9)

Example (4) comes from a pear story telling in which the speaker is commenting on the baskets of pears kept by the man in the initial scene of the film.[4] Here, the classifier is *-s'su^1*, which elsewhere appears simply as *-su^1*.

(4)   kåy^4='ë^{10} hu^5=wa^1 (a)   khay^2-s'su^1 öyng^{1}kewng^1-kanuy^1=a^1
       full=AND   DEM=LOC   uh   leave-AUGVCL   tree-bottom=LOC
       'They were full and there, uh, he kept a lot of them, under the tree.' (46.9)

In other cases, the classifier is not reduplicated, but the element has a longer, quasi-reduplicated form, as in (5), where the normal classifier form would be *-piw^1*, instead of the longer *-piw^{1}pa^1*, and in (6), where the classifier in the second line might instead have the form *-tliwng^1* rather than *-tliwng^{1}tlang^1*.

(5)   may^{5}yung^1 k'lüng^4-piw^{1}pa^1 kha^4 t'käng^5-kiwng^1
       thiwng^4=a^1

       coal   smear-AUGVCL   time fireplace-foundation inside=LOC
       khay^2-yo^3 thëng^{1}cë^{10}=lö^1
       leave-IMPFV   Thiengcie.LOC=TOP
       'They smeared coal on her, left her in the bottom of the fireplace, Thiengcie.' (24.51a)

(6)   mang^4 ampo^1=wö^1 të^4-k'å^{5}y'lå^2=c'=bä^5 samthöyng^5-t'va^2
       INTERJ father=EMOT   cook.NEG.-POT.SUPR-INSIST=EMOT   bamboo.cooker

       tho^2-tliwng^{1}tlang^1=håwy^1 sam^{1}på^2 may^1
       thick-AUGVCL =INST   bamboo.shavings   fire

       leng^3-tü^5-nö^3=tew^2=bä^5...
       burn-AUGVCL=NMLZ=COP=EMOT
       '"No, father, maybe it's not finished cooking yet. You've only set a bamboo shavings fire with a thick bamboo cooker..." (Bear's wife said.)' (31.183)

While speakers regard all verbal classifiers as having this potential for reduplicated or elongated forms, naturally occurring instances are fairly infrequent in the available text corpus, so there is little way to tell what the effect of using the longer forms is with certainty. From the available examples, there would appear to be some association of longer verbal classifier forms with intensification. For instance, in (3), the reduplication perhaps has to do with the effort required to catch the piece of deer meat, and in (4) it may be related to the large quantity or the distributed nature of the pears in the baskets; the action of smearing is thorough or intense in (5), and the longer form seen in (6) may have to do with the extreme size of the bamboo cooker

---

[4] For readers unfamiliar with the pear story, see Chafe (1980).

the speaker envisions. We will see below that elaborate expressions often are used in a context involving intensification. It is perhaps this nuance of intensification, which leads speakers to associate reduplicated or elongated verbal classifiers with elaborate expressions.[5]

There is also a clear sound symbolic facet to verbal classifiers. An examination of the vowels which occur in them reveals a tendency for more front vowels to be associated with the diminutive verbal classifier and back and low vowels to be associated with the augmentative verbal classifier for a given pair. See (7) for the attested correspondences between vowels of paired classifiers.

(7)   AUGVCL vowel: DIMVCL vowel:
        a   ë, öy, e, ö, ü, ä
        ay   e
        å   e, ë, ö, ä, ü
        u   ö
        iw   öy
        o   ë
        ew   ë
        u   ü

iw~öy and *ew~ë* would appear to be exceptions to the above generalization, but the diphthongs *iw* and *ew* in Khumi come from a recent modification to etymological **u* and **o*, respectively (cf. Proto-Kuki-Chin **bu'* and Khumi *biw²* 'cooked rice'; PKC **p'lo:ng* and Khumi *plewng¹* 'boat'.) These are thus not exceptional as long as one considers the vowels that these must have had as recently as a couple of hundred years ago. *ü* arguably comes from **i* (cf. PKC **sa-ri'* 'seven' > Khumi *s'rü²*, PKC **min* 'ripe' > Khumi *müng³*), which also would bring *u~ü* into line with the generalization.

It is worth mentioning that the origin of these verbal classifiers is in a long-recognized Kuki-Chin phenomenon: so-called *chiming*. Henderson (1965) first noted this phenomenon in Tedim Chin, defining it there as 'a specialized kind of reduplicated adverb, very common in the colloquial style, in which there is variation in the vowels of the adverb' (1965: 57), and it was later described in detail for Tedim by Bhaskararao (1989). As demonstrated for Tedim, and for Lai by Patent (1998), the phenomenon would appear to be an optional embellishment for making speech more vivid or aesthetically pleasing. Some examples are given in (8).

---

[5] It should be added, however, that the patterns found in elaborate expressions and reduplicated or elongated verbal classifiers are not identical. For verbal classifiers, in the cases detected so far, there is consistently replacement of the rhyme in the reduplicated portion, or total reduplication; in elaboration, as we will see shortly, there are numerous other possibilities, but never total reduplication. So, reduplication/elongation of verbal classifiers may not simply be subsumed under elaboration.

(8)   a. Tedim (Bhaskararao 1989: 113):
       ka^{2}la^{2}ou?^{1} a^1-san^2-gen^{2}gan^2 khat^1 hong^1-pai^2-gan^{2}gan^2-hi^1
       camel   3SG-tall-CHIME   one   VEN-go-CHIME-INDIC
       'The tall camel is coming in a gan-gan way.' (specific motion involving long
       legs or a strong body)

       b. Hakha Lai (Patent 1998: 156):
       saay   a-naal   zua'ma'
       elephant   3SG.SBJ-slip   IDEO
       'The elephant slipped (in a large cumbersome way).'

On the basis of my work with Khumi, I would say that it does not have an exclusively embellishing or decorative effect, and I would doubt that it really has such an effect in other Kuki-Chin languages either. In fact, as with the chiming elements of Tedim and the ideophonic ones of Lai, verbal classifiers in Khumi show such idiosyncratic associations with particular verbal predicates, and they convey such subtle nuances, independent of any aesthetic effect they may have, that I think they are better regarded simply as part and parcel of the language's word-formation resources.[6] For instance, while the -ka^1/-kö^1 elements seen in (1–2) indicate something about the object's relative size in each case, perhaps the more important contribution of this element is that the objects in each case *died*, so that a more faithful rendering of the sentences might include 'to death'. Whereas in the English lexicon we have a large number of specific predicates conveying informa-tion about the exact type of motion involved in a motion event (e.g., *stagger* vs. *saunter* vs. *walk*) or about specific characteristics of the participants, Khumi channels a large part of this expressiveness into specific verbal classifiers. Thus, the ability of a Khumi speaker to appropriately select a verbal classifier to go with a particular predicate in a specific discourse context is akin to the English speaker's ability to select just the right word for describing a given event.

From this perspective, it is not entirely clear that this aspect of Khumi grammar should be considered part of the aesthetics of Khumi grammar any more so than good word choice would be in other languages. However, the sound symbolic nature of the vocalism and the potentially reduplicative form of these elements, as well as their relationship with other phenomena we now turn to, suggest that they belong to the language's stock of devices motivated by aesthetics.

---

[6] Although he does not go quite this far, Patent (1998) seems to be thinking along highly similar lines in his discussion of Lai ideophones: 'the ideophones add rich semantic detail to the verb. In these canonical cases, it is hard to disentangle the semantics of the verb from the semantics of the ideophone' (1998: 157).

3 Elaborate expressions

A characteristic of Khumi speech that clearly has primarily aesthetic conse-
quences is frequent use of elaborate expressions.[7] I employ a definition of
elaborate expression which is crucially functional, although there is a marked
tendency for elaborate expressions in Khumi to assume a particular form, as in
other area languages that make use of them.

For my purposes, elaborate expressions are reduplicative or quasi-
reduplicative structures used for a particular aesthetic effect. Specifically, speakers regard use of them as a sign of good speaking. Elaborate expressions occur
in all discourse genres, but they are most frequent in narrative.

All elaborate expressions contain a head, the element that could occur by
itself were it not part of an elaborate expression; the other portion is the
elaboration. The primary sources for elaborations are nonce expressions or
semantically related items, which may be placed either to the left or to the
right of the head. In the absence of a more specific conventionalized elaboration,
a default reduplicative template involving total reduplication and replacement
of the final rhyme with *-i* is used; elaborate expressions utilizing the default
template are all right-headed. Rarely, elaborations are taken from another
language (generally Marma) or an auxiliary song language. A few examples
of each of these possible elaboration sources are given in (9).

(9)   a. nonce elaborations:
         amung⁵-amang¹ 'dream'
         ka¹¹si¹-taw¹¹kë¹ 'star'
         s'miwng¹-s'tang⁵ 'gayal'

      b. semantically related elaborations:
         ka¹¹si¹-lo² 'moon' (lit. star-moon)
         tuy¹-may¹ 'water' (lit. water-fire)
         uy¹-k'lay¹ 'dog' (lit. dog-monkey)

      c. default reduplicative elaborations:
         mi¹-may¹ 'fire'
         jåy¹ti¹¹-jåy¹tang⁵ 'marfa'
         t'ki¹-t'kay⁵ 'tiger'

      d. elaborations from borrowings or song language:
         nöyng¹¹-akhöyng¹ 'time' (*akhöyng¹* is from Marma)
         ksewng¹-khu⁵ray¹ 'flower' (*khu⁵ray¹* is from 'song language')

In principle, any part of speech could be elaborated, but the only elaborate
expressions attested in our corpus involve verbs and nouns, and the latter
dominate tremendously. They tend to fall into some specific semantic domains,

---

[7] Peterson (2010) provides a more extensive treatment of elaborate expressions in Khumi.

and there probably are both speaker-specific and item-specific preferences for what gets elaborated (e.g., $lä^1$-$'üng^1$ 'field-house', usually with the meaning 'field' in context, or aju^1-$cnå^4$ 'wife-child', usually meaning only 'wife', are quite familiar to speakers and show a strong tendency to be used, and biw^1-$'ang^1$ 'food' is technically no longer an elaborate expression, behaving more like a lexicalized compound).

In terms of function, examining the use of elaborate expressions over a large text corpus suggests that they tend to be employed in a few semantically similar situations. They are used when multiple participants are involved, e.g., as in (10).

(10) ca^1-$cung^4$=$b'lö^1$ $l'ung^4$=a^1 $aklüng^2$-$aklåy^1$=$b'lö^1$
        eat-FINISH=SEQ   area.next.to.houses=LOC   assemble-ELAB=SEQ
        ce^2=te^5 huy^2=te^5
        go=EVID   follow=EVID

        'When they finished eating, they gathered next to the houses, and they went,
        followed.' (35.48)

In this example, all the members of the village gather to hunt an elephant who has abducted a king's daughter.

Otherwise, there is a strong tendency for elaborate expressions to be invoked when an action is performed with intensity, or when a participant feels a particularly strong emotion. An example of the former, involving simply expression of intensity, is seen in (11), where a mother who has gone in search of her long-lost daughter hears loud celebratory sounds coming from the daughter's house.

(11) $t'ko^3$-$vä^3$ $t'ko^3$-$vä^3$=te^5 $måy^5$ $s'lëng^2$-$vä^3$=te^5=$yö^1$
        go-IMPFV   go-IMPFV=EVID   hill   cross-IMPFV=EVID=EMOT
        $nay^{11}b'lö^1$ $thay^3$=bo^3=te^5 ay^1ti^1-$ay^1töng^1$ $tüng^1$=$lö^1$ $ning^{11}ci^2$
        then   hear=REAL=EVID   ELAB-drum   sound=TOP   a.lot
        ang^1ngyi^1-$ang^1ngyëng^1$ $thay^3$=bo^3=te^5
        ELAB-cymbal   hear=REAL=EVID

        'They went and went, and crossed over the hill, and then she heard it, the drum,
        it was very noisy, she heard the cymbal ...' (1.100)

On the other hand, some instances where there is intensity of emotion for participants are given in (12) and (13). In (12), a man who is married to the magical deer-woman from the text discussed earlier bursts out in anger at his wife's pestering him to return home from drinking with friends; his speech to her contains a barrage of elaborate expressions:

(12) $p'khå^2$=$b'lö^1$ ti^2 $s'khi^4$ $daw^{11}kë^1$ muy^4-$ng'leng^5$=$nö^3$
        beat-SEQ   thus   deer   bamboo   stink-AUGVCL=NMLZ

lew^2 nåy^2=nö^3 khu^{1}lung^4 nåy^2=nö^3
word   numerous=NMLZ   song (ELAB)   numerous=NMLZ
ahåy^1=håy^1 ni^{1}puy^1=håy^1=pö^1 am^5-a^{1}ra^2 ne^1-thay^{12}-lä^3
friend=COM   ELAB=COM=also   rice.beer-rice.liquor   drink-POT-NEG
n'=pë^1=te^5 nökha^4=lö^1
QUOT=say=EVID   that.time=TOP

'He beat her at that time, and he said, "Deer, you stink! You talk a lot! I can't even drink with my friends!".' (8.9)

In the next example, several brothers express shocked disbelief at their brother's ability to find wives for them given that they live deep in the jungle:

(13)   tu^{1}nay^3 lew^2=tlay^1 thuy^3=lö^1 ma^4=ma^4 tita=a^1
        such   word=alone/strange   say=TOP   where=LOC   now/here=LOC
        day^{1}ci^1-dä^{1}räng^1 thiwng^4=a^1 m'nö^1 aju^1 nga^1-thay^3=mo^4
        jungle-ELAB   inside=LOC   how   wife   get-POT=Q

        "'Why would you say such a strange thing now? How would you be able to get wives in the jungle?'" (28.81)

This tendency for elaborate expressions to occur in conjunction with some sense of pluractionality or intensity is not grammatical in any strict sense, however. Khumi has many different ways to indicate such notions, which are more grammaticalized than this, such that elaboration is more purely decoration or embellishment than anything else. Of the phenomena considered here, this is also probably the most quintessentially Southeast Asian, although it does not necessarily involve structures identical to the elaboration manifested by other area languages.[8]

4   Mimetic elements

Another major area in which Khumi grammar appears to accentuate the aesthetic is in its large repertoire of mimetic elements. This repertoire is an apparently open class of predominantly reduplicative elements that convey the nature of sounds or motions involved in actions.[9] In fact, in the large corpus of forty-five lengthy texts, there are fewer than 100 different items attested; speakers' intuitions indicate that the class is virtually unlimited in size, however, with vast numbers of such elements yet to be uncovered.

---

[8] For what are usually considered more typical elaborate expressions in terms of form, see the discussions in Haas (1964), Matisoff (1973), and Solnit (1995), among others.
[9] So far there is no evidence that any mimetics in Khumi relate to other sensory impressions, as attested elsewhere (see, e.g., Diffloth 1976).

Some examples of mimetic elements relating to sound are given in (14–16). These examples illustrate the most common syntactic construction used for introducing elements like these. Specifically, they occur in a quotative construction, although the quotative complement is used adverbially rather than as the complement of a verb of speaking, as is usually the case. In (14), a tiger lifts a wooden pig trough in search of a girl who is hiding from him. The mimetic represents the creaking sound of the trough as he lifts it.

(14)   ew^{1}ku^1 khewng^1=nö^3 khri^{1}khrå^5-khri^{1}khrå^5-khri^{1}khrå^5=n'=te^5
        pig.trough   lift=NMLZ   (sound of lifting)   =QUOT=EVID

        bö^6-lä^3=te^5 ngo^6-lä^3=bë^4=te^5
        exist-NEG=EVID   get-NEG=next=EVID

        'He lifted the trough, (sound of lifting) it went, and she wasn't there, he didn't get her then.' (1.47)

(15) and (16) are located close to each other in a single text. Bear and Tiger have raised some human children they found abandoned in the jungle. Bear's daughter marries Tiger's son, but shortly after going to live at her father-in-law's house, Tiger eats her. Bear suspects Tiger has eaten his daughter and challenges him to a contest eating chillies and ginger. After the contest, they click their tongues at each other.[10] Bear is able to produce a proper click (in (15)). Tiger, on the other hand, since he has overeaten, produces an inferior click (in (16)), a telltale sign that he has eaten Bear's daughter.

(15)   ca^1 ca^1 ca^1 ca^1-bä^3-b'lö^1 t'vöng^5 p'lay^4 kö^{5}dang^1=nö^3=lö^1
        eat eat   eat   eat-exhaust-SEQ   bear   tongue   click=NMLZ=TOP

        tüng^1=lö^1 m'nö^1=må^4 n'=pë^1=b'lö^1
        sound=TOP   how=Q   QUOT=say=SEQ

        t'vöng^5 kö^{5}dang^1 kha^4=lö^1 tlang^{1}slang^1 n'=te^5
        bear   click   time=TOP   (good.click.sound)   QUOT=EVID

        'They ate and ate until they were finished, and the bear's tongue click, what was the sound like? When the bear clicked it was (alveolar click).' (3.73)

(16)   t'vöng^5 t'kay^5 kö^{5}dang^1 kha^4=lö^5=bo^3 tu^{1}t'ru^3=nö^3 vuy^3=te^5
        bear   tiger   click   time=TOP=REAL   (abnormal.sound)=QUOT   PFV=EVID

        nökha^4 sang^{1}khåy^1 may^{5}dë^1 a-niw^1-lå^3=te^5=ho^1
        that.time   hair.tuft   little.bit   MID-see=SUPR=EVID=DEIC

        'The bear (mistake) tiger clicked his tongue, "(abnormal click sound)" and at that time a little tuft of hair was seen.' (3.75)

---

[10] An alveolar click is essentially an interjection in Khumi (and several other languages of the area) signifying 'shut up' or 'get out', or indicating surprise, and the connotation in this context is that Bear and Tiger are showing their readiness to fight.

(17–18) give some instances where the mimetic in question primarily serves to depict motion rather than sound. Note that although sound is not the main thing invoked here, the quotative construction is nevertheless used for these, as in the case of auditory mimetics.

(17)   nay^{11}b'lö^1 tläm^3 sam^{1}på^2 may^1
        then   suddenly   bamboo.shavings   fire

        leng^3-tü^5=te^5=bo^3 hiw^1-hiw^1-hiw^2=nö^3
        burn-AUGVCL=EVID=REAL   (motion of flames)=QUOT

        sam^{1}på^2 may^1=lö^1
        bamboo.shavings   fire=TOP

        'Then suddenly he started a big fire with bamboo shavings (motion of flames), the bamboo shaving fire.' (31.179)

(18)   tlängm^3 k'lay^1 üng^1=ma^4 våy^4-yo^3=b'lö^1 alewng^5
        suddenly   monkey   house=LOC   return-IMPFV=SEQ   valley

        åm^2=te^5='e^{10} ni^5-mö^1-cë^5='ë^1 je^2-reng^1-nö^3=ma^4 töng^4=bo^3
        exist- EVID=AFF   3-FGD-P=GEN   live- IMPFV-NMLZ=ALL   arrive

        nökha^4='e   hu^{5}day^1-kiwng^1 li^{1}lång^5-li^{1}lång^5-li^{1}lång^5-li^{1}lång^5
        that.time=AFF   bamboo-tree   waving.motion.of.bamboo

        hu^{11} töm^4=bo^3 nay^{5}b'lö^1 puy^{5}khawng^1=moe^3 plå^2=te^5
        there   arrive   then   Puykhawng=FGD   call=EVID

        'Suddenly the monkeys returned home, there was a valley, and they arrived at the place they lived, and at that time then, arrived there with the bamboos waving [from their movement through them], and then Puykhawng called to them.' (18.79)

Mimetic elements having to do with sound that have been identified so far include those in (19), sorted into groups based on some of the salient categories represented.

(19)   animal sounds or calls:
         vång^{1}vång^{1}vång^1 'mosquito or fly sound'
         o^{1}wa^2'o^{1}wa^2 'sound made by crow or raven'
         bë^{1}trë^{1}bë^2 'sound made by a nightingale'
         t'ë^{1}trü^1'ü^1'a(m)bü^1'a(m)bü^1 'sound made by dove'
         ng(y)e^{1}ng(y)e^2 'sound of barking'
         bu^{11}'ung^1 'barking sound'
         pë^{11}rå^{11}pë^{11}råw^5 'sound of chickens who have been disturbed'

        sounds due to motion or other animal activities:
         så^{1}så^5 'sound of chickens pecking drying rice; rustling sound'
         khiw^{1}khiw^2 'sound of chickens pecking rice'
         ru^{1}ru^{1}ru^2 'sound of bear or other large creature moving through the jungle'

human sounds:

hüng^{1}hüng^5 'sound of irregular breathing'

tlang^{1}slang^1 'sound of a (good) alveolar click'

thuy^5 'spitting sound'

ri^{1}rå^{1}ri^{1}rå^1 'noisy sound, commotion, sound of a large gathering'

sounds of nature (water, wind, etc.):

ki^{1}kå^{11}ki^{1}kå^5 'sound of water entering into body, sinking sound'

bu^{1}bu^2 'sound of bubbling water (from boiling or other causes)'

rewng^{1}rewng^5 'sound of a rolling rock'

püng^1 'sound of wind blowing'

thlewng^{5}thlewng^5 'sound of rushing water or diarrhoea'

sounds associated with falling, hitting, or breaking:

tlöyng^{1}thöyng^1 'clattering sound'

thla^2 'breaking sound'

pha^5 'sound of large object breaking'

phe^5 'sound of small object breaking'

khang^1 'sound of beating'

thi^{1}thu^{1}thi^{1}thu^2 'sound of rope breaking'

piwng^5 'sound of large object falling'

kriwng^{1}kriwng^{1}kriwng^1 'sound of bamboo hitting something'

pu^2 'sound of foot going into a hole'

paw^5 'sound of something (fruit, dead bird) falling'

other common environmental sounds:

së^5 'sound of seeds being scattered (e.g., on a floor)'

sa^5 'sound of a large number of seeds being scattered'

sü^2 'sound of a bracelet'

kri^{1}kra^{1}kri^{1}kra^1 'sound of walking on bamboo, sound of grinding teeth'

sewng^{5}sewng^5 'sound of thatch being carried on the back'

When evaluating the sound symbolic nature of these items, it is useful to recall the vowel quality changes mentioned earlier: i.e., *iw* came from *$^*u$, *ew* from *$^*o$, and *ü* from *$^*i$. With these in mind, while nothing is absolute, lower/back and longer vowels tend to be associated with more resonant sounds and front/high short vowels associated with less resonant sounds. Unchecked tones also tend to be associated with more resonant sounds. For instance, consider the two mimetics related to dogs: *bu^{11}'ung^1* and *ng(y)e^{1}ng(y)e^2*. The first of these is used for a more extended howling sound, while the second is used for staccato barking.

(20)   quick motions:

yü^2 'motion of something passing quickly (including time)'

pruy^{1}pruy^{1}pruy^2 'quick motion'

phro^{11}phro^5 'quick motion'

lå^2 'darting motion, flashing motion'

sö² 'motion which is direct, without stopping'
phrü² 'quick climbing motion'

more specific motions:
li¹lång⁵li¹lång⁵ 'waving motion of bamboo'
phrång⁵phrång⁵ 'motion of many sparks flying from a fire,
                                    leaves falling from a tree, scattering motion'
pü¹ 'motion of disappearing'
dë¹dë² 'fluttering flight motion'
t'khew¹vew¹t'khew¹vew¹ 'running motion of a bear, porcupine, cow, large
                                    human'
hiw¹hiw¹hiw¹ 'motion of flames, feeling of getting angry'
phri¹phrü² 'motion of something going in and out'
prew¹prew¹prew⁵ 'motion of small creatures (e.g., mice)'
prewng⁵ 'spread out motion'

For motions, tone appears to be more important than segmental composition. Checked tones occur with mimetics depicting movements with shorter duration. Unchecked tones (and reduplicative forms) are seen for movements with longer duration.

There is one other important observation to make about mimetics. Compare examples (21) and (22). The element identified as a mimetic in the first sentence, *phri¹phrü²*, bears a striking resemblance to what is identified as a verbal classifier (*phrü²*) in the second.

(21)   phri¹phrü²   phri¹phrü²   phri¹phrü²   n'=te⁵
        (motion of going in and out)   QUOT=EVID

        h'ni³   k'do³-nö³   tüng¹-nö³   vuy³=te⁵=ho¹
        this   bubble-NZ   sound-NZ   PFV=EVID=DEIC

        thiwng¹⁰   angto²-nö³   tüng¹   k'do³-nö³   nö³   vuy³=bo³
        inside   move-NMLZ   sound   bubble-NMLZ   QUOT   PFV=REAL

        '(motion of Treeshrew going in and out) "This bubbling sound must be the
        sound of him moving around inside," he (Bear) (thought).' (31.181)

(22)   tuy¹   dew²=b'lö¹   dew²-phrü²   våy⁴-phrü²   dew²-phrü²
        water   fill=SEQ   fill-DIMVCL   return-DIMVCL   fill-DIMVCL

        våy⁴-phrü²=te⁵   tlëng⁵   nüng²   tlëng⁵   thung⁵=lö¹
        return-DIMVCL=EVID   time   two   time   three-TOP

        'She filled water, quickly filled and returned, filled and returned two or three
        times.' (33.99)

Generally verbal classifiers may not appear in the quotative construction we have seen in use with mimetics. Similarly, mimetics generally cannot appear in bound postverbal position and be interpreted as a verbal classifier. There are a handful of items, however, where there appears to be overlap between classifiers and mimetics. The verbal classifier in (22) involves a quick motion; similarly, the motion of the tree shrew in (21) is quick, and back-and-forth, which would also be a possible interpretation in (22), where there would be a back-and-forth motion associated with fetching water.

Other verbal classifiers exhibit a similar dual behaviour, although it is rare. For instance, sa^5, as seen in (23), may have the behaviour of a verbal classifier. In (24), on the other hand, we see that it also can have the behaviour of a mimetic element, even to the extent that it is introduced with the typical quotative construction. In both of these contexts, which occur immediately adjacent to each other in a single text, the element in question has to do with a large amount of rice seed being thrown, so it is quite clear that they are referring to the same event, although their morphosyntactic behaviour is quite distinct in the two instances.

(23)   tlängm³   ca⁵tüng¹   he²-sa¹=te⁵
         suddenly   seed.type   throw-AUGVCL =EVID

         na⁵si¹na⁵ra¹   åm²-pö²   khu⁵mi¹co¹ möy³-no²   anüng²=nö³
         house.spirit   exist-DIMVCL.IMPER child   eye-nose(ELAB)dirty=NMLZ

         vå¹khång⁵   a¹luy⁵   kamlöyng¹-puy¹   cöyng¹=nö³=ma⁴
         tomorrow   cock   mixed.colour-AUG sacrifice=NMLZ=CERT

         'Suddenly, they (the women) threw out lots of seeds (and the tigers said),
         "House spirit, be quiet! You'll get (them, the seeds) in the children's eyes!
         Tomorrow we'll sacrifice a big multi-coloured rooster to you."' (15.76)

(24)   si¹su¹ si¹su¹   si¹su¹   nö³   i²   sa⁵   nö³   he²-bë⁴
         tiger sleeping sound   QUOT sleep throwing.sound QUOT throw-NEXT

         na⁵si¹na⁵ra¹   åm²-pö²   nay³   thay¹²=kha³
         house.spirit   exist-DIMVCL.IMPER   QUOT   hear.NEG=Q

         khu⁵mi¹co¹   möy³-no²   anüng²=nö³   nay³ thay¹²=ʼa¹
         child   eye-nose (ELAB)   dirty=NMLZ   QUOThear.NEG=Q

         'They slept, (sound of tigers sleeping.) And they threw again, (sound of seeds
         being thrown.) "House spirit, be quiet! Don't you hear? You'll get them in the
         children's eyes! Don't you hear?"' (15.77)

Even for verbal classifiers, which do not exhibit this sort of ambiguous behaviour, it is highly usual for these to have nuances of either sound or motion. Other Kuki-Chin languages have comparable or even more extreme tendencies for related elements to refer to sound and motion.

5   Discourse-level parallelism

Aside from the three aesthetic devices seen so far, there is, as elsewhere in the area (cf. Solnit 1995), a strong preference for structures with parallel structures.

These include structures with exact repetition, or simply approximations or reports of similar occurrences. Their domains range from near proximity, to distinct episodes. To illustrate a few of these, in (25), a girl is giving gifts to her long-lost mother: a box of chicken, a box of beef, and a box of pork. When the girl's speech is reported, the story-teller chants, nearly singing these noun phrases in succession.

(25) ...k'ni^5 nüng^2 k'ni^5 thung^5 ång^2=b'lö^1 thuy^3-pë^1=te^5
      day   two   day   three stay=SEQ   say-BEN=EVID

      ane^3=yå^5 h'ni^3=lö^1 a^5-nga^1 adüng^5=ba^5
      mother=VOC   this=TOP   chicken-meat   container=EMOT

      h'ni^3=lö^1 sö^{5}ra^1-nga^1 adüng^5=ba^5
      this=TOP   cow-meat   container=EMOT

      h'ni^3=lö^1 ew^2-nga^1 adüng^5=ba^5 n'=pë^1=te^5
      this=TOP   pig-meat   container=EMOT   QUOT=BEN=EVID

'... two days, three days they stayed, and she (the daughter) said, "Mother, this is a box of chicken meat, this is a box of beef, this is a box of pork."' (1.106)

The same story-teller again almost sings the repeated portions of example (26), where the girl's husband delights in the death of his in-laws, who had abandoned his wife in her childhood:

(26) å^2 n'b'lö^1 kåm^2-nö^3 mewng^{1}ca^1=lö^1
      INTERJ   then   happy-NMLZ   son.in.law=TOP

      pi^4 döy^2 döy^2 pu^4 döy^2 döy^2
      mother.in.law die   die   father.in.law   die   die

      pi^4 döy^2 döy^2 pu^4 döy^2 döy^2
      mother.in.law die   die   father.in.law   die   die

      acå^2-l'lü^4 acå^2-l'lü^4 acå^2-l'lü^4-ra=ma^4
      jump- IMPFV   jump- IMPFV   jump- IMPFV-LOC.NMLZ=LOC

      ew^{1}ko^5 k'låy^4=ma^4 tla^1-yo^3=te^5 döy^2-yo^3=te^5
      deck   bottom=ALL   fall-IMPFV=EVID   die-IMPFV=EVID

'"Oh!" then they were so happy, and the son-in-law said, "Mother-in-law's dead, father-in-law's dead, m.-in-law's dead, f.-in-law's dead", he jumped and jumped and jumped such that he fell off the back of the deck and died.' (1.113)

In fact, a further parallelism follows shortly in the same text as the daughter herself almost sings the same lines as her now dead husband did, and then accidentally dies herself. A comparable sort of symmetrical ending is seen in (27), where one of the protagonists is cut by a magic gourd plant and dies when he goes out in the middle of the night. The same fate befalls his wife.

(27) j'vo⁵   areng¹   (a)   p'jung¹¹   athaw²='ë¹⁰
      husband   king   (mistake)   urinate.IRR   get.up=AND

      h'ni³=lö¹   a'ung⁴   bä²-nga¹   döy²-rö³
      this=TOP   gourd.plant   cut-AUGVCL   die-INCEPT

      aju¹=pö¹   t'khawng¹⁰   thaw²
      wife=also   pass.water.IRR get.up

      h'ni³=lö¹   a'ung⁴   bä²-nga¹   döy²-rö³
      this=TOP   gourd.plant   cut-AUGVCL   die-INCEPT

'The husband, the king, got up to pee, and this gourd plant cut him and he died.
The wife, also, passed water, and this, the gourd plant cut her, and she died.'
(24.163)¹¹

This parallelism is somewhat less local than that of the first two examples, since
(27) technically includes multiple independent sentences. However, the parallelism can be even more remote, as in examples (28) and (29), which occur
several lines from each other in the text, and don't even involve identical
situations, although they are almost identical.

(28) u²   ne¹²-lä³=ba⁵   b'hu⁵='å⁵   kay¹   vo²-nö³   ne¹²-lä³=ba⁵
      INTERJ   be- NEG-EMOT   dove= VOC   1s   cry- NMLZ   be-NEG-EMOT

      kay⁶   möy³=lö¹   p'thå²=mö³ ang-svë²-hay³=nö³=tew²=ba⁵
      1SG.GEN   eye=TOP   fly=FGD   AGR-spray-APP=NMLZ=COP=EMOT

      n'=pë¹=te⁵   å²   n'=pë¹=te⁵
      QUOT=ben=EVID   okay   QUOT=say=EVID

'"Oh, I'm not, dove, I'm not crying, a fly just sprayed my eye," she said,
"Okay," it said.' (1.102)

(29) kay⁶   möy³=lö¹   phay¹löyng¹=mö³
      1SG.GEN   eye=TOP   ant=DEF

      ang-kë²-tlå¹=nö³=tew²=ba⁵   n'=pë¹=te⁵
      AGR-bite-AUGVCL=NMLZ=COP=EMOT   QUOT=say=EVID

'"An ant bit me in the eye," he said.' (1.104)

In each of these examples, the parents of the abandoned child are overcome with
sentiment and begin to cry, but don't want to admit to crying.

Thus, Khumi narrative, in particular, is replete with parallel structures of
various sorts, in addition to the aesthetic devices already discussed. This
preference for parallel structures is not uncommon, of course, even in other
places, but it is nevertheless consistent with the prevalent repetition involved in
the reduplicative and quasi-reduplicative structures Khumi exhibits which *are*
more specific to Southeast Asian languages.

---

¹¹ For all major protagonists to die at the end of a Khumi story is not out of the ordinary.

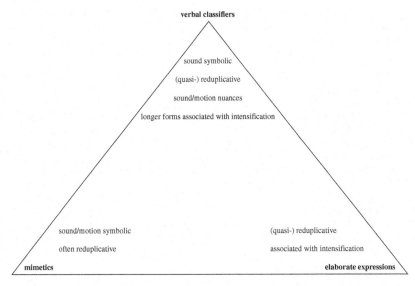

Figure 14.1 Aesthetic devices in Khumi

6   Conclusion

In conclusion, verbal classifiers, elaborate expressions, and mimetics are all discrete grammatical phenomena in Khumi. They show substantial formal and semantic overlap, and hence can cause confusion for speakers. Without careful consideration, they may not know at first glance quite how to categorize a given item.

Figure 14.1 summarizes some of the key features we have seen for the elements discussed in detail here. Clearly, there is overlap in their tendency (or potential) to have a reduplicated (or quasi-reduplicated) form. Verbal classifiers and mimetics are further similar in their tendency to express information about sound and motion, and in their clear sound symbolic tendencies. Verbal classifiers and elaborate expressions both appear to have a covert motivation in signalling intensification.

Possibly there are additional aspects of each type of element which could be considered, but even this relatively shallow level of analysis shows a remarkable level of interrelatedness between them, especially between verbal classifiers and mimetics. In Peterson (2008) I speculated that the verbal classifiers were able to develop their more dominantly augmentative/diminutive senses with the development of the mimetic lexical class; but it is also clear that there is a more direct relationship between mimetics and verbal classifiers, such as for sa^1, seen above. It is arguable that a number of verbal classifiers which do not have the freer distribution of mimetics actually grammaticalized from mimetic elements, and have simply preserved their mimetic auditory and motion semantics.

References

Bhaskararao, Peri. 1989. The process of chiming in Tiddim Chin. *Linguistics of the Tibeto-Burman area* 12(1): 110–132.
Chafe, Wallace. 1980. *The pear stories: cognitive, cultural, and linguistic aspects of narrative production*. Norwood, NJ: Ablex.
Diffloth, Gérard. 1976. 'Expressives in Semai'. In Philip N. Jenner, Laurence C. Thompson, and Stanley Starosta (eds.), *Austroasiatic studies*, Part I. (Oceanic Linguistics Special Publications, No. 13.) Honolulu: University of Hawaii Press, pp. 249–264.
Haas, Mary R. 1964. *Thai–English student's dictionary*. Palo Alto: Stanford University Press.
Henderson, E. J. A. 1965. *Tiddim Chin: a descriptive analysis of two texts*. London: Oxford University Press.
Matisoff, James. 1973. *The grammar of Lahu*. Berkeley: University of California Press.
Patent, Jason D. 1998. A willy-nilly look at Lai ideophones. *Linguistics of the Tibeto-Burman area* 21(1): 155–200.
Peterson, David A. 2008. Bangladesh Khumi verbal classifiers and Kuki-Chin 'chiming'. *Linguistics of the Tibeto-Burman area* 31(1): 109–138.
   2010. Khumi elaborate expressions. *Himalayan linguistics* 9(1): 1–20.
   to appear. 'Bangladesh Khumi'. In Alice Vittrant (ed.), *Southeast Asian areal phenomena*.
Solnit, David. 1995. 'Parallelism in Kayah Li discourse: elaborate expressions and beyond'. In Leela Bilmes, Anita Lang, and Weeraw Ostapirat (eds.), *BLS 21*, (Proceedings of the 21st Annual Meeting of the Berkeley Linguistics Society). Special session on discourse in Southeast Asian languages. Berkeley: University of California Press, pp. 127–140.

15 Delight in sound: Burmese patterns of euphony

Julian K. Wheatley

1 Introduction[*]

As a glance through a Burmese dictionary will show, the Burmese[1] lexicon, like that of the other languages described in this book, has a predilection for patterns of euphony involving features (or processes) such as repetition, pleonasm, alliteration ('chime'), and rhyme. The following examples illustrate a variety of the patterns.

(1) *θwédzín-θádzín*[2]
ေသွးချင်းသားချင်း[3]
'kith and kin'

(2) *təhóunhóun*
တဟုန်းဟုန်း
'swoosh' (descriptive of the wind or of a furious blaze)

(3) *teʰɔ́teidzi̤*
ချောကျိကျိ
'slick and slimy'

---

[*] This chapter has benefitted greatly from comments and corrections on a draft version from my former teachers, John Okell and U Saw Tun, and my former colleague, San San Hnin Tun. Errors that remain, of course, are my own.

[1] The official English language name of both the country and the language is Myanmar (*Mjəmà* in Burmese), a more formal version of *Bəmà*, which gave rise to the older English name, Burma. The older usage has the advantage of distinguishing the country, Burma, from the language, Burmese, so we continue to use it here.

[2] Burmese language material is presented in the broad phonetic transcription that is used in Watkins (2005), with the exception that nasalization is indicated by a final plain 'n' rather than the small cap 'en'. The standard IPA usage for representing tones can be confusing for those who previously used other transcriptions. In the current system, the four tones of Burmese (of which checked syllables constitute one) are marked over the main vowel sign as follows: low tone, with a grave accent (à); high, with an aigu (á); creaky with the sign for creaky voice (a tilde under the vowel); and checked, by the final glottal stop. A dot between syllables of a phonological phrase indicates a morpheme boundary. For ease of reading of the transcription, a hyphen is placed between the hemistichs of four and six-syllable compounds.

[3] To speed recognition of words for those who can read it, as well as to provide backup for the phonetic transcription, first mention of examples includes a rendering in Burmese script.

(4)   *dáuɴdəlù-máundəlù*
ဒေါင်းတလူ မောင်းတလူ
'high and mighty'

As you would expect, 'expressives', as we will call them, tend to occupy the adverbial and nominal positions in sentence structure, though as adverbials, they may be strongly tied to a verb (or verbal head), and translated by a single verb in English, as shown in (5).

(5)   *lè   təhóunhóun   tai?.tè*
wind swoosh   blow.REAL
လေ တဟုန်းဟုန်း တိုက်တယ်
'The wind roared.'

All the examples above are formed by reduplication or pleonasm. In some cases, the expression is designed only for the pleasure of its utterance. In other cases, though, the form echoes the sense, either by mimicking auditory aspects of the event (onomatopoeia), or where sound is not involved, subtly evoking visual or emotional responses (phonaesthesia). Example (1), *θwédzin-θádzin*, is a generic, formed from *θwéθá* 'flesh and blood' (*θwé* 'blood,' *θá* 'children') interleaved by the reciprocal formative, *tɛin*,[4] in a process that falls within the scope of what Chao termed 'ionization'.[5] The result is a euphonically balanced expression whose pleonastic form symbolizes its broad, generic meaning. *Təhóunhóun*, on the other hand, has an onomatopoeic stem (*hóun*); the compound mimics the sound of wind or fire ('with a swoosh') and, typically, acts as complement to more explicit verbs such as 'to blow (of wind)' or 'to burn (of fire)'. The example (3), *tɛhɔ́tɛidzi̱*, with stem *tɛhɔ́* 'slippery', is not onomatopoeic, but its affricate initials, arguably, reinforce the meaning of slipperiness. (It is probably not coincidence that the same repeated syllable also appears in the word for 'snail', *pɛ?tɕi̱*.)

Example (4), *dáundəlù-máundəlù*, is descriptive of self-importance (in speech, writing, or movement). Translating it as 'high and mighty' suggests both the pleonastic effect and the euphony of the Burmese compound. The repeated syllable *lù* probably derives from the verb 'to rise', while the initial syllables, *dáun* and *máun*, may be derived (with shift in tone, and with voicing) from the stems underlying expressions such as *tʰàundàun-máunmáun* (ထောင်ထောင်မောင်းမောင်း) 'tall and strapping'. A well-attested voicing process can

---

[4]   Voiceable initials (the stops, affricates, and fricatives) are voiced after non-checked syllables in close juncture.

[5]   Chao (1968: 159): 'There are various degrees and types of separation of morphemes which are usually bound to each other ... Because of the similarity to a part of a chemical compound floating around in the same solution with its partners ... the separated morphemes have been described as being ionized.'

account for the shift in initial manner of the initial syllable (t^h > d); the tonal shift (*dàun* to *dáun*) is less systematic. Like *tɕʰɔ́tɕidzi̞*, *dáundəlù-máundəlù* also seems to be informed by sound symbolism, with the long vowels of [dáun] and [máun], and the rhythmic gait of the two hemistichs suggestive of self-importance.

It is often possible to find English glosses like 'kith and kin' or 'high and mighty' that show a level of euphony, balance, or iconicity comparable to the Burmese. The difference is that in Burmese, such words – or compounds – not only have wide currency within spoken and written genres, but they also conform overwhelmingly to a relatively small repertoire of patterns, most of them involving repetition of sound or reduplication of meaning. While English exploits its rich repertoire of initial and final clusters and weak syllables to animate its lexicon (higgledy-piggledy, mumble and mutter), Burmese makes use of the preponderance of syllabic or sesquisyllabic words and the ease of compounding.[6] Both 'strategies' reflect the powerful communicative need to bridge the gap between the word and its referent, enlivening the discourse by colouring speech, 'stirring dull roots with spring rain'.

2 Terminology

For Burmese, I am using the term 'expressive' to cover not only the typically four- or six-syllable 'elaborate expressions' (Haas 1964) formed by partial repetition, pleonasm, rhyme or chime along the lines of *θwédzín-θádzín* or *dáundəlù-máundəlù*, but also the various types of ternary expressions such as *təhóunhóun* and *tɕʰɔ́tɕidzi̞* that are not usually termed 'elaborate'. Though the even-syllabled expressions, it could be argued, offer more material for expressive creativity, there is, in fact, overlap between the two types. For example: *shódó-shạndạ̀n* (ရှို့တိုး:ရှန့်တန့်) 'diffidently' (formed by rhyme and chime on the stem *shạ̀n* 'to flinch') is more or less synomymous with *shạndạndạ̀n* (ရှန့်တန့်တန့်), formed on the same stem.

The term 'expressive' is sometimes treated as synonymous with 'ideophone' (Diffloth 1976), but I prefer to reserve the latter term for those expressives which resemble the prototypical ideophones found in many African languages, as well as in Semai spoken on the Malay Peninsula, and in Lai Chin (illustrated below), all of which are strongly sound symbolic, and which mimic, or echo, often by nuanced manipulation of the sound substance, not only the auditory aspects of an event, but visual and emotional aspects as well. So in Burmese, it

---

[6] These same factors probably also account for the inclination towards various kinds of linguistic play involving spoonerisms, which, in Burmese, involve exchanging rhymes rather than initials (e.g. *ʔəsɑ̀jó* 'starts off clean' for *ʔəsójạ* 'government'). For discussion of spoonerisms and other 'disguised speech' in Burmese, see Haas (1969).

will be useful to classify some expressives as ideophones; but as a class, ideophones are not highly profiled in the language. While there are rich resources for onomatopoeia in Burmese, the more general architectural features of the language involve euphony (which includes rhythm and balance) rather than sound symbolism.

3 A poetic sample

As a point of departure, let me begin by looking for expressive language with the poets. Below is an excerpt from a poem by the contemporary poet Tin Moe (တင်မိုး) called *PəjiʔkauʔP* (ပုရစ် ကောက်) 'Picking Up Crickets:'[7]

ခုန်ကာပျံကာနဲ့	လမ်းပေါ်မှာ တရွရွ မဲမဲတုတ်၊	ပြူးတိပြူးကြောင်
kʰòun.gà-pjàn.gà.nɛ̰	lán.bɔ̰. m̥à dəjwa̰jwa̰ mɛ́mɛ́touʔ	pjúdḭ-pjúdʑàun
jump.ing-fly.ing.ADV	road.on.LOC teeming black-lump	eyes bulging

နှုတ်ခမ်းမွေး တထောင်ထောင်နဲ့	ပုရစ်ကောင်တအုပ်။	သံပြိုင်ဟစ်၍	တကျစ်ကျစ် တစီစီ၊
n̥əkʰánmwé tətʰàndàun.nɛ̰	pəjiʔ.kàun.təʔouʔ ॥	θànbjàin hiʔ.jwḛ	də dʑiʔdʑiʔ dəzìzì
antennae quivering.ADV	cricket.body.one.mass	chorus sing out.SUB	chirp drone

နားကွဲလုမျှ	စူးရှစွာ	အော်ပြီ။
ná.kwɛ́.lṵ.m̥ja̰	súʃa̰.zwà	ʔɔ̀.bì ॥
ear.split.about to.as if	shrill. ADV	clamour.PUNC

The poem illustrates various types of expressive material, packaged either in the three or four-syllable format. The excerpt opens with an expression in which a subordinate clause marker, *-kà* (voiced in closed juncture), rather than being placed in its paradigmatic position after a compound verb, is distributed evenly across it (in ionized fashion) to give it the form of an elaborate expression: *kʰòunpjàn* 'to jump high (jump + fly)' x *kà* 'SUB' → *kʰòun.gà-pjàn.gà*. This is common with grammatical formatives.

A true elaborate expression follows a few phrases afterwards, with first and third syllables identical: *pjúdḭ-pjúdʑàun* 'with eyes bulging', built on the stem *pjú* 'to bulge (of the eyes)'. The last syllable, *tɕàun* in citation form, is probably derived from the verb 'be odd, strange, dazed', that appears in phrases such as *tɕàuntàundàun* (ကြောင်တောင်တောင်) 'staring blankly' and *pjútɕàundʑàun* (ပြူးကြောင်ကြောင်) 'as if transfixed'. The second syllable is variable. Rather than *pjúdḭ-pjúdʑàun*, with creaky-toned *dḭ*, the main Burmese dictionaries[8] actually give *pjúdí-pjúdʑàun* (ပြူးတီးပြူးကြောင်), with high-toned *dí*. Variation between

[7] Tin Moe is the pen name of the poet Maung Ba Gyan (1933–2007). The complete Burmese version of the poem, with English translation, can be found in Win Pei (1978).

[8] I have relied mainly on the following dictionaries: Qin 1990 (Burmese-to-Chinese), Myanmar Language Commission 1993 (Burmese-to-English) and Myanmar Language Commission 1978–80

dị and *dí* is a pattern that recurs in a number of other elaborate expressions, for example: *jàundị-jàundàun* (ကောင်းတိုကောင်းတောင်) or *jàundí-jàundàun* (ကောင်းတို့းကောင်းတောင်), both 'not knowing what to do', with base *jàun* 'act in a dazed, absent-minded fashion' and chimed syllables; and *pɔ̣tị-pɔ̣sʰạ* (ပေါ့တိပေါ့ဆ) or *pɔ̣tí-pɔ̣sʰạ* (ပေါ့တို့းပေါ့ဆ) 'treat casually, carelessly', based on *pɔ̣sʰạ* 'be careless' (ultimately, from *pɔ̣* 'light' and *sʰạ* 'to estimate the weight of; ponder').[9]

There are other variants as well: *pjúdú-tɕàundàun* (ပြူးဒူးတေ့ကြောင်တောင်), with *dú*, and then *dàun* as a chiming syllable, seems to be equivalent to *pjúdị-pjúdzàun* and *pjúdí-pjúdzàun; pɔ̣bɔ̣-sʰạzạ* (ပေါ့ပေါ့ဆဆ), with each syllable of the base compound *pɔ̣sʰạ* repeated, seems to be synonymous with *pɔ̣tị-pɔ̣sʰạ / pɔ̣tí-pɔ̣sʰạ*. Exhaustive elicitation might reveal nuances of difference among such variants. But the proliferation of variants, with or without shades of semantic distinction, suggests a more general principle: that expressives are not immutable, and that these forms can be shaped by poets, by village story-tellers, or by anyone else who possesses linguistic flair. Assuming that Tin Moe made an intentional choice to use a creaky-toned syllable over the high-toned one, it would be interesting to know if he did so for rhythmic or musical reasons; to insert creaky-toned dissonance in a string of high tones, perhaps – or for some more subtle sensory effect.

The expression *pjúdị-pjúdzàun* highlights the bulginess of the beady, black, eyes of crickets. It achieves this effect because it – or its variants – are conventionally associated with the sort of meanings given in dictionaries, that is, 'with eyes bulging' supported, but not entirely accounted for by those constituent morphemes that are fairly transparent, *pjú* 'to bulge out' and *tɕàun* 'odd; staring'. In addition there may be some sound symbolic support for the meaning 'bulge' from the rhythmic protrusion of lips associated with the vowel of *pjú*, further set off by the shift from high tone to creaky, then high to low. The effect is not unlike English expressions such as 'higgledy-piggledy,' where the image of pigs in a sty combines with an evocative rhythm to support the meaning of 'jumbled'; or like topsy-turvy, where 'top' and obsolete 'turvy' (meaning 'turned') combine with a bouncy rhythm to support the sense of 'upside down'.

Continuing with the poem, beginning in the second measure, there are a number of reduplicated expressions with a *tə*- prefix (*də*- when followed by other than an aspirated stop). The crickets are teeming on the road: *dəjwạjwạ*; their antennae quiver: *tətʰàundàun*; they cry out in chorus: *dədziʔdziʔ* and *dəzìzì*. Okell, in his Burmese reference grammar writes that *tə* + repetition 'indicates constant or continuous action, sound, etc.' (Okell 1969: 412). The process is productive, which means that phonological effects of the whole are blended

---

(Burmese-to-Burmese). Qin 1990 is a particularly rich source of examples. However, I recognize the danger of relying too closely on dictionaries for nuances of meaning, and have tried to find examples in context as much as possible.

[9] I thank Saw Tun for bringing these examples to my attention.

with the meaning of the stem morpheme. In the case of *dədziʔdziʔ*, the stem (*dziʔ*) is onomatopoeic. Picking up the sound of the previous verb, *hiʔ* 'to call out, shout out', the compound renders quite well the sounds that crickets make, with the sibilant initials corresponding to the buzz, and the repeated checked syllables suggesting the beating or throbbing sensation characteristic of cricket noise. In addition to the sound of crickets, *dədziʔdziʔ* can also be applied to the chirping of birds, the squeaking of carts, or the endless whining of children.

Dəzìzì, on the other hand, gets its effect not only from the buzzing sound of the voiced fricatives, but also from the lexical association with the verb *sì* 'to line up, to place in a row', which is, apparently, the stem morpheme of the expression. If we translate *dədziʔdziʔ* with 'chirp', which in English is, by convention, the sound that crickets make, *dəzìzì* can be translated as 'droning', a word which, like the Burmese expression, combines features of sound and duration.

As with the four-syllable pleonastic type of expressions, *tə*-repetition often shows an array of options with small phonetic differences. In addition to *dədziʔdziʔ*, for example, dictionaries list *dədzìdzì* (တကျည်ကျည်), with low tone, descriptive of squeaking or crying, and *dədzɛʔdzɛʔ* (တကျက်ကျက်), with checked tone, descriptive of bickering. In addition to *dəzìzì*, there is *dəzàzà* (တစစ), with a low open vowel, descriptive of continuous calling, as in the sound of a hawker selling his wares, a child fussing or whining, or in combination with the verb *tɛɛʔ* (ကျက်) 'to learn by rote', students cramming for exams (*dəzàzà tɛɛʔ*).

Moving on to the other examples: *dəjwɑjwɑ* blends the sound symbolism of repeated creaky tone with the lexical meaning of the stem verb, *jwɑ*, 'to wriggle, squirm', to give a sense of 'seething in a mass, teeming'.[10] *Təthàundàun*, based on the stem *thàun* 'to place upright', is the least auditory (least onomatopoeic) of the four expressions, since it is applied to cricket antennae, which do not normally make noise. However, the image is so closely associated with sound, that one can almost hear the delicate 'boing boing' of their antennae quivering or vibrating as the crickets chirp and drone in a dark mass on the road.

The other descriptive phrase in the poem, *mémétouʔ*,[11] illustrates another ternary pattern, of the form XXY, with all syllables fully stressed. It is an augmented version of *métouʔ* (formed from *mé* 'black' and *touʔ*, the latter appearing in expressions meaning 'large, bulky, or stocky'), and denotes a dense black mass. The repetition of *mé* may offer some iconic support for the intensity of the seething black mass; but otherwise the phonological symbolism is restrained. Alternately, the repetition of the first syllable may also be a way to accommodate the rhythmic needs of the poet. The XXY pattern (cf. Okell 1969:

---

[10] Cf. *touʔtouʔ-jwɑjwɑ* 'teeming' (လှုပ်လှုပ်ရှရှ).
[11] Spelled မဲမဲတုတ် in my printed version of Tin Moe's poem, but မည်းမည်းတုတ် in standard spelling.

475; Okell and Allott 2001: 274–275), though not productive, is not uncommon. Here are two other examples.

(6)   *pjábjáwuʔ*   < *pjá* + *wuʔ*
        ပြားပြားဝပ်
        'in a cringing, meek manner' (< 'to prostrate oneself' + 'to crouch')

(7)   *pjébjésìn*   < *pjé* + *sìn*
        ပြဲပြဲဆင်
        'far and wide' (< 'wide' + 'be clear')

Near the end of the selection from the poem, the mildly alliterative, pleonastic, literary adverbial, *súʃa.zwà* 'shrilly' or 'piercing to the point of setting one's nerves on edge', has some expressive potential despite lacking the repetition seen in its colloquial equivalent, *súzú -ʃaʃa.nɛ* (ဆူးဆူးရှရှနဲ့). It is made up of *sú* 'to feel a prickly sensation (on the skin), be sharp, shrill (of the voice), experience glare (in the eyes)', and *ʃa* 'abrade; taste sharp', marked as an adverbial by *swà*, the literary equivalent of colloquial *nɛ*. This last example makes the point that to conjure up a particular image – even one in which sound is a dominant component – the poet, or the ordinary speaker, has a wide range of options from which to create the desired effect.

There are, of course, simplex words in Burmese with strong components of phonological symbolism, in which the sound evokes sensation, like English forlorn: 'the very word is like a bell to toll thee back from thee to my sole self'.[12] Both *hiʔ* and *ʔɔ̀*, the verbs of calling that end the poetic excerpt are suggestive, in their own ways, of loud speech; cf. *hɛʔ* (ဟက်) 'to gag' on the one hand, and *hɔ́* (ဟော) 'preach', *tɕɔ̀* (ေကြာ်) 'shout', on the other.[13] Many other words seem superficially well suited to their meanings: *ʔanʔɔ́* (အံ့ဩ) 'amazed'; *kəliʔ* (ကလိ) 'tickle'; *ɲiʔ* (ညှစ်) 'squeeze'; *ŋaʔ* (နှပ်) 'snot', and so on. Historical processes involving sound symbolism, semantic contamination, or morphological elaboration have also resulted in apparent word families or phonaesthetic groupings: *twé* (တွဲ) 'hang down', *sʰwé* (ဆွဲ) 'suspend', *lwè* (လွယ်) 'hang from the shoulder'; *ŋauʔ* (ငောက်) 'to project; stick up', *ŋɔ́* (ငေါ) 'bulge; stick up'; *ŋ2* (ငေါ့) 'to stick out'; *ŋɔ̀* (ငေါ်) 'stick up obliquely'; *ŋouʔ* (ငုတ်) '(tree) stump'. The variants thrown up by these processes are grist to the expressive mill, providing material for pleonastic elaboration and euphonic composition. Our attention, however, will remain primarily on the various types of expressive compounds that are particular to Burmese (and other languages of the region), and so well illustrated by Tin Moe's poem, and by other material cited below.

---

[12] Keats, 'Ode to a Nightingale'.
[13] Both *ʔɔ̀-hiʔ* and the reverse, *hiʔ-ʔɔ̀*, are compounded forms for 'to shout loudly'.

4   Three-syllable expressives

Most of the three-syllable expressives that appear in the poem are of the type with the unstressed ('weak') first syllable, *tə*. The one exception was *mémétou?* 'be darkly massing', with the repeated syllables in initial position. Missing from the poem, however, are examples of a type of augmented adjective, with fully stressed components, and with the repeated syllables in final position. This fully stressed type has two subtypes. One is restricted, consisting of an adjectival stem augmented by repeated syllables that begin with a dental stop [t] and that rhyme with the stem. An example is *pjútútú* (ဗျူးတူးတူး) 'bulgy; goggly (of eyes); pert or forward (of girls)', based on the familiar *pjú* 'to bulge out'. The other subtype is unrestricted, the repeated syllables neither rhyming with the stem, nor having a predictable initial consonant, but generally having identifiable lexical sources. An example is *ɲànsàzà* (ညံစာစာ) 'sound of birds, weeping, etc.; cheep; weep', with stems *ɲàn* 'be noisy' and *sà* 'be shrill'. The three types (*tə* + YY, Cx + txtx, and XYY) are discussed in more detail in the following sections.

4.1   *tə* + YY

The compounds of the *tə* + reduplication type illustrated in the poem are all onomatopoeic expressions. Other examples include: *təkʰwíkʰwí* (တခွေးခွေး), representing the snuffling sound of a wild boar – or the sniffling of a sleeping baby; *dəgwìgwì* (တဂွီဂွီ), representing the noise of stomach growling, or of a horn blasting (sic); *təla?la?* (တလပ်လပ်) 'pitter-patter', descriptive of the sound of the heart racing; or *tətu?tu?* (တတွတ်တွတ်) 'prattle', descriptive of endless talk. The pattern is not limited to onomatopoeic stems, however, as the following examples show: *təmjámjá* (တများများ) 'excessively', based on *mjá* 'many'; or *təlùlù* (တလူလူ) 'waving (in the wind); fluttering; curling upward (of smoke)', based on the verb *lù* 'to rise up (of smoke, dust)', seen also in *dáundəlù-máundəlù*. Neither imitates sound, and in fact, the only mimetic feature is reduplication, that provides sensory support for intensity, or for enduring or repeated events.

Phrases in the *tə* + YY format often combine with a general verb to create nuanced meanings (i.e. hyponyms of a more generic notion). Thus, *dədzìdzì ɲò-* (တကျည်ကျည် ငို-), with *ɲò-* 'cry', is 'to cry boo-hoo', that is 'to whine or whimper'; *dədzìdzì pjɔ́-* (တကျည်ကျည် ပြော-), with *pjɔ́* 'speak', is 'to yak on and on', or 'to drone on and on'. To match the Burmese, the English gloss should also have a generic verb such as 'to go' with an imitative object; but English does not offer the same range as Burmese. Thus, 'boo-hoo' lacks the high vowels that one would associate with a whine or whimper; yak suggests nonsense as well as long-windedness, which may not be implied by the Burmese. The following examples show the range available for the verb *jì* (~*jè*) (ရယ်) 'to laugh':

(8) təkʰiʔkʰiʔ jì-
 တခစခစ်
'to go tee-hee; to titter'

(9) təkʰįkʰį jì-
တခိခိ
'to go heh-heh; to giggle'

(10) tə háhá jì-
တဟားဟား
'to go ha-ha; to laugh uproariously'

(11) təhìhì jì-
တဟိဟိ
'to go hee-hee; to laugh lightly'

(12) təwáwá jì-
တဝါးဝါး
'to go ho-ho, hee-hee; to peal with laughter'

(13) təθɔ́θɔ́ jì-
တသောသော
'to go haw-haw-haw; to guffaw'

This is not to say that Burmese does not also provide metaphoric as well as imitative options for expressing nuances of laughter. *Wəlóungwé jì-* (ဝါးလုံးကွဲ ရယ်-) 'to crack up (bamboo-split laugh-)', for example, is formed by a regular process of incorporation, which in this case, combines the verb *kwé* 'split', and its complement, *wəlóun* 'bamboo', to form a nonce word that functions as an adverbial complement to *jì-* 'laugh', evoking the sound of sudden uproarious laughter. English, of course, makes a similar analogy in the colloquial expression 'to crack up'. In Burmese, however, the onomatopoeic (or otherwise, sound symbolic) options are very common, and are not associated only with colloquial registers.

4.2 Fully stressed types (Cx + txtx, XYY)

The fully stressed three-syllable compounds with final reduplication come in restricted and unrestricted forms. Examples of the first is *saʔtaʔtaʔ* (စပ်တပ်တပ်) 'rather hot or pungent (as chillies)', or 'smirking', an extension of *saʔ* 'spicy hot'; and *tɕéintéintéin* (ကျဉ်းတဉ်းတဉ်း) 'stinging (of eyes); on edge (of teeth)', with *tɕéin* 'to smart; set on edge' (as well as *pjútútú* cited above). Okell (1969: 478–479) characterizes the general meaning of the type as: "'-ish, partly, somewhat", indicating that the quality expressed by the base is imperfectly or only partially achieved, sometimes suggesting disapproval, contempt'. Like the English -ish suffix that applies productively to gradable adjectives with monosyllabic bases (Quirk et al. 1972: 1006) – tallish, poorish, smoothish – the *t*-rhyming process is productive enough that the resulting expressions do not need to be listed in dictionaries.

The unrestricted type (without the rhyme or *t*-initial) is not productive, but for certain types of adjectival verbs, such as those denoting colour and taste, the options are quite prolific. Thus, *saʔ* 'be hot (like chillies.)', a stem in the *t*-rhyme example given above (*saʔtaʔtaʔ*), is also the base of *saʔʃaʃa* (ဝပ်ရှရှ), *saʔʃéinʃéin* (ဝပ်ရှိမ်းရှိမ်း), both 'hot, spicy (taste)', and *saʔpʰjinbjin* (ဝပ်ကျဉ်းကျဉ်း) 'burning or smarting (of eyes, skin, etc.)'. In the *saʔ* examples just given, and many of the colour terms cited below, the source of the reduplicated 'augment' is not obvious. However, in other cases, the reduplicated morphemes are more transparent, as indicated in the following examples, built on the verb *pjàun* (ပြောင်), whose meanings range from 'shining' to 'brazen (bright, hard, like brass)' and 'to act without proper regard; to joke with':

(14)   *pjàuntɕʰɔ̀dzɔ̀*
        ပြောင်ချော်ချော်
        'frivolously' (with *tɕʰɔ̀* 'dross, scum; miss the point')

(15)   *pjàunsaʔsaʔ*
        ပြောင်ဝပ်ဝပ်
        'impishly' (with *saʔ* 'pungent')

(16)   *pjàunpʰjébjé*
        ပြောင်ဖြဲဖြဲ
        'impishly' (with *pʰjé* 'widen; exaggerate')

(17)   *pjàunshuʔshuʔ*
        ပြောင်ရွတ်ရွတ်
        'playfully' (with *shuʔ* 'jest; joke')

While in most cases, the first syllable of this type of expressive is a lexical root which can be given a clear meaning, there are also cases in which both the first syllable and the reduplicated syllable are onomatopoeic, as for example in the following two representations of musical sounds: *dùwèwè* (ဒူဝေဝေ), defined as the reverberating sound of the *tɕézì* (ကြေးစည်), the triangular brass gong that is beaten during calls for alms; and *dùhùhù* (ဒူဟူဟူ), the reverberating sound of a Burmese gong. It is worth noting that there is a rich tradition of rendering the sounds of musical instruments in the lyrics of classical Burmese songs, such as example (18), from the first song in the traditional collection, the *Məhàgìtạ*:

(18)   ထံတျာတောရှင်၊ ထံတျာတောရှင်၊ ချန်ချန်၊ ထံတျာတောရှင်။   ဒလုဒလု ထုံ့ချန်ချန်၊ ။
       tʰàndərà tè.ʃin tʰàndərà tèi.ʃin dəyan.dəyan tʰàndərà tè.ʃin dəlu.dəlu[14] tʰòun.dəyan.dəyan
       dum-di-dum, dum-di-dum   strum-strum dum-di-dum   drum-sound strum.strum

4.3   Colour expressives

The XYY pattern discussed in the last section is particularly well developed for colours (and for flavours). Here are two sets of examples. The first is based on *ɲò* (ညို), which is often glossed as 'brown', but Judson's general definition may be more appropriate: 'be dark in color, between blue and black; to be of a deep blue or green; to become dark'.

(19)   ɲòpouʔpouʔ ʃì-
       ညိုပုပ်ပုပ် ရှိ-
       'be dark, swarthy (of forest, skin, etc.)'

(20)   ɲòseinzein ʃì-
       ညိုစိမ့်စိမ့် ရှိ-
       'be light brown, a lustrous brown (of complexion)'

(21)   ɲòmwémwé ʃì-
       ညိုမွဲမွဲ ရှိ-
       'be dull brown'

As shown, such colour expressions often appear as complements to the verb *ʃì-* 'be; have', which makes them look like what in English would be called predicate adjectivals. The identity of the repeated syllables may be uncertain. Is *pouʔ* 'be rotten, putrid' a candidate for the first? Or is *sein* 'to ooze', also a noun, 'marsh, mire' possibly the source for the second? *Mwé*, in the third, is probably related to the stem of *mwétɕʰauʔtɕʰauʔ* (မွဲခြောက်ခြောက်) 'dull or wan (of complexion)'.

While *ɲò* is relatively constrained in its options, a second root, *nì* (နီ) 'red', engenders a riot of possibilities. The comprehensive Chinese–Burmese dictionary (Qin 1990) lists well over a dozen augmented adjectivals based on *nì*. The lexicographers seem hard pressed to distinguish many of them. The following, for example, are all lumped under a single entry, whose Chinese gloss translates as 'light red copper colour': *nìtɕindzin* (နီကြင်ကြင်), with creaky tone; *nìtɕindzìn* (နီကြင်ကြင်), with low tone; *nìtɕandzan* (နီကြန့်ကြန့်), with creaky 'a'

---

[14] Though in my version of the songbook, *lu* is written with the short vowel representing creaky tone (as shown), it seems to be sung on the high. Some of the words seem to suggest particular musical instruments, while others seem less committed.

[a̰]; *nìtɕàndzàn* (နီကြန်နီကြန်), with low 'a'; *nìpʰànbàn* (နီဖန်ဖန်); *nìtɕʰìndzìn* (နီချင်ချင်). Some of the augmented adjectivals involving the base 'red' are uncomplicated and seemingly transparent as examples (22a) and (22b) show.

(22a)   nìtìdì (နီတိတိ)
         nì + tì + dì
         red + XX + REDPL
         'reddish'

(22b)   nìsaʔsaʔ (နီစပ်စပ်)
         nì + saʔ + saʔ
         red + piquante + REDPL
         'ugly, raw red'

Other forms cluster together as shown by examples in Table 15.1 and 15.2, where there are gross semantic equivalents that convey nuances of difference.

Mixes of red and other colours also conform to the reduplicated format: *nìpjàbjà* (နီပြာပြာ) 'bluish red' (cf. *pjà* 'blue'); *nìwàwà* (နီဝါဝါ) 'yellowish red' (cf. *wà* 'yellow'). Looking beyond the reduplicated forms, one finds still more options, such as *nìtàyé* (နီတာရဲ) 'bright red; blood red'. In fact, the red of the root syllables has, in some cases, bled into the reduplicated syllables, so that *jétuʔ* (ရဲတွတ်), which is made up of the reduplicated syllables from *nìjéjé* and *nìtuʔtuʔ*, means 'bright red, scarlet'.

Burmese colour and flavour expressives come as close to the ideophonic ideal as any of the illustrations cited thus far. Diffloth (1976: 255) remarked on

Table 15.1 *Augmented adjectivals with the meaning 'brilliant red'*

နီတျာတျာ	နီရဲရဲ	နီတွတ်တွတ်
nìtəjàtəjà	nìjéjé	nìtuʔtuʔ
nì + təjà + təjà	nì + jé + jé	nì + tuʔ + tuʔ
red + XX + REDPL	red + bold + REDPL	red + XX + REDPL

Table 15.2 *Augmented adjectivals with the meaning 'dull red'*

နီပြဲပြဲ	နီဖျော့ဖျော့	နီနမ်းနမ်း	နီမွဲမွဲ
nìpjèbyè	nìpʰjɔbjɔ	nìɲánɲán	nimwémwé
nì + pjè + byè	nì + pʰjɔ + bjɔ	nì + ɲán + ɲán	nì + mwé + mwé
red + XX + REDPL	red + pale/faded + REDPL	red + 'be tinged with' + REDPL	red + dull + REDPL

the special profile of such colour and flavour words in Semai, where they consistently straddle two word classes: 'As a rule, all color terms and words for tastes are ambivalently expressives and stative verbs.' Closer to home, Lai Chin, a Tibeto-Burman language spoken in Chin State in the northwest of Burma, has a rich system of ideophones that offers some interesting analogues to the Burmese terms. Patent (1998) cites examples of the form adjectival + ideophone (for the roots 'spicy' and 'red') that suggest that the Burmese augmented adjectivals could also derive, originally, from similar, sound symbolic material.[15]

Lai-Chin ideophones Burmese augmented adjectivals

(23a) thak biaʔ-maʔ [(175)] (23b) saʔʃáʃá
 spicy IDEO
 'super spicy'

(24a) sen siir-siar [(145)] (24b) nìtìdì
 red IDEO
 'ever-so-slightly red'

(25a) sen dil-del [(96)] (25b) nìjéjé
 red IDEO
 'vividly red'

(26a) sen del-dul [(96)] (26b) nìmwémwé
 red IDEO
 'equally vivid, but darker'

Interestingly, in Chinese, colour and taste adjectivals are also frequently found in the XYY format: Burmese nìjéjé, Chinese hóngyànyàn (红艳艳), both 'bright red'; Burmese ŋàntɕɪdzɪ (ငန်ကြိကြိ,), Chinese xiánzīzī (咸滋滋), both 'rather salty'; and Burmese saʔpʰjínbjín (4.2 above), Chinese 热辣辣, both 'burning or smarting'. In the three cases cited, the Chinese repeated syllables correspond to independent morphemes; but such is not always the case.[16]

5 Sudden movement

Before leaving the ternary patterns, it is worth mentioning the vivid suffix kəné (ကနဲ)[17], which does not involve repetition, but forms adverbials that have the

[15] The superscript numbers in parenthesis following each Lai example are those in Patent's article.
[16] Bauer and Benedict (1997), §3.2, is an excellent discussion of sound symbolism in Cantonese, which has a richer array of colour and flavour expressives than standard Chinese (Mandarin).
[17] The first syllable of the suffix is often spelled with the aspirate stop, kʰ (ə). However, because the suffix is unstressed the distinction is neutralized. I follow Qin (1990) and others and write the plain initial.

250   *Julian K. Wheatley*

enlivening function of expressives. Example (27) is taken from the same source as those in the next section, the novel *Nga Ba*:

(27)   ြ က န့   ေသွး ေသွ   ပန့်ထွက်သည်။
       Pʰjà.gəné   θwé.dwe   pán.tʰwɛʔ.θì.
       radiate.sfx   blood.coll   spurt.out.real
       'Blood spurted out in a fan-like pattern.'

Okell (1969: 271) describes the *kəné* suffix as indicating 'vivid, often sudden, sensations, sounds, sights, etc.' In many cases, *kəné* is attached to imitative stems: *tʰwì.gəné* (ထွီ) *ptui*, descriptive of the sound of spitting; *wá.gəné* (ဝါး), descriptive of rain swilling down; *dò.gəné-dɛʔ.kanɛ* (ဒိုး/ဒက်) or *dò.gəné-dauʔ. kəné* (ဒိုး/ေဒါက်) 'with a snap of the fingers; instantly', descriptive of a quick, clever response. Other examples are descriptive of movement: *sʰaʔ.kəné* (ဆတ်), descriptive of a quick glance (cf. *sʰaʔ* 'brittle'); *swɛ.gəné* (ေဆ့) 'alley-oop', descriptive of an effortless lift or leap; *mɛ.gəné* (ေမ့), descriptive of eyelids suddenly drooping from tiredness (cf. *mɛ* 'forget; faint').

6   Elaborate expressions

The most pervasive expressives in the Burmese lexicon are the four or six-syllable elaborate expressions. Many involve reduplication, either clustered, or interleaved. Clustered repetition results from a regular process that forms adverbials from verbs.

(28)   *jìmó* (ရယ်ေမာ) 'to laugh' → *jìjì-mómó* 'with laughter'

(29)   *ʃouʔʃɛʔ* (ရှုပ်ရှက်) 'be in a mess' → *ʃouʔʃouʔ-ʃɛʔʃɛʔ* 'chaotically'

Single-syllable verbs may undergo the same process, resulting in two-syllable reduplications: *tò* (ေတာ်) 'be enough; proper; to fit' → *tòdò* 'rather; quite'. Irregularly, the same format occasionally shows a noun stem rather than a verb: *lùlù-θùθù* (လူလူသူသူ) 'decently, like a human', from *lùθù* 'humanity'.
    The repeated syllables may also be interleaved, either with reduced syllables, or with only full ones. In either case, alternate syllables are often related by rhyme and chime. Examples with reduced syllables are: *gəbò-kəyò* (ကပိုကရို) 'without bothering about appearance'; and *dəjì-dəjàin* (တယီးတယိုင်), or also *dəjéin-dejàin* (တယိမ်းတယိုင်), 'staggering'. With full (stressed) syllables, the repeated elements may be odd (first and third) or even (second and fourth), with the non-repeated syllables (from each hemistich) often related by rhyme or chime: *gəbàθù-gəbàθá* (ကမ္ဘာသူကမ္ဘာသား) 'mankind' (*gəbà* 'world', *θù* 'person', *θá* 'child; being') repeats first and third (full) syllables, and chimes second and fourth; *dòlì-mòlì* (တိုလီမိုလီ) 'hither and thither; odds and ends' repeats second and

fourth, and rhymes first and third. Within these major groupings there are also minor configurations, such as the one discussed earlier that has *tí* (sometimes varying with *tị*) in second position: *tuʔtí-tuʔtà* (တွတ်တီးတွတ်တာ) 'prattle (of talk); gambol (of walk)'.

Adverbials can also be formed regularly by prefixation, which adds to the repertoire of elaborate (looking) expressions: *sənìʔ tɛ̀ɑ* 'to be systematic (system drop)' → *sənìʔ-dədzɑ̀* (စနစ်တကျ) 'systematically'; *tɛ́ózá* 'to try, make an effort', → *tətɛ́ó-dəzá* (တကြိုးတစား), with nominalization of the first syllable: 'with great effort'; *kʰánná* 'splendid, magnificent' → *təkʰán-dəná* (တခမ်းတနား) 'with cere-mony'. The addition of a reduced syllable sometimes results in an odd number, as in *wódəwá* (ဝိုးတဝါး) 'indistinctly', based on *wówá* 'be indistinct', giving an anomalous form that can still be regarded as an expressive. But the four-syllable expression is the most common outcome, as in *wódó-wádá* (ဝိုးတိုးဝါးတား), which has the same meaning as *wódəwá*.

7 A prose excerpt

Most of the examples in this section are taken from a prose source, the popular novel, *Nga Ba* ('Rascal Ba'), written by Maung Htin and first published in 1947. Though the book is written in a light literary style (with the grammatical particles of the written language rather than the spoken), it is quite colloquial in its usage. *Nga Ba* is a humorous and, at times, poignant tale about a Burmese peasant farmer and his family, who suffer all sorts of indignities during the tumultuous years of World War II.

To save space, and to make the Burmese more accessible, I have stitched together a number of excerpts from an episode that covers a few pages in the book (pp. 147–151 in my 1957 edition), translated them as literally as practicable, and inserted the relevant Burmese phrases into the English text. The setting is as follows: Nga Ba's daughter, Mi Ni, has been lured into a room full of drunken soldiers, while Nga Ba's wife, Mi Ni's mother, Mi Hpaw, waits on her own in the dark beneath the house.

Time slid by (*dəjwɛjwɛ̀* /တရွေ့ရွေ့.) like a snail. From above, she could hear the sounds of bottles and glasses. From time to time (*tətɛʰɛʔ-tətɛʰɛʔ* /တချက်တချက်), a beam of light shone through a crack in the floor ... She heard the sounds of sandals skidding on the floor (*shaʔshaʔ-shaʔshaʔ* /ရှပ်) in an effort to resist (*sʰouʔsʰáinzáin* /ဆုပ်ဆိုင်းဆိုင်း). ... Mi Hpaw grew anxious (*jódó-jwɑ̀dɑ̀* /ရိုးတိုးရွတ) ... Indistinct (*məθé-məgwé* /မသဲမကွဲ) sounds like creaking (*tɛódzó-tɛwịdzwị* /ကျိုးကျိုးကွိုကွို), and the jostle and jounce (*bəjóun-bəjín* /ဗရုန်းဗရင်း) of a struggle put her in a state of excruciating (*məkʰàndzị-məkʰàndà* / မခံ့မခံသာ) anxiety. For a while, there was a pause in the cacophony (*ʔəθàn-bəlàn* / အသံဗလံ.). [A little later, the mother struggles with a man who is trying to stop her climbing up the stairs.] The two of them struggle and tussle (*bəlóun-bətʰwé* /ဗလုံးဗထွေး); then the young girl appears, her head covered with a towel, looking disheveled (*bòðì-baʔθì* / ဗုသိဘဘက်သိ). To Mi Hpaw, she appears blurry (*wódó-wádá* / ဝိုးတိုးဝါးတား); she calls out to her mum, and Mi Hpaw takes her hand.

A number of the phrases are clearly onomatopoeic: *shaʔshaʔ-shaʔshaʔ*, possibly just a repetition of the word *shaʔ* 'be flat', represents the scuffing sound of shoes; and *tɕódzó-tɕwìdzwì*, with *tɕó* possibly the verb 'break', imitates the sound of creaking floorboards. *Dəjwɛjwɛ* casts the verb *jwɛ* 'move' in the format that suggests continuous action to describe incremental movement, like a snail. Several other compounds of this form appear in the (long) lacunae within the excerpt: *təʔìʔì*, descriptive of sobbing; *dəgauʔgauʔ*, the noise of clogs; and *gəlauʔlauʔ*, with unstressed *gə* rather than *tə*, representing the sound of pouring liquid, 'glub-glub'. The only other ternary compound in the passage is *sʰouʔ-sʰáinzáin*, based on the stems *sʰouʔ* 'withdraw, wane' and *sʰáin* 'suspend' (cf. *sʰouʔsʰáin* 'hesitate').

The rest of the cited forms are all elaborate expressions. Several are ionized by the negative marker, *mə*: *məθέ-məgwέ*, from *θέgwέ* 'clear; distinct'; *məkʰàndzì- məkʰànðà*, formed from the stems *kʰàndzì* and *kʰànðà*, themselves both based on *kʰàn* 'to bear; endure'. *Bəlóun-bətʰwέ* 'tussling' inserts the otherwise meaningless *bə* into the compound *lóuntʰwέ* 'entangled'. *Bəjóun-bəjín* does the same to the pleonastic *jóunjín*, based on *jóun* 'to pull; struggle'. The *bə* suffix also appears in the rhyming supplement of the pleonastic *ʔəθàn-bəlàn* 'cacophony', based on the noun *ʔəθàn* 'sound'.

Still others have interlocking rhyme and chime rather than repeated syllables. *Jódó-jwàdà* 'anxious', based on the root *jwà* 'to itch; be restless; be antsy' (cf. *dəjwàjwà* 'teeming' in Tin Moe's poem), is formed by rhyme (*jwà → jwàdà*), and then chime (*jwàdà → jódó*). *Wódó-wádá* 'indistinct', seen later in the passage, is constructed with rhyming syllables, *dó* and *dá*, on the stem *wówá* 'be dim; obscure' (cf. *wódəwá* above). The same pattern appears in *kóyó-káyá* (ကိုးရိုးကားရား) 'in disorder; be a mess; higgledy piggledy' and *módó-maʔtaʔ* (မိုးတိုးမတ်တတ်) 'bolt upright; without sitting down'.[18] Finally, *bòðì-baʔθì* 'dishevelled (of hair, clothing)', with the stem probably *pò* 'in excess', and the chiming *baʔθì* added to a pseudo-stem, *bòðì*.

8   Conclusion

Sometimes you don't need to bother about appearance; you can be humdrum (making no effort to look good): *gəbò-kəyò.nɛ̀* (ကပိုကရိုနဲ့). But sometimes, you need some razzle-dazzle; you need to dress up 'with gold-dangling and silver-jangling': *ʃwètwélwé-ŋwètwélwé.nɛ̀* (ရွှေတွဲလွဲငွေတွဲလွဲနဲ့). All languages presumably

---

[18] Again, thanks to Saw Tun for bringing these examples to my attention.

have such resources, and in Burmese, they are used most effectively. As Whorf (1956: 267) observed:

If the sounds fit, the psychic quality of the sounds is increased, and this can be noticed by the layman. If the sounds do not fit, the psychic quality changes to accord with the linguistic meaning, no matter how incongruous with the sounds, and is not noticed by the layman.[19]

In other words, speakers can make do with sound that is only conventionally associated with meaning but they are drawn to sounds that fit the situation. Just what fits and what does not is harder to define. It may be rhythm; it may be euphony; it may be mimicry. Ultimately, if it sounds right, it is right: *kʰìnjà sʰwèmjó mèinjà híngáun* (ခင်ရာ ဆွေမျိုး၊ မိန်ရာ ဟင်းကောင်း) 'Whoever is close is family; whatever tastes good is good [food].'

References

Bauer, Robert S. and Paul K. Benedict. 1997. *Modern Cantonese phonology (Trends in Linguistics, Studies and Monographs 102)*. Berlin and New York: Mouton de Gruyter.

Chao, Yuen Ren. 1968. *A grammar of spoken Chinese*. Berkeley and Los Angeles: University of California Press.

Diffloth, Gérard. 1976. 'Expressives in Semai'. In Philip N. Jenner, Laurence C. Thompson, and Stanley Starosta (eds.), *Austroasiatic studies*, Part I. (Oceanic Linguistics Special Publications, No. 13.) Honolulu: University of Hawaii Press, pp. 249–264.

Haas, Mary R. 1964. *Thai–English student's dictionary*. London: Oxford University Press.

1969. Burmese disguised speech. *Bulletin of the Institute of History and Philology*, Academia Sinica (Taipei) 39(2): 277–86.

Judson, Adoniram. 1966. *Judson's Burmese–English dictionary*. Revised and enlarged version of the 1953 edition. Yangon: Baptist Board of Publications.

Maung Htin (pen name of Htin Fatt). 1957 [1947]. *Nga ba*. Yangon: People's Press.

Myanmar Language Commission. 1978–80. *Mranmā abhidhān akyañ:khyup [Abridged Myanmar dictionary]*. 5 volumes. Yangon: Myanmar Language Commission.

1993. *Mranmā-Aṅgalip abhidhān [Myanmar–English dictionary]*. Second edition. Myanmar: Myanmar Language Commission.

Okell, John. 1969. *A reference grammar of spoken Burmese*, Parts I and II. London: Oxford University Press.

Okell, John and Anna Allott. 2001. *Burmese/Myanmar dictionary of grammatical forms*. Richmond, Surrey: Curzon Press.

Patent, Jason D. 1998. A willy-nilly look at Lai ideophones. *Linguistics of the Tibeto-Burman area* 21(1): 155–200.

Qin, Senjie, general editor. 1990. *Mian-Han cidian*. Beijing: Commercial Press.

---

[19] I owe the citation to Waugh and Newfield (1995: 210).

Quirk, Randolf, Sidney Greenbaum, Geoffrey Leech, and Jan Svartvik. 1972. *A grammar of contemporary English*. London: Longman.

Saw Tun. 2010. The voicing rules in Burmese: an analysis of statements made by two Bama scholars. Unpublished manuscript.

Watkins, Justin (ed.). 2005. *Studies in Burmese linguistics* (Pacific Linguistics 570). Canberra: Pacific Linguistics, Research School of Pacific and Asian Studies.

Waugh, Linda and Madeleine Newfield. 1995. 'Iconicity in the lexicon and its relevance for a theory of morphology'. In Marge E. Landsberg (ed.), *Syntactic iconicity and linguistic freezes: the human dimension*. Berlin: Mouton de Gruyter, pp. 189–222.

Whorf, Benjamin L. 1956. *Language, thought and reality*, ed. John Carroll. Cambridge, MA: MIT Press.

Win Pe. 1978. *Modern Burmese poetry*. Yangon: Myawaddy Press.

16   Psycho-collocational expressives in Burmese

Alice Vittrant

1   Introduction

Burmese as part of the Mainland Southeast Asia linguistic area shares many linguistic features with other related and unrelated-related languages of the area. Since Henderson (1965) noticed striking similarities between Southeast Asian languages, Mainland Southeast Asia (henceforth MSEA) has been recognized as a *Sprachbund* (Migliazza 1996; Matisoff 2001; Enfield 2005; Vittrant 2010) or a 'zone of structural convergence' (Bisang 2006). The features shared belong to different domains (cf. Bisang 1991, 1996; Clark 1989; Matisoff 1986, 1991, for details). 'Expressive' is one of these features, at the crossroad of the phonetic, morphosyntactic, and semantic domains. This feature also illustrates the aesthetic components of the grammar of MSEA languages, being a productive and significant device to express emotion, feelings, and mental states in these languages. Two kinds of expressive are found in MSEA languages: elaborate expressions and psycho-collocations. The purpose of this chapter is to present Burmese psycho-collocations, focusing on their forms, their syntactic behaviours, their similarities and differences with psycho-collocations in other languages of the area.

2   About expressives or how to express emotional phenomena

2.1   What is an expressive?

Many languages of the world have a lexical category referred to as expressives (Fudge 1970), phonoaesthetics (Henderson 1965[1]), or ideophones to refer to noise, animal cries, mental states, physical states, and actions. Expressives may be divided in sub-categories. For instance Antilla (1977) distinguished three classes of words: 'onomatopoeic' for words describing animal cries and noise, 'descriptive' for those referring to physical states and actions, and 'affective' for

---

[1] Henderson (1965) labelled 'phonaesthetic' words for descriptive noises and sudden darting movement (instead of onomatopoeic).

mental states words; whereas Diffloth (1972, 1976,[2] 2001) defines ideophones and onomatopoeic words as sub classes of 'expressives'. Expressive is sometimes considered as a distinguished part-of-speech category. Most recently, Potts et al. (2009) have discussed expressives as a class of emotive morphemes, words, and constructions.

However they are labelled, expressive words have a tendency in a wide range of languages to be associated with structural and phonological peculiarities, although these are not sufficient conditions for defining this category cross-linguistically. For instance, Henderson (1965: 460) evokes secondary phonological pattern of 'affective' language whereas Mithun (1984)[3] notices that expressives are 'particularly resistant to regular phonetic change'.

As for the syntactic patterns exhibited by expressives, Clark (1996: 535) and Goddard (2008: 89) point out the non-standard or reverse order of components in expressive compounds. Jaisser (1990: 160) reports on syntactic device for differentiating the locus of emotion from a single organ in Hmong language, whereas Diffloth (1972, 1976) and Mithun (1984) noted unusual syntactic properties of these expressives.[4]

Expressives are regularly omitted in grammars, and generally neglected although they constitute a fundamental word class in many Asian languages. They are however extremely difficult to elicit in the field as noted by Diffloth (2001: 267).[5] They indeed rarely appear in declarative and neutral speech as they represent an attempt by the speaker to transmit a sensation to the hearer as

---

[2] Diffloth (1976: 264): 'Onomatopoeic forms are those displaying acoustic symbolism and having syntactic and morphological properties totally different from those of verbs and nouns. *Ideophones* are words displaying phonological symbolism of any kind (acoustic, articulatory, structural) and having distinct morphosyntactic properties; ideophones include onomatopoeic forms as a subclass. *Expressives* have the same morphosyntactic properties as ideophones, but their symbolism, if such exists, is not necessarily phonological; expressives contain ideophones as a subclass.'

[3] Expressive words found in related Iroquoian languages do not exhibit the expected sound correspondences for cognates.

[4] Diffloth (1972: 445) noticed unusual negative properties in negative sentences containing ideophones, a 'morphology that is semantically and formally unlike anything found in nouns and verbs' (1976: 251); whereas, Mithun (1984: 50) wrote about Iroquoian languages: 'Expressive terms are characterized by special syntactic, morphological ... patterns. Their syntactic patterns are quite limited. They do not enter into the same kinds of grammatical constructions as other lexical items. Instead, they occur either as complete, independent utterances, or as the objects of a verb like *say*.'

[5] Diffloth (2001: 267): '*De façon plus générale, comment faire pour récolter les expressifs? Il serait toujours possible de oser une question du genre: "Y a-t-il un mot comme XXX? ... On pourra aussi pêcher au hasard et demander à satiété : "Quel expressif, quel mot utiliseriez-vous si vous voulez transmettre la sensation x, l'impression y, z, etc.," en suggérant peut-être divers contextes. L'interrogé restera en général perplexe. ... Il faut donc guetter les expressifs, les attraper au vol; mais dans le feu de l'action et de la discussion animée où ils naissent, qui aurait le culot d'interrompre tout le monde afin de pouvoir vérifier une voyelle, un sens, une intention?*'

directly as language allows. This is why they may sometimes be considered interjections (see Headley 1977).

In this paper, expressives are considered to be idiomatic forms that display special phonological and structural properties with often a 'direct' or 'unmediated' relation to meaning.

2.2   Expressives and body-part terms

According to Wierzbicka (1999), who looks for universal parameters in the definition of emotions and their linguistics coding, all languages describe emotions, to a certain degree, via bodily symptoms (blush) or sensations (feeling hot as a reaction to an emotional situation). Body is also central in decoding other people's emotions: there is a range of physiological characteristics such as smiles, eyebrow shapes by which we judge if a person is happy, sad, etc. The human body is moreover frequently used as metaphorical source domain across languages (Fedry 1976; Vandeloise 1986; Sweetser 1990). Therefore, body parts, either internal or external, may easily be conceptualized as the locus of emotions and mental states. As such, they are regularly invoked in the description of these processes. This is particularly true for East and Southeast languages as noted by Matisoff (1986a), Clark (1996), Wayland (1996), Yu (2002), Musgrave (2006), and Compton (2007 inter alia).

Example (1) contains an internal body-part term and illustrates a mental state. Emotions are expressed with internal body-part terms in examples (2), (3), and (4b) and with external body-part terms in (4a) and (5).

(1)   Hmong from Jaisser (1990: 167)
a.   nkag   **siab**
         crawl   **liver**
         'to understand (lit. to crawl into the liver)'
b.   txiav   **siab**
         cut   **liver**
         'to decide, make a decision'

(2)   wolof from Becher (2003) [cited by Verhoeven (2007: 92)]
         Sama   **xol**   dafa   tang
         poss.1.sg   **heart**   subj.3.sg   be hot
         'I am angry.' (lit. : 'My heart is hot.')

(3)   Kambera from Klamer (2002: 369)
         mbaha – naya – ka   na   **eti** – na   na   maramba
         be.wet – 3sg.subj – perf   art   **liver** – 3sg.poss   art   king
         'The king is pleased.' (lit. : 'The king's liver is wet.')

(4)   CHINESE from Yu (2002)
a.   hui – **tou**   tu – **lian**
        grey/dusty – **head**   earthy – **face**
        '(dial) dejected; despondent, depressed'
b.   **gan – chang**   yu – duan
        liver – intestines   about.to split
        'be heartbroken; be deeply grieved'

(5)   BURMESE[6]
a.   ခြေနိုင်လက်နိုင် ။
        $c^h e^2$ – naiN^2– lɛʔ – naiN^2
        foot   can   **hand** can
        'within one's means or capacity'
b.   လက်လွယ် ။
        lɛʔ –   lwɛ^2
        hand   free
        'generous, open-handed'

(6)   THAI from Matisoff (1986: 41, 45)
a.   dii   nýa   dii   caj
        good   flesh   good   heart, breath
        'glad, delighted'
b.   caj   hǎaj   caj khwâm
        heart, breath vanish   **id**. overturn
        'get scared out of one's wits'

2.3   Expressives in Asia: elaborate expressions and psycho-collocations

In many Asian languages, expressives appear with a specific form, intermediate
in structure between ordinary compound and reduplication. Known as 'elaborate expressions', a term coined by Mary Haas (1964) talking about Thai literary
four-syllable expressions, this type of construction is typical of East and
Southeast Asian languages. Matisoff (1973: 81) describes them as a 'compound
containing four (usually monosyllabic) elements, of which either the first and
third or the second and fourth are identical (A-B-A-C or A-B-C-B) [and that]
characteristically convey a rather formal or elegant impression'.

---

[6] About Burmese transcription: my phonemic transcription roughly follows Bernot's (1980) proposal,
with some minor changes for tones and diphthongs. Tones are indicated by superscript numbers at
the end of the syllable: [^{1}] stands for brief, high and creaky tone; [^{2}] stands for long, low and breathy
tone; [^{3}] stands for long, clear, high-falling tone. The fourth tone corresponds to a glottal stop. Atonal
(and unmarked) syllables may appear in disyllabic words with [ə] as the main vowel. Capital letters
stand for stops that can be realized as voiced or unvoiced depending on the phonological (and
morphosyntactic) context. Most of the grammatical morphemes start with a capital letter, given that
they are usually (but not always) syntactically closely related to the preceding morpheme.

The two non-reduplicated elements of the quadrisyllabic expression are usually referred to as an 'elaborate couplet', i.e. a pair of phonologically different but roughly synonymous or antonymic morphemes that conventionally appear together. The same couplet may appear in a large number of different expressives, simply by varying the reduplicated element. Examples (7) and (8) from Burmese provide illustrations.

(7a)   မနီး မဝေး ။

      mə –   ni^3 –   mə –   wɛ^3

      NEG   close   NEG   far

      'not so far, (to be) at a good distance'

(7b)   အတော် အတန့် ။

      ʔə -tɔ^2 ʔə –taN^2

      NMLZ – be sufficient, fit NMLZ -be worth, fit

      'fairly, moderately'

(8a)   ခြေချော်လက်ချော် ။

      c^{h}e^2 – C^{h}ɔ^2 –   lɛʔ – C^{h}ɔ^2

      foot miss   **hand** miss

      'accidentally, inadvertently'

(8b)   ခြေစလက်စ ။

      c^{h}e^2 – Sa^1 –   lɛʔ – Sa^1

      foot begin **hand** begin

      'aptitude, qualification'

Although elaborate quadrisyllabic expressions may be characteristic of formal speech in some languages such as Thai, they are part of everyday language in others such as Hmong languages (Jaisser 1990: 160) or Dong, a Tai-Kadai language spoken in China (Gerner 2004, 2005). They usually function as adverbials, but as shown by the Burmese and Hmong examples, respectively (8b) and (9b), they may form nominal compounds or other parts of speech.

(9)   HMONG (Mortensen 2003)

       a. nrawm – caj   nrawm – tuag

          fast   alive   fast   dead

          'very quickly'

       b. ntxhais – um   ntxhais – tswv

          girl   official girl   lord

          'princess'

However, the psycho-collocation is another kind of expressive found regularly in Asian languages, containing body-part or organ terms and expressing emotional states and other mental activities. As psycho-collocations are at the core of this chapter, the next sections will be dedicated to this second kind of expressive. Section 3 presents the phenomenon and its important place in Asian languages and Section 4 is dedicated to the phenomenon in Burmese, highlighting its peculiarities in this language.

3   About psycho-collocations

3.1   Defining psycho-collocation

The 'psycho-collocation' areal feature, described for a number of MSEA languages (Matisoff 1986; Jaisser 1990; Oey 1990; Clark 1996; VanBik 1998), refers to a collocation, i.e. a conventionalized combination of words that may become idiomatic to differing degrees. These polymorphemic expressions make an explicit reference to body parts or organs as the locus of emotions or psychological states. The term 'psycho-collocation' was coined by Matisoff (1986) to describe expressions that involve metaphorical uses of high frequency adjectives (or verbs) explicitly collocated with person part terms to refer to psychological phenomenon.

Psycho-collocation [is] a polymorphemic expression referring as a whole to a mental process, quality, or state, one of whose constituents is a psycho-noun, i.e. a noun with explicit psychological reference (translatable by English words like heart, mind, spirit, soul, temper, nature, disposition, mood). The rest of the psy[cho]-collocation contains morphemes (usually action verbs or adjectives) that complete the meaning. This element we call the psycho-mate. (Matisoff, 1986: 7)

Psycho-collocations may be classified from several points of view; (1) semantic, (2) morphological, or (3) syntactic. The following features may be used to distinguish different sub-types of psycho-collocations:
1. – the particular kind of mental activity that the collocation refers to (cf. Matisoff 1986: 7ff.),
   – the physical or metaphorical states (Clark 1989),
   – the type of psycho-noun: body part or abstract noun (VanBik 1998);
2. – the part of speech of the psycho-noun, i.e. common noun or nominalized verb (VanBik 1998);
3. – the syntactic status of the psycho-noun, i.e. subject or object of the predicate (Matisoff 1986: 11; Goddard 2008: 89),
   – the compositionality or non-compositionality of the expressions (Bickel 1997: 141ff.),
   – the status of the expression: compound or incorporation (Clark 1989).

3.2   Psycho-collocation in Asian languages

Metaphorical expressions involving body parts or organs are found in many of the world's languages (English: 'Take **heart**'; 'to one's **heart's** content'; 'big-**hearted**', French: '*sans cœur*' (heartless); '*écœuré*' (be disgusted, be sicken); '*cœurd'artichaut*' (someone who falls in love with every girl/boy he/she meets); '*avoir les foies* [liver]' (to be scared to death), Spanish 'echar los higados' [liver] (to sweat one's guts out)). In the major European languages (French, English among others), the expression of mental activities or emotional states is typically treated as a covert class: nothing in the words '*espérer*'/ hope, or '*furieux*'/angry, or '*heureux*'/happy tells us they refer to psychological or mental phenomena.

On the other hand, Asian and MSEA languages tend to treat the expression of emotional and mental states or processes much more like an overt class. When describing physical and emotional feelings, i.e. psychological phenomena, Southeast Asian languages (and to a certain extent East Asian languages[7]) commonly use a distinctive construction consisting of a body-part term and a stative/adjective verb; a construction that has been labelled a 'psycho-collocation,'[8] by Matisoff (1986). Although these 'body part-adjective' expressions may be seen as part of a universal metaphorical tendency – closely related to French expressions such as '*avoir le sang chaud*'/'hot-blooded,' *avoir le cœur gros/*'fat-hearted', there seems to be a qualitative difference in the extremes to which MSEA[9] languages carry this tendency: most of these languages cannot express mental activities, emotion, or character features without referring to a body part, as noted by VanBik (1998: 227) about Lai, a Tibeto-Burman language of Burma: 'Psycho-collocations are essential in the daily use of Lai. It is impossible to discuss the life of the mind without them.'

This construction is widespread in all languages of the area whatever the linguistic family they belong to. It is therefore found in Sino-Tibetan languages (ST), Tai-Kadai languages (TK), Hmong-Mien languages (HM), Austroasiatic languages (AA), and Austronesian (AN) languages, as shown by examples

---

[7] See for instance Yoon (2003) on uses of *maum* ('heart, mind') in Korean as in 마음이 가다 (*maumi kata*: lit. *maum* goes): 'tend to be attracted'.

[8] Psycho-collocation constructions are also known as 'experiential collocation' (Verhoeven 2007), or compositional and non-compositional collocations (Bickel 1997).

[9] This is particularly true for languages of Mainland Southeast Asia, and under discussion for the insular languages, such as those of the Western Malayo-Polynesian grouping. While Oey (1990) illustrates the phenomenon for Malay, Musgrave (2006) reports about two construction types for emotion predicates in the area. According to the latter author, Western Malayo-Polynesian (Indonesian, Balinese) typically uses simple predicates to denote emotional states, whereas Eastern Indonesian languages use complex predicates involving body-part terms. However, Donahue (2004: 223) demonstrates the pervasiveness of the construction in Western Malayo-Polynesian languages.

(10)–(14). This construction is also known as one of the numerous features shared by languages of the MSEA Sprachbund. However it does exist in SEA languages of the islands such as Bahasa Indonesia, Malay (Oey 1990; Goddard 2008; Siahaan 2008), and in languages belonging to the Papuan linguistic family (cf. Klamer 2002; Musgrave 2006; Gaby 2008).

(10)   Sino-Tibetan
a.   LAI (VanBik 1998: 213)
ka – luŋ – na – tliŋ
1SG.POSS-**heart** -3SG.OBJ-complete
'I am satisfied.' *(lit. : 'My heart is complete.')*
b.   BURMESE
ဝမ်းသာတယ် ။
waN³ θa²   Tɛ²
belly pleasant REAL
'(I) am pleased.'
c.   BELHARE (Bickel 1997: 143)
a-niuta ta-he
1SG.POSS-**mind** activate-PT
'I am pleased.'

(11)   Tai-Kadai
a.   THAI from Jenny (2011)
thuùk – cay
correct – **heart**
'please, satisfy'
b.   SHAN[10]

tʰuk² tsaɯ
be suitable – **mind**
'be pleased, be pleased with, like'

(12)   Austroasiatic
a.   MON from Jenny (2011)
cɒt – klɛʔ
heart – short'
'short tempered'
b.   WA (from Watkins to appear)
ʔạt – rʰɔm
heart – salty
'angry'

---

[10] From the online version of Dr J. N. Cushing's Shan-English Dictionary (1881, Rangoon) http://sealang.net/shan/.

(13)   Hmong-Mien
a.   HMONG from Jaisser (1990: 159, 163)
         tus   kwv   mas   siab   ncjag
         CLF   younger brother   TOP   liver   straight
         'Youngest brother, you are honest.' (lit. : 'Younger brother, (your) liver is
         straight.'
b.   siab – luv
         liver – short
         'impatient, short tempered'

(14)   Austronesian
a.   MALAY from Donahue (2004: 223)
         saya   hati   senang
         1SG   **liver** content
         'I am content'
b.   NIAS from Laiya 1985 (cited by Donahue 2004)
         a-fõkhõ tõdõ   nia   khõ-gu
         STAT-sick **liver** 3SG.GEN   DAT-1SG.GEN
         'He is jealous of me.'

To sum up, whatever language is studied, psycho-collocation constructions are
always peculiar in terms of their structure, conveying either figurative or
metaphorical meanings. However, studies of the phenomenon bring out two
opposite properties of these psycho-collocations: there is cross-cultural or
universal status of the metaphors involved in these psycho-collocations while
there are also culture-specific ways of combining psycho-nouns and psycho-
mates, i.e. body-part terms and predicates.

   The conceptualization of body parts or organs as the locus of emotional and
mental activities reveals different cultural models, derived sometimes from
cultural tradition or ethnic religious beliefs (Siahaan 2008: 48): every language
has its favourite location for psychological states and feelings, either the heart as
in English and Thai (see example (11a)), the liver as in Malay and Hmong (see
examples (14a) and (13)), or the guts or the stomach as in Vietnamese (see
example (15)).

(15)   VIETNAMESE from Clark (1996: 538)
         Nàng đau lòng   lắm
         3SG sick intestines/guts very
         'She's heart-broken.'

So what about Burmese? What are the body-part terms found in Burmese
psycho-collocations? What is the favourite locus of emotions and feelings for
Burmese speakers? What about the syntactic behaviour of these polymorphemic expressions? These are all issues that will be addressed in the next section.

4   Psycho-collocations in Burmese

Spoken in Burma by nearly 50 million speakers (Wheatley 2003: 195), Burmese is a member of the Sino-Tibetan linguistic family, but also clearly a Southeast Asian language, sharing many features with languages spoken in the MSEA area (Vittrant 2010): tonal system, tendency to monosyllabicity, classifier device, serial verb constructions, etc. ... and of course expressives. Elaborate quadrisyllabic expressions and psycho-collocations are therefore found in Burmese, the latter type of expression being the only means of expressing emotions, psychological states in this language, unlike what is found in Vietnamese (Clark 1989: 537) or Indonesian (Musgrave 2006).

In this section, I will first present the body-terms used to express emotions and psychological states in Burmese within the context of what is found in other Asian languages. Then, I will focus on the preferred body-part term of Burmese psycho-collocation, that is to say *ɓ́ɕ sei?*, tracing back its origin and examining the predicates it combines with. Then I will end by observing some of the peculiarities of Burmese psycho-collocations.

4.1   The organs and body-part terms in expressive constructions

Looking at organs and body-part terms in Burmese polymorphemic expressions reveals an impressive list, containing either elaborate and quadrisyllabic expressions and psycho-collocations.

4.1.1 Body-part term in quadrisyllabic and elaborate expressive constructions   As seen in Section 2.2, body-part terms may be used in Burmese elaborate expressions (cf. examples (5) and (8)). Bernot's Burmese-French dictionary (1978–1992) – henceforth BFDic – gives around fifteen quadrisyllabic constructions containing the couplet 'foot ~ hand' (and four with the reverse order 'hand ~ foot'), most of them referring to mental or psychological states. Although some of them exhibit the expected structure ABAC or ABCB (cf. (16)), others are just quadrisyllabic expressions containing a couplet of body-part terms (cf. (17)). Apart the couplet <foot ~ hand>, the following combinations <mind ~ belly>, <mind ~ heart>, <mind ~ hand>, <mind ~ body (corpse)> are also common in Burmese expressives. Table 16.1 indicates the number of expressions found for each association in Bernot's Burmese-French dictionary.[11]

---

[11] I do not claim that BFDic provides an exhaustive list of this type of expressions. However, other dictionaries such as Burmese–English (1993) or Burmese–Burmese (1991) dictionaries published in Yangon (Myanmar) by the Department of the Myanmar Language Commission, give similar or shorter lists of expressions for these couplets. Moreover, as shown by the couplet <mind/heart>, some expressions are not listed at all in dictionaries. Therefore, the number of expressions given here for each couplet is only indicative.

Table 16.1 *Frequency of body-part couplets in Burmese from BFDic*

Couplet of	Body-terms	Number of tokens found	Illustration
<hand ~ foot>	လက်ခြေ /lɛʔ- $C^h e^2$/	18+4 expressions listed in *BFDic*	Cf. examples (5) and (8)
<mind ~ belly>	စိတ်ဝမ်း /sɛiʔ- waN^3/	6 expressions listed in *BFDic*	စိတ်ဝမ်းကွဲ sɛiʔ waN^3 kwɛ^3 mind-belly – be broken 'become desunited'
<mind ~ heart>	စိတ်နှလုံး /sɛiʔ- ŋəloN^3/	7 expressions given by informants[12]	Cf. examples (18)
<mind ~ hand>	စိတ်လက် /sɛiʔ- lɛʔ/	10 expressions listed in *BFDic*	Cf. examples (16) and (17)
<mind ~ body (corpse)>	စိတ်ကိုယ် /sɛiʔ- ko^2/	5 expressions listed in *BFDic*	စိတ်နောက်ကိုယ်ပါ sɛiʔ naɔʔ ko^2 pa^2 mind- soon-body-accompany 'impulsively, rashly'
<mind~nature (corpse)>	စိတ်သဘော /sɛiʔ- θəbɔ^3/	2 expressions listed in *BFDic*	စိတ်တူသဘောတူ sɛiʔ tu^2 θəbɔ^3 tu^2 mind- similar-nature-similar 'in agreement (adv.)'

- < mind ~ hand>, စိတ်လက် , sɛiʔ- lɛʔ

(16a) စိတ်ပါလက်ပါ ။
　　　sɛiʔ　pa^2　　lɛʔ　　　　pa^2　　sɛiʔ
　　　mind be with, accompany **hand** idem
　　　'willingly'

(16b) စိတ်ပျက် လက်ပျက် ။
　　　sɛiʔ　pyɛʔ　　　　lɛʔ　　pyɛʔ
　　　mind be destroyed **hand** idem
　　　'in disappointment, dejectedly'

(17a) စိတ်ပြေလက်ပြောက် ။
　　　sɛiʔ　pye^2　　lɛʔ　　pyaɔʔ
　　　mind be relieved **hand** drop
　　　'for a change, a respite'

---

[12] None of these expressions are listed in the BFDic, nor in the two dictionaries published in Yangon (Myanmar) by the Department of the Myanmar Language Commission. They have been elicited from Burmese informants.

(17b) စိတ်လှုက်ရှု
      sɛiʔ   lo²   lɛʔ   ya¹
      mind be destroyed **hand** idem
      'willingly, voluntarily'

Some of these elaborate expressions may be psycho-collocations. As noted by Matisoff (1986), the structure of the psycho-collocation may be made complex by using compounding, reduplication of one component (either the psycho-noun or the psycho-mate) and elaborate couplets (with quasi-synonymous or related nouns).

* <mind ~ heart>, စိတ်နှလုံး, sɛiʔ- ŋəloN³

(18a) စိတ်နှလုံး အေးချမ်းတယ်။
      sɛiʔ – ŋəloN³   ʔe³   CʰaN³   Tɛ²
      mind – heart   be cool   be cold   REAL
      '(He) feels at peace.' (lit. : '(His) mind and heart are cool.')

(18b) စိတ်နှလုံးညှိုးနွမ်းတယ်။
      sɛiʔ   -ŋəloN³   ɲto³   ŋwaN³   Tɛ²
      mind   -heart   wither   be outdated   REAL
      '(He) is sad [because of a love-story].' (lit. : '(His) mind and heart are withered, outdated.')

4.1.2 Body-part terms in Burmese psycho-collocations A first study of Burmese psycho-collocations (Matisoff 1986) lists the most common psycho-nouns used in this language, that is to say, some internal organs such as 'heart', 'liver', 'belly', and some nouns with explicit psychological reference like 'mind', 'nature/disposition', 'consciousness'. However, other organs and body-part terms may be part of a collocation with mental or emotional connotations, as shown by Table 16.2.

For instance, the word 'ear' may be combined with motion verbs (i.e. 'enter, turn, drop') or stative verbs (i.e. 'be far, be good, be hot, be clear, be heavy') to convey psychological process as 'understand' or emotional state (cf. (19)). As for the word 'eye', its collocation with the verb 'turn' means 'find someone confusing'. Other examples are given in (20) and (21).

(19) a. ear + turn   နား လည်   *Understand, know, comprehend*
                   na³ + lɛ²

      b. ear + enter နား ဝင်   *Accept, be convinced*
                   na³ + wiN²

      c. ear + (be) hot နား ပူ   *Be distressingly noisy, be irritated by*
                   na³ + pu²   *hearing something repeatedly, worry*
                           somebody for a favour

Table 16.2 *List of Burmese psycho-nouns*

INTERNAL ORGANS		
heart	နှလုံး	ŋəloN³
liver	အသည်း	ʔəθɛ³
belly	ဝမ်း	waN³
intestines, guts	အူ	ʔu²
EXTERNAL ORGANS / BODY PARTS		
hand	လက်	lɛʔ
foot	ခြေ	cʰe²
ear	နား	na³
nose	နှာ	ŋa²
eye	မျက်စိ	myɛʔ.si¹
face (eye-nose)	မျက်နှာ	myɛʔ. ŋa²
PSYCHOLOGICAL REFERENCE		
mind	စိတ်	sɛiʔ
nature	သဘော	θəbɔ³
consciousness	သတိ	θəTi¹

(20) a. eye + turn   မျက်စိ လည်   *Find someone confusing*
                              myɛʔ si¹ + lɛ²

      b. eye + (be) clear   မျက်စိ ရှင်   *Be sharp-eyed*
                              myɛʔ si¹ + ʃiN²

      c. eye + (be) opened   မျက်စိ ပွင့်   *Be sophisticated*
                              myɛʔ si¹ + pwiN¹

(21) a. face + (be) dark   မျက်နှာ မည်း   *Dislike, disapproval*
                              myɛʔ.ŋa² + mɛ³

      b. face + destroy   မျက်နှာ ဖျက်   *Damage or mar the reputation of a*
                              myɛʔ.ŋa² + pʰyɛʔ   *person; soil a person's good name*

      c. face + (be) opened မျက်နှာ ပွင့်   *Be popular*
                              myɛʔ.ŋa² + pwiN¹

4.2 Origin of the most productive body-part terms in Burmese psycho-collocations

4.2.1 Origin of the main psycho-nouns   Two origins could be reconstructed for Burmese nouns used in psycho-collocations. Most of them are inherited Tibeto-Burman terms as listed in Table 16.3, with cognates in languages that also make use of psycho-collocations such as Lai (Haka Chin). Examples

Table 16.3 *Inherited Tibeto-Burman terms (from Matisoff 2003)*

Burmese term	Matisoff Transliteration <	Proto-Tibeto-Burman term
<heart> နှလုံး / nəloN³/	hnəlûm	*s-niŋ (cf. Benedict 1972: 217)
<liver> အသည်း /ʔəθɛ³/	ʔəsâñ	*m-sin
<belly> ဝမ်း /waN³/	wâm	*pʷam [stomach]
<hand> လက် /lɛʔ/	lak	*lak
<eye> မျက် /myɛʔ/	myak	*mik ~*myak
<ear> နား /na³/	nâ	*g-na
<nose> နှာ / ŋa²/	hna	*s-na

(22) and (23) show Lai and Burmese cognate psycho-nouns for 'heart' and 'ear'.

(22)   a. LAI from VanBik (1998: 217)

     na   **niŋ**   ʔa   hŋal
     2SG.POSS **heart** 2SG. SUBJ know-I
     'You are presumptuous.'

     b. BURMESE

     မပြောချင်ဘူး ၊ ဒီကောင်နှလုံးနာလွန်းလို့ ။

     mə   pyɔ   ChiN Pu   di   KaɔN²   **nəloN³**   na²   lwaN³   lo¹
     NEG talk   wish NEG DEM guy   **heart**   hurt in excess
     SUB:because
     '(I) don't want to talk (about that). Because (I) can't stand this guy.'
     (lit. : 'I don't want to talk. Because, this guy, heart is hurting in excess.')

(23)   a. LAI from VanBik (1998: 217)

     ka   **hna**   ʔa   ŋam
     1SG.POSS **ear**   3SG. SUBJ at home-I
     'I am content/ I am not worried.' (lit. 'My ear is at home.')

     b. BURMESE

     တစ်ချိန်မှာ သူ ကျွန်တော်ကို နားလည်လာမှာပါ ။

     tə-chɛiN² Ma² θu² cənɔ²   Ko²   **na²-lɛ²**   la²   mə²
     Pa²
     one-time LOC 3SG 1SG (H.P) OBJ understand **(ear.turn)** AUX:inchoat IRR
     POL
     'Once, he will begin to understand me.'

As noted in Table 16.3, Tibeto-Burman terms found in psycho-collocations refer to body parts and organs. On the other hand, abstract and psychological nouns used as psycho-nouns such as 'mind', 'nature/ disposition', or 'attention/ consciousness' (သတိ θəTi¹), are not inherited; they are mainly loanwords from Pali as Table 16.4 demonstrates.

Table 16.4 *Loanwords from Pali used as psycho-nouns*

Burmese term	Transliteration <	Pali	Meaning in Pali
< mind> စိတ် /sɛiʔ/	cit	citta	*heart (psychologically), i. e. the centre & focus of man's emotional nature*
<nature / disposition> သဘော /θəbɔ³/	sabhô	sabhāva	*state of mind, nature, condition; character, disposition; truth, reality*
<attention / consciousness> သတိ /θəTi¹/	satí	sati	*memory, recognition, consciousness*

4.2.2 'Mind' versus 'liver': the Burmese choice   Contrary to the Hmong languages (Jaisser 1990), the Austronesian languages (Siahaan 2008), and some Tibeto-Burman languages (see VanBik 1998, 2010 about Lai), the most productive psycho-noun used in psycho-collocations in Burmese is not 'liver' but the word စိတ် /sɛiʔ/ that could be translated by 'mind, the seat of emotion or life'. စိတ် /sɛiʔ/ is indeed very productive. The Burmese–French Dictionary gives nearly eighty psycho-collocations (sixty entries in Burmese–English Dictionary), whereas 'heart' နှလုံး ŋəloN[3] is found in about thirty psycho-collocations and 'liver' အသည်း /ʔəθɛ³/ barely in about fifteen. Moreover, as seen in the previous section, it combines with many other body-part terms to produce elaborate expressions.

The word စိတ် /sɛiʔ/ (transliterated *cit*) comes from Pali *citta*, via Mon. Burmese has also borrowed many religious and political words (and concepts) from these two languages during the Pagan period (eleventh to fourteenth centuries), with the influence of the Pali being more substantial than that of Mon.[13]

Interestingly, the same etymon is found as a psycho-noun in other Southeast Asian languages, such as Mon or Khmer. However the meaning of the word is both perceptibly and noticeably different in the three languages. Whereas Burmese dictionaries give 'mind' as the first meaning for စိတ် /sɛiʔ/, both Mon /cɒt/, and Khmer /cət/ have 'heart' as the main meaning (see definitions in (25)).

Notice that Southeast Asian cultures differ from Western ones, which clearly distinguish heart and mind (spirit) as illustrated by this French maxim: 'Le cœur

---

[13]   On Mon and Pali loanwords in Burmese, see Hla Pe (1961, 1967), Kasevitch (1994). On Mon and/or Pali influence on Burmese language, see Yanson (1994), Næss and Jenny (2011) and Jenny (2011).

a ses raisons que la raison ne connaît pas' ('The heart has reasons that reason does not comprehend').

(24)   KHMER from Clark (1996: 553)
         tŋay nih kñom sapbaay **cət**   nah
         day DEM ISG happy   **heart** very
         'Today, I'm very happy.'

(25)   a. Definition of Burmese စိတ် /sɛiʔ/   b. Definition of Khmer 'cət, **cetta?'**
         from Myanmar–English Dictionary   *from Cambodian–English*
         (1993),   *Dictionary by Robert K. Headley,*
         Myanmar Language Commission;   *Kylin Chhor, Lam Kheng Lim, Lim*
         republished 1996, Dunwoody Press   *Hak Kheang, and Chen Chun*
                                                        (1977), http://sealang.net/khmer/
                                                        dictionary.htm

         1. n. mind; thought; consciousness;   1. n. heart (as the seat of emotions),
            heart   feelings, emotions; mind, spirit,
         2. n. desire; will; interest   will (power); intention; thought,
         3. n. preoccupation   opinion; nature, disposition; is
                                                           often paired with 'liver' to empha-
                                                           size the totality of the emotion or
                                                           trait)

4.2.3 စိတ် sɛiʔ and its psycho-mates   What about the psycho-mates, i.e. the predicates used with *စိတ် sɛiʔ*? We found stative verbs (equivalent to adjectives in other languages) and action verbs in equal proportion. Stative verbs are often high-frequency verbs, associated with physical properties (hot, cold, big, small, dirty, clean, etc.).

One sub class of active verbs regularly found with psycho-nouns is motion verbs. Example (26) illustrates the combination of *စိတ် sɛiʔ* 'mind' with the verb လည် *lɛ²* 'to rotate, go around', a verb that also combines with 'ear', 'eye' (cf. (19), (20), (23)).

Indeed, the same psycho-mate may appear with different psycho-nouns, with relatively/quite distinct meanings. For instance, *စိတ်ဆိုး sɛiʔ shoᵌ* ('mind + be bad') and *သဘောဆိုး θəbɔᵌ shoᵌ* ('nature + be bad') mean respectively 'be angry' and 'be bad natured'. See also example (27) where the stative verb ပေါက် *paɔʔ* combines with *စိတ် sɛiʔ* 'mind', ရ *ʔuᵌ* 'intestines', and သဘော *θəbɔᵌ* 'nature'.

(26)   သူ့စိတ်(ပြန်)လည်လာပြီ ၊ အရင်လိုမစိမ်းကားတော့ဘူး ။
         θuᵌ¹ sɛiʔ-   (pyaNᵌ²)-lɛ²   la²   Piᵌ² ʔəyiNᵌ².loᵌ² mə saiNᵌ³.Kaᵌ³ Tɔ¹ Phuᵌ³
         3SG.GEN mind (again) rotate INCHOAT CRS hurry.NEG be distant   ASP NEG
         '(He) reverts to a former opinion. He is not as distant as before (towards me).'

(27)

a.	mind + be broken, explode	စိတ် ပေါက် sεiʔ paɔʔ	*Become angry, lose one's head*
b.	intestines + be broken, explode	အူ ပေါက် ʔu^2 paɔʔ	*Digress, ramble*
c.	nature + be broken, explode	သဘော ပေါက် θəbɔ^3 paɔʔ	*Realize, comprehend*

A last peculiarity about psycho-mates is the existence of psycho-collocations using both members of causative verb pairs. These pairs of verbs, realized with a consonantal or tonal alternation, reflect an earlier process of causativisation. Many Tibeto-Burman languages have preserved a few pairs of verbs, and Burmese still possesses a lot of them alongside a morphological process to form causatives.[14]

(28)

a. ကျမအသည်းကို မခွဲပါနဲ့ ။

cəma^1	ʔəθε^3	ko^2	mə	**k^{h}wε^3**	Pa^2	nε^1
ISG	liver	OBJ	NEG	break/split	POL	INJ

'(Please), don't break my heart.'

b. အသည်းခွဲတယ်
ʔəθε^3 – **kwε^3** Tε^2
liver – be broken REAL
'(I) am heart-broken.'

c. အသည်းခွဲတယ်
ʔəθε^3 – **k^{h}wε^3** Tε^2
liver – break REAL
'(I) broke (his) heart.'

4.3 *Structure and properties of Burmese psycho-collocations*

Several issues emerge as we examine utterances containing psycho-collocations: firstly, the number and nature of the arguments; secondly, the syntactic functions of these arguments, and the way the language expresses the grammatical roles they fulfil; and thirdly, the relationship between stative verb and body-part term, and the possibility of noun incorporation into the verb.

4.3.1 Nature and number of psycho-collocation's arguments

Arguments of an emotional predicate containing a psycho-noun are various: simple nominal phrase (NP) as in (22) where the NP is marked for its syntactic/pragmatic function (cf. (23), (29a)) as a nominalized clause (cf. (29b)), sub-ordinated clause (cf. (29c)) or with no overt argument (cf. (18a)).

(29)

a. **...သူ့အဖေ သူ့အပေါ်မှာ စိတ်ကုန်သွားပြီ** ။

...θu^1	ʔəphe^2	θu^1	ʔə-pɔ^2	m̥a^2	**sεiʔ -koN^2**	θwa^3	Pi^2
3SG.GEN	father	3SG.GEN	NMLZ-above	LOC	**mind-run out**	ASP.PRFS	CRS

'His father is fed up with him [because. . ..]'

[14] Vittrant (1998) lists eighty-three pairs in Burmese, showing either aspiration or tonal alternations. Gyurme (1992: 258) gives a list of ninety-six pairs for literary Tibetan, specifying that it is not an exhaustive list.

b. ကျမ ဒီလို နိုင်းတာ စိတ်မရှိပါနဲ့ ခင်ဗျား ။

cəma^1	di^2	lo^2	k^{h}aiN^3-Ta^2		sɛiʔ-mə	-ʃi^1	Pa^2	nɛ^1
1SG.FEM	DEM.	like	order-NMLZ.REAL		mind-NEG-happen	POL	INJ	

kəbya^3
2SG.MASC.POL

'Don't be angry if I give you such orders.'
(lit. : 'Don't be angry [with the fact that] I order you like this.')

c. သူ စာရေးဆရာဖြစ်ဖို့ စိတ်သန်နေတယ် ။

θu^2	sa^2.ye^3-s^{h}əya^2	p^{h}yiʔ	pho^1	sɛiʔ	-θaN^2	ne^2	Tɛ^2
3SG	writing-master	be	SUB:for	mind	-be strong	IPFV	REAL

'He really wants to be a writer.'

Notice also that the number of arguments varies for these psycho-collocations; some are strictly intransitive where the expressive meaning 'to be mixed up, confused' စိတ် ရှုပ် /sɛiʔ ʃoʔ/ ('mind + be complex') can occur with a unique argument marked as a topic or a subject (/ka^1/) and will not permit a NP marked as an object with ကို /ko^2/ – that is to say a second argument, as shown by the examples in (30).

(30)　a. သူ (က) စိတ်ရှုပ်နေတယ် ။

θu^1	(Ka^1)	sɛiʔ	- ʃoʔ	ne^2	Tɛ^2
3SG.GEN	(TOP/S)	mind	- be complex	IPFV	REAL

'(As for him), he is confused.'

b. *သူ ကို စိတ်ရှုပ်နေတယ် ။

θu^1	Ko^2	sɛiʔ	- ʃoʔ	ne^2	Tɛ^2
3SG.GEN	OBJ	mind	- be complex	IPFV	REAL

On the other hand, some expressives need two arguments, whether they are overt or not. Sentences in (32) contain the expressive စိတ်တို /sɛiʔ to^2/ meaning 'to be short-tempered, lose one patience'. In (32a), one argument (the source of the irritation) appears in the sentence and it is marked as an object. In (32b), although two participants are needed to fulfil the process of irritating, none of them is expressed. Whereas in (32c), the sentence contains a unique argument marked as the topic or subject of the expressive predicate: the sentence is ungrammatical with a stative reading. As shown by (32d), the intransitive reading requires another structure, a topic–comment structure, which is very common in Asian and Southeast Asian languages (Goddard 2008: 126ff). This kind of information structure is indeed reported by Matisoff for Lahu, which language exhibits sequences containing a noun followed by a 'transhemistichial compound', i.e. a noun and a verb semantically tight: some sequences that are clearly related to constructions of the type: 'NP$_{TOPIC}$ + N-V' (see (31)).

(31)   LAHU from Matisoff (1973: 310)
       áp-pò? chi í-kâ? nê?   ve
       shirt DEM water be wet IND
       'As for this shirt, it is water-wet.'

(32)   a. သူ့ကို စိတ်ရှုပ်နေတယ် ။
          θu¹   Ko² sɛi? - to²   Tɛ²
          3SG.GEN OBJ **mind** - **be short** REAL
          'He gets on (my) nerves.'

       b. စိတ်တိုလာတယ် ။
          sɛi? -to²   la   Tɛ²
          mind - be short INCHOAT REAL
          '(You) get on my nerves more and more.' or '(You)'re becoming really
             irritating.'

       c. *ဒီအသံက စိတ်တိုတယ် ။
          di   ?əθaN² Ka¹ sɛi? - to²   Tɛ²
          DEM noise TOP/S **mind** - **be short** REAL
          (*intend* : this noise is irritating.)

       d. ဒီအသံက စိတ်တိုစရာကောင်းတယ် ။
          di   ?əθaN² Ka¹ **sɛi?** -to²   -Səya kɔN   Tɛ²
          DEM noise TOP/S **mind** - **be short** - NMLZ be good   REAL
          'This noise is irritating.'
          (lit. : 'This noise, it is good in causing one feeling "short-tempered".')

4.3.2 Functions of the psycho-collocation's arguments   Psycho-collocation
constructions raise two questions regarding grammatical relationships and
functions among components of the sentences. One is the question of the
relationship between the verb and the body-part term and the status of the
latter as being incorporated into the verb. By incorporation we mean that
the incorporated noun and the verb which incorporates it function as a
single grammatical unit.[15] The second question deals with the relation of
inalienability between the subject whole and the body part: what is the
relationship between the body part used as a psycho-noun and the possessor
of this body part?

Although psycho-nouns do not have argument status in sentences like (33)
for instance – the two argument positions in (33) are already occupied by NPs
marked syntactically as the main arguments by က /Ka¹/ and ကို /Ko²/ – there
are several reasons to hesitate considering psycho-collocations as having incorporated nouns as noticed by Clark (1996) for other Southeast Asian languages.
Among these reasons, the probability of incorporation is ruled out by the

---

[15] On noun incorporation, see Mithun (1984) and Clark (1996: 541ff).

existence of sentences like (34) and (35). In the former, the psycho-noun is treated as an argument, being syntactically marked, and therefore separated from the psycho-mate, whereas in the latter example, psycho-noun and verb are separated by negation. Then the typological nature of Burmese also argues against incorporation since this language has no morphological indication and few phonetic clues for incorporation: sandhi will occur only in the case of tight relationship, and only under specific phonetic conditions.

As stated by Mithun (1984: 948ff.) in her discussion of noun incorporation, different types of noun incorporation exist and represent historical development of incorporation, the first type being a sort of lexical compounding and the last one being distinguished by possessor promotion. Different stages co-exist in Burmese. It should be noted, however, that compounding is very productive in Burmese, and Type I of noun incorporation (defined as loose-bound simple juxtaposition type) in which the noun loses its syntactic status as an argument of the sentence, seems to be the most frequent. This peculiar syntactic behaviour is emphasized by Matisoff's (1973: 309ff.) definition of transhemistichial compound that points out the existence of 'specifying nouns' (N_{spec}) that 'are neither subjects nor objects, but simply limiters of the unspecified generality of the naked verb'.

(33) မိုးမိုးက သူ့ကို စိတ်ကုန်သွားပြီ ။
mo^3 mo^3 Ka^1 θu^1 Ko^2 **sɛiʔ** **- koN^2** θwa^3 Pi^2
Moe Moe TOP/S 3SG.GEN OBJ **mind** **- run out** ASP.PRF CRS
'Moe Moe can't stand him any longer.'

(34) a. စိတ်ကို တိုသွားတာဘဲ ။
sɛiʔ- Ko^2 **-to^2** θwa^3 Ta^2 bɛ^2
mind OBJ/FOCUS **be short** ASP.PRF REAL DM
'(He) really gets on (my) nerves [when he says that].'

b. သူ့ကို လုပ်ချင်တာ အသဲကို ယားနေတာဘဲ ။
θu^1 Ko^2 loʔ C^{h}iN^2 Ta^2 **ʔəθɛ^3** **Ko^2** **-ya^3** **ne^2**
3SG.GEN OBJ work wish NMLZ.REAL **liver** OBJ/FOCUS **itch** PRF
Ta^2 bɛ^2
REAL DM
'(I) am dying to make something [hit] to him.'
(lit.) : (My) liver is itching to the fact (I) wish to make [something] to him.

(35) ဝေဝေ့မှာ တွေးမိတိုင်း စိတ်မချမ်းသာ …။ from Bernot et al. (2001:17)
we^2 we^1 m̥a^2 twe^3 mi^1 TaiN^2 **sɛiʔ-** mə **-c^{h}aN^3** θa^2
Wewe LOC consider NON-VOLITION each **mind** NEG be rich . . .
'Each time WeWe thought about it, she was not in peace.'

4.3.2.1 Possessor and body part Psycho-collocations involve also the relationship between the body part used as a psycho-noun and the possessor of this body part. In other Southeast Asian languages such as Vietnamese, a body-part term may be treated as being possessed (see example (36a)), but the possessor might also be promoted from its position of modifier of the possessee (body part) to first argument of the sentence (36b).

(36)   VIETNAMESE from Clark (1996: 544)
a.   bụng   tôi   (bi)   đau
        stomach   1SG   suffer   sick
        'My stomach aches.'
b.   Tôi   (bi)   đau   bụng
        1SG   suffer   sick   stomach
        'I ache/am sick in the stomach.' (< 'I stomach-ache.')

Although the two strategies coexist in Vietnamese where sentences with possessed body part or promoted subject (with body-part compound with verb) are given as equivalent, it is not the case in Burmese. None of my examples contains a body-part term marked for possession, although it is difficult sometimes to distinguish possessor due to specific phonetic rules.[16]

5   Conclusion

This discussion of Burmese expressives aims to show the aesthetic qualities of constructions used to express emotional or mental process, trying also to reveal the place of aesthetics in Burmese grammar. Two kinds of expressives have been discussed and distinguished as for their functions, their forms, and their semantics in this chapter. The first category of expressives, i.e. elaborate expressions, described more extensively by Wheatley in this volume, tend to be used as adverbial or sometimes nominal, whereas the second ones, psycho-collocations, are generally verbal predicates referring to mental and emotional process.

Regarding their forms, elaborate expressions and psycho-collocations differ in respect of their phonological pattern, their internal structure and number of syllables, although body-part terms are found in both categories of expressives. Elaborate expressions have a predilection for patterns involving rhyme, repetition, and alliteration, which are not aspects of the construction of psycho-collocations.

As for their structure, elaborate expressions are generally four-syllable expressions, although three-syllable expressions do occur frequently in Burmese as also discussed by Wheatley in his contribution to this volume. They are also polymorphemic expressions that often combine, in special

---

[16] Syntactic dependency is often marked in Burmese by a short-high and creaky tone (tone 1) that replaces the original lexical tone of the last syllable of the word. However, this tone is noticeable only on syllables whose original tone is low (tone 2). In other terms, if the possessor is expressed with a high-falling tone (tone 3) or high-creaky tone (tone 1), the modifier status of the possessor won't be marked.

patterns (ABAC, ABCB), semantically related morphemes (synonymous, antonymous, generic/specific, etc.). On the other hand, psycho-collocations are mostly bisyllabic (and bi-morphemic) expressions formed with a body-part or organ term and a verbal lexeme, either static or dynamic. Semantically, elaborated expressions may create nuanced meanings, imitative or evocative sounds (onomatopoeic), whereas psycho-collocations describe emotions, feelings, mental states, or processes.

Among these idiomatic expressions that display special structural and phonological properties, I focus on the ones containing body-part or organ terms and expressing mental and physical states. My study of Burmese psycho-collocations shows that these expressions are numerous and part of everyday language. A general picture of the terms used as psycho-nouns in Burmese reveals that the most common and productive term found in psycho-collocations is the word meaning 'mind' (cit = *sei?*) unlike what is frequently found in other Southeast Asian languages, such as Lai (VanBik 1998) or Hmong (Jaisser, 1990). In these two languages, the most frequent psycho-noun is the term for 'liver'. However, as I examine the origin of the term စိတ် *sei?*, I found the same etymon in Khmer and Mon psycho-collocations.

This study of a particular type of expressive in Burmese, i.e. psycho-collocations, leads us to the conclusion that the aesthetic component is clearly visible in the sonorous and rhythmic quality of elaborated expressions, but less obvious in psycho-collocations. However, shouldn't we consider also the poetic images generated by collocation of psycho-nouns and psycho-mates, as revealing the aesthetic of this language, as reflecting the Burmese worldview?

References

Antilla, Raimo. 1977. Toward a semiotic analysis of expressive vocabulary. *Semiosis* 5 (1): 27–40.

Benedict, Paul. 1972. *Sino-Tibetan : a conspectus*. Cambridge University Press.

Bernot, Denise. 1978–1988. *Dictionnaire birman–français*, vol. 1 to 11. Paris: Société d'Études Linguistiques et Anthropologiques de France.

1980. *Le prédicat en birman parlé*. Paris: Société d'Études Linguistiques et Anthropologiques de France.

1988–1992. *Dictionnaire birman–français*, vol. 12 to 15. Paris: Société d'Études Linguistiques et Anthropologiques de France/PEETERS.

Bernot, Denise, Marie-Hélène Cardinaud and Yin Yin Myint Marie. 2001. *Grammaire birmane–manuel du birman*. vol. 2. Paris: L'Asiathèque (Langues et Mondes).

Bickel, Balthazar. 1997. 'The possessive of experience in Belhare'. In D. Bradley (ed.) *Tibeto-Burman languages of the Himalayas*, Papers in Southeast Asian linguistics no. 14, Canberra: Pacific Linguistics, pp. 135–155.

Bisang, Walter. 1991. 'Verb serialization, grammaticalization and attractor positions in Chinese, Hmong, Vietnamese, Thai and Khmer'. In Hansjakob Seiler and

Waldfried Premper (eds.), *Partizipations–Das sprachliche Erfassen von Sachverhaltten*. Tübingen: Narr, pp. 509–562.

1996. Areal typology and grammaticalization: processes of grammaticalization based on nouns and verbs in East and mainland South East Asian languages. *Studies in language* 20: 517–597.

2006. Contact-induced convergence: typology and areality. In Keith Brown (ed.), *Encyclopedia of language and linguistics, volume 3*. Oxford: Elsevier, pp. 88–101.

Clark, Marybeth. 1989. 'Hmong and areal South-East Asia'. In David Bradley (ed.), *Southeast Asian syntax*. Papers in Southeast Asian linguistics no. 11. Canberra: Pacific Linguistics, pp. 175–230.

1996. 'Where do you feel? Stative verbs and body-parts terms in Mainland Southeast Asia'. In H. Chappell and W. McGregor (eds.), *Grammar of alienability*. Berlin: Mouton de Gruyter, pp. 529–564.

Compton, Carol J. 2007. 'Four-word phrases in Lao discourse: Yuu4 4 Dii2 2 Mii3 3 HEEN3 3'. In Ratree Wayland et al. (eds.), *SEALS XII Papers from the 12th Annual Meeting of the Southeast Asian Linguistics Society 2002*. Canberra: The Australian National University, pp. 23–35.

Diffloth, Gérard. 1972. 'Notes on expressive meaning'. *Papers from the Eighth Regional Meeting of the Chicago Linguistics Society*. Chicago Linguistics Society, pp. 440–447.

1976. 'Expressives in Semai'. In Philip N. Jenner, Laurence C. Thompson, and Stanley Starosta (eds.), *Austroasiatic studies*, Part I. (Oceanic Linguistics Special Publications, No. 13.) Honolulu: University of Hawaii Press, pp. 249–264.

2001. Les expressifs de Surin et où cela conduit. *Le Bulletin de l'École Française d'Extrême-Orient* 88: 261–269.

Donahue, Mark. 2004. Typology and linguistic areas. *Oceanic linguistics* 43: 221–239.

Enfield, Nick J. 2005. Areal linguistics and Mainland Southeast Asia. *Annual review anthropology* 34: 181–206.

Fedry, Jacques. 1976. L'expérience du corps comme structure du langage – essai sur la langue Sàr (tchad). *L'homme*, No. XVI (1): 65–107.

Fudge, Erik. 1970. Phonological structure and 'expressiveness'. *Journal of linguistics* 6(2): 161–188.

Gaby, Alice. 2008. 'Gut feelings: locating intellect, emotion, and lifeforce in the Thaayorre body'. In Farzad Sharifian, René Dirven, Ning Yu and Suzan Niemeier (eds.), *Body, culture and language: conceptualizations of internal body organs across cultures and languages*. Berlin: Mouton de Gruyter, pp. 27–44.

Gärtner, Uta and Jens Lorenz (eds.). 1994. *Tradition and modernity in Myanmar*. Berlin: LIT Verlag.

Gerner, Matthias. 2004. Expressives in Kam (Dong): a study of sign typology (part I). *Cahiers de linguistique d'Asie Orientale* 33(2): 159–202.

2005. Expressives in Kam (Dong): a study of sign typology (part II). *Cahiers de linguistique d'Asie Orientale* 34(1): 25–67.

Goddard, Cliff. 2008. 'English heart and Malay hati'. In Farzad Sharifian, René Dirven, Ning Yu, and Suzan Niemeier (eds.), *Body, culture and language: conceptualizations of internal body organs across cultures and languages*. Berlin: Mouton de Gruyter, pp. 75–102.

Gyurme, Kesang. 1992. *Le clair miroir: enseignement de la grammaire Tibetaine*. Paris: Éditions Prajña.

Haas, Mary R. 1964. *Thai–English student's dictionary.* Stanford University Press

Headley, R. 1977. *Cambodian–English dictionary.* Washington, DC: Catholic University of America Press.

Henderson, Eugenie J. A. 1965. Final –k in Khasi: a secondary phonological pattern. *Lingua* 14: 459–466.

Hla Pe. 1961. Some adapted Pali loan-words in Burmese. *Burma Research Society Fiftieth Anniversary Publication* I: 71–100.

1967. A tentative list of Mon loan words in Burmese. *Journal of Burma Research Society* 50(1): 71–94.

Jaisser, Annie C. 1990. DeLIVERing an introduction to psycho-collocations with SIAB in Hmong. *Linguistics of the Tibeto-Burman area* 13: 159–178.

Jenny, Mathias. 2011. Burmese syntax in Mon – external influence and internal development. In Sophana Srichampa, Paul Sidwell, and Kenneth Gregerson (eds.), *Austroasiatic studies: papers from ICAAL4. Mon-Khmer studies journal special issue* No. 3, 48–64.

Kasevitch, Vadim B. 1994. 'Buddhist tradition and some aspects of the Burmese political vocabulary'. In Uta Gärtner and Jens Lorenz (eds.), *Tradition and modernity in Myanmar.* Berlin: LIT Verlag, pp. 373–379.

Klamer, Marian. 2002. Typical features of Austronesian languages of Central Eastern Indonesia. *Oceanic linguistics* 41: 363–83.

Matisoff, James A. 1973. *The grammar of Lahu.* Berkeley: University of California Press.

1983. 'Linguistic diversity and language contact in Thailand'. In John McKinnon and Wanat Bhruksasri (eds.), *Highlanders of Thailand.* Oxford University Press, pp. 56–86.

1986. Hearts and minds in South-East Asian languages and English: an essay in the comparative lexical semantics of psycho-collocation. *Cahiers de linguistique d'Asie Orientale* 15(1): 5–57.

1991. 'Areal and universal dimensions of grammatization in Lahu'. In Elizabeth C. Trangott and Bernd Heine (eds.), *Approaches to grammaticalization*, vol. II. Amsterdam: John Benjamins, pp. 383–453.

2001. 'Genetic versus contact relationship: prosodic diffusibility in South-East Asian languages'. In Alexandra Y. Aikhenvald and R. M. W. Dixon (eds.), *Areal diffusion and genetic inheritance: problems in comparative linguistics.* Oxford University Press, pp. 291–327.

2003. *Handbook of Proto-Tibeto-Burman.* Berkeley: University of California Press.

2004. 'Areal semantics–is there such a thing?' In Anju Saxena (ed.), *Himalayan languages, past and present.* Berlin: Mouton de Gruyter, pp. 347–393.

Migliazza, Brian. 1996. Mainland Southeast Asia : a unique linguistic area. *Notes on linguistics* 75: 17–25.

2005. Some expressives in So. *Ethnorêma* 1(1): 1–18.

Mithun, Marianne. 1984. The evolution of noun incorporation. *Language* 60: 847–894.

Mortensen, David. 2003. Hmong elaborate expressions are coordinate compounds. Unpublished manuscript, University of California, Berkeley.

Musgrave, Simon. 2006. 'Complex emotion predicates in eastern Indonesia: evidence for language contact?' In Y. Matras, A. Mcmahon, and Nigel Vincent (eds.), *Linguistic areas: convergence in historical and typological perspective.* Hampshire: Palgrave, pp. 227–243.

Næss, Åshild and Mathias Jenny. 2011. Who changes language? Bilingualism and structural change in Burma and the Reef Islands. *Journal of language contact* 4: 217–49.

Oey, Eric. 1990. Psycho-collocations in Malay. *Linguistics of the Tibeto-Burman area* 13 (1): 141–158.

Potts, Christopher, et al. 2009. Expressives and identity conditions. *Linguistic inquiry* 40 (2): 356–366.

Siahaan, Poppy. 2008. 'Did he break your heart or your liver? A contrastive study on metaphorical concepts from the source domain organ in English and in Indonesian'. In Farzad Sharifian, René Dirven, Ning Yu, and Suzan Niemeier (eds.), *Body, culture and language: conceptualizations of internal body organs across cultures and languages*. Berlin: Mouton de Gruyter, pp. 45–74.

Stanford, James N. 2007. Sui adjective reduplication as poetic morpho-phonology. *Journal of East Asian linguistics* 16: 87–111.

Sweetser, Eve. 1990. *From etymology to pragmatics: the mind-as-body metaphor in semantic structure and semantic change*. Cambridge University Press.

VanBik, Kenneth. 1998. Lai psycho-collocation. *Linguistics of the Tibeto-Burman area* 21(1): 201–232.

— 2010. The syntax of psycho-collocations in Hakka Lai. *Linguistics of the Tibeto-Burman area* 33(2): 137–150.

Vandeloise, Claude. 1986. *L'espace en français*. Paris: Editions du SEUIL.

Verhoeven, Elizabeth. 2007. *Experiential constructions in Yucatec Maya: a typologically based analysis*. Amsterdam: John Benjamins.

Vittrant, Alice. 1998. Sémantique et syntaxe des paires verbales en birman. Unpublished manuscript, Université Vincennes-Saint-Denis/ Paris 8.

— 2010. Aire linguistique Asie du sud-est continentale: le birman en fait-il partie? *Moussons* 16(1): 7–38.

Watkins, Justin. in press. Wa language. In Alice Vittrant and Justin Watkins (eds.), *The languages of the Southeast Asian sprachbund*. Mouton de Guyter.

Watson, Richard L. 2001. 'A comparison of some southeast Asian ideophones with some African ideophones'. In F. K. E. Voeltz and C. Kilian-Hatz (eds.), *Ideophones*. Amsterdam: John Benjamins, pp. 385–405.

Wayland, Ratree. 1996. Lao expressives. *Mon Khmer studies* 26: 217–231.

Wheatley, Julian. 2003. 'Burmese'. In Graham Thurgood and Randy Lapolla (eds.), *The Sino-Tibetan languages*. London: Routledge, pp. 196–207.

Wierzbicka, Anna. 1999. *Emotions across languages and cultures: diversity and universals*. Cambridge University Press.

Yanson, Rudolf. 1994. 'Mon and Pali influence on Burmese: how essential was it?' In Uta Gärtner and Jens Lorenz (eds.), *Tradition and modernity in Myanmar*. Hamburg: Lit Verlag, pp. 365–372.

Yoon, Kyung-Joo. 2003. 'Korean *maum* vs. English *heart* and *mind*: contrastive semantics of cultural concepts'. In *Proceedings of the 2003 Conference of the Australian Linguistic Society*.

Yu, Ning. 2002. 'Body and emotion: body parts in Chinese expression of emotion'. In Nick Enfield and Anna Wierzbicka (eds.), special issue 'The body in description of emotion: cross-linguistic studies', *Pragmatics and cognition* 10: 341–367.

17   Grammatical aesthetics of ritual texts in Akha

Inga-Lill Hansson

1   Introduction

For many decades there has been an ongoing debate about the creation and transmission of oral literature, whether still only in oral form or written down recently or a long time ago. The literature in this field is huge, with a significant percentage being reactions to the thesis put forward by Parry and Lord based on Homeric studies (mainly by Parry) and on their common research on Jugoslavian oral literature (Lord 1960).[1] The debate contends with many issues, the main ones being the question of the possibility of verbatim oral transmission over long periods of time through memorization contrasted with theories of transmission through the use of stock phrases or formulas. In this second scenario, each performance is then partly a creation anew but of course based on remembered poetry or narratives. The roles of repetition, contrasting lines, stock phrases, and other structural features also continue to be debated with the camps organized around views that these features are signs of an oral origin and transmission in contrast to a written composition, or that such features are stylistic choices which are possible in both oral and written literature. It is also for very obvious reasons extremely difficult to judge the ancientness of an unwritten text or of course also that of a written text prior to being written down, not forgetting the problems in deciding for many early written texts exactly when they were written down the first time and in which shape. The reader or hearer cannot be certain if the version that she/he is reading or listening to is one unchanged for generations or one that is being elaborated upon constantly. In the mouths of the Akha reciter, his words are not his own, but 'words of old, words of the ancestors'.

In this chapter I will look into the devices used in the ritual language of the Akha, comparing the ritual text with a modern rendition, to see how the language copes with the rules of a metric system.

---

[1] See e.g. the summary of the theories and criticism of them, including further studies, by Finnegan (1977, 1988) and Foley (1981, 1988), where there also are ample bibliographies. The latest research presented – as far as I know – is by Minna Skafte Jensen: *Writing Homer* (2011), which just got into my hands.

2   Background to Akha

The Akha, a Tibeto-Burman people, live in the border region between China, Burma, Thailand, Laos, and Vietnam. Most of them live in the southwestern part of the Yunnan province in China, forming part of the Hani nationality, and adjacent areas in Burma. In Thailand, where I did my main fieldwork, they are reported to have arrived from Burma only at the beginning of the last century.

Until very recently, the Akhas have not had any writing system. Missionaries developed a transcription system in Burma in the 1960s and the New Testament was printed in Rangoon in 1968. Other Christian literature and some Akha songs and proverbs, have been published in this system (1989). During the same period, Catholic missionaries in Thailand developed a writing system based on Thai letters. So far, only some Christian Akhas can use these orthographic systems.[2] In China, a transcription system based on the Chinese pinyin was made for Hani in 1957, with one dialect chosen as standard, and is used in a few schools in China. The Hani in China are now publishing some very interesting literature in the Hani script, usually accompanied by Chinese translations. Only a few thousand Hani are reported to be literate in their own language.

In the mythology and oral history of the Akhas, it is said that they once had a script, written on buffalo skin, but during a fight they got hungry and ate it up, so now they remember everything in their hearts while others have to rely on writing. From their literature it can be seen that they have had contacts, presumably since a long time ago, with among others the Shan and the Han Chinese. The Shan script is also mentioned in some texts. In these narratives, the Akha comment about the Chinese only that they are numerous and wise; no mention is made of their writing. I think it can be safely said that writing has not so far played a part in the transmission of Akha literature, but will probably do so in the future, especially in China (for Hani) and Thailand.

3   Akha texts

The Akha have several types of texts, which are broadly defined and conceptualized as follows:

1. Ritual texts recited by the *phirma*,[3] recited in connection with personal rituals at death, sickness, and securing of good health.

---

[2] A parallel situation holds with the Jarai in Vietnam whereby the Catholic Missions developed the first Jarai orthographies and those Jarai who adopted Catholicism were the only ones, consequently, who were literate.

[3] The transcription system, decided by the Akha at a meeting in 2011, has the main features: (i) it represents the three tones, high, middle, and low, which are represented by the letters: -r for high tone, none for mid tone, and -q for low tone; (ii) laryngealization is marked with a -v before the tonal marking; and, (iii) some vowels have specialized representations as *an* < -ang / *e* < ˙ (based on Pinyin) / *ei* < e.

2. Ritual texts recited by the *nyirpaq* 'shaman' in connection with personal rituals at sickness.
3. Ritual texts recited by the *dzoeqma* 'village leader' in connection with yearly rituals concerning the village.
4. Ritual songs sung by everybody at specific occasions, as e.g. mourning songs at death, wedding songs, songs at the singing festival, thematic songs describing seasonal activities, songs at planting. Each kind of song has its own rhythm or melody.
5. Songs sung by everybody, e.g. at the dancing place in the evening, going to the fields, while working, love songs, nursery songs.
6. Stories, myths, riddles, told by everybody.

The greatest body of texts belong to the office of *phirma*, and they are claimed to be 'words of the ancestors', transmitted through lines of *phirma*, the names of which are part of the texts. The longest single text is the one recited at the occasion of the death of an elder. It goes on for three nights, sometimes more, and is in the version I have more than 6,000 lines long. The various healing texts amount to even more, all remembered by the *phirma*. The *phirma* I have been working with is definitely not literate, neither was his teacher. The interesting thing about these *phirma* texts is that they are formally taught, using a technique, called *naeq ke ke* in Akha, which I have had the chance to observe several times. The *phirma* gathers in evening time his *pirzaq* 'apprentices', and other men (the *phirma* is always a man) who want to take part, in his house, and they settle down formally around a table, set with some liquor and small things to eat, special leaves stuck behind their ears, and the *phirma* starts to recite in a special teaching rhythm. The apprentices follow suit a few syllables behind. It may continue for hours, sometimes the whole night, and for many nights during the year. For the ones who seriously want to become *phirma*, the training process continues for years. Additionally, they assume formal apprenticeships and assist with rituals, taking part in reciting. *Phirma aqbawr Gaw* – who died in 2010 – was in his forties before he could manage a complete death ritual by himself. It is a feat of memorization, and it is said by the *phirma* that one has to have a heart for it, be clear thinking, and be able to concentrate. It is important that the words are correct. In these times of rapid change in the lives of the Akhas, with many Akhas leading a new life abolishing their rituals, the remaining *phirma*'s are afraid of forgetting their texts, not having occasion to recite as often as before. I have seen *aqbaw Gaw* many evenings lying by himself in his house reciting, just to keep on remembering the texts. In larger villages in former times, the *phirma* could spend most of his time on rituals, getting a bigger share of the sacrificed animal. He was also though usually working in the fields like any villager.

The Death Ritual Text used here deals with getting the dead on the right road back to the ancestors. It gives the names of the rivers the Akha have passed on their migration routes, reciting them backwards. It describes Akha life from conception to death, telling about growing up, finding a mate, going far away for buying salt, getting old and eventually dying. It is a great source for information on the area also from a geographical point of view (Hansson 1983, 1997; Alting von Geusau 1983).

Does the *phirma* then recite the same text each time? I checked with *Phirma aqbaw Gaw* several times, based on my transcribed text, asking him again by e.g. giving him some lines in a section, making him continue, and he recited the identical text. Sometimes there has been a passage of many years between the first time we worked on a text and my questioning him again. The lines may end in a row of final particles, the number of which depends on the speed of recitation, and they may vary, but the bulk of the lines is the same. Apprentices are known for having some initial words of hesitation, recited slowly, while they desperately try to remember the next line! I have also checked passages with another *phirma* from the same line of teachers. The two have never met each other, but they come up with the same lines. The text may vary in length, and I don't know if there is a longest possible version. The length depends on the *phirma*'s skill, his willingness to recite that day, his health and mental energy at the moment, but there is a shortest possible version to ensure that the ritual is fulfilled. According to the *phirma*, there is a road he must take, but he can decide himself on how many sideroads he wants to go into, always coming back to the main road though. I have participated in a *naeq ke ke* where *phirma* from different villages took turns in reciting, easily taking over from each other.

Are the recited texts then the 'words of old', faithfully transmitted? The names in the geneaologies show that the office of *phirma* is probably very old, but we of course do not know what they recited. The language of the present texts is not easy to understand for anybody else but *phirma* and trained laymen. I have taught the text to young Akhas, literate in Thai, still fluent in Akha and able to sing the common Akha songs, but they could not understand the language of the texts. They were not even able to comprehend the lines when listening to a tape recording – to the dismay of an attending *phirma*! After some days of training they made progress and were able to manage not too difficult passages.

4   Features and analyses of Akha ritual texts

The main features that set the category of ritual texts apart from vernacular Akha discourse can be summarized in the following way.

1. Akha ritual texts are organized into lines based on iambic feet with a degenerate final foot.
2. Akha ritual texts exhibit some differences in grammar, especially in the occasional absence of noun and verb particles.

3. Akha ritual texts evidence monosyllabic replacement forms in nouns.
4. Akha ritual texts evidence a high frequency of obsolete or archaic vocabulary.[4]

The combination of these structural features in the ritual texts makes them salient as distinct forms, enriching their aesthetic value while also contributing to the opacity of meaning. Equally, the fact that many young Akhas do not participate in the traditional ritual life makes it difficult for them to understand the content of the texts. A further complication is the fact that some passages in the texts are not understood by the *phirma* himself any longer, while others are only partially understood. In these cases, the *phirma* cannot discern the meaning word by word.

Is this then a sure sign of age or of a traditional skill handled by *phirma*'s over generations, adding to the text as time goes by? The pattern is not difficult to reproduce – I have had success in producing lines in this fashion accepted by the *phirma* with his laughing comment that I got it right, but it is also clear to me that he himself doesn't try deliberately to include new material. He sees himself as a faithful transmitter of memorized texts, not as a composer of new texts. In the following sections, I explore these factors in more detail providing illustrative material from the Death Rituals of the Akha *phirma*'s repertoire.

4.1   *Metrical structure and constituent order*

As mentioned previously, the metric pattern of the ritual language makes it deviate from the modern language and thereby difficult to understand. I have studied the structure of Akha ritual texts to determine whether the organization of lines in them differs from that found in everyday, modern Akha discourse.[5] Briefly it can be said that each line is built upon what I call a *rhythm pair*, i.e. two syllables with the second one more stressed.

Each line contains a row of such pairs + one last syllable, making each line in slow recitation consist of an uneven amount of syllables.

There are also restrictions placed on what types of grammatical forms can be in which position within the pair, e.g. the negation can only be in the first

---

[4] These features certainly point to the longevity of the form, but it is not easy to judge how ancient the texts themselves might be.

[5] The preliminary results are reported by Hansson (1991).

position, noun and verb particles only in the second, etc. The language solves this problem through use of e.g. prefixes, suffixes, and filler syllables when needed to ensure the right placement of the words. The grammar of the ritual language is basically the same as that of the modern, vernacular language, but it means that the language has to a certain extent been manipulated or stretched in its possibilities to make it fit into the requirements of the metrical pattern.

All noun and verb particles must be in the second position, while negation must be in the first position. If e.g. the structure of a line is: object – negation – verb, and the object is monosyllabic, it has to be extended by an affix or a filler syllable to enable the negation to come first in the next slot as shown in examples (1a) and (1b).

(1a)   hawq   maq   dzaq
         rice   NEG   eat
         Not eat rice (vernacular Akha)

(1b)   hawq   law   maq   dzaq
         rice   filler δ   NEG   eat
         Not eat rice (ritual Akha)

4.2   Vocabulary differences

Many words that are disyllabic in the modern language are replaced by monosyllabic forms in the ritual language, increasing the difficulty in comprehension for the untrained. This may be accomplished through syncopation of forms, not uncommon in many languages of the Southeast Asian mainland. In some cases, the lexical items are not subject to syncope, but instead a process of total replacement applies. Table 17.1 provides some examples of both solutions to the problem.

In the following example, the text deals with an aspect of everyday life, trying to get a hen to lay eggs in a basket, where the process of monosyllabic replacement is evidenced.

Table 17.1 *A comparison of ritual and everyday vocabulary in Akha*

Gloss	Ritual	Everyday	Process
'thatch'	iq	uqjir	Syncope
'shoulderbag'	tangr	pehrtangr	Syncope
'road'	gar	garma	Syncope
'below'	bi	uqmovq	Replacement
'Shan'	chmq bi	miqchmq	Syncope
'basket'	tur	puqtur	Syncope

(2a)   Modern vernacular
jauv maq ka anr-eq / yaciv ya guir / yawq ngaevq / pavq gar
egg NEG lay in VP / chicken basket / empty /   tie   place

(2b)   Ritual variety
uv law /   maq ka /   ya   guir /   yawq ngaevq /   pavq mir
egg elab / NEG lay/ chicken basket /   empty/   tie   place
'Where the empty basket is tied, no eggs are laid.'

In this example, *mir* 'place' is replaced by the more common vernacular form *gar*. In the construction *uv law* 'egg + filler syllable' is chosen instead of *ya uv* 'chicken + egg', which does occur in other verses. This slot has to be filled with two syllables, as the following negation '*maq*' must be in the first place in a slot. Finally, the form *-eq* is added, marking a relative clause.

Example (3) compares a ritual and modern version of a text concerning the importance of child-bearing in Akha culture.

(3a)   Akha ritual variety
    (i)   uq civq
        night
    (ii)   naevq haw
        spirit look
    (iii)   maq mawr
        NEG see
    (iv)   nan ghanr
        daytime
    (v)   tsawr haw
        people look
    (vi)   maq xiq
        NEG know
    (vii)   lar   aer
        come ADV P

(3b)   Modern Akha version
    (i)   uqcivq   paw
        night side   spirit
    (ii)   naevq haw   ngeh
        look   when
    (iii)   maq   mawr   nya
        NEG see   able
    (iv)   nan ghanr   paw
        daytime   side
    (v)   tsawr haq haw   ngae
        people   see   when
    (vi)   maq xiq
        NEG know

(vii)   lar ni
        come PREP
(viii) ghae e   mae
        do   VP   SP
'At night spirits looking cannot see it (that the woman is pregnant) in the
daytime people looking can't find out about it.'

Comparing these two versions evidences several differences between grammatically aesthetic Akha ritual language and the daily vernacular. For instance,
the conjunction *ngae* is added to the text in the modern version.

Structure: The conjunction 'ngae – when/while' is added in the modern
version. In the second line, – the first line can also be said to be part of
this construction – the first phrase is constructed adverbially to a general verb
'ghae-e do'. Literally translated: In daytime, people doing as if seeing without
knowing.

In the next text, a young man who is looking for a wife proclaims his
willingness to do his utmost as a husband.

(4a)   Ritual Akha version
        (i)   mi   jav
               knife   have
        (ii)   khaq jir
               man
        (iii) yar   law
               field filler δ
        (iv)   maq myaq
               NEG clear
        (v)   mawvq-eu
               want   -VP
        (vi)   maq nger
               NEG be

(4b)   Modern Akha version
        (i)   mi   caer jav   -awr
               knife   have   -VP
        (ii)   yar   maq   myaq   mawvq   -e
               field   NEG   clear   want   -VP
        (iii) maq   nger
               NEG   be
        'I am not a man who, if having a machete, would not clear the hill field.'

In comparing the ritual text with its modern, vernacular counterpart, several
salient features are involved. In the ritual text, *yar* is elaborated with the filler
syllable *law* to make the following negation appear in the correct position. This
is not needed in the modern Akha version. The ritual text also makes use of an

archaic variant for 'man,' *khaq jir*. The modern text employs the markers *awr* to signal the continuation of verbal action to the next one. While the ritual text should also have such a marker, there is no place for it given the strictures of the metrical form.

5   Conclusion

As can be seen from the examples and discussion above, the ritual language cannot be said to be extremely divergent from the modern vernacular. In translating between ritual language and the Akha vernacular, it is not always a matter of literal replacement. Instead, there is an aesthetic of brevity in word structure. Without contention is the fact that becoming competent in Akha ritual genres requires considerable training and repetition for the *phirma*. It is a remarkable feat of memorization and ability to concentrate and probably requires a kind of life that is rapidly disappearing. There are though movements among the Akha in various countries to preserve the rituals, by now using video to document the old traditions. On my last trip I heard that in one village, where there was no *phirma* in residence, they used a tape recording of the text instead. When the *phirma*'s in other villages heard of this action, they were not pleased.

References

Alting von Geusau, Leo. 1983. 'Dialectics of Akhaza: the interiorization of a perennial minority group'. In John McKinnon and Wanat Bhruksasri (eds.), *Highlanders of Thailand*. Oxford University Press, pp. 243–277.

Finnegan, Ruth. 1977. *Oral poetry: its nature significance and social context*. Cambridge University Press.

—— 1988. *Literacy and orality: studies in the technology of communication*. Oxford: Blackwell.

Foley, John Miles. 1981. *Oral traditional literature: a festschrift for Albert Bates Lord*. Columbus: The Ohio State University Press.

—— 1988. *The theory of oral composition*. Bloomington: Indiana University Press.

Hansson, Inga-Lill. 1979. Sound changes in Akha, paper at the 13th ICSTLL, Paris.

—— 1983. 'Death in an Akha village'. In John McKinnon and Wanat Bhruksasri (eds.), *Highlanders of Thailand*. Oxford University Press, pp. 279–290.

—— 1991. The language of Akha ritual texts. *Linguistics of the Tibeto-Burman area* 14(2): 155–167.

—— 1997. Orally transmitted texts of the minorities in East and Southeast Asia: suggestions for research across borders. *Asia Pacific viewpoint* 38(2): 145–153.

Jensen, Minna Skafte. 2011. *Writing Homer. A study based on results from modern fieldwork*. Scientia Danica. Series H, Humanistica, 8 vol. 4, Det Kongelige Danske Videnskabernes Selskab.

Lord, Albert. 1960. *The singer of tales*. Cambridge University Press.

Index